Scheduling Divisible Loads in Parallel and Distributed Systems

Veeravalli Bharadwaj
Concordia University, Montreal

Debasish Ghose
Indian Institute of Science, Bangalore

Venkataraman Mani
Indian Institute of Science, Bangalore

Thomas G. Robertazzi
State University of New York, Stony Brook

IEEE Computer Society Press
Los Alamitos, California

Washington • Brussels • Tokyo

Library of Congress Cataloging-in-Publication Data

Scheduling divisible loads in parallel and distributed systems/
    Veeravalli Bharadwaj ... [et al.].
        p.   cm.
    Includes bibliographical references (p.   ).
    ISBN 0-8186-7521-7
    1. Parallel processing (Electronic computers).   2. Electronic data
processing—Distributed processing.   3. Computer capacity—Planning.
I. Bharadwaj, Veeravalli.
QA76.58.S345 1996
005.4 ' 3—dc20
                                                    96-177
                                                    CIP

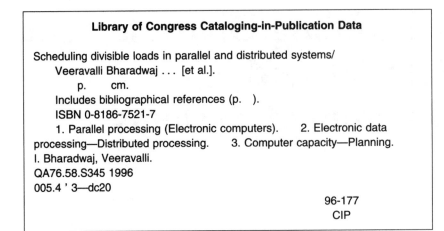

IEEE Computer Society Press
10662 Los Vaqueros Circle
P.O. Box 3014
Los Alamitos, CA 90720-1264

IEEE Computer Society Press Order Number BP07521
Library of Congress Number 96-177
ISBN 0-8186-7521-7

Additional copies may be ordered from:

IEEE Computer Society Press	IEEE Service Center	IEEE Computer Society	IEEE Computer Society
Customer Service Center	445 Hoes Lane	13, Avenue de l'Aquilon	Ooshima Building
10662 Los Vaqueros Circle	P.O. Box 1331	B-1200 Brussels	2-19-1 Minami-Aoyama
P.O. Box 3014	Piscataway, NJ 08855-1331	BELGIUM	Minato-ku, Tokyo 107
Los Alamitos, CA 90720-1264	Tel: +1-908-981-1393	Tel: +32-2-770-2198	JAPAN
Tel: +1-714-821-8380	Fax: +1-908-981-9667	Fax: +32-2-770-8505	Tel: +81-3-3408-3118
Fax: +1-714-821-4641	mis.custserv@computer.org	euro.ofc@computer.org	Fax: +81-3-3408-3553
Email: cs.books@computer.org			tokyo.ofc@computer.org

Assistant Publisher: Matt Loeb
Technical Editor: Jon Butler
Acquisitions Editor: Bill Sanders
Acquisitions Assistant: Cheryl Smith
Advertising/Promotions: Tom Fink
Production Editor: Lisa O'Conner
Cover Design: Alex Torres
Printed in the United States of America by BookCrafters

 The Institute of Electrical and Electronics Engineers, Inc

Contents

Preface

In the past decade there have been several books dealing with various aspects of parallel and distributed processing systems aimed at users at different levels and with varying interests. Those that are designed as text books are usually meant for final year undergraduate students or graduate students in computer science. These usually provide a general treatment of a variety of topics. The coverage is wide but normally restricted to fundamental concepts and results. Others, which are mainly intended to be research monographs, provide an in-depth study of some specific aspect of parallel and distributed systems. This book belongs to the latter category and is concerned with a class of problems in the general area of load sharing and balancing in parallel and distributed systems.

Load scheduling/sharing has attracted a considerable amount of attention in the computer science literature in recent times. It is one of the many ways of exploiting the power of multiprocessor/multicomputer systems. However, most research reported in the literature on parallel computing, attempts to achieve this goal algorithmically—that is, by designing new and more efficient parallel algorithms in place of the conventional sequential algorithms. A recently developed research direction has concentrated on exploiting possible parallelism in the data so that it can be partitioned optimally and assigned to several processors, in order to be processed in the shortest possible time. This leads us directly into the domain of what is known as *divisible loads*. Research in this area is concerned with identifying interrelationships among various data points in a computational load, and using this knowledge, along with information about system-dependent constraints, to partition the data into optimally sized segments for each processor. The simplest such load is the one that is arbitrarily divisible, that is, one that can be divided into any number of segments of any desired fractional size. Such loads are commonly encountered in applications involving image processing, signal processing, processing of massive experimental data, and so on. Design and analysis of strategies for distribution of such arbitrarily divisible loads is the primary goal of this book. Another important objective of this book is to study the trade-off relationships between communication and computation since an important bottleneck in most load sharing problems is that of communication overheads due to delays. This is the first book in this area and it is hoped that it will spur further research in this direction thus enabling these ideas to be applied to a more general class of loads.

Research in this area is quite recent and is spread over both the mainstream computer science literature as well as other literature not usually referred to by computer scientists. This book collects all these results in one place and presents them in a logically connected manner. Although most of the material in the book has been developed mainly by two research groups, at the Indian Institute of Science and at the State University of New York at Stony Brook, it also covers results by other researchers that have either appeared or are due to appear in the literature.

The level of presentation in the book is of a research monograph. However, one of the strengths of the book is that, unlike most such research monographs, it provides relevant but easily understandable numerical examples and figures to illustrate important concepts. We trust that this will improve the readability of the book to a great extent and make it accessible to a large number of computer scientists and engineers. Considering that this is a research monograph, the mathematical sophistication expected of the reader is quite modest. Though we present formal and rigorous proofs to all the results obtained here, the treatment is such that a reasonable grasp of the basic concepts of linear algebra and discrete mathematics is sufficient to understand them. Also, at one or two places (Lemmas 5.7 and 5.12 in Chapter 5), some elementary results in mathematical analysis have been used.

The computer scientists and engineers who will find the book useful are researchers interested in the problem of load scheduling/sharing and load balancing, software engineers developing codes for these problems, and researchers in the application areas of image processing, signal processing, distributed sensor systems, and the like, who find it beneficial to exploit the power of multicomputer systems to process massive data files more efficiently. To a limited extent, the book will also be of interest to operations research specialists and management scientists, since many practical problems of production and resource management involving transportation and distribution of unfinished goods to manufacturing units may be modeled similarly.

Presently evolving computer science curricula in many universities have begun to give considerable importance to the area of load scheduling and balancing in parallel and distributed systems. Advanced graduate level courses treat this topic either independently or as part of a course on distributed processing. The area of scheduling divisible loads provides a new and practically useful paradigm for analyzing such problems from a perspective that is different from the conventional one. Hence, this book, being the first in this area, can be a useful inclusion in such courses.

In this book we present the design and analysis of load distribution strategies for arbitrarily divisible loads in multiprocessor/multicomputer systems subject to system-constraints in the form of communication delays. In particular, two system architectures—(a) Single-level tree or Star network, and (b) Linear network—

are selected for thorough analysis. We study two different cases, one of processors with front ends (communication coprocessors) and the other of processors without front ends. We wish to stress that the book concentrates mainly on load distribution strategies and their performance analysis, and does not cover issues related to implementation of these strategies on any specific parallel or distributed computing system. Moreover, since this is the first attempt to formulate and analyze problems in the area of scheduling divisible loads, we have adopted a simplified system model for study.

The material in the book is organized into 13 chapters. A brief description of the salient features of each chapter is given below.

In Chapter 1, we begin with a brief description of a multiprocessor/multicomputer system and discuss the load scheduling/sharing problem associated with such systems. We provide a formal classification of various kinds of computational loads from the viewpoint of divisibility. The communication delay is introduced as a crucial system-dependent constraint in the context of load sharing. A few instances of applications involving arbitrarily divisible loads are discussed along with an illustrative example taken from the image processing literature. The chapter concludes with an informal discussion on divisible load theory and its applications to scheduling problems.

In Chapter 2, we present the mathematical models adopted for the processors and the communication links in a network. Simplifying assumptions made to obtain these models are also discussed. The chapter concludes with definitions of frequently used terms in the book and a numerical example illustrating important features of a simple load distribution scheme for an arbitrarily divisible load.

In Chapter 3, we carry out a preliminary study of load distribution in linear networks having arbitrary load origination points. Some rationale for obtaining optimal load distribution is discussed and a set of recursive equations are developed. Some important features are demonstrated through an extensive numerical study that forms the motivation for a rigorous analytical treatment in later chapters. An analysis to obtain performance bounds is carried out using a processor equivalence concept. In Chapter 4, we present a similar study for general tree networks.

In Chapter 5, we present a proof for obtaining an optimal load distribution in single-level tree and linear networks. Here, too, we use the concept of an equivalent processor-link pair, but in a different sense than in Chapters 3 and 4. This chapter forms the theoretical basis for the rest of the book. We conclude the chapter with a critical appraisal of the model adopted here.

In Chapter 6, we obtain closed-form solutions for optimal load distribution in a linear network and prove some important results regarding the sequence of load distribution. These proofs provide an analytical basis to many of the numerical results obtained in Chapter 3.

In Chapter 7, we show that further improvement in the performance of single-level heterogeneous tree networks can be achieved by a hierarchy of steps involving an optimal sequence of load distribution and an optimal architectural rearrangement policy (wherever it is possible). Based on the analytical results obtained in earlier chapters we carry out a rigorous analysis to precisely identify this optimal sequence and rearrangement.

In Chapter 8, we address the problem of obtaining the performance bounds with respect to network parameters and the number of processors for both linear and single-level tree networks. We also conduct an analytical study to demonstrate the effect of communication delays on the system performance and the trade-off relationships between communication and computation. We show that these results are endorsed by numerical results given in Chapters 3 and 4.

In Chapter 9, we address the task of utilizing the front ends of the processors in a linear network in a more efficient way than in the strategy adopted in earlier chapters. For this, we propose an alternate strategy in which a processor begins computation as soon as its front end receives its own load fraction and does not wait for the load fractions of its successors. A complete analysis is carried out to obtain results on optimal sequence of load distribution and the location of the load origination processor for a special class of networks. Its applicability to a general class of linear networks is also demonstrated through an illustrative example. An asymptotic performance analysis is also presented.

In Chapter 10, we design a multi-installment load distribution strategy for single-level tree networks that improves the performance considerably over single installment strategies used in earlier chapters. In fact, we show that the adverse effect of communication delays can be circumvented to a large extent by using this strategy. Closed-form solutions and asymptotic results are obtained.

In Chapter 11, we present a multi-installment load distribution strategy for linear networks. However, the equations developed here turn out to be only partially tractable and many of the asymptotic results are obtained computationally.

All of the above studies considered the distribution of a single arbitrarily divisible load. In Chapter 12, we apply these results to a practical scenario where a number of loads arrive at a processor in a bus network and are processed one after the other. An efficient algorithm is presented to compute the optimal load distribution.

In Chapter 13, we conclude the book with a discussion of certain problems that arise naturally from the results presented, and point to a number of new open problems in this area of research.

Each chapter ends with bibliographic notes citing the relevant references related to the material covered in the chapter.

During the preparation of the manuscript, the authors have benefited from the help of many individuals. The first three authors would especially like to thank L. Anand for his timely help, which considerably lightened the task of manuscript preparation for them. T.G. Robertazzi would like to thank his former graduate students (Y.-C. Cheng, S. Bataineh, T. Hsiung, and J. Sohn) who collaborated with him over the years on this topic. The comments provided by the reviewers of the manuscript were also useful in vastly improving the presentation. Thanks are due to Professors B. Shirazi, K.M. Kavi, J. Blazewicz, M. Drozdowski, and H.J. Kim for sending us material from their recent publications. Thanks are due to M. Singhal and J. Butler for their editorial support. Thanks are also due to Catherine Harris and Lisa O'Conner and the staff of CS Press for their very professional efforts in seeing this work to fruition. The work of the copy editor, Martha Balshem, is also very much appreciated.

D. Ghose and V. Mani would like to acknowledge the financial support for manuscript preparation received from the Curriculum Development Cell (Centre for Continuing Education) established at the Indian Institute of Science, Bangalore, by the Ministry of Education and Culture, Government of India. They would also like to thank their colleagues in the Department of Aerospace Engineering for providing them with an environment that encourages research in interdisciplinary areas.

At a personal level, V. Bharadwaj would like to thank his father, brother, sister-in-law, and Raja, for their encouragement during the book writing process. D. Ghose would like to express his gratitude to his family, and in particular to his wife Swati for her patience and understanding, and also to three-year-old Debraj who refused to understand what his father was up to! V. Mani would like to thank his family members and friends for their support and encouragement throughout his career and especially to his wife Raji for her love and affection. T.G. Robertazzi would like to thank his wife and children for their support and encouragement during the course of this work.

ACKNOWLEDGMENTS

The authors would like to thank the following publishers for the permission granted to use material from papers published in their journals.

The Institute of Electrical and Electronics Engineers (IEEE), Inc.

[1] Bataineh, S. and T.G. Robertazzi, "Bus Oriented Load Sharing for a Network of Sensor Driven Processors," *IEEE Trans. Systems, Man, and Cybernetics*, Vol. 21, 1991, pp. 1202–1205.

[2] Bataineh, S., T. Hsiung, and T.G. Robertazzi, "Closed Form Solutions for Bus and Tree Networks of Processors Load Sharing a Divisible Job," *IEEE Trans. Computers*, Vol. 43, 1994, pp. 1184–1196.

[3] Bharadwaj, V., D. Ghose, and V. Mani, "Optimal Sequencing and Arrangement in Distributed Single-Level Networks with Communication Delays," *IEEE Trans. Parallel and Distributed Systems*, Vol. 5, 1994, pp. 968–976.

[4] Bharadwaj, V., D. Ghose, and V. Mani, "Multi-installment Load Distribution in Tree Networks with Delays," *IEEE Trans. Aerospace and Electronic Systems*, Vol. 31, 1995, pp. 555–567.

[5] Mani, V. and D. Ghose, "Distributed Computation in Linear Networks: Closed-Form Solutions," *IEEE Trans. Aerospace and Electronic Systems*, Vol. 30, 1994, pp. 471–483.

[6] Robertazzi, T.G., "Processor Equivalence for a Linear Daisy Chain of Load Sharing Processors," *IEEE Trans. Aerospace and Electronic Systems*, Vol. 29, 1993, pp. 1216–1221.

[7] Cheng, Y.C. and T.G. Robertazzi, "Distributed Computation with Communication Delays," *IEEE Trans. Aerospace and Electronic Systems*, Vol. 24, 1988, pp. 700–712.

[8] Cheng, Y.C. and T.G. Robertazzi, "Distributed Computation for a Tree Network with Communication Delays," *IEEE Transactions on Aerospace and Electronic Systems*, Vol. 26, 1990, pp. 511–516.

[9] Sohn, J. and Robertazzi, T.G., "Optimal Divisible Job Load Sharing for Bus Networks," *IEEE Trans. Aerospace & Electronic Systems*, Vol. 32, 1996, pp. 34–40.

Elsevier Science Ltd.

[10] Bharadwaj, V., D. Ghose, and V. Mani, "An Efficient Load Distribution Strategy for a Distributed Linear Network of Processors with Communication Delays," *Computers and Math. with Applications*, Vol. 29, 1995, pp. 95–112.

Academic Press

[11] Ghose, D. and V. Mani, "Distributed Computation with Communication Delays: Asymptotic Performance Analysis," *J. of Parallel and Distributed Computing*, Vol. 23, 1994, pp. 293–305.

CHAPTER 1

Introduction

The need for load scheduling/sharing arises in many real-world situations. Common examples include the scheduling of processing loads in distributed computing systems, the scheduling of production loads in manufacturing systems, and the scheduling of available resources among many users. By and large, a scheduling problem addresses the following question: *What is the best possible way to organize a given work load so that it can be completed in the shortest possible time?* In a distributed computing system, processing loads arrive from many users at random time instants. A proper scheduling policy attempts to assign these loads to available processors so as to complete the processing of all loads in the shortest possible time.

In recent years, with the advent of sophisticated and complex parallel and distributed computing systems, research in the area of load scheduling has gained considerable momentum. This book is a contribution in one particular area in the broad field of load sharing in parallel and distributed computing systems. Specifically, it addresses issues associated with the distribution of *arbitrarily divisible loads* among processors in a distributed computing system subject to communication delays. Here we shall assume the words *sharing*, *scheduling*, and *distribution* to be synonymous, although in a strict sense this need not be true, and use them interchangeably throughout the book.

1.1 MULTIPROCESSOR AND MULTICOMPUTER SYSTEMS

Both multiprocessor and multicomputer systems are characterized by the presence of several processors in the system. Multiprocessor systems are usually considered as computer systems that have several processors, but are serviced by a single set of peripherals. Hence, these processors are not autonomous and such systems are also known as *parallel processing systems* (PPS). In contrast, multicomputer systems consist of several autonomous processors connected via communication links. Such multicomputer systems are also known as *distributed computing systems* (DCS). These definitions are not rigid, and there exist a large number of systems that may not be easy to classify as one or the other. For example, loosely coupled multiprocessor systems (where each processor has a memory of its own, in contrast to tightly coupled multiprocessor systems where the processors share a common memory) mimic many of the characteristics of multicomputer systems and are also classified as distributed computing systems. A general distributed computing system normally has physically well-separated autonomous processors connected via communication links (Figure 1.1). In general, an entire parallel and distributed computing system, or a part of it, may have one of a number of known topologies, such as: bus, star, linear, tree, hypercube, ring, mesh, and so on.

Such systems may or may not be dedicated to a specific application. The main purpose of a DCS is to offer a variety of services to the users. In a DCS, the processing loads may arrive at many sites. A load submitted by a user at some site may be processed right there or at a different site, depending upon the availability of resources and the type of service demanded. When a job has to be processed at

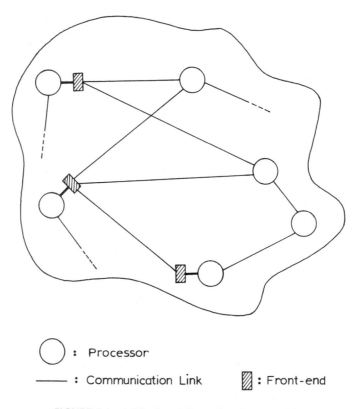

◯ : Processor

—— : Communication Link   ▨ : Front-end

FIGURE 1.1 A Distributed Computing System (DCS)

a different site, it is transferred via communication links. Since the processors are physically well separated in a DCS, it takes a certain amount of time for the load to reach its destination; that is, load transfer from one site to another is subject to nonzero communication delays. Each processor in the network may be engaged in processing its own load, while simultaneously involved in communication with other processors. This is accomplished through dedicated communication coprocessors, often called *front ends*, attached to the processors. These front ends are shown as boxes in Figure 1.1. When a processor is not equipped with such front ends, it has to perform the tasks of both communication and computation.

A parallel processing system attempts to exploit the inherent parallelism in a problem by identifying those modules that can run concurrently so that the solution is obtained in the shortest possible time. Quite frequently, this may involve transfer and exchange of data from one processor to another. Communication overheads due to delays associated with these operations can become substantially high and degrade system performance unless an efficient scheduling policy is adopted.

In subsequent sections, we present a brief account of various aspects of load scheduling/sharing. This discussion is intended to give an overview of some of the important topics addressed in the literature on scheduling theory and is not meant to be exhaustive as these topics are not directly relevant to the specific problem—scheduling arbitrarily divisible loads—addressed in this book.

1.2 THE LOAD SCHEDULING/SHARING PROBLEM

In a broad sense, load scheduling/sharing problems can be classified in many ways. One of the possible classifications is

- Static
- Dynamic

It is also possible to classify them as

- Deterministic
- Stochastic

In *static scheduling*, the objective is to find an optimal schedule of a given number of loads to a set of processors. No dynamics of the system are taken into consideration. The scheduling of, for example, n loads to a set of m processors so that the time required to process all the loads is a minimum is one such problem. On the other hand, if the dynamics of the process are considered, then the scheduling is said to be *dynamic*. In the above example, if loads arrive at arbitrary time instants, and the scheduling policy at any instant in time depends on the current state of the system, then the scheduling is dynamic. It should be noted that the difference in the above two classifications lies in the consideration of the time factor.

In the case of *deterministic scheduling*, all the characteristics of the processing loads, such as their execution times and arrival times, are deterministic quantities and are known a priori. On the other hand, if the arrival of the loads is a random process and/or the execution times are random variables with some known probability distribution, then the scheduling of loads is said to be *stochastic*.

Static scheduling can be either deterministic or stochastic depending on whether the execution times of the loads are known exactly or only in a stochastic sense. However, most static scheduling problems are considered to be deterministic and are usually solved using graph-theoretic techniques. Similarly, dynamic scheduling problems could also be deterministic or stochastic, though they have usually been considered in the stochastic framework and are solved using queueing-theoretic techniques.

Another related problem is called *load balancing*. It uses similar analytical and computational techniques, but its primary objective is to ensure that all the processors in the system are more or less equally loaded.

All the scheduling problems described above may be either preemptive or nonpreemptive. In the case of *preemptive scheduling*, interruption and subsequent resumption of execution of a load, either in the same processor or elsewhere, is permitted. In *nonpreemptive scheduling* the currently executing load is allowed to run till completion without any interruption.

In general, the formulation of a scheduling problem consists mainly of four steps.

  (i) Modeling the system
 (ii) Defining the type of processing load
(iii) Formulating an objective function (or cost function)
 (iv) Specifying the constraints

The model describes the system, the type of network, the number of processors, whether they are equipped with front ends or not, the topology of the network, and so on. The type of processing load determines the scheduling algorithm. Different types of loads are defined in the next section. In general, the objective of the scheduling problem (the objective function) is as follows: *Given a set of loads and a system, what is the best possible mapping of these loads onto the processors such that the desired cost function is optimized?* As an example, the objective function could be the minimization of the following:

$$\text{Total cost} = \text{computation cost} + \text{communication cost} \qquad (1.1)$$

Here the total cost refers to the processing time of a load or a set of loads. As can be seen from Equation (1.1), the total cost takes into account both the computation and the communication costs. The constraints for this problem may be the limitations on the availability of processors and communication channels in the system. Another objective could be to find the bounds on the number of schedules that satisfy certain constraints on communication only. There is another class of scheduling problems in which the objective is to optimally partition a multiprocessor system into smaller subsystems and to then schedule loads onto these subsystems such that the processing time is a minimum.

1.3 CLASSIFICATION OF LOADS

By and large, the scheduling problems discussed in the literature do not attempt to formulate scheduling policies based on the type of jobs submitted by a user, except perhaps where resource constraints are involved. Usually, the stress has been on designing efficient parallel algorithms in place of conventional sequential algorithms. This requires identification of parallelism in an algorithm and is known as *function parallelism*. However, there is another kind of parallelism that occurs in the data and is called *data parallelism*. This is usually found in computational-intensive tasks with computational loads that consist of large numbers of data points that must be processed by programs, copies of which are resident in all the processors in the system (for example, the SIMD architecture). This adds a new dimension to the scheduling problem. Such loads can be split into several parts and assigned to many processors. But the manner in which this partitioning (or load division) can be done depends on the type of load. In this section we classify computational loads based on their *divisibility property*.

Scheduling of loads has also been categorized as either *job scheduling* or *task scheduling*. A job is defined to be composed of a number of tasks. If a job in its entirety is assigned to a processor, it is called job scheduling, as in distributed computing systems. If different tasks are assigned to different processors, it is called task scheduling, as in parallel processing systems. Thus, the kind of scheduling depends primarily on the type of load being processed. In Figure 1.2 we show a classification of loads based upon their divisibility property, that is, the property that determines whether a load can be decomposed into a set of smaller loads or not.

1.3.1 Indivisible Loads

These loads are independent, indivisible, and, in general, of different sizes. This means that a load cannot be further subdivided and has to be processed in its entirety in a single processor. These loads do not have any precedence relations and in the context of static/deterministic scheduling, these problems are considered to be

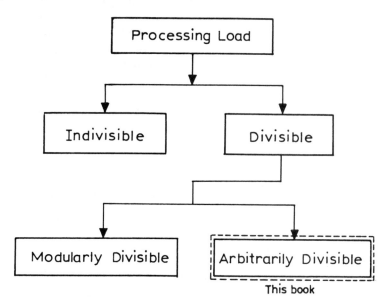

FIGURE 1.2   Classification of Processing Loads

analogous to *bin-packing* problems discussed in the literature. These problems are known to be NP-complete and hence only heuristic algorithms can be proposed to obtain suboptimal solutions in reasonable time. On the other hand, in the case of dynamic/stochastic scheduling schemes, these loads arrive at different time instants and the problem is to schedule them based on the availability and speed of the processors or only on the state of the system.

1.3.2 Modularly Divisible Loads

These loads are a priori subdivided into smaller loads or tasks based on some characteristics of the load or the system. These smaller loads are also called tasks/subtasks or modules, and hence the name. The processing of a load is said to be completed when all its modules are processed. Usually these loads are represented as graphs whose vertices correspond to the modules, and whose edges represent interaction between these modules. This modular representation of a load is known as *Task Interaction Graph* (TIG) in the literature. If these modules are subject to precedence relations, then a directed graph is used. On the other hand, if the graph is not directed, though the modules may exchange information, then it is assumed that they can be executed in any order. They can also be totally independent, in which case they may be modeled as indivisible loads, each consisting of a single module.

1.3.3 Arbitrarily Divisible Loads

This kind of load has the property that all elements in the load demand an identical type of processing. These loads can be arbitrarily partitioned into any number of load fractions. These load fractions may or may not have precedence relations. For example, in the case of Kalman filtering applications, the data is arbitrarily divisible but precedence relations exist among these data segments or load fractions. On the other hand, if the load fractions do not have precedence relations, then each load fraction can be independently processed. This book addresses the problem of scheduling arbitrarily divisible loads, which do not have precedence relations, among several processors. Such loads are encountered in many applications. We describe some of them below.

1.4 DIVISIBLE LOADS: APPLICATIONS

Feature extraction and edge detection in image processing. In computer vision systems, image feature extraction is an extremely important function. This basically consists of two levels of processing, namely, a local computation followed by a nonlocal interprocessor communication and computation. The first level of computation partitions the given image into many segments. Each of these segments is processed locally and independently on different processors. This is done to extract local features of the image from different segments. In the second level of computation, these local features from different processors are exchanged and processed to extract the desired feature. It is at the first level of computation that the load can be considered to be arbitrarily divisible without any precedence relations. Similarly, edge detection is a very well-known problem in image processing. Here the objective is to detect the edge or boundary of an image. As before, the given image can be arbitrarily partitioned into several subframes of varying sizes (that is, each may contain a different number of pixels) and each of these subframes can be processed independently.

A practical situation in which processing of such data may frequently be necessary involves the space shuttle orbiter, which collects massive volume of image data that has to be communicated to the earth station for processing (by a parallel or distributed computing system). This kind of data also has the potential of arbitrary divisibility. The data can be partitioned and sent directly for processing to a number of processors situated at various geographical points on the surface of the earth, in which case they incur considerable communication delay. Depending on the location of the processing units the communication delays will be different.

Signal processing.   A simple application involves the problem of recovering a signal buried in zero-mean noise. The raw data consists of a large number of measurements that can be arbitrarily partitioned and shared among several processors. Another application involves passing a very long linear data file through a digital filter. This might be for frequency shaping purposes (that is, passing the data through a low pass filter) or for pattern matching (that is, passing the data through a matched filter designed to find a particular pattern). In either case the data file may be partitioned among a number of processors. Each processor runs the same filter on its segment of the data. Some care must be taken at the partition boundaries (overlapping the segments slightly is one possibility) when the results are reported back to the originating processor. For the frequency shaping case the output is a filtered data record while for the pattern matching case the results are the location(s) in the data file where the desired pattern was found.

Here we will briefly describe a feature extraction problem in which the arbitrary divisibility property of the image data is exploited to expedite processing. Consider an image in the form of a cluster of pixels that may be a subset of the original image array. The primary task of image feature extraction is to process this data to generate a representation that facilitates higher level symbolic manipulations. It is possible to exploit data parallelism at this stage of processing by assigning different portions of the image array to each of the processors in a parallel or distributed processing system. There could be several subtasks that must be executed to achieve this goal. For example, computation of Hough transforms and region moments are two universally recognized tasks that have to be performed in a majority of situations. In addition, these tasks allow us to exploit data parallelism to the full extent.

To illustrate the above point, consider the Hough transform of straight lines in an image. It is given as an array $B(\rho, \theta)$, each element of which represents the number of pixels whose spatial coordinates (x, y) in the given image array satisfy the equation

$$\rho = x \, \cos\theta \, + \, y \, \sin\theta \qquad (1.2)$$

For each pair (x, y), the value of ρ is computed for a set of discrete values of θ. Thus, each point in the (x, y) plane generates a curve in the (ρ, θ) plane. Based on the nature of these curves and their relative positions one can identify $B(\rho, \theta)$ and obtain information about the features in the given image array. Note that the computation of Hough transform for each point in the image array is done independent of any of the other points. This aspect makes the data (image array) arbitrarily divisible.

Similarly, the $(k + l)$th order region moment of a cluster of image data is computed as

$$m_{kl} = \sum_{x} \sum_{y} x^k y^l I(x, y) \tag{1.3}$$

where $I(x, y)$ is the image intensity of the pixel (x, y). The complete set of moments of order n consists of all moments of order less than or equal to n. Here, too, it is apparent that the data can be arbitrarily divided among the processors to carry out the required computations.

As an illustrative example, let us assume that the data to be processed in the above manner is stored in a (512×512) image array. Let the computations done on a single pixel take 1 unit of time in any of the processors in a network consisting of four identical processors (p_0, p_1, p_2, p_3) connected through a bus and having separate local memories (shown in Figure 1.3). The data to be processed is resident in p_0, which can communicate segments of the data, one at a time, to the other processors. If the communication delay in sending the data is negligible then it is wise to distribute the data in four equal parts. For example, each processor can be assigned 128 rows (see Figure 1.4, left side), thus incurring a processing time of $(1 \times 128 \times 512)$ time units. This strategy is normally recommended in the literature. However, when the communication delay is not negligible, as when the processors are well separated, then this strategy is no longer optimal. Suppose the time delay for communicating one pixel from one processor to another is 10 percent of the computation time per pixel. Then the times taken by each processor to complete its computation is $(1 \times 128 \times 512)$ time units for p_0, $(1.1 \times 128 \times 512)$ time units for p_1, $(1.2 \times 128 \times 512)$ time units for p_2, and $(1.3 \times 128 \times 512)$ time units for p_3. Thus, the processing of the complete data is over only after processor p_3 completes its computation. Hence, the presence of communication delay has increased the processing time by 30 percent. But it is obvious that we can exploit the arbitrary divisibility property of the data to improve performance. For example, let us allocate 147 rows to p_0, 134 rows to p_1, 121 rows to p_2, and 110 rows to p_3 (see Figure 1.4, right side). Then the processing time for each processor is $(1 \times 147 \times 512)$ time units for p_0, $(1.1 \times 134 \times 512)$ time units

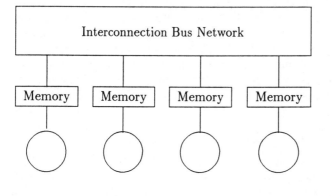

Processor 0   Processor 1   Processor 2   Processor 3

FIGURE 1.3 Bus Network with Four Processors

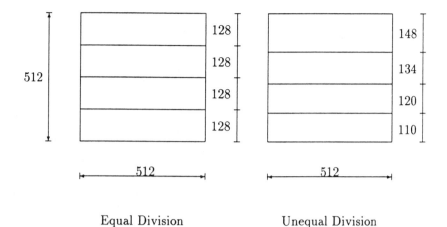

Equal Division   Unequal Division

FIGURE 1.4   Partitioning of Data for Image Feature Extraction

for p_1, $(0.1 \times 134 \times 512 + 1.1 \times 121 \times 512)$ time units for p_2, and $(0.1 \times 134 \times 512 + 0.1 \times 121 \times 512 + 1.1 \times 110 \times 512)$ time units for p_3. From the above, we find that p_1 takes the maximum time to complete its computation. For comparison, we can rewrite this time as $(1.152 \times 128 \times 512)$ time units and note that this strategy has produced a 15 percent reduction over the naive equal division strategy.

The above example demonstrates how the arbitrary divisibility property of the data can be exploited to enhance the performance of a real-world image feature extraction algorithm. However, note that since we have allocated data in terms of rows, the data is not arbitrarily divisible in the true sense, but may be considered to be so for large volumes of data. We shall clarify this point in detail in Chapter 2.

Although we use the words scheduling, sharing, and distribution interchangeably in the context of an arbitrarily divisible load, which is shared or distributed among several processors, the phrases *load sharing* and *load distribution* appear to be more appropriate.

1.5 COMMUNICATION DELAY

As demonstrated in the example given in the above section, a crucial aspect in the modeling of a parallel and distributed computing system is the communication delay incurred during transfer of load through the links. These delays, in general, are due to communication processing time, queueing time, transmission time, and propagation time. In order to evaluate the performance of a system, the mathematical model must take into account all these delays. However, for the ease of analysis, approximate models can be employed.

When a load, or a part of it, is communicated to other processors via communication links, the delay (the time it takes to reach the destination) incurred is reflected in the objective function as communication costs, as shown in Equation (1.1). A good scheduling policy must take into account these communication delays. In the case of scheduling modularly divisible loads, it is assumed that the communication costs between two interacting modules are known a priori. In the literature, many

computational-intensive loads have been considered arbitrarily divisible, and are usually partitioned and distributed equally among several identical processors. As shown
above in the discussion of Figure (1.4), this equal partitioning is optimal if one considers a system where communication delays are negligible. However, if the same
application were to be carried out in a system where communication delays were
significant, the load distribution strategy would have to take this delay into account.

1.6 DIVISIBLE LOAD THEORY

Most of the parallel processing literature concentrates on identifying and exploiting
inherent parallelisms in sequential programs and on producing parallel programs that
can run on multiprocessor systems. However, there is another kind of parallelism
that can be exploited. This is the parallelism inherent in large *computational loads*.
There exists a large class of loads that involve very large data files that must be
processed by programs, copies of which are resident in all the processors in the
system. In general, such a load (data file) can be one of the types mentioned in
Section 1.3 or a mix of some or all of them; that is, some segments of the load
can belong to one category while the others belong to a different category. Identification of these segments in a given load will be the first step toward exploiting
parallelism in the data. This knowledge, coupled with system-dependent constraints,
like communication delays and processor characteristics, can then be used to partition
and share the load optimally among the processors in the network. There is no well-
established theory in the literature that helps a user to accomplish this goal. But, judg-
ing from its applicability from the viewpoint of scheduling computational-intensive
loads, such a theory will indeed be useful. We will call this theory, which identifies
and exploits data parallelism in a computational load, *Divisible Load Theory* (DLT).
We wish to add a word of caution that the theory cannot yet be considered complete, but is rather at an incipient stage. However, many key concepts that form the
basis of DLT have been studied extensively in the literature on scheduling and load
balancing.

It is not our intention to cover divisible load theory in this book, but rather
to apply some of its fundamental concepts to the problem of scheduling arbitrarily
divisible loads in which each data point receives independent processing. Though
there has been a considerable body of literature dealing with scheduling/sharing of
indivisible and modularly divisible loads, until recently arbitrarily divisible loads and
loads of the mixed type have not received much attention. Only very recently has
there been interest in the scheduling of arbitrarily divisible loads. Studies in this area
address the following question:

Given an arbitrarily divisible load without precedence relations and a multi-
processor/multicomputer system subject to communication delays, in what proportion
should the processing load be partitioned and distributed among the processors so
that the entire load is processed in the shortest possible time?

One of the major issues is that of computation-communication trade-off relationships. The answer to the above question depends entirely on this issue and we
will devote considerable attention to it here. Since this is the first attempt in this
direction, we adopt a simplified linear system model for study. This yields a continuous mathematical formulation and provides a flexible analytical tool. Like previous

linear models in other areas (for example, electric circuit theory and queueing theory) this leads to tractable analysis and a rich set of results.

Apart from the applications specified in Section 1.3.3 for arbitrarily divisible loads, there are situations in which one may need to process a large volume of data in almost real time. Such applications include target identification, problems in search theory, and processing of data in distributed sensor networks. In these applications, processing the load in the shortest possible time is a most crucial requirement, and these are precisely the situations in which divisible load theory becomes even more important. However, not all such loads need be arbitrarily divisible. In general, these loads are of a mixed kind.

Finally, we stress that this book presents important theoretical developments concerning scheduling strategies for arbitrarily divisible loads, but does not cover issues related to implementation of these strategies on any specific parallel or distributed computing system. Implementation issues, which are a subject of study in themselves, are beyond the scope of this book.

BIBLIOGRAPHIC NOTES

Section 1.1 The taxonomy of multiprocessor/multicomputer systems can be found in Hwang and Briggs (1989). An excellent overview of parallel and distributed systems and their many salient features is available in Bertsekas and Tsitsiklis (1989), Bokhari (1987), and Lewis et al. (1992). A specific instance of a distributed system made up of several high performance work stations interconnected by a high speed network, for solving computationally-intensive tasks, is described in Atallah et al. (1992). Parallel and distributed systems, their mapping into various kinds of architectures, and their salient features are dealt with in many books [Hwang and Briggs (1989), Siegel (1990), DeCegama (1989)]. In addition, Coulouris and Dollimore (1988) present a comprehensive description of several distributed architectures, their communication networks and protocols, and provide case studies on many real-world architectures. Sloman and Kramer (1987) also address many of the above aspects of distributed systems but with primary emphasis on communications issues. Leighton (1992) describes in detail techniques to implement various mathematical algorithms in linear arrays, trees, and hypercube architectures.

Section 1.2 One of the first papers to provide a classification of scheduling methods in distributed computing systems is by Casavant and Kuhl (1988). Tzafestas and Triantafyllakis (1993) provide an extensive survey of deterministic scheduling policies. Stankovic et al. (1995) also provide a classification of scheduling policies. In addition, they present an excellent account of the applicability of classical scheduling theory to real-time systems. Some recent representative papers that model the scheduling problems in several different ways are Anger et al. (1990), Fernandez-Baca (1989), Krishnamurti and Ma (1992), Lee et al. (1992), Nation et al. (1993), Price and Salama (1990), Shin and Chen (1990), and Veltman et al. (1990). A comprehensive discussion on load sharing policies in multicomputer systems is available in Shivaratri et al. (1992). An excellent collection of papers providing a broad coverage of topics related to scheduling and load balancing in parallel and distributed computing systems is available in Shirazi et al. (1995). The papers in this collection are grouped into chapters based on important issues such as static scheduling; task granularity and partitioning (though in a different context than that addressed in the present book); scheduling tools for parallel processing; load balancing in distributed systems; task migration; and load indices. The introductory notes provided by the editors, prefacing each group of papers, are especially enlightening. Another source of information on current work in this area is the special issue on scheduling and load balancing published by the *J. of Parallel and Distributed Computing* [Shirazi and Hurson (1992)].

Section 1.3   The concept of data parallelism and function parallelism, in the context of a SIMD architecture, is given in Kim et al. (1991). Job scheduling and task scheduling are defined explicitly in Tantawi and Towsley (1985). The formal classification of loads from the viewpoint of divisibility is of recent origin [Bharadwaj (1994)]. Static scheduling of indivisible loads has been addressed by Coffman (1976) and Coffman et al. (1978), among many others. Stankovic (1985) and Weber (1993) discuss certain problems associated with dynamic/stochastic scheduling policies for such loads. Norman and Thanisch (1993), in a survey paper, discuss scheduling of modularly divisible loads. Task interaction graphs have been used extensively in Lee et al. (1992). Jobs with precedence relationships have been discussed by Murthy and Selvakumar (1993), Peng and Shin (1993), Price and Salama (1990), and Xu (1993), while those without precedence relationships have been considered in a paper by Stone (1977) and later extended by Lee et al. (1992). Scheduling of a collection of independent tasks in a multiprocessor system, and some related issues, are discussed in Swami et al. (1992). The literature on these topics is vast and we have cited only a few representative references. The problem of scheduling arbitrarily divisible loads was first considered by Cheng and Robertazzi (1988).

Section 1.4   Edge detection and feature extraction problems in image processing that expressly use divisible loads have been described in Carlson et al. (1994), Choudhary and Ponnusamy (1991), and Gerogiannis and Orphanoudakis (1993), among others. The data processing requirements for the space shuttle orbiter is a recent area of research and development and a brief account of this work can be found in Binder (1994). The image feature extraction problem given here for illustration is taken from Gerogiannis and Orphanoudakis (1993), where the arbitrary divisibility property of the data has been used to implement a load balancing algorithm, based on an efficient redistribution scheme, on an iPSC/2 hypercube (a MIMD machine) and the CM-2 (a SIMD machine) to obtain significant improvements in performance. However, the communication delays are not considered in any of these studies.

Section 1.5   A general model of communication delay is given in Bertsekas and Tsitsiklis (1989). However, many approximations depending on the application have been discussed in the literature, for example, Stone (1977), Lee et al. (1992), Fernandez-Baca (1989), Norman and Thanisch (1993), and Reed and Grunwald (1987).

Section 1.6   The first paper that uses divisible load theory is by Cheng and Robertazzi (1988) and was motivated by data fusion application in distributed sensor networks [Tenney and Sandell (1981)]. However, the definition of divisible load theory given here is the first attempt to provide a functional, but not a complete, description of the theory.

CHAPTER 2

The System Model

As mentioned in Chapter 1, the solution of a scheduling problem in a multiprocessor/multicomputer system requires a model of the system, identification of the type of loads, formulation of an objective function, and specification of the constraints. In this chapter, we present the various network component models adopted in this book. These models are universally used in most studies on arbitrarily divisible loads. It is assumed that the processing loads considered here are of the arbitrarily divisible kind, in which each data element requires an independent and identical type of processing. Our aim is to obtain an optimal partition of the processing load such that the entire load can be distributed to several processors and processed in the shortest possible time. Thus, we define the objective function to be the time taken to process the entire load, and we frequently refer to this as the *time performance* of the system.

2.1 PROCESSOR MODEL

It is assumed that the load arrives at only one particular processor in the network, known as the *originating processor* or the *root processor*. The scheduling operation involves partitioning and distribution of the processing load to all the processors. The processing of a load is said to be complete only when all its load fractions have been processed by the processors to which they are assigned. The next load, if any, is taken up for processing only after processing of the current load is complete. Of course, in certain situations, it may be advantageous to relax this condition. We shall discuss this in Chapter 12.

In general, the processors in a network may be classified as *identical, uniform,* or *unrelated*. The processors in the network are said to be *identical* if they have identical speeds, that is, if they take the same amount of time to compute a given load. Processors in the network are said to be *uniform* if they have different speeds, but the speeds are independent of the type of load. For example, if a processor p_1 takes time t_1 to process any given load, and processor p_2 takes time t_2 to process the same load, then the ratio t_1/t_2 is a constant for all loads. In fact, this ratio is equal to unity for identical processors. Thus, identical processors are also uniform, but the converse may not be true. The processors in a network are said to be *unrelated* when the speed of the processors is dependent on the type of load submitted for processing, that is, when the ratio t_1/t_2, defined above, varies with the type of load. When the loads are of the same type, the unrelated processors act like uniform processors. In this book we will assume the processors to be either identical or uniform.

We will denote the parameter that characterizes a processor's speed by a symbol w_i for a processor p_i. This parameter is defined as

$$w_i = \frac{\text{Time taken by processor } p_i \text{ to compute a given load}}{\text{Time taken by a standard processor to compute the same load}}$$

Obviously, for a standard processor, used for reference, the value of this parameter is equal to one. The standard processor referred to here may be any existing processor in the network, or some fictitious processor that serves as a convenient reference. Thus, the parameter w_i is inversely proportional to the speed of the processor p_i. In reality, w_i is not a deterministic quantity—a processor may not devote its full time to process a given load (for example, in a time-sharing system) or the processors may be subject to degraded performance. In such cases, it may be more realistic to model w_i as a stochastic quantity with some assumed probability distribution. However, in this book, we assume w_i to be a deterministic quantity. This is supported by the fact that even in an analysis based on a stochastic framework the expected values of the performance measures of interest are obtained with acceptable accuracy by replacing the random variable w_i by its mean.

We define another parameter denoted by T_{cp} as

$$T_{cp} = \text{Time taken to process a unit load by the standard processor}$$

The quantity $w_i T_{cp}$ represents the time taken by the processor p_i to process a unit load. Therefore, if α_i is the fraction of load assigned to p_i, then the time taken to compute this fraction by processor p_i is given by $\alpha_i w_i T_{cp}$. Thus, the time required to process a given load is proportional to the amount of load given to the processor. In subsequent chapters, we make the assumption that all processors are available for computation right from the start. We will relax this assumption partially in Chapter 12. Note that though this is a strong assumption for a general distributed system, it is usually true for a dedicated system. This assumption also leads to a simplification of the analysis, but yields results that are not qualitatively different from the results obtained by relaxing the assumption. Moreover, the analytical techniques used in this book can be easily extended to cases where this assumption is relaxed.

As mentioned in Chapter 1, the processors in a distributed computing system may or may not be equipped with front ends or communication coprocessors. Although such dedicated front ends usually exist there may be instances where this may not be true. This is a distinct possibility since the front ends are normally separate machines attached to the main processor and are subject to failure. When this happens, the main processor takes over the task of communication in addition to its computational task. Further, fast communication channels may help in dispensing with front ends altogether. This provides the rationale for considering processor models with and without front ends. We assume that the processors or the front ends have adequate buffer (memory) capacity to store processing loads.

2.2 COMMUNICATION LINK MODEL

As in the case of processors, we may characterize communication links as either *identical* or *uniform*. The concept of *unrelated* links is not relevant here since the speed of a link does not depend on the type of load it carries. In general, in the case of parallel processing systems, the communication time between any two processors is modeled as the sum of the *communication start-up time* and the *transmission time* (or *transit time*). The start-up time is usually a constant, whereas the transmission time is a function of the size of the load and the bandwidth (or the speed) of the link connecting the two processors. Similarly, the communication delay model in a distributed computing system involves the following components:

(i) *Communication processing time t_C*: This is the delay involved in getting the information ready for transmission. It consists of the time taken to organize the load into packets, append source and destination addresses and control codes to the packets, ascertain the availability of a link on which to transmit each packet, and store the packets in buffers.

(ii) *Queueing time t_Q*: Before the start of transmission the packets may have to wait in a queue in the link buffer. This can happen because of temporary non-availability of the communication link due to priority, contention resolution, temporary resource constraints, non-readiness of the destination node, and various other operational reasons. In general, queueing time is random in nature and is difficult to quantify, but approximate models are usually sufficient to yield meaningful results.

(iii) *Transmission time t_T*: This is the time it takes for the complete information to be transmitted from the source.

(iv) *Propagation time t_P*: This is the time it takes for a single bit in the packet to travel from the source to the destination.

Hence, in general, the overall communication delay can be expressed as

$$\text{Communication delay} = t_C + t_Q + t_T + t_P$$

where t_C is the time required for preparing the information for transmission, t_Q is the time that the packets of information spend in the queue, t_T is the time required to transmit all the information, and t_P is the time taken by the last bit in the information to travel from the source to the destination. In addition, there could be another delay component arising from the necessity to process the received data before it is ready for computation. This component can be easily incorporated in t_C.

One may also consider the communication delay to be the sum of a component proportional to the size of the load, a constant component, and a stochastic component independent of the size of the load. The proportional part is mainly due to the transmission time and partly due to the communication processing time (since the number of packets depends on the size of the information, and each of them requires the same kind of preprocessing). The constant part of the communication delay is due to the propagation time. The stochastic part depends mainly on the queueing time. Depending upon the given system and its function, one or more of the above may be neglected. Usually, the queueing time may be neglected for systems that are not affected by resource constraints.

In this book we consider two types of networks, namely, single-level tree or star networks and linear networks. In both networks we use the *single-port* communication regimen, in which each processor can send the load to at most one of its neighbors at a time. Further, the constant part of the delay (propagation delay) is assumed to be negligible since the amount of load that is communicated to one processor by the other is very large. It is assumed that the communication delay is only due to the transmission time of the load over the link, and hence is proportional to the size of the load. Later, in Chapter 5, we will justify our model.

As in the processor model, we denote the parameter that characterizes the communication link speed as z_i for link l_i in a distributed computing system. For a given amount of load this parameter is defined as

$$z_i = \frac{\text{Time taken by the link } l_i \text{ to communicate the given load}}{\text{Time taken by a standard link to communicate the same load}}$$

Obviously, for a standard link, used for reference, the value of this parameter is equal to one. It may be noted that the standard link referred to here may be any existing link in the network, or some fictitious link that serves as a convenient reference. Thus, the parameter z_i is inversely proportional to the speed of the link l_i. As in the processor model, z_i is, in reality a stochastic quantity, but we assume it to be a deterministic one. This assumption is again supported by similar arguments given for the processor model.

We define another parameter denoted by T_{cm} as

$$T_{cm} = \text{Time taken to communicate a unit load on a standard link}$$

The parameter $z_i T_{cm}$ is the time taken to communicate a unit load over the link l_i. Hence, if α_i is the fraction of the total unit load that is to be sent to a processor via the link l_i, then the time taken to communicate this load is given by $\alpha_i z_i T_{cm}$. Thus the communication time is proportional to the amount of load that is to be transferred over a link.

Note that it is possible to have more than one communication link from one processor to another. This could be either for fault tolerance or for increased capacity. Although we assume that there is a single communication link between two processors, multiple links can be modeled as a single link with an equivalent communication capacity.

In a network, if all the processors have the same speeds and all the links have the same speeds, then the network is referred to as a *homogeneous* network. According to our earlier classification, we see that the processors and links in a homogeneous network are identical. On the other hand, a network that does not satisfy the above property is referred to as a *heterogeneous* network. Thus, we can only say that these processors and links belong to the uniform category.

2.3 SOME DEFINITIONS

Throughout the book the following important basic definitions will be used frequently. In both the architectures considered, we assume that there are $(m + 1)$ processors $(p_0, p_1, \ldots, p_m)$ and m links $(l_1, \ldots, l_m)$.

(i) *Load distribution (LD)*: This is defined as an ordered $(m + 1)$tuple α given by

$$\alpha = (\alpha_0, \alpha_1, \ldots, \alpha_m) \tag{2.1}$$

where α_i is the load fraction assigned to p_i. Further,

$$\sum_{i=0}^{m} \alpha_i = 1 \tag{2.2}$$

and

$$0 \leq \alpha_i \leq 1, \quad i = 0, 1, \ldots, m \tag{2.3}$$

The set of all such load distributions is denoted by L. Obviously, L is a closed, bounded, and convex set. This simple definition will be modified in later chapters to suit different types of load distribution.

(ii) *Finish time*: The finish time of p_i, denoted by $T_i(\alpha)$, for a given load distribution $\alpha \in L$, is defined as the time difference between the instant at which the ith processor stops computing and the time instant at which the root processor initiates the process.

(iii) *Processing time*: For a given $\alpha \in L$, this is defined as

$$T(\alpha) = max\{T_0(\alpha), \ldots, T_i(\alpha), \ldots, T_m(\alpha)\} \tag{2.4}$$

where $T_i(\alpha)$ is the finish time of the processor p_i. In other words, $T(\alpha)$ is the time at which the entire load is processed. This is referred to as the time performance of the network for a given load distribution α.

(iv) *Idle time*: The idle time for a processor p_i is defined as the time interval between the instants at which the root processor initiates the load distribution process and the time instant at which the processor p_i starts its computation or communication, and is denoted as $T_{idle(i)}$.

(v) *Minimum processing time*: This is defined as

$$T^* = \min_{\alpha \in L} T(\alpha) \tag{2.5}$$

(vi) *Optimal load distribution*: This is defined as the $(m + 1)$tuple $\alpha^* \in L$ such that the processing time is a minimum, that is,

$$\alpha^* = \arg \min_{\alpha \in L} T(\alpha) \tag{2.6}$$

Further, we define the parameter δ as

$$\delta = \frac{T_{cm}}{T_{cp}} \tag{2.7}$$

and the parameter σ as,

$$\sigma = \frac{zT_{cm}}{wT_{cp}} \tag{2.8}$$

The parameter σ is defined only for homogeneous networks and is the ratio of the communication delay to the computation time of a unit load and is frequently referred to as the *network parameter*. The time performance of homogeneous networks can be expressed as a function of this network parameter.

Though the processing load is assumed to be arbitrarily divisible, there are some practical limitations to this assumption. A processing load consists of a collection of a large number of data units and it is not possible to divide a data unit any further. Hence, in reality, each load fraction assigned to a processor must be an integer multiple of the data unit. It may also happen that each load fraction must be an integer multiple of a fixed number of data points (as in the example in Section 1.4, where each load fraction was assumed to consist of an integral number of rows in the given image matrix). Thus, one may define a *divisibility factor d* as the fundamental unit, so that each load fraction n is nd units in length, with n taking integer values. Although this imposes a theoretical restriction on the arbitrary divisibility property of the processing load, in practice large loads can be safely assumed to be arbitrarily divisible without any significant loss of accuracy. In fact, in the rest of this book, we shall assume that the load fraction can take any real value between 0 and 1 as in Equation (2.3). This is the limiting case with $d \to 0$. For loads with a very large number of data points this assumption is quite reasonable.

2.4 AN ILLUSTRATIVE EXAMPLE

The following illustrative example is used to clarify the definitions in the previous section. Note that here, unlike in the example given in Section 1.4, we assume the load to be arbitrarily divisible in the true sense, that is, load fractions can take any real value between 0 and 1.

Example 2.1

We consider a two processor system as shown in Figure 2.1. The speed parameters of the processors p_0 and p_1 are given by $w_0 = 0.5$ and $w_1 = 0.2$, respectively. The link speed parameter is $z_1 = 0.1$. Further, we assume $T_{cp} = T_{cm} = 1.0$. Let a unit load originate at processor p_0. Also, let us assume that the processor p_0 is equipped with a front end for communications offloading. The load, being arbitrarily divisible, is divided into two subloads, which we denote as α_0 and α_1. Since we have assumed a unit load, there are infinite ways in which the load can be divided as α_0 and α_1 and distributed between p_0 and p_1. Each such division constitutes a tuple, that is, (α_0, α_1), such that $\alpha_0 + \alpha_1 = 1$, and is a *load distribution (LD)*. The set of all such LD is the set L. In the context of the image feature extraction problem discussed in Section 1.4, which had a total load of (512×512) pixels, a load fraction of α_i constitutes a load of $(\alpha_i \times 512 \times 512)$ pixels, $i = 1, 2$. Of course, the result should be rounded off appropriately such that the total load processed is (512×512).

We shall call p_0 as the root processor. The root processor starts computing the load fraction α_0 and simultaneously communicates the load fraction α_1 to p_1 via the

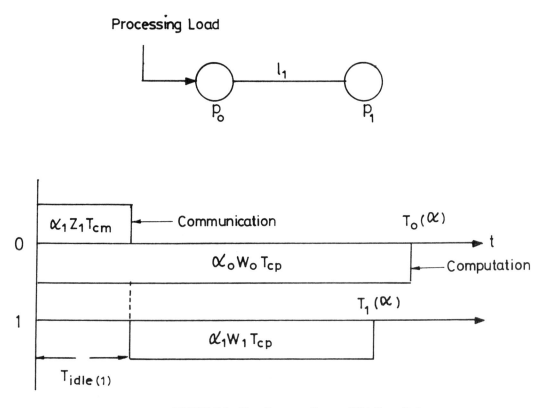

FIGURE 2.1   Two Processor System: With Front End

link l_1. The processor p_1 starts computing immediately upon receiving the load fraction α_1. The processors p_0 and p_1 finish their computations at time instants $T_0(\alpha)$ and $T_1(\alpha)$, where $\alpha \in L$. This process of communication and computation of the respective processors is shown by means of a timing diagram in Figure 2.1. This timing diagram gives a simple pictorial representation of the process of load distribution and computation through a *Gantt-chart*-like diagram. In this timing diagram the communication is shown above the time axis and the computation is shown below the time axis for all processors in the network. That convention is followed throughout this book. It can be seen from this figure that the entire load is processed at a time instant given by the maximum of the two completion times. This completion time is the *processing time* of the load, denoted as $T(\alpha)$. Also, from Figure 2.1 it can be seen that $T_{idle(1)}$ is the time for which the processor p_1 remains idle. This is because during this time the processor p_1 receives the load fraction α_1 via the link l_1 from p_0.

Table 2.1 shows some of the LDs, the corresponding values of the processor's finish times, the idle time of p_1, and the processing time of the load. The expressions for the finish times $T_0(\alpha)$ and $T_1(\alpha)$ of the processors are obtained from the timing diagram shown in Figure. 2.1 as

$$T_0(\alpha) = \alpha_0 w_0 T_{cp} \tag{2.9}$$

$$T_1(\alpha) = \alpha_1 z_1 T_{cm} + \alpha_1 w_1 T_{cp} \tag{2.10}$$

$$T_{idle(1)} = \alpha_1 z_1 T_{cm} \tag{2.11}$$

TABLE 2.1   A Two Processor DCS: Example 2.1

$T_{cm} = T_{cp} = 1$,		$w_0 = 0.5$,	$w_1 = 0.2$,	$z_1 = 0.1$	
Case	α_0	α_1	T_0	T_1	$T_{idle(1)}$	$T = \max(T_0, T_1)$
A	0.6	0.4	0.30	0.12	0.04	0.30
B	0.5	0.5	0.25	0.15	0.05	0.25
C	0.4	0.6	0.20	0.18	0.06	0.20
D	0.35	0.65	0.175	0.195	0.065	0.195
E	0.3	0.7	0.15	0.21	0.07	0.21

From Table 2.1, it can be seen that for Cases A, B, and C the processing time is contributed by p_0. But, in Cases D and E, the processing time is contributed by p_1. The respective idle times are also shown for each case. It may be observed that equal division of the load (Case B) gives a time performance that is worse than the time performance for unequal divisions (Cases C, D, and E). From Table 2.1, it appears that there exists a specific load distribution for which the processing time is contributed by processors p_0 and p_1 both, that is, they stop computing at the same time instant. Such a division of load turns out to be the *optimal load distribution* α^*, yielding the minimum processing time, and is given by $\alpha^* = (0.375, 0.625)$. The corresponding finish times are $T_0(\alpha^*) = T_1(\alpha^*) = 0.1875$, with $T_{idle(1)} = 0.0625$. Hence, comparing the processing times of all the cases with this LD $\alpha^* \in L$, we see that only for this LD the processing time is a minimum. Thus, $T^* = 0.1875$.

In the above example, if the processor p_0 is not equipped with a front end, then the timing diagram is as shown in Figure 2.2. Without a front end a processor may either compute or communicate, but not both simultaneously. Here, p_0 first communicates the load fraction α_1 to p_1, and then starts computing. For this case, the optimal LD α^* is given by $\alpha^* = (0.2857, 0.7143)$, the minimum processing time is $T^* = 0.2143$, and $T_{idle(1)} = 0.07143$. It can be again verified that this minimum

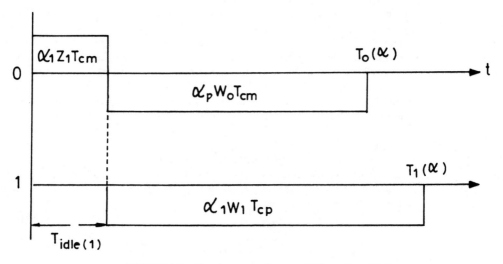

FIGURE 2.2   Two-Processor System: Without Front End

processing time is obtained by dividing the load in such a way that the processors finish computing at the same instant in time.

2.5 CONCLUDING REMARKS

The following are the highlights of this chapter:

- The mathematical models adopted in this book for processors and communication links were presented.
- Some frequently used terms were defined.
- A numerical example was used to illustrate these definitions.

In the next chapter we present a preliminary study of load distribution in linear networks. Most of the study will be carried out through numerical examples, which are expected to serve as a motivation for the analytical results to be presented in the subsequent chapters.

BIBLIOGRAPHIC NOTES

Section 2.1   The classification of processors is standard and has been explained well in the survey paper by Norman and Thanisch (1993).

Section 2.2   The various components of the communication delay have been discussed in many places, for instance, Saad and Schultz (1989) and Bertsekas and Tsitsiklis (1989). The single port communication regimen is discussed in Bhatt et al. (1993).

Section 2.3   The definitions given here have been used earlier only in the context of arbitrarily divisible loads.

Section 2.4   Gantt charts have been widely used in scheduling problems in operations research and in parallel and distributed computing; for example, see Hwang and Briggs (1989).

CHAPTER 3

Load Distribution in Linear Networks

In this chapter, we conduct a preliminary study of the problem of optimally distributing an arbitrarily divisible load in a linear network of processors connected via communication links. Two different cases are considered, one in which the processing load originates at a processor situated at one extreme end of the network (referred to as the *boundary case*); and one in which it originates at an interior processor in the network (referred to as the *interior case*). In each of these situations, we consider two cases, one in which all processors are equipped with front ends (*with-front-end case*); and one in which none of the processors have front ends (*without-front-end case*). First, we formulate the general load distribution equations by expressing the finish times of the processors as functions of the load fractions. Next, we give a simple motivational example to support the intuitive result that for optimality all processors must stop computing at the same instant in time. Based on this optimality condition, we obtain the recursive equations for a general linear network and present a computational technique along with some numerical results. Then, we consider a situation where the results of the computation must be sent back to the load originating processor. Finally, we present the concept of processor equivalence, which helps in grouping together several adjacent processors and provides an alternate proof for the optimality condition, and follow this by a study of the ultimate performance limits of a linear network.

For ease in understanding, the contents of each section in this chapter have been further sectionalized in terms of the cases being considered (boundary/interior and with/without front end).

3.1 GENERAL DESCRIPTION AND PROBLEM FORMULATION

A linear network of processors connected via communication links is shown in Figure 3.1. The load origination for the boundary and interior cases are shown in Figure 3.1a and 3.1b, respectively. The processor at which the load originates is referred to as the *root processor*. When we consider the *with-front-end* case, we assume that *all* processors in the network are equipped with front ends while in the *without-front-end* case we assume that *none* of the processors are equipped with front ends. Each processor in the network keeps a portion of the load it receives and communicates the rest to its immediate successor. If the processors are equipped with front ends, they can compute their own load fraction and communicate the rest of the load to their successors simultaneously. When they are not equipped with front ends, the processors first perform the function of load communication and then begin computation of their own load fractions. In this book, the process of load distribution is represented by Gantt-chart-like timing diagrams. As in the example in Chapter 2, the communication time is shown above the time axis and the computation time is shown below the time axis. This is the convention that we will follow throughout the book. Another convention that we follow is that the load originating at the root processor is assumed to be normalized to unit load.

3.1.1 Load Distribution Equations: With Front End (Boundary Case)

The timing diagram for a given load distribution α is shown in Figure 3.2. The root processor p_0 keeps the load α_0 and communicates the remaining load $(1 - \alpha_0)$ to its successor p_1. Similarly, the processor p_i keeps the load α_i and communicates the remaining load $(1 - \alpha_0 - \alpha_1 - \cdots - \alpha_i)$ to its successor p_{i+1}. This process continues till the last processor gets its share of load. From the timing diagram, the finish times

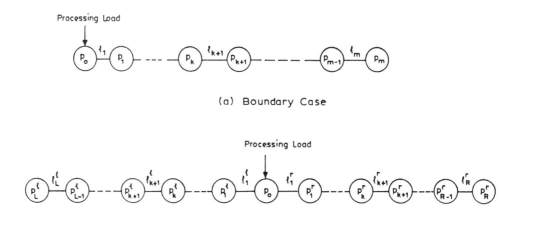

(a) Boundary Case

(b) Interior Case

FIGURE 3.1   Linear Network with Communication Links

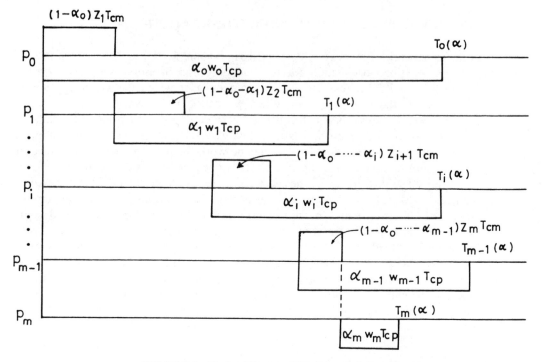

FIGURE 3.2   Timing Diagram: With Front End (Boundary Case)

for processors p_i $(i = 0, \ldots, m)$ can be written as

$$T_0(\alpha) = \alpha_0 w_0 T_{cp} \tag{3.1}$$

For $i = 1, \ldots, m$

$$T_i(\alpha) = \begin{cases} 0, & \text{if } \alpha_i = 0 \\ \sum_{k=1}^{i} \left\{ 1 - \sum_{j=0}^{k-1} \alpha_j \right\} z_k T_{cm} + \alpha_i w_i T_{cp}, & \text{if } \alpha_i \neq 0 \end{cases} \tag{3.2}$$

Note that $\alpha_0 + \alpha_1 + \cdots \alpha_m = 1$. In Equation (3.2), the first term represents the communication delay, that is, the time duration between the time instant at which the root processor initiates the load distribution process and the time instant at which the ith processor begins computing its load α_i. The second term represents the computation time of α_i by p_i. Also note that the root processor does not have any communication delay. Now from Equations (3.1) and (3.2) we can obtain the processing time of a load for any given load distribution α, by using Equation (2.4). These equations are also the fundamental equations based on which the optimal load distribution will be obtained later. The representation of load distribution given above serves our purpose and conforms to the definition of load distribution given in Chapter 2. However, one can also represent this load distribution differently. Let D_i be the load that processor p_i receives and let $\hat{\alpha}_i D_i$ $(0 \leq \hat{\alpha}_i \leq 1)$ be the amount of load retained by p_i for computing and $(1 - \hat{\alpha}_i)D_i$ be the amount of load communicated by p_i to its successor. Then the relation between α_i $(i = 0, \ldots, m)$ and $\hat{\alpha}_i$ $(i = 0, \ldots, m)$ can be written as

$$\alpha_0 = \hat{\alpha}_0$$

$$\alpha_i = \left\{ \prod_{j=0}^{i-1} (1 - \hat{\alpha}_j) \right\} \hat{\alpha}_i, \quad i = 1, \dots, m$$

(3.3)

Also, note that in this scheme $\hat{\alpha}_m = 1$ always, since the last processor has to compute all the load that it receives. Substituting these in the finish time equations above we can obtain the finish times of the processors in this alternative scheme. Though both schemes are identical so far as load distribution is concerned, the latter helps in decentralized decision-making since p_i needs to know only the value of $\hat{\alpha}_i$ regardless of the amount of load that actually originates at the root. In contrast, in the first scheme, p_i has to know both α_i and the amount of load originating at the root to calculate how much of the load it receives should be retained for computation.

3.1.2 Load Distribution Equations: Without Front End (Boundary Case)

The load distribution follows steps similar to the with-front-end case except for the fact that a processor begins computing its load fractions only after communicating to its successor. The timing diagram for a given load distribution α is shown in Figure 3.3.

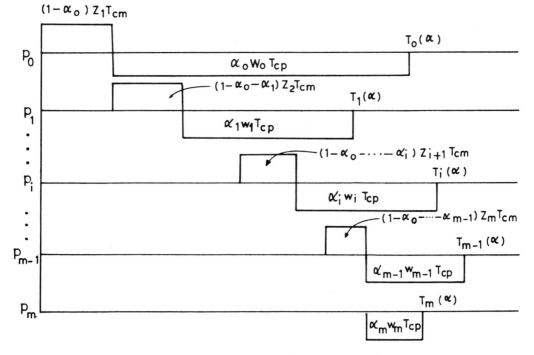

FIGURE 3.3 Timing Diagram: Without Front End (Boundary Case)

As in the with-front-end case, we write the finish times of the processors as follows: For $i = 0, \ldots, m - 1$,

$$T_i(\alpha) = \begin{cases} 0, & \text{if } \alpha_i = 0 \\ \sum_{k=0}^{i} \left\{ 1 - \sum_{j=0}^{k} \alpha_j \right\} z_{k+1} T_{cm} + \alpha_i w_i T_{cp}, & \text{if } \alpha_i \neq 0 \end{cases} \quad (3.4)$$

For $i = m$,

$$T_m(\alpha) = \begin{cases} 0, & \text{if } \alpha_m = 0 \\ \sum_{k=0}^{m-1} \left\{ 1 - \sum_{j=0}^{k} \alpha_j \right\} z_{k+1} T_{cm} + \alpha_m w_m T_{cp}, & \text{if } \alpha_m \neq 0 \end{cases} \quad (3.5)$$

where $\alpha_0 + \alpha_1 + \cdots + \alpha_m = 1$. In this case all the processors including the root have the communication delay component. This is due to the absence of front ends. Using Equations (3.4) and (3.5) we can obtain the processing time of the entire load using Equation (2.4). As mentioned above, these equations will be used later to obtain the optimal load distribution.

As in the with-front-end case, if we use $\hat{\alpha}_i$ $(i = 0, \ldots, m)$ to represent load distribution then we may again use the transformation given in Equation (3.3).

3.1.3 Load Distribution Equations: With Front End (Interior Case)

In this case, the load originating processor (that is, the root processor) lies at the interior of the network. There are L processors on the left and R processors on the right of the root (see Figure 3.1b). It is assumed that the front end of the root processor can transmit in only one direction at a time. Note that the interior case can also be considered as a situation in which the load distribution occurs in a ring topology with the load originating at one of the processors. The root processor first distributes β_l of the unit load to its left immediate neighbor, then β_r of the unit load to its right immediate neighbor, and keeps the load $\alpha_0 = (1 - \beta_l - \beta_r)$ for itself to compute. Upon receiving the load, the left immediate neighbor (the first processor on the left of the root) keeps the load α_1^l for itself to compute and communicates the remaining loads $(\beta_l - \alpha_1^l)$ to its successor. In general, the ith processor on the left (p_i^l) keeps the load α_i^l and communicates the remaining load $(\beta_l - \alpha_1^l - \cdots - \alpha_i^l)$ to its successor p_{i+1}^l. This process continues until the Lth processor on the left gets its share of the load. An exactly similar process of load distribution takes place in the processors on the right side of the root. The timing diagram for a given load distribution is shown in Figure 3.4. Note that once the root has distributed the load fractions β_l and β_r, the processors on the left or on the right of the root processor can be considered as in the boundary case, with the conditions $\sum_{i=1}^{L} \alpha_i^l = \beta_l$ and $\sum_{i=1}^{R} \alpha_i^r = \beta_r$.

Thus, as in the with-front-end (boundary) case, we can write the finish time equations of the processors as follows: For $i = 1, \ldots, L$,

$$T_i^l(\alpha) = \begin{cases} 0, & \text{if } \alpha_i^l = 0 \\ \beta_l z_1^l T_{cm} + \sum_{k=1}^{i} \left\{ \beta_l - \sum_{j=1}^{k-1} \alpha_j^l \right\} z_k^l T_{cm} + \alpha_i^l w_i^l T_{cp}, & \text{if } \alpha_i^l \neq 0 \end{cases} \quad (3.6)$$

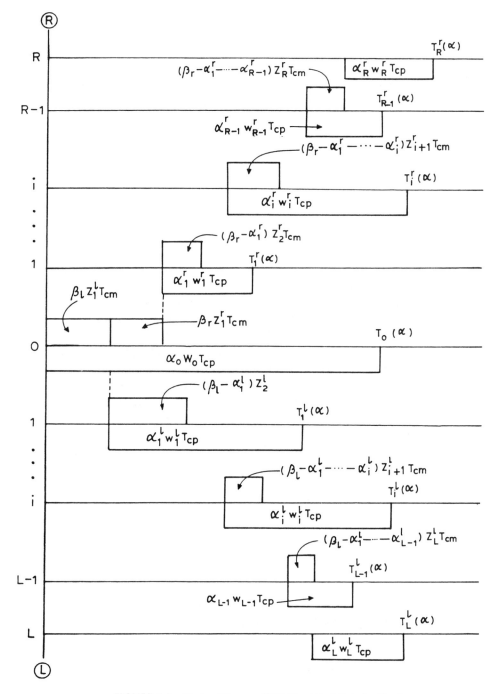

FIGURE 3.4   Timing Diagram: With Front End (Interior Case)

and for $i = 1, \ldots, R$,

$$T_i^r(\alpha) = \begin{cases} 0, & \text{if } \alpha_i^r = 0 \\ \beta_l z_1^l T_{cm} + \beta_r z_1^r + \sum_{k=1}^{i} \left\{ \beta_r - \sum_{j=1}^{k-1} \right\} z_k^r T_{cm} + \alpha_i^r w_i^r T_{cp}, & \text{if } \alpha_i^r \neq 0 \end{cases}$$

(3.7)

where the subscripts l and r refer to the left and right hand side, respectively. The finish time of p_0 is given by

$$T_0(\alpha) = \alpha_0 w_0 T_{cp} \tag{3.8}$$

It may be noted that

$$\alpha_0 + \beta_l + \beta_r = 1 \tag{3.9}$$

$$\sum_{i=1}^{L} \alpha_i^l = \beta_l \tag{3.10}$$

$$\sum_{i=1}^{R} \alpha_i^r = \beta_r \tag{3.11}$$

Note that the communication delay component is more for the processors on the right side than for the processors on the left side of the root. This is because the root processor first communicates to the left and then to the right. Using the above equations, the processing time for any given load distribution can be obtained by taking the maximum of all the finish times.

Even here, one can formulate an alternative but equivalent scheme as follows: The root communicates $\hat{\beta}_l$ of the unit load it receives to its left immediate neighbor and $\hat{\beta}_r$ to its right immediate neighbor, and retains $\hat{\alpha}_0 = 1 - \hat{\beta}_l - \hat{\beta}_r$ for itself to compute. Each processor p_i^l on the left retains $\hat{\alpha}_i^l$ fraction of the load it receives and communicates the rest to its successor. Similarly, each processor p_i^r on the right keeps $\hat{\alpha}_i^r$ fractions of the load it receives and communicates the rest to its successor. Obviously,

$$\beta_l = \hat{\beta}_l, \quad \beta_r = \hat{\beta}_r, \quad \alpha_0 = \hat{\alpha}_0$$

$$\alpha_i^l = \hat{\beta}_l \left\{ \prod_{j=1}^{i-1} (1 - \hat{\alpha}_j^l) \right\} \hat{\alpha}_i^l, \quad i = 1, \ldots, L \tag{3.12}$$

$$\alpha_i^r = \hat{\beta}_r \left\{ \prod_{j=1}^{i-1} (1 - \hat{\alpha}_j^r) \right\} \hat{\alpha}_i^r, \quad i = 1, \ldots, R \tag{3.13}$$

Here, $\hat{\alpha}_L^l = \hat{\alpha}_R^r = 1$ always, since the last processor on either side computes all the load it receives. Substituting these expressions in Equations (3.6) and (3.7) we get the finish time equations under this scheme.

3.1.4 Load Distribution Equations: Without Front End (Interior Case)

The timing diagram for this case for a given load distribution α is shown in Figure 3.5. The load distribution process follows the same steps as that of the with-front-end case

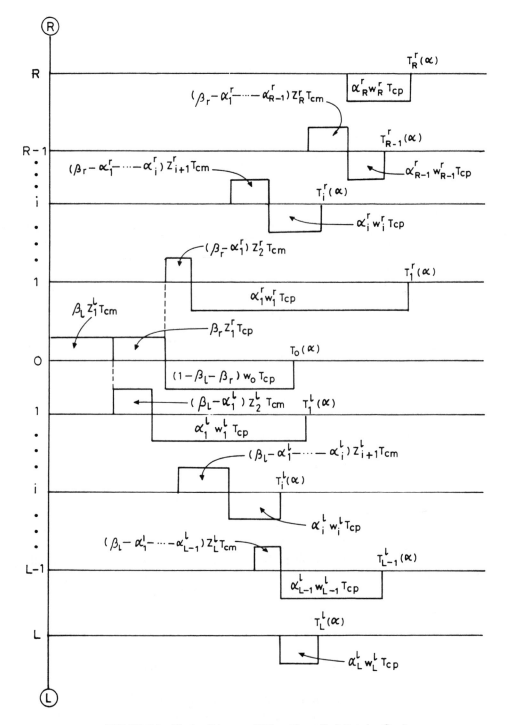

FIGURE 3.5   Timing Diagram: Without Front End (Interior Case)

and the finish time expressions are as follows: For $i = 1, \ldots, L - 1$,

$$T_i^l(\alpha) =$$
$$\begin{cases} 0, & \text{if } \alpha_i^l = 0 \\ \beta_l z_1^l T_{cm} + \sum_{k=1}^{i} \left\{ \beta_l - \sum_{j=1}^{k} \alpha_j^l \right\} z_{k+1}^l T_{cm} + \alpha_i^l w_i^l T_{cp}, & \text{if } \alpha_i^l \neq 0 \end{cases} \quad (3.14)$$

and for $i = L$,

$$T_L^l(\alpha) =$$
$$\begin{cases} 0, & \text{if } \alpha_L^l = 0 \\ \beta_l z_1^l T_{cm} + \sum_{k=1}^{L-1} \left\{ \beta_l - \sum_{j=1}^{L-1} \alpha_j^l \right\} z_{k+1}^l T_{cm} + \alpha_L^l w_L^l T_{cp}, & \text{if } \alpha_L^l \neq 0 \end{cases} \quad (3.15)$$

Similarly, for $i = 1, \ldots, R - 1$,

$$T_i^r(\alpha) =$$
$$\begin{cases} 0, & \text{if } \alpha_i^r = 0 \\ \beta_l z_1^l T_{cm} + \beta_r z_1^r T_{cm} + \sum_{k=1}^{i} \left\{ \beta_r - \sum_{j=1}^{k} \alpha_j^r \right\} z_{k+1}^r T_{cm} + \alpha_i^r w_i^r T_{cp}, & \text{if } \alpha_i^r \neq 0 \end{cases}$$
$$(3.16)$$

and for $i = R$,

$$T_R^r(\alpha) =$$
$$\begin{cases} 0, & \text{if } \alpha_R^r = 0 \\ \beta_l z_1^l T_{cm} + \beta_r z_1^r T_{cm} + \sum_{k=1}^{R-1} \left\{ \beta_r - \sum_{j=1}^{R-1} \alpha_j^r \right\} z_{k+1}^r T_{cm} + \alpha_R^r w_R^r T_{cp}, & \text{if } \alpha_R^r \neq 0 \end{cases}$$
$$(3.17)$$

The finish time of p_0 is given by

$$T_0(\alpha) = \begin{cases} 0 & \text{if } \alpha_0 = 0 \\ \beta_l z_1^l T_{cm} + \beta_r z_1^r T_{cm} + (1 - \beta_l - \beta_r) w_0 T_{cp}, & \text{if } \alpha_0 \neq 0 \end{cases} \quad (3.18)$$

The processing time can be obtained by taking the maximum of all the finish times. Note that finish times of p_L^l (given by Equation (3.15)) and of p_{L-1}^l (given by Equation (3.14) with $i = L - 1$) have identical delay components. This is also true for the last two processors on the right. Here, too, Equations (3.9) through (3.11) hold. If we use the alternative scheme of load distribution then the transformations given in Equations (3.12) and (3.13) will give the required finish time equations.

So far we have obtained the finish times of the processors for each of the cases discussed above. It is possible to have infinitely many load distributions that satisfy the above equations. To obtain the optimal load distribution, we shall impose certain conditions on these finish time expressions. The next section provides a motivation for formulating these conditions.

3.2 MOTIVATION FOR OPTIMAL LOAD DISTRIBUTION

It is intuitively clear that one of the properties that the optimal load distribution (which minimizes the processing time) should satisfy is that none of the processors should be able to complete its computation and then remain idle while other processors are still engaged in computation. It is important to understand that, due to the presence of communication delay, this property is not satisfied by an equal division of load between processors even for a homogeneous network.

3.2.1 Equal Division of Load

Example 3.1

Consider a homogeneous linear network consisting of $(m+1)$ processors equipped with front ends in which the processing load originates at the boundary. Let us consider a case where the processing load is equally divided among the $(m+1)$ processors, that is, $\alpha_0 = \alpha_1 = \cdots = \alpha_m = 1/(m+1)$. Following the methodology of load distribution explained in Section 3.1, the timing diagram for $m = 4, z = 1, w = 1$ is shown in Figure 3.6a.

From the timing diagram, it can be seen that the processing time of the entire load is given by the finish time of the last processor. In general, for the $(m+1)$ processor linear network with front ends, the equal-division load distribution is $\alpha = (\frac{1}{m+1}, \ldots, \frac{1}{m+1})$. Thus the processing time is given by

$$T(\alpha) = T_m(\alpha) = \frac{zT_{cm}}{m+1}\{m + (m-1) + \cdots + 1\} + \frac{wT_{cp}}{m+1}$$

(3.19)

$$= \frac{mzT_{cm}}{2} + \frac{wT_{cp}}{m+1}$$

The corresponding timing diagram for the without-front-end case (with $m = 4, z = 1, w = 1$) is given in Figure 3.6b. From the figure it may be verified that the processing time given by (3.19) holds for the without-front-end case, too.

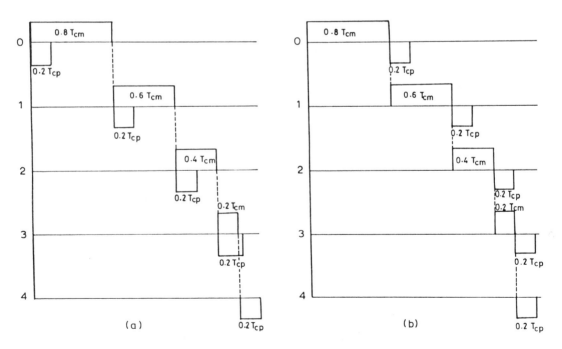

FIGURE 3.6 Timing Diagram for Equal Division of Load (a) with Front End; (b) without Front End

To minimize $T(\alpha)$ with respect to m, Equation (3.19) can be differentiated and equated to zero to yield

$$zT_{cm}(m+1)^2 - 2wT_{cp} = 0 \qquad (3.20)$$

Of course, we assume here that $T(\alpha)$ is a continuous function of m, where m takes values on the positive real line. Solving Equation (3.20) yields the value of m that minimizes the processing time. This optimum value of m is given by

$$m = \sqrt{\frac{2}{\sigma}} - 1 \qquad (3.21)$$

where $\sigma = zT_{cm}/(wT_{cp})$ is the network parameter defined in Chapter 2. Since the function $T(\alpha)$ is convex and unimodal with respect to m, one or both of the adjacent integer values of m given by Equation (3.21) are optimum. Note that for $\sigma \geq 2$, $m = 0$ is the optimum (that is, only the root processor in the network is used). For $0.5 \leq \sigma < 2$, $m = 0$ or 1 is the optimum. For $\sigma < 0.5$ we get optimal values of $m > 1$. From here, we observe that for equal division and a given value of σ, there is an optimal number of processors up to which the load can be shared. Hence, for best results, we have to leave some processors unused. This is obviously an unsatisfactory state of affairs.

It can be seen from the timing diagram in Figure 3.6a that the root processor finishes computing its load fraction much sooner than the last processor in the network does. In fact, in the example, its computation is over even before its front end finishes communicating to p_1. On the other hand, if p_0 is assigned a larger fraction of the load (that is, greater than $\frac{1}{m+1}$) the communication time by its front end would reduce. This would allow p_1 to start its computation earlier in time. It can easily be seen that this gain in time percolates down the network and that the processing of the total load is completed much earlier in time than given by Equation (3.19).

The above example clearly illustrates the situation in which equal division of the processing load is not satisfactory. This basically provides the motivation for obtaining an optimal load distribution. In the next section we shall show that in order to minimize the processing time, the load distribution must be such that all processors must stop computing at the same instant in time. The proof is motivated by the intuitive reasoning that, while distributing arbitrarily divisible loads, one should keep all the processors utilized until the last moment in order to obtain best results.

3.2.2 Optimal Division of Load

Now we will prove the optimality criterion that for a minimum time solution all the processors must stop computing at the same time instant. For simplicity, we consider the boundary case in a homogeneous linear network with front ends ($w = 1$ and $z = 1$). We prove this by first taking into account only the last two processors (p_m and p_{m-1}). We will prove that for a minimum time solution both should stop computing at the same time instant. One can extend this argument to processors p_{m-2} and p_{m-1}.

Consider the two rightmost processors—that is, the $(m-1)$th and the mth. The $(m-1)$th processor keeps a fraction $\hat{\alpha}$ of the data D it has received and transmits the remaining fraction $(1 - \hat{\alpha})$ to the mth processor. There are two possible cases, and both are discussed below. We assume the time reference to be the instant at which p_{m-1} begins computation. We also drop the argument α from the finish time notation for simplicity.

Case i. The mth processor stops first.   The finish times for these two processors are given by

$$T_{m-1} = \hat{\alpha} D T_{cp} \tag{3.22}$$

$$T_m = (1 - \hat{\alpha}) D (T_{cm} + T_{cp}) \tag{3.23}$$

Therefore,

$$\hat{\alpha} D T_{cp} \geq (1 - \hat{\alpha}) D (T_{cm} + T_{cp}) \tag{3.24}$$

From Equation (3.24) we have

$$\hat{\alpha} \geq \frac{T_{cm} + T_{cp}}{T_{cm} + 2T_{cp}} \tag{3.25}$$

The minimum processing time is achieved when T_{m-1} is minimized. Thus,

$$\begin{aligned} \min(T_{m-1}) &= \min(\hat{\alpha}) D T_{cp} = \left\{ \frac{T_{cm} + T_{cp}}{T_{cm} + 2T_{cp}} \right\} D T_{cp} \\ &= (1 - \min(\hat{\alpha})) D (T_{cm} + T_{cp}) = T_m \end{aligned} \tag{3.26}$$

In Equation (3.26) it can be seen that T_m is the finish time one obtains by minimizing $\hat{\alpha}$.

Case ii. The $(m-1)$th processor stops first.   In this case we obtain

$$\hat{\alpha} D T_{cp} \leq (1 - \hat{\alpha}) D (T_{cm} + T_{cp}) \tag{3.27}$$

From (3.27) we have

$$\hat{\alpha} \leq \frac{T_{cm} + T_{cp}}{T_{cm} + 2T_{cp}} \tag{3.28}$$

where the maximum value of $\hat{\alpha}$ is obtained when (3.28) has strict equality. Thus, the minimum processing time is obtained when T_m is minimized.

$$\begin{aligned} \min(T_m) &= (1 - \max(\hat{\alpha})) D (T_{cm} + T_{cp}) = \left\{ 1 - \frac{T_{cm} + T_{cp}}{T_{cm} + 2T_{cp}} \right\} D (T_{cm} + T_{cp}) \\ &= \max(\hat{\alpha}) D T_{cp} = T_{m-1} \end{aligned} \tag{3.29}$$

From Equations (3.26) and (3.29) it is apparent that it is preferable to stop the processors simultaneously rather than stop the mth or the $(m-1)$th processor first. This result shows that the minimum processing time is obtained when both processors stop at the same time instant. This result can be extended to the $(m-2)$th processor by replacing the $(m-1)$th and the mth processors by an equivalent processor with processing time $\hat{\alpha} D T_{cp}$. In this way this result can be generalized to a large linear homogeneous network. In Section 3.5 we shall provide a recursive proof of the optimality criterion for a heterogeneous linear network.

When front-end processors are not present, there are certain parameter values for which distributing the computational load to other processors does not result in a time saving. To see this, consider two adjacent processors p_1 and p_2 with speed parameters w_1 and w_2, connected via a link with speed parameter z. Let p_1 keep α_1

of the total unit load it receives and distribute the rest to p_2. The finish times of the first and second processors are

$$T_1 = (1 - \alpha_1)zT_{cm} + \alpha_1 w_1 T_{cp} \tag{3.30}$$

$$T_2 = (1 - \alpha_1)zT_{cm} + (1 - \alpha_1)w_2 T_{cp} \tag{3.31}$$

Consider these two equations as functions of α_1. The second equation has a negative slope. The first equation has a positive slope if $w_1 T_{cp} > zT_{cm}$ and a negative slope if $w_1 T_{cp} < zT_{cm}$. In the former case there is a value of $\alpha_1 (0 < \alpha_1 < 1)$ that minimizes the computation time. In the latter case computation time is minimized when α_1 equals one. This corresponds to the situation in which p_1 does not distribute any computational load to p_2. Intuitively, the condition for distribution of the computational load, $w_1 T_{cp} > zT_{cm}$, means that the communication time between processors must be less than the computation time of the first processor in order to achieve a net saving through distribution of the processing load.

3.3 RECURSIVE EQUATIONS FOR OPTIMAL LOAD DISTRIBUTION

Based on the optimality criterion discussed above, we shall develop recursive equations for each of the cases discussed in Section 3.1 and present numerical results. Using these, we demonstrate the behaviour of the minimum processing time with respect to the total number of processors in the network (in the boundary case) and with respect to the position of the root processor (in the interior case). Since we assume that all the processors have equal finish times, it is implied that all of them get nonzero load. This fact should be kept in mind while using the finish time equations given in Section 3.1.

3.3.1 Load Origination at the Boundary: With Front End

Optimal load distribution is determined by the requirement that all the processors stop computing at the same instant in time (that is, their finish times are equal). Figure 3.7 shows such a load distribution.

It can be seen that the processing time $\alpha_i w_i T_{cp}$ of the ith processor equals the transmission time $(1 - \alpha_0 - \alpha_1 - \cdots - \alpha_i)z_{i+1}T_{cm}$, from the ith processor to the $(i + 1)$th processor plus the processing time $\alpha_{i+1}w_{i+1}T_{cp}$, of the $(i + 1)$th processor, where α_is are the actual fraction of the load assigned to the ith processor. Thus,

$$\alpha_i w_i T_{cp} = (1-\alpha_0-\alpha_1-\cdots-\alpha_i)z_{i+1}T_{cm}+\alpha_{i+1}w_{i+1}T_{cp}, \quad i = 0, 1, \ldots, m-1 \tag{3.32}$$

These equations, along with the normalizing equation $\sum_{i=0}^{m} \alpha_i = 1$, form a system of $(m + 1)$ linear equations in $(m + 1)$ unknowns. These can be solved computationally by exploiting the recursive nature of the equations as follows: For $i = 0$, we have

$$\alpha_0 w_0 T_{cp} = (1 - \alpha_0)z_1 T_{cm} + \alpha_1 w_1 T_{cp} \tag{3.33}$$

From which we obtain

$$\alpha_1 = \left\{ \frac{w_0 T_{cp} + z_1 T_{cm}}{w_1 T_{cp}} \right\} \alpha_0 - \frac{z_1 T_{cm}}{w_1 T_{cp}} = A_1 \alpha_0 + B_1 \tag{3.34}$$

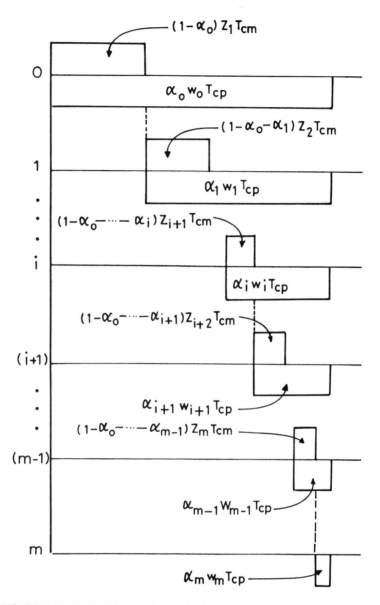

FIGURE 3.7 Timing Diagram for Optimal Load Distribution: With Front End (Boundary Case)

where

$$A_1 = \frac{w_0 T_{cp} + z_1 T_{cm}}{w_1 T_{cp}} \tag{3.35}$$

$$B_1 = -\left\{ \frac{z_1 T_{cm}}{w_1 T_{cp}} \right\} \tag{3.36}$$

For $i = 1$, we have

$$\alpha_1 w_1 T_{cp} = (1 - \alpha_0 - \alpha_1) z_2 T_{cm} + \alpha_2 w_2 T_{cp} \qquad (3.37)$$

Substituting the expressions for α_1 and solving, we get

$$\alpha_2 = A_2 \alpha_0 + B_2 \qquad (3.38)$$

where

$$A_2 = \frac{A_1(w_1 T_{cp} + z_2 T_{cm}) + z_2 T_{cm}}{w_2 T_{cp}} \qquad (3.39)$$

$$B_2 = \frac{B_1(w_1 T_{cp} + z_2 T_{cm}) - z_2 T_{cm}}{w_2 T_{cp}} \qquad (3.40)$$

Continuing like this we can express all the α_i $(i = 1, \ldots, m)$ in terms of α_0 as

$$\alpha_i = A_i \alpha_0 + B_i \qquad (3.41)$$

Each pair (A_i, B_i) can be calculated using (A_{i-1}, B_{i-1}) and the speed parameters of the processors and links. Substituting these in the normalizing equation, we can compute α_0. Using this value of α_0 and Equation (3.41), all the other load fractions can be computed easily. In general, for $i = 3, \ldots, m$,

$$A_i = \frac{A_{i-1}(w_{i-1} T_{cp} + z_i T_{cm}) + (1 + \sum_{j=1}^{i-2} A_j) z_i T_{cm}}{w_i T_{cp}} \qquad (3.42)$$

$$B_i = \frac{B_{i-1}(w_{i-1} T_{cp} + z_i T_{cm}) + (\sum_{j=1}^{i-2} B_j - 1) z_i T_{cm}}{w_i T_{cp}} \qquad (3.43)$$

An alternative way to compute these load fractions is by using $\hat{\alpha}_i$ $(i = 0, \ldots, m)$ defined in Section 3.1. This yields

$$\hat{\alpha}_i w_i T_{cp} = (1 - \hat{\alpha}_i) z_{i+1} T_{cm} + (1 - \hat{\alpha}_i) \hat{\alpha}_{i+1} w_{i+1} T_{cp}, \quad i = 0, 1, \ldots, m - 2 \qquad (3.44)$$

and

$$\hat{\alpha}_{m-1} w_{m-1} T_{cp} = (1 - \hat{\alpha}_{m-1}) z_m T_{cm} + (1 - \hat{\alpha}_{m-1}) w_m T_{cp} \qquad (3.45)$$

From the above equations, and through some simple algebraic manipulations, $\hat{\alpha}_i$ $(i = 0, \ldots, m - 1)$ may be recursively expressed as

$$\hat{\alpha}_i = \frac{z_{i+1} T_{cm} + \hat{\alpha}_{i+1} w_{i+1} T_{cp}}{w_i T_{cp} + z_i T_{cm} + \hat{\alpha}_{i+1} w_{i+1} T_{cp}}, \quad i = 0, \ldots, m - 2 \qquad (3.46)$$

$$\hat{\alpha}_{m-1} = \frac{z_m T_{cm} + w_m T_{cp}}{w_{m-1} T_{cp} + z_m T_{cm} + w_m T cp} \qquad (3.47)$$

The $\hat{\alpha}_i$'s can be solved recursively, and the optimal processing time is

$$T(\alpha) = \alpha_0 w_0 T_{cp} = \hat{\alpha}_0 w_0 T_{cp} \qquad (3.48)$$

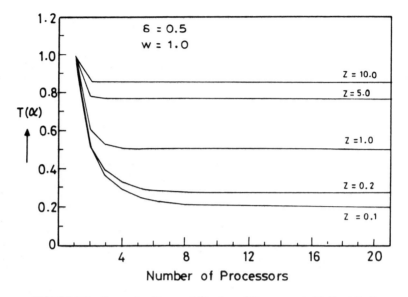

FIGURE 3.8   Processing Time and Number of Processors (with Front End)

In Figure 3.8, this processing time is plotted against the number of processors in a homogeneous linear network with $w_i = 1$ (for all i), $T_{cp} = 1$, and $T_{cm} = 0.5$. The five performance curves are obtained with $z_i = 0.1, 0.2, 1, 5, 10$ (for all i), respectively. As shown in the figure, the larger the communication delay, the longer the processing time. Note that the optimal processing time levels off after a certain number of processors.

3.3.2 Load Origination at the Boundary: Without Front End

Here, too, the load distribution is governed by the requirement that all processors stop computing at the same time instant. It is assumed that the network satisfies the condition $w_i T_{cp} > z_{i+1} T_{cm}$, for all $i = 0, \ldots, m-1$. The timing diagram of the entire process is shown in Figure 3.9. It can be seen that the computing time of the ith processor $\alpha_i w_i T_{cp}$ equals the transmission time $(1 - \alpha_0 - \alpha_1 - \cdots - \alpha_{i+1})z_{i+2} T_{cm}$ between the $(i+1)$th and the $(i+2)$th processor plus the computation time $\alpha_{i+1} w_{i+1} T_{cp}$ of the $(i+1)$th processor. Thus,

$$\alpha_i w_i T_{cp} = (1 - \alpha_0 - \alpha_1 - \cdots - \alpha_{i+1})z_{i+2} T_{cm} + \alpha_{i+1} w_{i+1} T_{cp},$$

$$i = 0, \ldots, m-2$$

$$\alpha_{m-1} w_{m-1} T_{cp} = \alpha_m w_m T_{cp} \tag{3.49}$$

These equations, along with the normalizing equation $\sum_{i=0}^{m} \alpha_i = 1$, form a system of $(m+1)$ linear equations with $(m+1)$ unknowns. Using a procedure similar to that given in the previous subsection, each α_i can be expressed as a function of α_0,

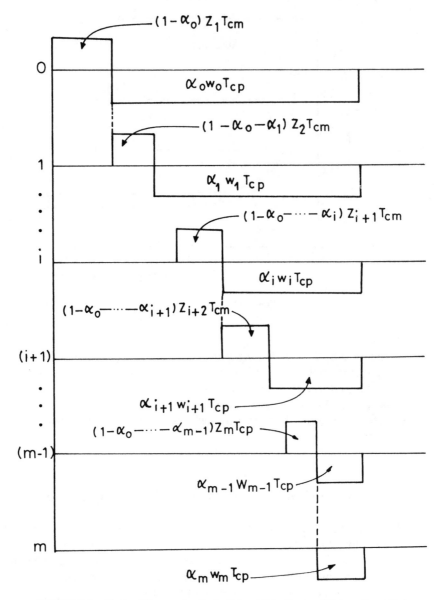

FIGURE 3.9 Timing Diagram for Optimal Load Distribution: Without Front End (Boundary Case)

as

$$\alpha_i = C_i \alpha_0 + D_i \tag{3.50}$$

where

$$C_1 = \frac{w_0 T_{cp} + z_2 T_{cm}}{w_1 T_{cp} - z_2 T_{cm}} \tag{3.51}$$

$$D_1 = \frac{-z_2 T_{cm}}{w_1 T_{cp} - z_2 T_{cm}} \tag{3.52}$$

$$C_2 = \frac{C_1(w_1 T_{cp} + z_3 T_{cm}) + z_3 T_{cm}}{w_2 T_{cp} - z_3 T_{cm}} \tag{3.53}$$

$$D_2 = \frac{D_1(w_1 T_{cp} + z_3 T_{cm}) - z_3 T_{cm}}{w_2 T_{cp} - z_3 T_{cm}} \tag{3.54}$$

and, in general, for $i = 3, \ldots, m - 1$,

$$C_i = \frac{C_{i-1}(w_{i-1} T_{cp} + z_{i+1} T_{cm}) + (\sum_{j=1}^{i-2} C_j + 1) z_{i+1} T_{cm}}{w_i T_{cp} - z_{i+1} T_{cm}} \tag{3.55}$$

$$D_i = \frac{D_{i-1}(w_{i-1} T_{cp} + z_{i+1} T_{cm}) + (\sum_{j=1}^{i-2} D_j - 1) z_{i+1} T_{cm}}{w_i T_{cp} - z_{i+1} T_{cm}} \tag{3.56}$$

$$C_m = C_{m-1} \frac{w_{m-1}}{w_m} \tag{3.57}$$

$$D_m = D_{m-1} \frac{w_{m-1}}{w_m} \tag{3.58}$$

These can now be substituted in the normalizing equation to obtain the individual load fractions. The minimum processing time $T(\alpha)$ is

$$T(\alpha) = (1 - \alpha_0) z_1 T_{cm} + \alpha_0 w_0 T_{cp} \tag{3.59}$$

An alternative way to compute the load fraction is to use $\hat{\alpha}_i$ ($i = 0, \ldots, m$), defined in Section 3.1. Substituting Equation (3.3) in Equation (3.49) we get

$$\hat{\alpha}_i w_i T_{cp} = (1 - \hat{\alpha}_i)(1 - \hat{\alpha}_{i+1}) z_{i+2} T_{cm} + (1 - \hat{\alpha}_i)\hat{\alpha}_{i+1} w_{i+1} T_{cp},$$
$$i = 0, 1, \ldots, m - 2 \tag{3.60}$$

$$\hat{\alpha}_{m-1} w_{m-1} T_{cp} = (1 - \hat{\alpha}_{m-1}) w_m T_{cp} \tag{3.61}$$

From the above, and through some simple algebraic manipulations, $\hat{\alpha}_i$s may be recursively expressed as,

$$\hat{\alpha}_i = \frac{(1 - \hat{\alpha}_{i+1}) z_{i+2} T_{cm} + \hat{\alpha}_{i+1} w_{i+1} T_{cp}}{w_i T_{cp} + (1 - \hat{\alpha}_{i+1}) z_{i+1} T_{cm} + \hat{\alpha}_{i+1} w_{i+1} T_{cp}}, \quad i = 0, 1, \ldots, m - 2 \tag{3.62}$$

From Equation (3.61)

$$\hat{\alpha}_{m-1} = \frac{w_m}{w_{m-1} + w_m} \tag{3.63}$$

The $\hat{\alpha}_i$'s can be solved recursively and the optimal processing time is

$$T(\alpha) = (1 - \hat{\alpha}_0) z_1 T_{cm} + \hat{\alpha}_0 w_0 T_{cp} \tag{3.64}$$

In Figure 3.10, the optimal processing time is plotted against the number of processors in a homogeneous linear network for the same network parameters as in Figure 3.8. Again, the larger the communication delay, the longer the processing time; and the minimum processing time, too, levels off after a certain number of processors. For the same parameters the minimum processing time is more than in the case of the network equipped with front-end processors (see Figure 3.8).

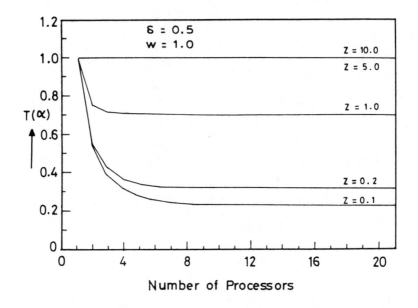

FIGURE 3.10   Processing Time and Number of Processors (without Front End)

3.3.3 Load Origination at the Interior: With Front End

The process of load distribution is the same as described in Section 3.1.3. However, the individual load fractions are such that all the processors stop computing at the same instant in time. The timing diagram of the entire process is shown in Figure 3.11. From this diagram, it can be seen that the processing time $(1 - \beta_l - \beta_r)w_0 T_{cp}$ of the root processor equals the transmission time $\beta_l z_1^l T_{cm}$ of the fraction β_l of the load transmitted to its left immediate neighbor p_1^l plus the processing time $\alpha_1^l w_1^l T_{cp}$ of p_1^l. The computation time $\alpha_1^l w_1^l T_{cp}$ of p_1^l also equals the communication time $\beta_r z_1^r T_{cm}$ from the root processor to the first processor on the right, p_1^r, plus the computation time $\alpha_1^r w_1^r T_{cp}$ of p_1^r. Both equations are given below:

$$\alpha_0 w_0 T_{cp} = (1 - \beta_l - \beta_r)w_0 T_{cp} = \beta_l z_1^l T_{cm} + \alpha_1^l w_1^l T_{cp} \qquad (3.65)$$

$$\alpha_1^l w_1^l T_{cp} = \beta_r z_1^r T_{cm} + \alpha_1^r w_1^r T_{cp} \qquad (3.66)$$

The rest of the equations can be written in a manner similar to that for the boundary case with front end, as follows:

$$\alpha_i^l w_i^l T_{cp} = (\beta_l - \alpha_1^l - \cdots - \alpha_i^l)z_{i+1}^l T_{cm} + \alpha_{i+1}^l w_{i+1}^l T_{cp}, \quad i = 1, \ldots, L - 1. \quad (3.67)$$

$$\alpha_i^r w_i^r T_{cp} = (\beta_r - \alpha_1^r - \cdots - \alpha_i^r)z_{i+1}^r T_{cm} + \alpha_{i+1}^r w_{i+1}^r T_{cp}, \quad i = 1, \ldots, R - 1. \quad (3.68)$$

where $\beta_l = \sum_{i=1}^L \alpha_i$ and $\beta_r = \sum_{i=1}^R \alpha_i$. The normalizing equation is

$$\alpha_0 + \sum_{i=1}^L \alpha_i^l + \sum_{i=1}^R \alpha_i^r = 1 \qquad (3.69)$$

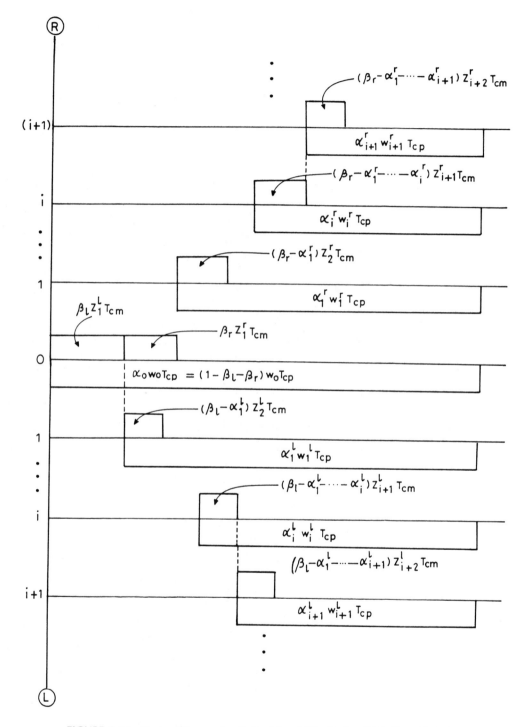

FIGURE 3.11 Timing Diagram for Optimal Load Distribution: With Front End (Interior Case)

Equations (3.65) through (3.69) form a system of $(R + L + 1)$ linear equations with $(R + L + 1)$ unknowns and can be solved computationally by exploiting their recursive structure as in the previous section. Using Equation (3.68), we express each α_i^l $(i = 1, \ldots, L)$ as

$$\alpha_i^l = A_i^l \alpha_0 + B_i^l \beta_l \tag{3.70}$$

where

$$A_1^l = \frac{w_0}{w_1^l} \tag{3.71}$$

$$B_1^l = \frac{z_1^l T_{cm}}{w_1^l T_{cp}} \tag{3.72}$$

$$A_2^l = \frac{A_1^l (w_1^l T_{cp} + z_2^l T_{cm})}{w_2^l T_{cp}} \tag{3.73}$$

$$B_2^l = \frac{B_1^l (w_1^l T_{cp} + z_2^l T_{cm}) - z_2^l T_{cm}}{w_2^l T_{cp}} \tag{3.74}$$

In general, for $i = 3, \ldots, L$, we have

$$A_i^l = \frac{A_{i-1}^l (w_{i-1}^l T_{cp} + z_i^l T_{cm}) + (\sum_{j=1}^{i-2} A_j^l) z_i^l T_{cm}}{w_i^l T_{cp}} \tag{3.75}$$

$$B_i^l = \frac{B_{i-1}^l (w_{i-1}^l T_{cp} + z_i^l T_{cm}) + (\sum_{j=1}^{i-2} B_j^l - 1) z_i^l T_{cm}}{w_i^l T_{cp}} \tag{3.76}$$

Similarly, we express each α_i^r $(i = 2, \ldots, R)$ as

$$\alpha_i^r = A_i^r \alpha_1^r + B_i^r \beta_r \tag{3.77}$$

where

$$A_2^r = \frac{(w_1^r T_{cp} + z_2^r T_{cm})}{w_2^r T_{cp}} \tag{3.78}$$

$$B_2^r = \frac{-z_2^r T_{cm}}{w_2^r T_{cp}} \tag{3.79}$$

$$A_3^r = \frac{A_2^r (w_2^r T_{cp} + z_3^r T_{cm}) + z_3^r T_{cm}}{w_3^r T_{cp}} \tag{3.80}$$

$$B_3^r = \frac{B_2^r (w_2^r T_{cp} + z_3^r T_{cm}) - z_3^r T_{cm}}{w_3^r T_{cp}} \tag{3.81}$$

In general, for $i = 4, \ldots, R$, we have

$$A_i^r = \frac{A_{i-1}^r (w_{i-1}^r T_{cp} + z_i^r T_{cm}) + (\sum_{j=2}^{i-2} A_j^r + 1) z_i^r T_{cm}}{w_i^r T_{cp}} \tag{3.82}$$

$$B_i^r = \frac{B_{i-1}^r (w_{i-1}^r T_{cp} + z_i^r T_{cm}) + (\sum_{j=2}^{i-2} B_j^r - 1) z_i^r T_{cm}}{w_i^r T_{cp}} \tag{3.83}$$

From the above relations the values of A_i^l, B_i^l ($i = 1, \ldots, L$), and A_i^r, B_i^r ($i = 2, \ldots, R$) can be computed recursively. We know that

$$\beta_l = \alpha_1^l + \cdots + \alpha_L^l = \left(\sum_{i=1}^{L} A_i^l \right) \alpha_0 + \left(\sum_{i=1}^{L} B_i^l \right) \beta_l \qquad (3.84)$$

From this we get

$$\beta_l = K \alpha_0 \qquad (3.85)$$

where

$$K = \frac{\sum_{i=1}^{L} A_i^l}{1 - \sum_{i=1}^{L} B_i^l} \qquad (3.86)$$

which can be easily computed since we know the values of A_i^l and B_i^l. Using this we obtain

$$\alpha_i^l = (A_i^l + K B_i^l)\alpha_0, \quad i = 1, \ldots, L \qquad (3.87)$$

We also know that

$$1 - \beta_l - \beta_r = \alpha_0 \qquad (3.88)$$

from which, by substituting Equation (3.85), we obtain

$$\beta_r = 1 - (1 + K)\alpha_0 \qquad (3.89)$$

Now, using Equations (3.89) and (3.70) in Equation (3.66), we obtain

$$\alpha_1^r = E_1 \alpha_0 + F_1 \qquad (3.90)$$

where

$$E_1 = \frac{(A_1^l + K B_1^l)w_1^l T_{cp} + (1 + K)z_1^r T_{cm}}{w_1^r T_{cp}} \qquad (3.91)$$

$$F_1 = -\frac{z_1^r T_{cm}}{w_1^r T_{cp}} \qquad (3.92)$$

Substituting in Equation (3.77) we immediately obtain, for $i = 2, \ldots, R$,

$$\begin{aligned} \alpha_i^r &= A_i^r(E_1 \alpha_0 + F_1) + B_i^r \{1 - (1 + K)\alpha_0\} \\ &= \left\{ A_i^r E_1 - B_i^r(1 + K) \right\} \alpha_0 + (F_1 A_i^r + B_i^r) \end{aligned} \qquad (3.93)$$

By this procedure we have succeeded in expressing each α_i^l and α_i^r in terms of α_0. By substituting these in the normalizing equation we can obtain the actual value of α_0 and then, by back substitution, obtain all the other load fractions, too.

The alternative load distribution using $\hat{\alpha}_i^l$ and $\hat{\alpha}_i^r$ can also be computed using these equations. The optimal processing time is given by

$$T(\alpha) = (1 - \beta_l - \beta_r)w_0 T_{cp} \qquad (3.94)$$

In Figure 3.12, the minimum processing time is plotted against the position of the processors in a linear network of 21 processors with the same network parameters as in Figure 3.8. As shown in the figure, the larger the communication delay, the longer the processing time. It also appears that the processing time is the least when

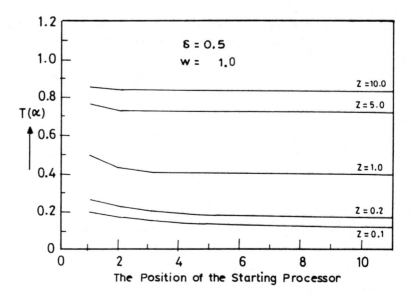

FIGURE 3.12   Processing Time and Position of the Starting Processor (with Front End)

the load originating processor is at the center of the linear network, though this point shows a shallow minimum. In Chapter 5, we will support this observation through rigorous analysis.

3.3.4 Load Origination at the Interior: Without Front End

Here, the root processor first divides the processing load into three smaller parts, and then communicates the fraction β_l of the total load to its left immediate neighbor, the fraction β_r to its right immediate neighbor, and starts the computation of the remaining fraction $(1 - \beta_l - \beta_r)$. The timing diagram showing the load distribution process is given in Figure 3.13. From the timing diagram the load distribution equations are as follows:

$$\alpha_0 w_0 T_{cp} = (1 - \beta_l - \beta_r) w_0 T_{cp}$$
$$= (\beta_r - \alpha_1^r) z_2^r T_{cm} + \alpha_1^r w_1^r T_{cp} \qquad (3.95)$$

$$\alpha_0 w_0 T_{cp} + \beta_r z_1^r T_{cm} = (\beta_l - \alpha_1^l) z_2^l T_{cm} + \alpha_1^l w_1^l T_{cp} \qquad (3.96)$$

The rest of the equations can be written similarly to the boundary case as

$$\alpha_i^l w_i^l T_{cp} = (\beta_l - \alpha_1^l - \cdots - \alpha_{i+1}^l) z_{i+2}^l T_{cm} + \alpha_{i+1}^l w_{i+1}^l T_{cp}, \quad i = 1, \ldots, L - 1 \qquad (3.97)$$

$$\alpha_i^r w_i^r T_{cp} = (\beta_r - \alpha_1^r - \cdots - \alpha_{i+1}^r) z_{i+2}^r T_{cm} + \alpha_{i+1}^r w_{i+1}^r T_{cp}, \quad i = 1, \ldots, R - 1 \qquad (3.98)$$

The above equations form a system of $(R + L + 1)$ linear equations with $(R + L + 1)$ unknowns. A procedure exactly similar to that used in the previous section is used to first express each α_i^l ($i = 2, \ldots, L$) in terms of α_1^l and β_l; and each α_i^r ($i = 2, \ldots, R$)

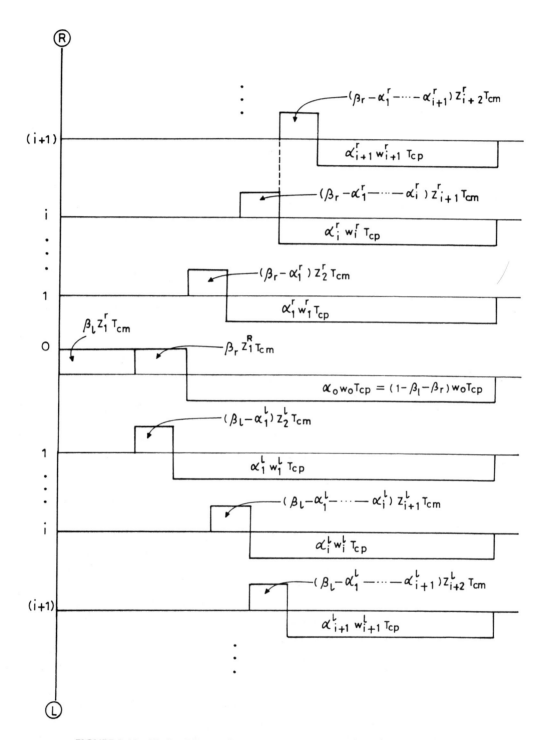

FIGURE 3.13 Timing Diagram for Optimal Load Distribution: Without Front End (Interior Case)

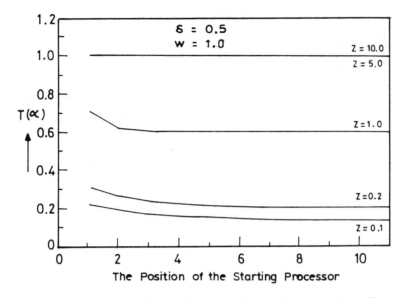

FIGURE 3.14   Processing Time and Position of Starting Processor (without Front End)

in terms of α_1^r and β_r. These are substituted in the equations $\sum_{i=1}^{L} \alpha_i^l = \beta_l$ and $\sum_{i=1}^{R} \alpha_i^r = \beta_r$ to obtain β_l and β_r in terms of α_1^l and α_1^r, respectively. Substituting these in Equation (3.95) and (3.96) followed by some algebraic manipulations, allows one to express each α_i^l $(i = 1, \ldots, L)$ and α_i^r $(i = 1, \ldots, R)$ in terms of α_0. Using the above in the normalizing equation yields α_0 and subsequently all the other load fractions. An alternative way of obtaining $\hat{\alpha}_i^l$ and $\hat{\alpha}_i^r$ can be formulated similarly.

The minimum processing time is

$$T(\alpha) = (1 - \beta_l - \beta_r)w_0 T_{cp} + \beta_l z_1^l T_{cm} + \beta_r z_1^r T_{cm} \qquad (3.99)$$

In Figure 3.14, the optimal processing time is plotted against the position of the processors in a linear network of 21 processors with the network parameters given in Figure 3.8. Again, the larger the communication delay, the longer the processing time. Here, too, it appears that the processing time is least when the root is at the center of the network. As in the with-front-end case, this point is a shallow minimum. These observations will be supported by rigorous proofs in Chapter 5. By comparing Figures 3.12 and 3.14 it can be seen that a linear network equipped with front ends performs better than one without.

3.4 INCLUSION OF SOLUTION TIME

Until now we have discussed only the distribution and processing of computational load. However, once the processors finish computing their load fractions, it may be necessary for the solution (that is, the result of their computation) to be sent back to the root processor to construct the complete solution to the problem. The previous sections do not consider this. It is beyond the scope of this book to consider this for all the cases discussed above. We shall do so for only one of these cases, that is, for a linear network with front ends (boundary case).

The timing diagram for a given load distribution α, which includes the time required to propagate the solution back to the originating processor, is shown in Figure 3.15. For the sake of simplicity, we will assume that the time taken by a processor to send the solution to its immediate predecessor is a constant of T_s time units. When the mth processor finishes its computation, it starts sending back the solution to its left immediate neighbor, the $(m-1)$th processor. This transmission takes T_s time units. Upon receiving this solution, the $(m-1)$th processor transmits this solution and its own solution to its left immediate neighbor, the $(m-2)$th processor. This transmission takes $2T_s$ time units. Similarly, the ith processor takes $(m-i+1)T_s$ time units to transmit all the solutions of its successors, combined

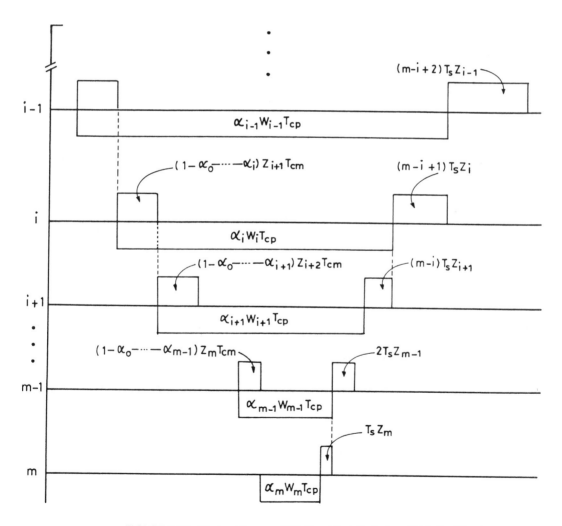

FIGURE 3.15   Timing Diagram: With Front End (Inclusion of Solution Time)

with its own solution, to its predecessor the $(i-1)$th processor. The solution sending process continues until all the solutions are sent back to the root processor.

Intuitively, an optimal load distribution should be such that a processor p_i should continue to compute its load fraction until it finishes receiving the cumulative solution from all the processors p_{i+1} to p_m via the link l_{i+1}. From the timing diagram, the computation time of the processor p_i is obtained as

$$\alpha_i w_i T_{cp} = (1 - \alpha_0 - \alpha_1 - \ldots - \alpha_i)z_{i+1}T_{cm} + \alpha_{i+1}w_{i+1}T_{cp} + (m-i)z_{i+1}T_s,$$

$$i = 0, 1, \ldots, m-1 \tag{3.100}$$

The above equation along with the normalizing condition can be recursively solved to obtain the individual load fractions of the processors. The processing time is given by

$$T(\alpha) = \alpha_0 w_0 T_{cp} \tag{3.101}$$

It must be noted that there could be several other models for propagation of the solution back to the root processor. For instance, the solution time might be proportional to the size of the load processed by a processor, or the solution time might be some other known function of the load fractions. For both cases, a similar set of linear equations can be formed and α_i's and $T(\alpha)$ can be obtained. In the same manner, we can derive the recursive equations and obtain optimal load fractions for all the cases considered in earlier sections. However, if the time for communicating the results to the root processor is negligible (for example, when the results occupy a significantly smaller memory space than the actual computational load) then the optimal load fractions and the processing time, for all practical purposes, will be the same as in the case when the solution time is not included in the formulation (as in the previous section). Since this assumption is true in most realistic situations where massive data is processed, we will, in our subsequent studies of the linear network, dispense with the delay due to sending back the results of the computations.

3.5 PROOF OF OPTIMALITY VIA PROCESSOR EQUIVALENCE CONCEPT

The proof of optimality given in Section 3.2.2 has been obtained by assuming specific values for the speed of processors and links. Now we shall provide a complete proof for a general heterogeneous linear network. To do so, we introduce the concept of collapsing two or more processors and associated links into a single processor with an equivalent speed parameter. Since the concept involves collapsing two processors at a time, it is sufficient to consider the boundary case alone (both with and without front-end cases) and then extend the results to the interior case.

3.5.1 Load Origination at the Boundary: With Front End

We will focus our attention on the $(m-1)$th and mth processors, as given in Figure 3.16. The time reference for this figure is the instant at which the communication (that is, the load transfer) from p_{m-2} to p_{m-1} ends. The processing load received by p_{m-1} from p_{m-2} is $(\alpha_{m-1} + \alpha_m)$. Assume that p_{m-1} keeps the fraction $\hat{\alpha}_{m-1}$ of

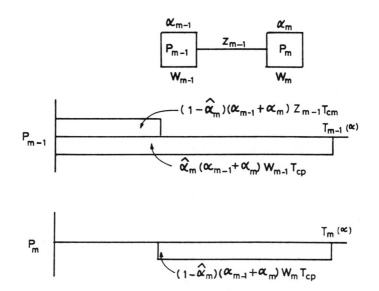

FIGURE 3.16   Timing Diagram for $m-1$ and mth Processors: With Front End (Boundary Case)

this load and transmits the remaining fraction $(1 - \hat{\alpha}_{m-1})$ to p_m. The finish times are given by

$$T_{m-1}(\alpha) = \hat{\alpha}_{m-1}(\alpha_{m-1} + \alpha_m)w_{m-1}T_{cp} \tag{3.102}$$

$$T_m(\alpha) = (1 - \hat{\alpha}_{m-1})(\alpha_{m-1} + \alpha_m)(z_m T_{cm} + w_m T_{cp}) \tag{3.103}$$

In order to prove that the minimum processing time is obtained when p_{m-1} and p_m stop at the same time instant, the possibilities that $T_{m-1} \geq T_m$ and $T_{m-1} \leq T_m$ must be examined. Let us assume that $T_{m-1} > T_m$. Some simple algebraic manipulation of Equation (3.102) and (3.103) yields

$$\hat{\alpha}_{m-1} \geq \frac{z_m T_{cm} + w_m T_{cp}}{w_{m-1}T_{cp} + z_m T_{cm} + w_m T_{cp}} \tag{3.104}$$

with equality occurring when both processors stop computing at the same instant in time. Minimizing the processing time $T(\alpha) = T_{m-1}(\alpha)$ clearly demands the minimum value of $\hat{\alpha}_{m-1}$, that is,

$$\min \; T(\alpha) = (\min(\hat{\alpha}_{m-1}))(\alpha_{m-1} + \alpha_m)w_{m-1}T_{cp} \tag{3.105}$$

It can be seen that the minimum value of $\hat{\alpha}_{m-1}$ occurs when the inequality in Equation (3.104) is replaced with an equality sign. The quantity $(\alpha_{m-1}+\alpha_m)$ is not involved in the minimization, since the value of $\hat{\alpha}_{m-1}$ is unaffected by the load $(\alpha_{m-1} + \alpha_m)$ delivered to p_{m-1}. Actually, the minimization process involves only the ratio of the load being allocated between p_{m-1} and p_m and not the total load allocated to these processors. A similar analysis for $T_{m-1} \leq T_m$ can be carried out.

Thus, from Figure 3.16, p_{m-1} and p_m may be replaced by a single equivalent processor with an equivalent speed parameter. It should be noted that this is possible only when the processors stop computing at the same time instant. From Figure 3.16, we can write

$$(\alpha_{m-1} + \alpha_m) w_{eq}^{fe} T_{cp} = \hat{\alpha}_{m-1} (\alpha_{m-1} + \alpha_m) w_{m-1} T_{cp} \qquad (3.106)$$

from which we obtain

$$w_{eq}^{fe} = \hat{\alpha}_{m-1} w_{m-1} \qquad (3.107)$$

where w_{eq}^{fe} denotes speed of the equivalent processor (superscript *fe* denotes the with-front-end case). This means that if instead of the two processors p_{m-1} and p_m in the linear network we have only one equivalent processor with speed w_{eq}^{fe}, the processing time of the load remains the same. In this manner, starting from $(m-1)$th and mth processors, the entire linear network can be collapsed (by considering two processors at a time) into a single equivalent processor. Thus, one can show that for a network of $(m+1)$ processors, the optimal processing time is obtained when all the processors stop computing at the same instant in time.

3.5.2 Load Origination at the Boundary: Without Front End

Here too, we consider the $(m-1)$th and the mth processors, shown in Figure 3.17. The mode of load distribution remains the same. The finish times are given by

$$T_{m-1}(\alpha) = (1 - \hat{\alpha}_{m-1})(\alpha_{m-1} + \alpha_m) z_m T_{cm} + \hat{\alpha}_{m-1}(\alpha_{m-1} + \alpha_m) w_{m-1} T_{cp} \qquad (3.108)$$

and

$$T_m(\alpha) = (1 - \hat{\alpha}_{m-1})(\alpha_{m-1} + \alpha_m)(z_m T_{cm} + w_m T_{cp}) \qquad (3.109)$$

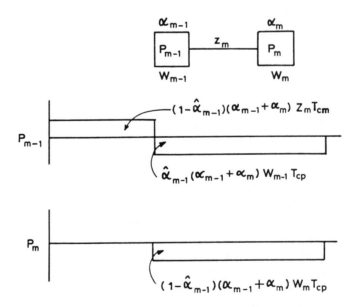

FIGURE 3.17   Timing Diagram for $m-1$ and mth processors: Without Front End (Boundary Case)

Once again, to prove that the optimal processing time requires both processors to stop at the same time, the cases $T_{m-1} \geq T_m$ and $T_{m-1} \leq T_m$ can be considered. For $T_{m-1} \geq T_m$, simple algebraic manipulation results in

$$\hat{\alpha}_{m-1} \geq \frac{w_m}{w_{m-1} + w_m} \tag{3.110}$$

with equality occurring when both the processors stop at the same time instant. From the above the processing time can be written as

$$T(\alpha) = T_{m-1}(\alpha) = (\alpha_{m-1} + \alpha_m)z_m T_{cm} + \hat{\alpha}_{m-1}(\alpha_{m-1} + \alpha_m)(w_{m-1}T_{cp} - z_m T_{cm}) \tag{3.111}$$

The sign of the term $(w_{m-1}T_{cp} - z_m T_{cm})$ now becomes important. If it is positive, minimizing $T(\alpha)$ is equivalent to minimizing $\hat{\alpha}_{m-1}$ and the optimal solution occurs at equality in Equation (3.110). In other words, if $w_{m-1}T_{cp} > z_m T_{cm}$, the distribution of load is economical. Again, $(\alpha_{m-1} + \alpha_m)$ is not involved in the minimization.

On the other hand, if $(w_{m-1}T_{cp} - z_m T_{cm})$ is negative, then minimizing $T(\alpha)$ is equivalent to maximizing $\hat{\alpha}_{m-1}$ (for instance, $\hat{\alpha}_{m-1} = 1$). That is, when communication speed is slow relative to computation speed, it is economical for p_{m-1} to process the entire load itself rather than to distribute a part of it to p_m. The argument for the case where $T_{m-1} \leq T_m$ proceeds along similar lines.

3.5.3 When to Distribute Load

A practical problem for the without-front-end case is to compute the equivalent computation speed of a linear network when, in fact, the optimal solution may not make use of all processors because of communication speeds that are too slow. When looking at two adjacent processors, say the $(i-1)$th and the ith one (where the ith processor is an equivalent processor for processors $p_i, p_{i+1}, \ldots, p_m$), we must determine whether or not it is economical to distribute load. That is, we seek the faster of two solutions: either that with both processors, T_{both}, or that with just a single $(i-1)$th processor, T_{single}:

$$T_{both}(\alpha) = (1 - \hat{\alpha}_{i-1})(\alpha_{i-1} + \alpha_i)z_i T_{cm} + \hat{\alpha}_{i-1}(\alpha_{i-1} + \alpha_i)w_{i-1}T_{cp} \tag{3.112}$$

$$T_{single}(\alpha) = (\alpha_{i-1} + \alpha_i)w_{i-1}T_{cp} \tag{3.113}$$

Here, the fraction $\hat{\alpha}_{i-1}$ of the total load, $(\alpha_{i-1} + \alpha_i)$, is assigned to processor $(i-1)$ and the fraction $(1 - \hat{\alpha}_{i-1})$ is assigned to processor i. If $T_{single} \leq T_{both}$, that is, $w_{i-1}T_{cp} \leq z_i T_{cm}$, then the ith processor is removed from consideration and the equivalent processing speed parameter, with no front end (*nfe*), is,

$$w_{eq}^{nfe} = \frac{(\alpha_{i-1} + \alpha_i)w_{i-1}T_{cp}}{(\alpha_{i-1} + \alpha_i)T_{cp}} = w_{i-1} \tag{3.114}$$

If $T_{single} > T_{both}$, that is, $w_{i-1}T_{cp} > z_i T_{cm}$, then the load distribution to p_i is economical. Then the two processors are collapsed into a single equivalent processor with an equivalent speed parameter,

$$w_{eq}^{nfe} = \frac{(1 - \hat{\alpha}_{i-1})z_i T_{cm} + \hat{\alpha}_{i-1}w_{i-1}T_{cp}}{T_{cp}} \tag{3.115}$$

where, from Equation (3.110),

$$\hat{\alpha}_{i-1} = \frac{w_i}{w_{i-1} + w_i} \tag{3.116}$$

Hence,

$$w_{eq}^{nfe} = \frac{w_{i-1}(z_i T_{cm} + w_i T_{cp})}{(w_{i-1} + w_i)T_{cp}} \tag{3.117}$$

By keeping track of whether Equation (3.113) or (3.113) is smaller, it is possible to determine which processors to remove from the original network.

   Note that the above procedure can be applied to the situation in which the load originates at a processor that is located in the interior of the network. The parts of the network to the left and to the right of the originating processor can be collapsed into equivalent processors following the procedure given here. The network now contains the remaining three processors (left, originating, right). Naturally, we must check to see whether the inclusion of one or both of the left or right equivalent processors leads to a faster solution. This architecture is a single-level tree network and will be dealt with in the next two chapters.

3.6 ULTIMATE PERFORMANCE LIMITS

A difficulty with the linear network architecture is that as more and more processors are added to the network, the amount of improvement in the network's time performance (and thus, in the equivalent speed) approaches a saturation limit. This is apparent from numerical studies reported previously in this chapter.

   It is possible to develop simple expressions for the equivalent processing speed of an infinite homogeneous network. These provide a limiting value on the performance of this architecture. The technique is similar to that used for infinitely large electrical networks to determine equivalent impedance.

3.6.1 Boundary Case: With Front End

Here, the basic idea is to write an expression for the speed parameter of the equivalent processor for processors $p_0, p_1, p_2, \ldots$. This is a function of the speed parameters of the root processor p_0 and the single equivalent processor for processors $p_1, p_2, \ldots$. However, these two speeds should be equal since both involve an infinite number of processors. We can simply solve for this speed. Let the network consist of p_0 and an equivalent processor p_{eq} for processors $p_1, p_2, \ldots$. Then, the speed of the equivalent processor is given by

$$w_{eq}^{fe} = \hat{\alpha}_0 w \tag{3.118}$$

But from Equation (3.104) with equality, and making the above assumption,

$$w_{eq}^{fe} = \left(\frac{z T_{cm} + w_{eq}^{fe} T_{cp}}{w T_{cp} + z T_{cm} + w_{eq}^{fe} T_{cp}} \right) w \tag{3.119}$$

Solving for w_{eq}^{fe} results in

$$w_{eq}^{fe} = \frac{-z T_{cm} + \sqrt{(z T_{cm})^2 + 4 w z T_{cm} T_{cp}}}{2 T_{cp}} \tag{3.120}$$

The processing time for such an infinite network is simply given by

$$T(\alpha) = w_{eq}^{fe} T_{cp} \tag{3.121}$$

3.6.2 Boundary Case: Without Front End

For the boundary case, an expression for the equivalent speed of a linear network with an infinite number of processors without front ends (nfe) can be determined in a similar manner:

$$w_{eq}^{nfe} = \sqrt{wz(T_{cm}/T_{cp})} \tag{3.122}$$

The processing time for this infinite network is simply given by $T(\alpha) = w_{eq}^{nfe} T_{cp}$.

The last expression is somewhat intuitive. Doubling w and z doubles w_{eq}^{nfe}. Doubling either w or z alone increases w_{eq}^{nfe} by a factor of $\sqrt{2}$. These results agree very closely with the numerical results presented in Section 3.3. It is straightforward to show that $w_{eq}^{fe} < w_{eq}^{nfe}$. We will present more detailed analytical results on the asymptotic performance of these networks in Chapter 8.

3.6.3 Interior Case: With Front End

It is possible to use the above results to calculate the limiting performance of an infinite network when the load originates at the interior. The infinite chain of processors to the right and left of the root processor can be replaced with a single processor with equivalent speed constants w_{eql}^{∞} and w_{eqr}^{∞}, respectively. Obviously, $w_{eql}^{\infty} = w_{eqr}^{\infty} = w_{eq}$. This three-processor network is shown in Figure 3.18a. The timing diagram of the reduced network is shown in Figure 3.18b. The following are the basic equations governing the system:

$$T_{fei}^{\infty} = \beta_c w T_{cp} \tag{3.123}$$

$$T_{fei}^{\infty} = \beta_l z T_{cm} + \beta_l w_{eq}^{\infty} T_{cp} \tag{3.124}$$

$$T_{fei}^{\infty} = (\beta_l + \beta_r) z T_{cm} + \beta_r w_{eq}^{\infty} T_{cp} \tag{3.125}$$

$$T_{fei}^{\infty} = w_{eqs}^{\infty} T_{cp} \tag{3.126}$$

$$\beta_c + \beta_r + \beta_l = 1 \tag{3.127}$$

where $T_{fei}^{\infty}(\alpha)$ is the processing time at which the load originates at the interior and w_{eqs}^{∞} is the equivalent processor speed parameter for the network. Here w_{eq}^{∞} is given by Equation (3.120). Using the above equation, an expression to calculate w_{eqs}^{∞} can be obtained as,

$$w_{eqs}^{\infty} = \frac{w(zT_{cm} + w_{eq}^{\infty} T_{cp})}{zT_{cm} + w_{eq}^{\infty} T_{cp} + wT_{cp} + \frac{ww_{eq}^{\infty} T_{cp}^2}{zT_{cm} + w_{eq}^{\infty} T_{cp}}} \tag{3.128}$$

where w_{eq}^{∞} is given by Equation (3.120). The processing time is

$$T_{fei}^{\infty} = w_{eqs}^{\infty} T_{cp} \tag{3.129}$$

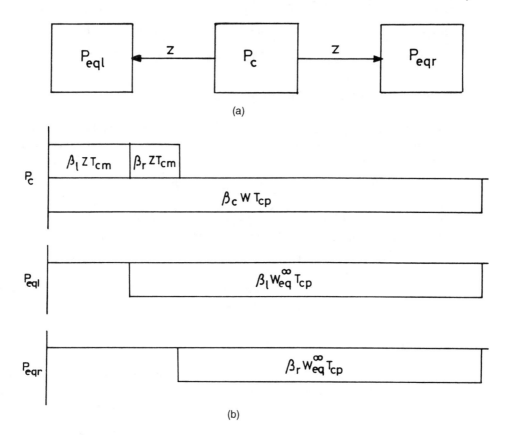

FIGURE 3.18   (a) A Reduced Linear Network (Interior Case) (b) Timing Diagram (with Front End)

3.6.4 Interior Case: Without Front End

The timing diagram for a given load distribution is shown in Figure 3.19. We obtain the following equations from the timing diagram.

$$T_{nfei}^{\infty} = (\beta_l + \beta_r)zT_{cm} + \beta_c w T_{cp} \tag{3.130}$$

$$T_{nfei}^{\infty} = \beta_l zT_{cm} + \beta_l w_{eq}^{\infty}T_{cp} \tag{3.131}$$

$$T_{nfei}^{\infty} = (\beta_l + \beta_r)zT_{cm} + \beta_r w_{eq}^{\infty}T_{cp} \tag{3.132}$$

$$T_{nfei}^{\infty} = w_{eqs}^{\infty}T_{cp} \tag{3.133}$$

Using the above equations together with Equation (3.122), an expression to calculate w_{eqs}^{∞} can be obtained, and is given by,

$$w_{eqs}^{\infty} = \frac{w(zT_{cm} + w_{eq}^{\infty}T_{cp})^2}{(w_{eq}^{\infty}T_{cp})^2 + w_{eq}^{\infty}T_{cp}\,^2 w + wT_{cp}(zT_{cm} + w_{eq}^{\infty}T_{cp})} \tag{3.134}$$

Then, the processing time T_{nfei}^{∞} can be calculated using Equation (3.133).

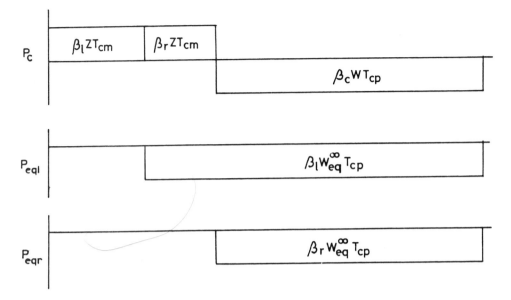

FIGURE 3.19   Timing Diagram for Reduced Linear Network: Without Front End (Interior Case)

3.7 CONCLUDING REMARKS

The following are the highlights of this chapter:

- The finish time equations for any given load distribution in a general linear network were developed. These were done for both with- and without-front-end cases, and also for load origination at the boundary and at the interior of the network.

- The equal-division load distribution strategy was shown to be inefficient in the presence of communication delay. This was used to motivate the criterion for optimal load distribution.

- It was shown that optimal division of the load occurs when the load distribution is such that all the processors stop computing at the same time instant. This was first done for a specific homogeneous network and was then extended to a general heterogeneous network by using a new concept of processor equivalence. In the without-front-end case an additional condition for load distribution was derived.

- The recursive equations were developed to obtain the optimal load distribution for a general linear network. Numerical results were presented to show the effect of number of processors and of communication delay on processing time.

- A method of incorporating the solution back-propagation time was also discussed.

- A study using the processor equivalence concept was conducted to obtain the ultimate performance limits with respect to the number of processors.

In this chapter, we mainly present the basic load distribution equations for a linear network. We also provide some insight into the load distribution process through computational results. In subsequent chapters we will develop analytical results to support many of these observations. We will also provide more detailed expositions of the analytical results in this chapter.

BIBLIOGRAPHIC NOTES

Section 3.1   The timing diagram representing the load distribution process and the development of the recursive load distribution equations were first introduced in Cheng and Robertazzi (1988). This was also the first paper to consider the problem of distributing arbitrarily divisible loads in distributed computing networks with communication delays.

Section 3.2   The issue of equal division of load and the optimal number of processors in this scheme was also addressed by Cheng and Robertazzi (1988). This paper also proves the optimality criterion, that all processors must stop computing at the same time instant, for homogeneous networks with all speed parameters equal to unity.

Section 3.3   The computational results reported here are also from Cheng and Robertazzi (1988). An alternative computational scheme can be found in Mani and Ghose (1994).

Section 3.4   The load distribution scheme that includes the propagation of computational results back to the load originating processor was also proposed in Cheng and Robertazzi (1988).

Section 3.5   The concept of processor equivalence was presented in Robertazzi (1993) and was used to prove the optimality criterion for linear networks.

Section 3.6   The ultimate performance limits of a linear network, using the processor equivalence concept, were obtained by Bataineh and Robertazzi (1992).

CHAPTER 4

Load Distribution in Tree and Bus Networks

In the previous chapter we presented a preliminary study of the load distribution problem in linear networks. Here, we present a similar study for a tree network of processors. For this purpose, we consider a general tree network and derive load distribution equations for two types of nodes—those whose child processors are terminal nodes and those whose child processors are nonterminal nodes. We do this for both with- and without-front-end cases. This is followed by a simple motivational example to demonstrate the intuitively appealing notion that for optimal performance all processors should stop computing at the same time instant. Based on this consideration we derive the optimal load distribution equations. Next, we consider the situation in which the processors have to send back the results to the load originating processor. We then extend the analysis to bus networks, which can be considered as a special case of a single-level tree network. We consider three types of bus architectures and present numerical results. Finally, we introduce the concept of processor equivalence, to obtain some optimality results and to study the ultimate performance limits.

As in the previous chapter, we have taken care to sectionalize the material in terms of architectural specialities (with/without-front-end, tree/bus networks).

4.1 GENERAL DESCRIPTION AND BASIC EQUATIONS

A general tree network of communicating processors is shown in Figure 4.1. As in Chapter 3, where we consider the with-front-end case, it is assumed that *all* the processors are equipped with front ends. On the other hand, for the without-front-end case, we assume that *none* of the processors in the tree network are equipped

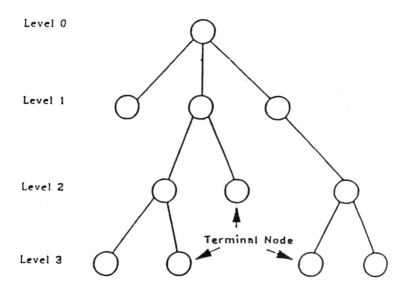

FIGURE 4.1 A General Tree Network

with front ends. It is assumed that the processing load always originates at the root processor (situated at level zero).

Following the model adopted in Chapter 2, the load distribution process proceeds as follows. The root processor (at level zero) keeps some fraction of the total processing load for itself to compute and divides and distributes the remaining load one by one to its child processors at the next level. The processors at this level perform the same operation with the load they receive. This process continues until the processors located at the terminal nodes of the tree are assigned their share of the processing load. For simplicity, in this chapter we will denote the finish times as T_i instead of $T_i(\alpha)$ in most of the equations where the load distribution α is well defined.

4.1.1 Load Distribution Equations: With Front End

The load distribution equations are derived by considering two basic types of subtrees. They are:

> Case i: those whose child processors are terminal nodes of the tree;
> Case ii: those whose child processors are not terminal nodes.

Note that a node is a *terminal node* when it has no child processors.

Consider a subtree of the network that consists of one parent processor p_i and $(i-1)$ child processors that are terminal nodes of the network (that is, Case i). The parent processor that has received some data D from *its* parent processor keeps a fraction α_i for itself to compute and divides and communicates the remainder to its children. The first child receives a fraction α_1 of D, the second child receives a fraction α_2 of D, and so on until the child $(i-1)$ receives a fraction α_{i-1} of D. The timing diagram of the entire process is shown in Figure 4.2. The finish times of the

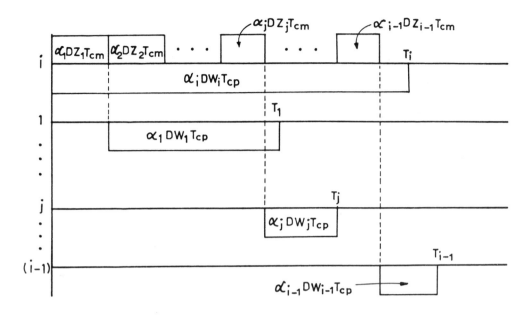

FIGURE 4.2   Timing Diagram: Subtree with Terminal Nodes (with Front End)

parent processor p_i and the child processors p_j $(1 \leq j \leq i - 1)$ are given by

$$T_i = \alpha_i D w_i T_{cp} \tag{4.1}$$

For $j = 1, 2, \ldots, i - 1$

$$T_j = \begin{cases} 0, & \text{if } \alpha_j = 0 \\ \sum_{k=1}^{j} \alpha_k D z_k T_{cm} + \alpha_j D w_j T_{cp}, & \text{if } \alpha_j \neq 0 \end{cases} \tag{4.2}$$

$$\sum_{k=1}^{i} \alpha_j = 1 \tag{4.3}$$

For the type of processor arrangement (Case ii) where child processors are not terminal nodes of the network, consider a subtree of the network consisting of one parent processor p_k and $(k - 1)$ child processors. As above, the parent processor that has received some data D from *its* parent processor keeps β_k fraction of D for itself to compute and divides and transmits the remainder to its children. The first child receives a fraction β_1 of D, the second child receives a fraction β_2 of D, and so on until the $(k - 1)$th child receives a fraction β_{k-1} of D. Upon receiving the β_1 fraction of D, the first child keeps γ_1 fraction of what it has just received and transmits the remainder to its l_1 child processors. In general, the jth child keeps γ_j of what it has received, that is, β_j of D, and transmits the remainder to its l_j child processors. Here, l_j is the number of children of the jth child processor and the processing load allocated to the jth child processor is $\gamma_j \beta_j D$. The timing diagram is shown in Figure 4.3. The finish times of the parent processor p_k and its child processors p_j $(1 \leq j \leq k - 1)$ are given by

$$T_k = \beta_k D w_k T_{cp} \tag{4.4}$$

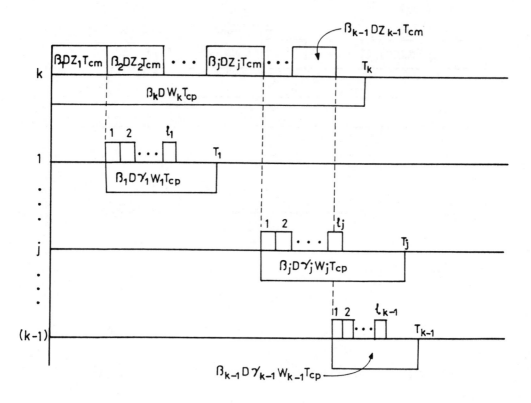

FIGURE 4.3 Timing Diagram: Subtree with Nonterminal Nodes (with Front End)

For $j = 1, \ldots, k-1$

$$T_j = \begin{cases} 0, & \text{if } \beta_j = 0 \text{ or } \gamma_j = 0 \\ \sum_{q=1}^{j} \beta_q D z_q T_{cm} + \gamma_j \beta_j D w_j T_{cp}, & \text{if } \beta_j \neq 0 \text{ and } \gamma_j \neq 0 \end{cases} \tag{4.5}$$

$$\sum_{q=1}^{k} \beta_q = 1 \tag{4.6}$$

$$\gamma_j + \gamma_1 + \cdots + \gamma_{l_j} = 1 \tag{4.7}$$

Note that there is a slight abuse of notation in the above equations. Using this set of Equations (4.1) to (4.7), we can obtain the finish times of all the processors in the network for a given load distribution. Also, a mix of these equations can be used judiciously to cater to the situation when a node has both terminal and nonterminal nodes as children. The processing time of the entire load can be found by taking the maximum of all the finish times.

4.1.2 Load Distribution Equations: Without Front End

We follow the same methodology as above. For Case i, the timing diagram is shown in Figure 4.4. The finish times for the parent processor p_i and child processors

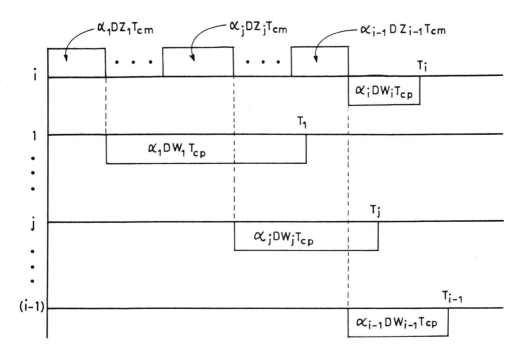

FIGURE 4.4   Timing Diagram: Subtree with Terminal Nodes (without Front End)

p_j ($1 \le j \le i - 1$), are given by

$$T_i = \begin{cases} 0, & \text{if } \alpha_i = 0 \\ \sum_{k=1}^{i-1} \alpha_k Dz_k T_{cm} + \alpha_i Dw_i T_{cp}, & \text{if } \alpha_i \ne 0 \end{cases} \tag{4.8}$$

For $j = 1, \ldots, i - 1$

$$T_j = \begin{cases} 0, & \text{if } \alpha_j = 0 \\ \sum_{p=1}^{j} \alpha_p Dz_p T_{cm} + \alpha_j Dw_j T_{cp}, & \text{if } \alpha_j \ne 0 \end{cases} \tag{4.9}$$

For Case ii consider a subtree of the network consisting of one parent node p_k and ($k - 1$) child processors that are not terminal nodes of the network. The parent processor, which has received some data D from *its* parent processor, keeps a fraction β_k of D for itself to compute and transmits the remainder of the load to its children. Since the parent processor does not have a front end, it first communicates to its children and then starts computing its load fraction β_k. The rest of the processors (that is, the child processors) repeat the same procedure. The timing diagram for the process is shown in Figure 4.5. It is assumed, as in the previous case, that each of the child processors p_j ($1 \le j \le k - 1$) has l_j children. From the timing diagram, we obtain the finish time expressions for the processors as

$$T_k = \begin{cases} 0, & \text{if } \beta_k = 0 \\ \sum_{p=1}^{k-1} \beta_p Dz_p T_{cm} + \beta_k Dw_k T_{cp}, & \text{if } \beta_k \ne 0 \end{cases} \tag{4.10}$$

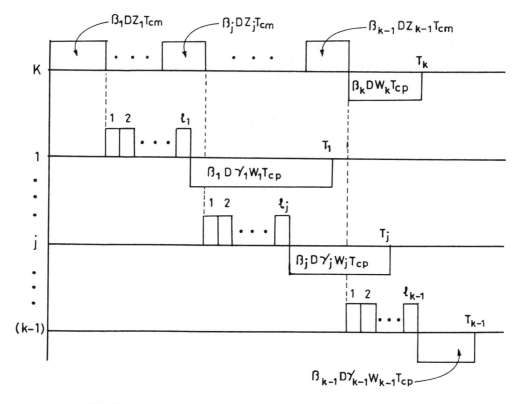

FIGURE 4.5   Timing Diagram: Subtree with Nonterminal Nodes (without Front End)

For $j = 1, \ldots, k - 1$,

$$T_j = \begin{cases} 0, & \text{if } \beta_j = 0 \text{ or } \gamma_j = 0 \\ \sum_{q=1}^{j} \beta_q D z_q T_{cm} + \sum_{s=1}^{l_j} \delta_s \beta_j D z_s T_{cm} + \beta_j \gamma_j D w_j T_{cp}, & \text{if } \beta_j \neq 0 \text{ and } \gamma_j \neq 0 \end{cases}$$

(4.11)

where δ_s is the fraction of the load sent by the processor p_j $(1 \leq j \leq k - 1)$ to its child processor p_s $(1 \leq s \leq l_j)$. Using the set of Equations (4.8) through (4.11) we obtain the finish times of all the processors in the network. By taking the maximum of all finish times we obtain the processing time of the entire load for a given load distribution.

4.2 MOTIVATION FOR OPTIMAL LOAD DISTRIBUTION

In this section we present a motivating example for obtaining the optimal load distribution.

Example 4.1

Let us consider a tree network equipped with front ends and consisting of a root processor and two child processors, as shown in Figure 4.6. Let the speed parameters of the network be given as $w_0 = w_1 = w_2 = 0.2$, $z_1 = z_2 = 1.0$, $T_{cm} = T_{cp} = 1.0$. Let

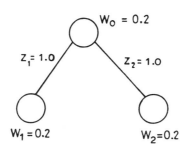

FIGURE 4.6   Two-Level Tree Network
(Example 4.1)

us assume that the processing load is divided equally among the processors in the network. This means $\alpha = (0.3333, 0.3333, 0.3333) \in L$. Using Equations (4.1) and (4.2), we obtain the finish times of the individual processors as $T_0(\alpha) = 0.0666$, $T_1(\alpha) = 0.396$, $T_2(\alpha) = 0.738$. Now, by taking the maximum of all the finish times, we obtain the processing time of the entire load as $T(\alpha) = 0.738$.

Now consider another distribution $\alpha' = (0.8372, 0.1395, 0.0233)$. Using Equations (4.1) and (4.2) we obtain the finish times as $T_0(\alpha') = T_1(\alpha') = T_2(\alpha') = 0.1674$. In this example, all processors have equal finish times, that is, they all stop computing at the same time instant. Comparing with the equal distribution case, we see that $T(\alpha') < T(\alpha)$. In fact, it may be verified that for any other load distribution, the processing time is greater than $T(\alpha')$. We shall provide a formal proof for this observation in the next chapter.

The above example clearly illustrates that, as in the case of linear networks, choosing a load distribution that ensures equal finish times for all processors (that is, all processors stop computing at the same time instant) is a viable strategy to achieve optimality. One can also provide an intuitive explanation for this reasoning through contradiction as follows: Suppose that in the optimal load distribution, processors stop at different time instants. Then, towards the end of computation, some processors are idle while others are still busy. It seems reasonable to assume that the processing time can be improved by transferring some of the load from the busy processors to the idle processors, provided that the communication delay incurred is not high. This contradicts the original assumption of an optimal solution.

For the rest of this chapter we shall assume the intuitive assumption (that all processors must stop computing at the same time instant) to be true and derive the load distribution equations. This intuitive assumption is indeed true for a large class of tree networks.

However, the intuitive explanation given above is actually not true for the general class of tree networks. For certain network parameter values optimal performance is not achieved if all processors are made to stop computing at the same time instant. In fact, in these networks some of the processors may not receive any processing load at all when the load is distributed optimally. This fact will be proved through a rigorous analysis in the next chapter.

In this chapter, we will be careful to consider only those networks in which optimality is achieved when all processors participate in load processing and stop computing at the same time instant for optimal performance. In fact, the network chosen for Example 4.1 satisfies this requirement. One of the reasons for deriving these load distribution equations is that these can also be used, with minor modifications, for a general tree network (as we shall show in the next chapter). The above discussion holds both for the with- and without-front-end cases.

4.3 OPTIMAL LOAD DISTRIBUTION: RECURSIVE EQUATIONS

Based on the intuitive result discussed in the previous section, we will obtain recursive equations for both the with- and without-front-end cases. This is done by equating the finish times of the processors (that is, by making the processors to stop computing at the same time instant). This assumption also implies that each processor receives a nonzero load to compute. This fact should be kept in mind when the finish time equations given in the previous section are used.

4.3.1 With-Front-End Processors

The timing diagram for a given load distribution α for the case when the subtree has terminal nodes is shown in Figure 4.7. From the timing diagram, we can write the following load distribution equations:

$$\alpha_i w_i T_{cp} = \alpha_1 z_1 T_{cm} + \alpha_1 w_1 T_{cp} \tag{4.12}$$

$$\alpha_j w_j T_{cp} = \alpha_{j+1} z_{j+1} T_{cm} + \alpha_{j+1} w_{j+1} T_{cp}, \qquad j = 1, \ldots, i-2 \tag{4.13}$$

Note that D gets cancelled from both sides. The normalizing equation is

$$\alpha_1 + \alpha_2 + \cdots + \alpha_i = 1 \tag{4.14}$$

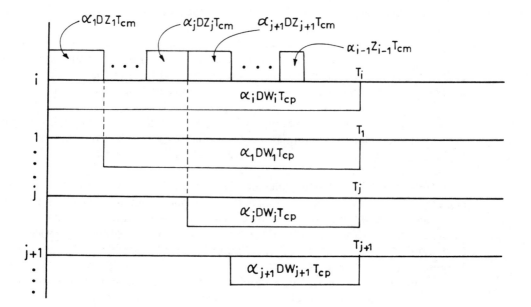

FIGURE 4.7   Timing Diagram: Optimal Division for Subtree with Terminal Nodes (with Front End)

These form a system of i linear equations with i unknowns. As in Chapter 3, one can exploit the recursive nature of these equations and obtain a computational solution.

For the case when the subtree consists of nonterminal nodes, the timing diagram is shown in Figure 4.8. For the intuitive result to hold, the parent processor should compute its fraction of the processing load during the entire processing period. If the parent processor is the root processor, then the processing time equals its computing time. From Figure 4.8, we can write the following load distribution equations:

$$\beta_k w_k T_{cp} = \beta_1 z_1 T_{cm} + \beta_1 \gamma_1 w_1 T_{cp} \tag{4.15}$$

$$\beta_j \gamma_j w_j T_{cp} = \beta_{j+1} z_{j+1} T_{cm} + \beta_{j+1} \gamma_{j+1} w_{j+1} T_{cp}, \qquad j = 1, \ldots, k-2 \tag{4.16}$$

with the normalizing equation

$$\beta_1 + \beta_2 + \cdots + \beta_k = 1 \tag{4.17}$$

If all the γ_j's are known then the above equations form a set of k linear equations with k unknowns. The β_j's can then be solved using a computational technique similar to the one given in Chapter 3. Note that the γ_j's would have been previously determined from the next level below. If a node in the next level is a terminal node, then the corresponding value of γ_j can be obtained from Equations (4.12) through (4.14), where γ_j is the corresponding α_i. If a node at the next level is a nonterminal node then γ_j can be obtained from Equations (4.15) through (4.17), where γ_j is the

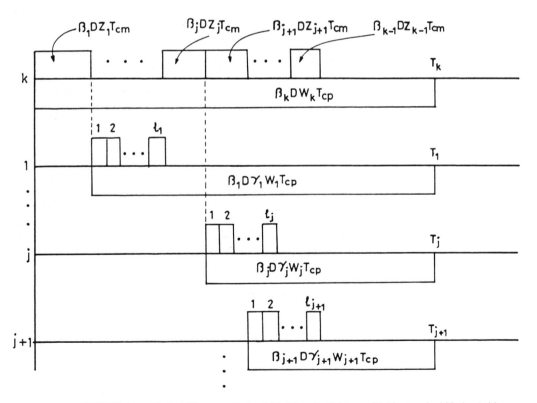

FIGURE 4.8 Timing Diagram: Optimal Division for Subtree with Nonterminal Nodes (with Front End)

corresponding β_k. The essential idea is to start from the bottom-most level and work upwards computing the fraction (of the load D) that each processor retains for itself. Here, D is the load that the processor has received from its parent. This procedure is practical since at each processor node the number of equations will be the same as the number of unknowns (which is equal to the number of child processors that the node has plus one).

If a subtree of the network consists of one parent processor and *both* terminal node and nonterminal node children, the γ_j's of the terminal node processors should be unity, since these processors keep all of what they have received. The γ_j's of the nonterminal node processors can be obtained either from Equations (4.12) through (4.14) or from Equations (4.15) through (4.17) depending on whether their next levels are the lowest or not.

4.3.2 Without-Front-End Processors

The timing diagram for a given load distribution α for the case when the subtree has terminal nodes is shown in Figure 4.9. From the timing diagram, we obtain the following recursive equations:

$$\alpha_i w_i T_{cp} = \alpha_{i-1} w_{i-1} T_{cp} \tag{4.18}$$

$$\alpha_j w_j T_{cp} = \alpha_{j+1} z_{j+1} T_{cm} + \alpha_{j+1} w_{j+1} T_{cp}, \; j = 1, 2, \ldots, i-2 \tag{4.19}$$

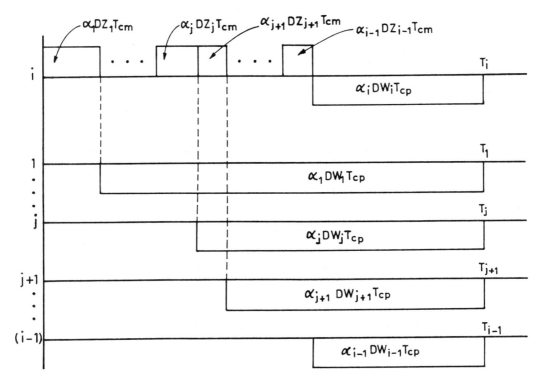

FIGURE 4.9   Timing Diagram: Optimal Division for Subtree with Terminal Nodes (without Front End)

Together with the normalizing equation (4.14), there are a total of i linear equations with i unknowns. The α_j's can thus be determined following a similar computational procedure.

For the case when the subtree has nonterminal nodes, the timing diagram is shown in Figure 4.10. Following the methodology adopted in Section 4.3.1, we obtain the following recursive equations from the timing diagram.

$$\beta_k w_k T_{cp} = \beta_{k-1} w_{k-1} \gamma_{k-1} T_{cp} \tag{4.20}$$

$$\sum_{q=1}^{l_j} \beta_j \delta_q z_q T_{cm} + \beta_j \gamma_j w_j T_{cp} = \beta_{j+1} z_{j+1} T_{cm} + \sum_{p=1}^{l_{j+1}} \beta_{j+1} \delta_p z_p T_{cm} + \beta_{j+1} \gamma_{j+1} w_{j+1} T_{cp},$$

$$j = 1, \ldots, k-2 \tag{4.21}$$

Here $p_j (1 \le j \le k-1)$ has l_j child processors. If the δ_p's and γ_j's are known, then along with the normalizing equation (4.17) there are k linear equations with k unknowns. The β_j's can thus be determined computationally. The γ_j's and δ_p's would have been previously determined from the next level below. If the next level is the lowest level, then the value of γ_j's can be obtained from Equations (4.14)

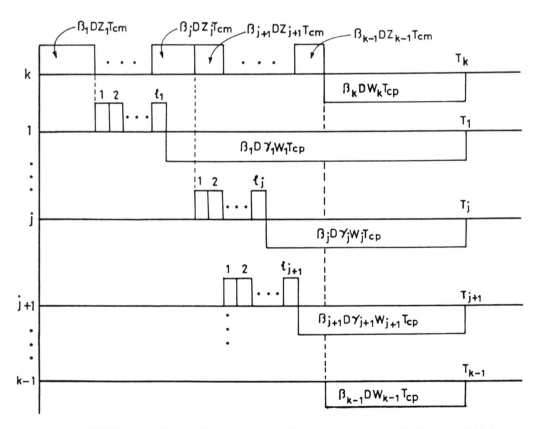

FIGURE 4.10 Timing Diagram: Optimal Division for Subtree with Nonterminal Nodes (without Front End)

through (4.16). However, if the next level is not the lowest level, then γ_j's and δ_p's can be obtained from Equations (4.17) through (4.18).

4.3.3 An Illustrative Example

In this section, we shall demonstrate the above procedure for obtaining optimal load distribution through an example.

Example 4.2

Consider a tree network such as that shown in Figure 4.11a. The root processor (node 8) distributes its processing load to other processors in the tree with $T_{cp} = 1$ and $T_{cm} = 1$. The processors are equipped with front ends. All the processors have the same computing capability with $w_i = 1$. Similarly, the channel speed between the processors are assumed to be the same with $z_i = 1$. There are essentially three sub-trees A, B, and C. Sub-trees A and B have terminal nodes as child processors. Sub-tree C has non-terminal nodes as child processors. The fraction of load that each processor in subtree A processes from what it has received can be calculated first using Equations (4.12) through (4.14) as

$$\alpha_4 = \alpha_1 + \alpha_1$$
$$\alpha_1 = \alpha_2 + \alpha_2$$
$$\alpha_2 = \alpha_3 + \alpha_3 \qquad (4.22)$$
$$\alpha_1 + \alpha_2 + \alpha_3 + \alpha_4 = 1$$

These equations can be solved to yield $\alpha_1 = 0.267, \alpha_2 = 0.1333, \alpha_3 = 0.067$, and $\alpha_4 = 0.5333$. The fraction of load that processors in subtree B keep from what they have received can be calculated in a similar manner using Equations (4.12) through (4.14) as

$$\alpha_7 = \alpha_5 + \alpha_5$$
$$\alpha_5 = \alpha_6 + \alpha_6 \qquad (4.23)$$
$$\alpha_5 + \alpha_6 + \alpha_7 = 1$$

These equations can be solved to yield $\alpha_5 = 0.286, \alpha_6 = 0.143$, and $\alpha_7 = 0.571$. Substitute γ_{l1} and γ_{r1} with α_4 and α_7, respectively. The fraction of load that each processor in subtree C keeps from what it has received can be calculated using Equations (4.15) through (4.17) as

$$\beta_3 = \beta_1 + \beta_1\alpha_4$$
$$\beta_1\alpha_4 = \beta_2 + \beta_2\alpha_7 \qquad (4.24)$$
$$\beta_1 + \beta_2 + \beta_3 = 1$$

The β_i's can be solved to obtain $\beta_1 = 0.348, \beta_2 = 0.118$, and $\beta_3 = 0.5333$. Here, β_1 is the fraction of load that root (node 8) processor sends to node 4, β_2 is the fraction of load root sends to node 7, and β_3 is the fraction of load that the root processes itself. The actual fractions of load that each processor processes are shown in Figure 4.11b with the time normalized with respect to T_{cp}. Hence, $\delta = T_{cm}/T_{cp}$ in this figure. The total processing time is just the processing time of the root processor, $\beta_3 T_{cp}$, which equals 0.5333.

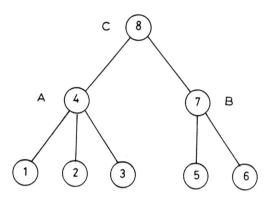

(a)

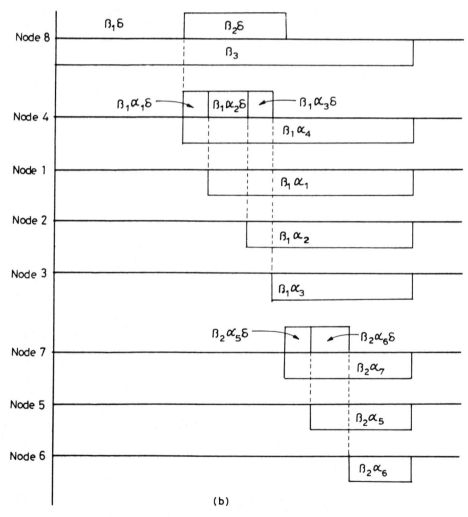

(b)

FIGURE 4.11 Example 4.2 (a) Tree Network (b) Timing Diagram (with Front End)

4.4 INCLUSION OF SOLUTION TIME

It may be noted that in Section 3.4, the inclusion of solution time was discussed for linear networks. Similarly, as an example, we consider a load distribution that incorporates the solution back propagation time in tree networks with front ends.

As in Chapter 3, here the solution transmission time from each of the processors is assumed to be of the same length. Each of the processors in the network may have different computing capabilities and the channel capacities between the processors may be different. The root processor of the tree network receives the processing load. The entire process is similar to the one in Section 4.3.1, except for the inclusion of T_s.

For the subtrees in the network whose child processors are terminal nodes, the parent processor distributes the processing load to its $(i - 1)$ child processors. When the $(i - 1)$th child processor finishes its computation, it sends back the solution to the parent processor. The choice is arbitrary; the first child processor could have reported back first. The transmission takes time T_s. The $(i - 2)$th child processor finishes its computation and transmits the solution to the parent when the $(i - 1)$th child processor finishes its solution transmission. This transmission takes another T_s. The solution sending process repeats itself until the solutions from all the $(i - 1)$ child processors are sent back to the parent processor. The timing diagram of the entire process is shown in Figure 4.12. The load distribution equations are:

$$\alpha_i w_i T_{cp} = \alpha_1 z_1 T_{cm} + \alpha_1 w_1 T_{cp} + T_s + (i - 1)T_s \qquad (4.25)$$

$$\alpha_j w_j T_{cp} = \alpha_{j+1} z_{j+1} T_{cm} + \alpha_{j+1} w_{j+1} T_{cp} + T_s, \quad j = 1, 2, \ldots, i - 2 \qquad (4.26)$$

and

$$\alpha_1 + \alpha_2 + \cdots + \alpha_i = 1 \qquad (4.27)$$

There are a total of i equations and i unknowns. Thus the α_j's can be determined.

For the subtrees in the network whose children are not terminal nodes, the parent processor distributes the processing load to its $(k - 1)$ child processors and the jth child processor distributes what it has received to its l_j child processors. The situation is illustrated in Figure 4.13.

When all the l_{k-1} child processors of the subtree for which the $(k - 1)$th child processor is the root processor report their solutions back to the $(k - 1)$th child processor, the $(k - 1)$th child processor starts sending the solutions of its children and its own solution back to the parent processor. It stops computing just prior to transmitting its own solution. The $(k - 2)$th processor starts transmitting the solutions of its l_{k-2} child processors to its parent when the $(k - 1)$th processor finishes its solution transmission. The $(k - 2)$th processor stops computing just prior to transmitting its own solution. The solution sending process repeats itself until all the solutions from the $(k - 1)$ child processors are sent back to the parent processor. The timing diagram of the entire process is shown in Figure 4.14.

As with the subtrees whose child processors are terminal nodes of the network, in order to obtain a minimum time solution, the parent processor should compute its fraction of the processing load during the entire processing period.

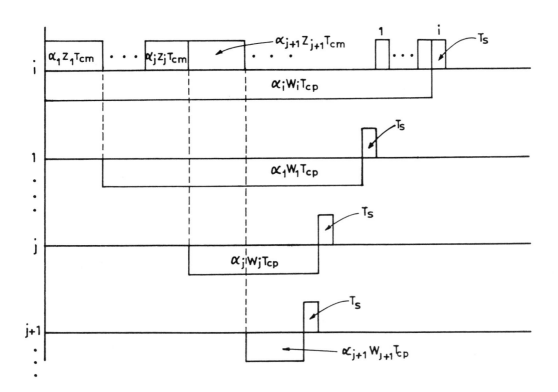

FIGURE 4.12   Timing Diagram: Inclusion of Solution Time for Subtree with Terminal Nodes (with Front End)

Let N_k be the number of children of the kth processor. From the timing diagram, the load distribution equations are:

$$\beta_k w_k T_{cp} = \beta_1 z_1 T_{cm} + \beta_1 w_1 \gamma_1 T_{cp} + T_s + N_k T_s \tag{4.28}$$

$$\beta_j w_j \gamma_j T_{cp} = \beta_{j+1} z_{j+1} T_{cm} + \beta_{j+1} w_{j+1} \gamma_{j+1} T_{cp} + T_s + N_j T_s \tag{4.29}$$

and

$$\beta_1 + \beta_2 + \cdots + \beta_k = 1 \tag{4.30}$$

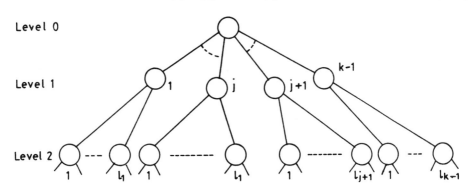

FIGURE 4.13   A Sample Tree Network

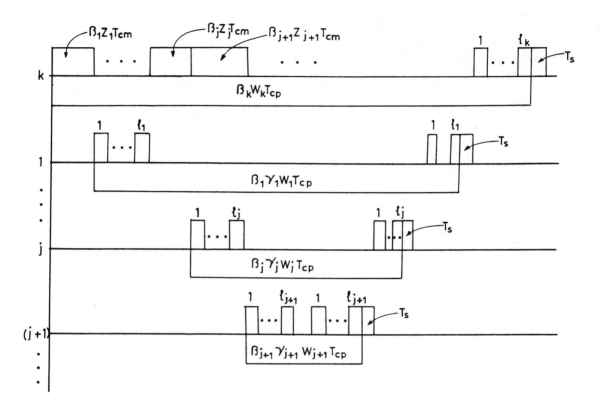

FIGURE 4.14 Timing Diagram: Inclusion of Solution Time for Subtree with Nonterminal Nodes (with Front End)

These are k linear equations with k unknowns. Thus the β_j's can be obtained. The γ_j's would have been previously determined from the next level below. If the next level is the lowest of the tree, the value of γ_j can be obtained from Equations (4.25) through (4.27), where α_i corresponds to γ_j. If the next level is not the lowest level of the tree, then γ_j can be obtained from Equations (4.28) through (4.30) where γ_j corresponds to β_k. The above process is repeated until the fraction of data that the first level processors process is determined.

For the subtree for which the starting processor is the root, the timing relation between the parent (root) processor and its k child processors is similar to the timing relation of other subtrees except that the parent processor does not have to retransmit the solution of its child processors. In this case Equation (4.28) is replaced by

$$\beta_k w_k T_{cp} = \beta_1 z_1 T_{cm} + \beta_1 \gamma_1 w_{l_1} T_{cp} + T_s \qquad (4.31)$$

for the starting processor rooted subtree. By using Equation (4.31) along with Equations (4.29) and (4.30) the fraction of data that the starting processor processes can be determined.

If a subtree of the network consists of one parent processor and *both* terminal node and nonterminal node children, the γ_j's of the terminal node processors should be unity, which indicates that these processors keep all of what they have received. The γ_j's of the nonterminal node processors can be obtained either from Equations (4.25) through (4.27) or from Equations (4.28) through (4.31) depending on whether their next levels are the lowest or not.

Note that in subsequent studies we will not take into account the time for sending the solution back to the root, for reasons given in Section 3.4.

4.5 APPLICATION TO BUS NETWORKS

In this section, we consider a special case of the tree network discussed so far. This is a single-level tree network (level 0 and level 1) with identical links. This network models a bus network and is shown in Figure 4.15. However, in this case, the root processor is considered to be a control processor, which only distributes the load fractions to other processors. In general, a bus network may or may not have a control processor. Accordingly we have the following three architectures:

Architecture 1: Bus network with control processor.

Architecture 2: Bus network without control processor; processors equipped with front ends.

Architecture 3: Bus network without control processor; processors not equipped with front ends.

In Architecture 1 the load is assumed to originate at the control processor, whereas in Architectures 2 and 3 the load is assumed to originate at one extreme end of the network. We now present the load distribution equations for all three cases. We assume that the network consists of m processors.

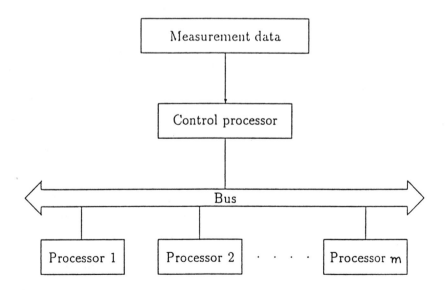

FIGURE 4.15 Bus Network with a Control Processor

4.5.1 Architecture 1: Bus Network with Control Processor

Consider the timing diagram shown in Figure 4.16, for a given load distribution α for a network of m processors. The finish time expressions are given by

$$T_i(\alpha) = (\alpha_1 + \alpha_2 + \cdots + \alpha_i)zT_{cm} + \alpha_i w_i T_{cp}, \quad i = 1, \ldots, m-1 \qquad (4.32)$$

We will show that for optimal load distribution, all processors must stop computing at the same instant in time. For this we will first show that $T_1(\alpha) = T_2(\alpha)$ for an optimal solution and then extend it to show that $T_1(\alpha) = T_2(\alpha) = \cdots = T_m(\alpha)$, for optimality.

Case i. Consideration of $T_1(\alpha)$ and $T_2(\alpha)$　Here, the rest of the finish times $T_3(\alpha), T_4(\alpha), \ldots, T_m(\alpha)$ will not be considered and will be assumed to have arbitrary values. That is, the fractions $\alpha_3, \alpha_4, \ldots, \alpha_m$, are assumed to have arbitrary constant values. Define

$$C_2 = \alpha_3 + \alpha_4 + \cdots + \alpha_m \qquad (4.33)$$

Then

$$\alpha_1 + \alpha_2 = 1 - C_2 \qquad (4.34)$$

Hence, for all feasible values of α_2,

$$0 \leq \alpha_1 \leq 1 - C_2 \qquad (4.35)$$

Then $T_1(\alpha)$ and $T_2(\alpha)$ can be represented as follows:

$$T_1(\alpha) = (zT_{cm} + w_1 T_{cp})\alpha_1 \qquad (4.36)$$

$$\begin{aligned} T_2(\alpha) &= (\alpha_1 + \alpha_2)zT_{cm} + \alpha_2 w_2 T_{cp} \\ &= (1 - C_2)(zT_{cm} + w_2 T_{cp}) - \alpha_1 w_2 T_{cp} \end{aligned} \qquad (4.37)$$

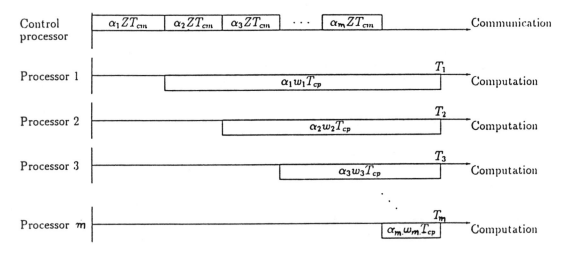

FIGURE 4.16　Timing Diagram: Bus Network with Control Processor

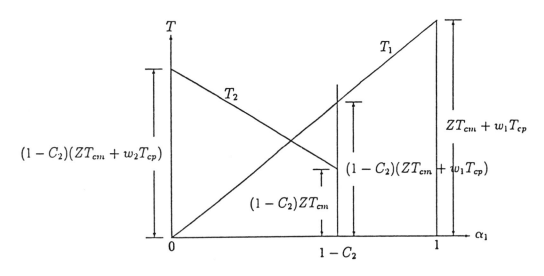

FIGURE 4.17 T_1 and T_2 as Functions of α_1

Note that these are linear equations in $\alpha_1 \in [0, 1 - C_2]$ and

$$T_1(\alpha_1 = 0) = 0 < T_2(\alpha_1 = 0) = (1 - C_2)(zT_{cm} + w_2T_{cp}) \qquad (4.38)$$

$$T_1(\alpha_1 = 1 - C_2) = (1 - C_2)(zT_{cm} + w_1T_{cp})$$
$$> T_2(\alpha_1 = 1 - C_2) = (1 - C_2)zT_{cm} \qquad (4.39)$$

From the above, we conclude that there always exists a crossover point for these two lines where $T_1(\alpha) = T_2(\alpha)$. Further, since $T_1(\alpha)$ has a constant positive slope and $T_2(\alpha)$ has a constant negative slope, this crossover point also determines the value of α_1 which gives the optimal processing time for p_1 and p_2, that is, which minimizes $\max\{T_1(\alpha), T_2(\alpha)\}$. See Figure 4.17 for illustration. Thus, from Equations (4.36) and (4.37), with $T_1(\alpha) = T_2(\alpha)$ we have

$$\alpha_2 = \left(\frac{w_1 T_{cp}}{zT_{cm} + w_2T_{cp}} \right) \alpha_1 = k_1\alpha_1 \qquad (4.40)$$

where $k_1 = w_1T_{cp}/(zT_{cm} + w_2T_{cp})$ denotes the ratio in which the load $(1 - C_2)$ must be shared between p_1 and p_2, irrespective of the load in the other processors, in order to minimize the processing time of these two processors.

Case ii. Consideration of $T_1(\alpha)$, $T_2(\alpha)$, and $T_3(\alpha)$ Now we will examine the optimal processing time when $T_1(\alpha)$, $T_2(\alpha)$, and $T_3(\alpha)$ are considered. Let

$$C_3 = \alpha_4 + \alpha_5 + \cdots + \alpha_m \qquad (4.41)$$

Then

$$\alpha_1 + \alpha_2 + \alpha_3 = 1 - C_3 \qquad (4.42)$$

and

$$\alpha_3 = (1 - C_3) - (\alpha_1 + \alpha_2) = (1 - C_3) - (1 + k_1)\alpha_1 \qquad (4.43)$$

since $\alpha_2 = k_1\alpha_1$. Now for all feasible values of α_3,

$$0 \le \alpha_1 \le \frac{1-C_3}{1+k_1} \tag{4.44}$$

Then, $T_1(\alpha)$, $T_2(\alpha)$, and $T_3(\alpha)$ can be represented as follows:

$$T_1(\alpha) = T_2(\alpha) = (zT_{cm} + w_1T_{cp})\alpha_1 \tag{4.45}$$

$$T_3(\alpha) = (\alpha_1 + \alpha_2 + \alpha_3)zT_{cm} + \alpha_3 w_3 T_{cp} \tag{4.46}$$

$$= (1 - C_3)(zT_{cm} + w_3T_{cp}) - (1 + k_1)\alpha_1 w_3 T_{cp} \tag{4.47}$$

As before, we note that these are linear equations in $\alpha_1 \in \left[0, \frac{(1-C_3)}{(1+k_1)}\right]$ and

$$T_1(\alpha_1 = 0) = T_2(\alpha_1 = 0) = 0$$
$$< T_3(\alpha_1 = 0) = (1 - C_3)(zT_{cm} + w_3T_{cp}) \tag{4.48}$$

$$T_1\left(\alpha_1 = \frac{1-C_3}{1+k_1}\right) = T_2\left(\alpha_1 = \frac{1-C_3}{1+k_1}\right) = \frac{(zT_{cm} + w_1T_{cp})(1-C_3)}{1+k_1}$$
$$> T_3\left(\alpha_1 = \frac{1-C_3}{1+k_1}\right) = (1 - C_3)zT_{cm} \tag{4.49}$$

The inequality in Equation (4.49) can be easily verified by substituting the value of k_1 from Case i here. From the above, we conclude that there always exists a crossover point for the lines $T_1(\alpha)(=T_2(\alpha))$ and $T_3(\alpha)$ at a point where $T_1(\alpha) = T_2(\alpha) = T_3(\alpha)$. Further, since $T_1(\alpha) = T_2(\alpha)$ has a constant positive slope and $T_3(\alpha)$ has a constant negative slope, this crossover point also determines the value of α_1 that gives the optimal processing time for p_1, p_2, and p_3, that is, that which minimizes $\max\{T_1(\alpha), T_2(\alpha), T_3(\alpha)\}$ (see Figure 4.18 for illustration). From Equations (4.37),

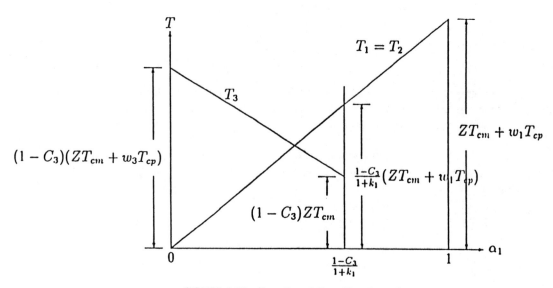

FIGURE 4.18 $T_1 = T_2$ and T_3 as Functions of α_1

(4.40), and (4.46), α_3 can be expressed as a function of α_2 and α_1 since $T_1(\alpha) = T_2(\alpha) = T_3(\alpha)$,

$$\alpha_3 = \left(\frac{w_2 T_{cp}}{z T_{cm} + w_3 T_{cp}} \right) \alpha_2 = k_2 \alpha_2 = k_2 k_1 \alpha_1 \tag{4.50}$$

where $k_2 = w_2 T_{cp}/(z T_{cm} + w_3 T_{cp})$ denotes the ratio in which an optimal load distribution between p_2 and p_3 should be done. Note that k_1 and k_2 together determine the ratio of optimal load distribution between p_1, p_2 and p_3.

Case iii. Consideration of $T_1, T_2, \ldots, T_i$ Based on the results of the previous cases, one can extend the proof to show that $T_1 = T_2 = \cdots = T_i$ achieves the optimal solution. Let

$$C_i = \alpha_{i+1} + \alpha_{i+2} + \cdots + \alpha_m \tag{4.51}$$

Then,

$$\alpha_1 + \alpha_2 + \cdots + \alpha_i = 1 - C_i \tag{4.52}$$

and

$$\begin{aligned} \alpha_i &= (1 - C_i) - (\alpha_1 + \alpha_2 + \cdots + \alpha_{i-1}) \\ &= (1 - C_i) - (1 + k_1 + k_1 k_2 + \cdots + k_1 k_2 \cdots k_{i-2}) \alpha_1 \end{aligned} \tag{4.53}$$

Now, for all feasible values of α_1

$$0 \le \alpha_1 \le \frac{1 - C_i}{1 + k_1 + k_1 k_2 + \cdots + k_1 k_2 \cdots k_{i-2}} = C \tag{4.54}$$

Then $T_1, T_2, \ldots, T_i$ can be represented as follows:

$$T_1 = T_2 = \cdots = T_{i-1} = (z T_{cm} + w_1 T_{cp}) \alpha_1 \tag{4.55}$$

$$\begin{aligned} T_i &= (\alpha_1 + \alpha_2 + \cdots + \alpha_i) z T_{cm} + \alpha_i w_i T_{cp} \\ &= (1 - C_i) z T_{cm} + \alpha_i w_i T_{cp} \end{aligned} \tag{4.56}$$

Using Equations (4.52) and (4.53) and simplifying, we get

$$\begin{aligned} T_i &= (1 - C_i) z T_{cm} + \{(1 - C_i) - (1 + k_1 + k_1 k_2 + \cdots + k_1 k_2 \cdots k_{i-2}) \alpha_1\} w_i T_{cp} \\ &= (1 - C_i)(z T_{cm} + w_i T_{cp}) - (1 + k_1 + k_1 k_2 + \cdots + k_1 k_2 \cdots k_{i-2}) w_i T_{cp} \alpha_1 \end{aligned} \tag{4.57}$$

As before we note that these are linear equations in $\alpha_1 \in [0, C]$ and

$$T_i(\alpha_1 = 0) = \cdots = T_{i-1}(\alpha_1 = 0) = 0 < T_i(\alpha_1 = 0) = (1 - C_i)(z T_{cm} + w_i T_{cp}) \tag{4.58}$$

$$T_i(\alpha_1 = C) = \cdots = T_{i-1}(\alpha_1 = C) = (z T_{cm} + w_1 T_{cp}) C > T_i(\alpha_i = C)$$

$$= (1 - C_i) z T_{cm} \tag{4.59}$$

The inequality of Equation (4.59) can be easily verified by substituting $k_j = \alpha_{j+1}/\alpha_j$, $(j = 1, 2, \ldots, i - 2)$. Hence, from Equations (4.58) and (4.59) we conclude that there always exists a crossover point for the lines $T_1 = T_2 = \cdots = T_{i-1}$ and T_i at a point where $T_1 = T_2 = \cdots = T_i$. Further, since $T_1 = T_2 = \cdots = T_{i-1}$ has a constant positive slope with respect to α_1, and T_i has a constant negative slope with respect to α_1, this crossover point determines the value of α_1 that gives the optimal processing time for $p_1, p_2, \ldots p_i$, that is, that which minimizes $\max\{T_1, \ldots T_i\}$. See Figure 4.19 for illustration. It is easy to see that by mathematical induction one can prove that $T_1 = \cdots = T_m$ is necessary to minimize the processing time. Hence, the minimum processing time is obtained if all processors stop computing at the same time instant.

From Equations (4.55) and (4.56), α_i can be expressed as a function of α_{i-1}, $\alpha_{i-2}, \ldots, \alpha_1$ since $T_1 = T_2 = \cdots = T_i$:

$$\alpha_i = k_{i-1}k_{i-2}\cdots k_1\alpha_1, \quad 2 \le i \le m \quad (4.60)$$

where

$$k_j = \frac{\alpha_{j+1}}{\alpha_j} = \frac{w_j T_{cp}}{z T_{cm} + w_{j+1} T_{cp}}, \quad 1 \le j \le m - 1 \quad (4.61)$$

Substituting in the normalization equation, we get

$$\alpha_1 = \frac{1}{1 + k_1 + k_1 k_2 + \cdots + k_1 k_2 \cdots k_{m-1}} \quad (4.62)$$

From the above the optimal values of α_i's that the originating processor (the control processor) should calculate in order to achieve the minimal solution time can be computed by the following algorithm:

$$\textit{Step 1:} \quad k_j = \frac{w_j T_{cp}}{z T_{cm} + w_{j+1} T_{cp}}, \quad 1 \le j \le m - 1 \quad (4.63)$$

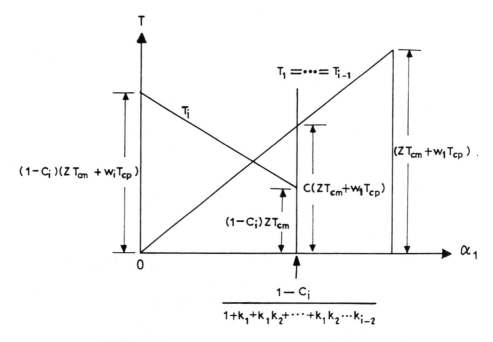

FIGURE 4.19 $T_1 = T_2 = \cdots = T_{i-1}$ and T_i as Functions of α_1

$$Step \ 2: \quad \alpha_1 = \frac{1}{1 + \sum_{i=1}^{m-1} \prod_{j=1}^{i}(k_j)} \quad (4.64)$$

$$Step \ 3: \quad \alpha_i = \left(\prod_{j=1}^{i-1} k_j\right)\alpha_1, \quad 2 \le i \le m \quad (4.65)$$

Interestingly, the solution for the optimal load allocation is of a *product form*. That is, the solution of α_i in Equation (4.65) can be expressed as a product of system constants k_i's and a normalization constant, α_1, which is also a function of k_i's.

4.5.2 Architecture 2: Bus Network without Control Processor (with Front End)

Here we consider another bus oriented architecture in which the control processor is absent and the load distribution is done by one of the processors which is also assumed to be the load originating processor (here it is assumed to be p_1). Since this processor is equipped with a front end it can simultaneously communicate and compute. The timing diagram for a given load distribution α is shown in Figure 4.20 for a network of m processors. From the timing diagram we obtain the following recursive equations

$$\alpha_i w_i T_{cp} = \alpha_{i+1} z T_{cm} + \alpha_{i+1} w_{i+1} T_{cp}, \ i = 1, \ldots, m-1 \quad (4.66)$$

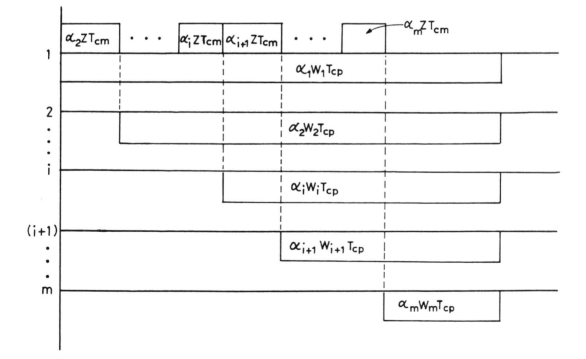

FIGURE 4.20   Timing Diagram: No Control Processsor (with Front End)

Using the normalization equation and following the procedure adopted in the previous
section, we obtain the individual α_i's. The processing time is given by $\alpha_1 w_1 T_{cp}$. It
may be observed that we have implicitly assumed that for optimal solution all the processors must stop computing at the same time. This result can be proved in a similar
manner by following the procedure in the previous section. Note that this architecture
can also be treated as a single-level tree network with identical link speeds.

4.5.3 Architecture 3: Bus Network without Control Processor (without Front End)

This architecture is similar to Architecture 2, except for the fact that the load originating processor is not equipped with a front end. Hence, it has to wait until the
communication is over before beginning its own computation. Here we assume that
the load originating processor is p_m. The timing diagram for a given load distribution
α is shown in Figure 4.21 for a network of m processors. From the timing diagram
we obtain the following recursive equations.

$$\alpha_i w_i T_{cp} = \alpha_{i+1} z T_{cm} + \alpha_{i+1} w_{i+1} T_{cp}, \quad i = 1, \ldots, m-2 \tag{4.67}$$

$$\alpha_{m-1} w_{m-1} T_{cp} = \alpha_m w_m T_{cp} \tag{4.68}$$

The proof for the optimal time solution can be obtained in a manner similar to that
shown in the previous section.

4.5.4 Position of Processors in Bus Networks

Now that we have studied the procedure to find the optimal division of the processing
load, it is natural to ask whether the position of the processors in the network affects
the processing time or not. To check this, we consider a system with three processors
($m = 3$) with a control processor. Solving the set of recursive equations obtained

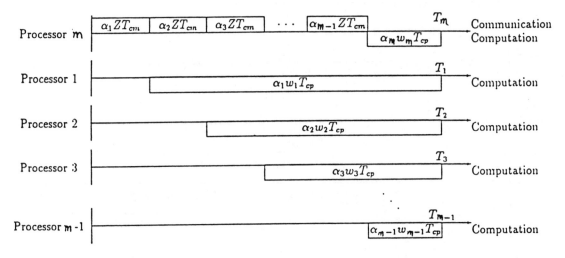

FIGURE 4.21   Timing Diagram: No Control Processor (without Front End)

from the timing diagram shown in Figure 4.16, we obtain

$$T(\alpha) =$$

$$\left\{ \frac{(zT_{cm} + w_2 T_{cp})(zT_{cm} + w_3 T_{cp})}{(zT_{cm})^2 + (zT_{cm}T_{cp})(w_1 + w_2 + w_3) + (T_{cp})^2(w_1 w_2 + w_1 w_3 + w_2 w_3)} \right\} w_1 T_{cp}$$

$$(4.69)$$

Thus we see that the finish times are symmetric in w_1, w_2, w_3, implying that the position of the processors on the bus is not important. Thus, a processor can be placed anywhere on the bus or any two processors can be interchanged without affecting the minimum processing time. These results will be proved in the context of a more general tree network in Chapter 7.

4.5.5 Numerical Results

In this section, we present some interesting computational results when the bus network has a control processor. The behavior of minimum processing time with respect to the number of processors is shown in Figure 4.22 for $T_{cm} = 0.5$, $T_{cp} = 1.0$, $w_i = 1$ for all i. Six performance curves are given for $z = 0.1, 0.2, 0.5, 1.0, 10.0$, and 20.0. As shown in the figure the minimum finish time levels off to zT_{cm} as more processors are added. This can be proved as follows: We know that for the last processor,

$$T_m(\alpha) = zT_{cm} + \alpha_m w_m T_{cp} \qquad (4.70)$$

Clearly, as the number of processors increases, the load assigned to each processor

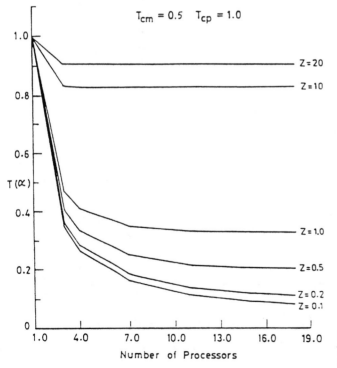

FIGURE 4.22 Minimum Processing Time and Number of Processors (Different Link Speeds)

becomes smaller. In other words as $m \to \infty \Rightarrow \alpha_m \to 0$, therefore,

$$\lim_{m \to \infty} T_m(\alpha) = zT_{cm} \tag{4.71}$$

Figure 4.22 implies that only a small number of processors are needed to come close to the minimum processing time. Figure 4.22 also supports the intuitive result that the minimum processing time increases as the value of z increases and decreases as the number of processors increases.

In Figure 4.23, the effect of different processor speeds is examined, while keeping the bus speed constant. The optimal processing time is plotted against the number of processors in the network with $T_{cm} = 0.25$, $T_{cp} = 1.0$, $z = 1.0$. Five performance curves are obtained for $w_i = 0.05, 0.1, 0.2, 0.5, 1.0$ (for all $i = 1, 2, \ldots, m$). As Figure 4.23 reveals, if a large number of processors is used, the minimum finish time is independent of the speed of the processors. That is, for any speed of the processors, the minimum finish time will level off to zT_{cm}. The second point to observe is that using a small number of fast processors to solve the computational problem is as good as using a large number of slow processors.

Now consider Architecture 2 (bus network without control processor; processors equipped with front ends), which has the same model as a single-level tree network with identical links. An examination of the processing time $T(\alpha)$ given in Table 4.1

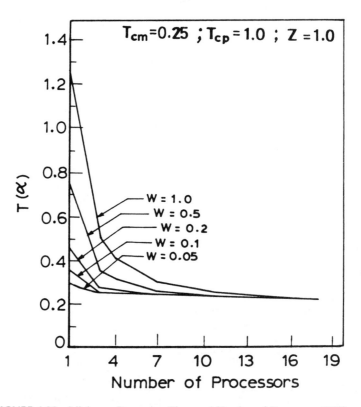

FIGURE 4.23   Minimum Processing Time and Number of Processors (Different Processor Speeds)

TABLE 4.1 Minimum Time Solution ($T_{cm} = 0.5$, $T_{cp} = 1.0$).

z	w_1	w_2	w_3	w_4	α_1	α_2	α_3	α_4	$T(\alpha)$
1.0	0.2	0.5	0.8	1.0	0.7588	0.1518	0.0584	0.0311	0.1518
1.0	0.5	0.2	0.8	1.0	0.5311	0.3794	0.0584	0.0311	0.2656
1.0	1.0	0.2	0.8	0.5	0.3541	0.5058	0.0778	0.0623	0.3541
1.0	1.0	0.8	0.2	0.5	0.3541	0.2724	0.3113	0.0623	0.3541
0.1	1.0	1.0	1.0	1.0	0.2686	0.2558	0.2436	0.2320	0.2686
0.5	1.0	1.0	1.0	1.0	0.3388	0.2710	0.2168	0.1734	0.3388
1.0	1.0	1.0	1.0	1.0	0.4154	0.2769	0.1846	0.1231	0.4154
2.0	1.0	1.0	1.0	1.0	0.5333	0.2667	0.1333	0.0667	0.5333

indicates that, for best performance, the processor with the fastest computation speed should distribute the load. A computational verification of this is given in the first four rows of Table 4.1. The third and fourth rows show that the order of the processors, excepting the one that distributes the load, does not affect the processing time. The last four rows of Table 4.1 show that the time performance is best when the bus speed is maximum. In Chapter 7, we shall analytically prove these observations to be true.

Next we consider an architecture in which the processors are not equipped with front ends (that is, Architecture 3). In Figure 4.24 the minimum finish time is plotted against the number of processors in the network with $T_{cm} = 0.5$, $T_{cp} = 1.0$, $w_i = 1$ and seven performance curves were obtained for $z = 0.1, 0.2, 0.5, 1.0, 1.8, 2.0$ and 2.1. From this figure we can make two important observations. The first is that the minimum processing time function levels off to a certain value after a small number of processors. The second is that there is a threshold value that limits the speed of communication. Beyond this value, using more than one processor to compute the load would take more time than when only one processor is used. This is because of the time that is wasted in slow communication.

In the following we will calculate the value at which the processing time levels off and the threshold value of z. Based on the fact that the optimal processing time is achieved when all processors stop at the same time, we have

$$T_1 = (1 - \alpha_1)z_{cm} + \alpha_1 w_1 T_{cp} = z T_{cm} + \alpha_1 (w_1 T_{cp} - z T_{cm}) \qquad (4.72)$$

As $m \to \infty$ we have $\alpha_1 \to 0$ and so $T_1 \to z T_{cm}$. The following inequality must hold; otherwise the minimum finish time will be less than $z T_{cm}$, which is not possible.

$$w_1 T_{cp} - z T_{cm} \geq 0$$

and hence

$$z \leq \frac{w_1 T_{cp}}{T_{cm}} \qquad (4.73)$$

This implies that the threshold value of z is

$$z_{th} = \frac{w_1 T_{cp}}{T_{cm}} \qquad (4.74)$$

Both the previous results are verified in Figure 4.24, where, if $z > 2$, it is more efficient for the originating processor to process the entire load itself rather than to distribute it, because of the slow communication. A more detailed analysis of optimal load distribution conditions will be carried out in Chapter 5.

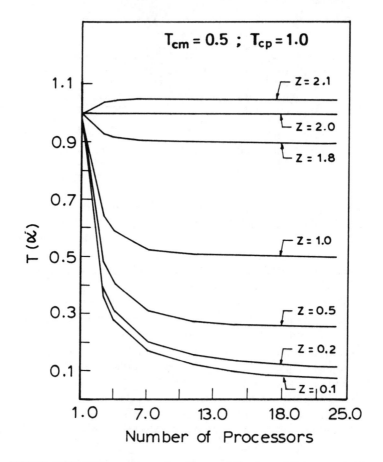

FIGURE 4.24 Minimum Processing Time and Number of Processors (without Front End)

4.6 EQUIVALENT PROCESSORS IN HOMOGENEOUS TREE NETWORKS

As is true of processor equivalence in homogeneous linear networks, here, too, we can collapse a homogeneous tree network into one equivalent processor that preserves the characteristics of the original tree network in terms of its minimum processing time. This allows an easy examination of large tree networks. In addition, it becomes possible to find a closed-form solution for the optimal amount of load that is to be assigned to each processor in order to obtain minimum processing time. We present the analysis for with- and without-front-end processors below.

4.6.1 With-Front-End Processors

A general homogeneous tree network is shown in Figure 4.25a. The tree is assumed to be a balanced one. We will begin collapsing the tree from the terminal nodes (Level N-1) and move up to the root processor (Level 0). On our way up, every parent processor and its children will be replaced by one equivalent processor. This

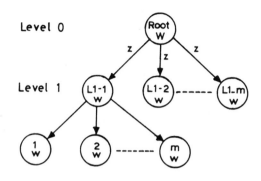

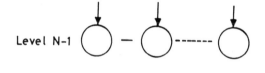

(a)

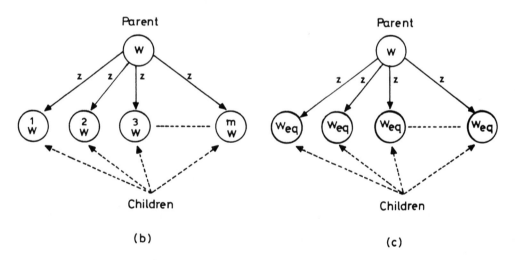

(b)   (c)

FIGURE 4.25   (a) A Homogeneous Tree Network (b) A Subtree with Terminal Nodes (c) A Subtree with Nonterminal Nodes

process will continue until the root processor and its children are collapsed to one equivalent processor. In this aggregation process, only two cases are possible: the first case occurs at the last two levels, where all of the processors have the same speed, as shown in Figure 4.25b; the second case occurs for the children at level k and their parents at level $k-1$, $k = 0, 1, \ldots, N-2$ where all processors except the parent have the same speed, as shown in Figure 4.25c.

The timing diagram for the first case is the same as the bus network shown in Figure 4.20. We solve this set of recursive equations (4.66) together with the normalization equation and obtain

$$T(\alpha) = wT_{cp}\left\{\frac{r^{m-1}(r-1)}{r^m - 1}\right\}\tag{4.75}$$

where

$$r = \frac{wT_{cp} + zT_{cm}}{wT_{cp}}\tag{4.76}$$

We now equate Equation (4.75) and $w_{eq}T_{cp}$ to obtain

$$w_{eq} = w\left\{\frac{r^{m-1}(r-1)}{r^m - 1}\right\}\tag{4.77}$$

The timing diagram for the second case is the same as Figure 4.20 with $w_1 = w$ and $w_2 = \cdots = w_m = w_{eq}$. With this, we obtain the finish time of processors as

$$T_i(\alpha) = (\alpha_2 + \alpha_3 + \cdots + \alpha_i)zT_{cm} + \alpha_i w_{eq}T_{cm}, \quad i = 2,\ldots,m\tag{4.78}$$

$$T_1(\alpha) = \alpha_1 wT_{cp}\tag{4.79}$$

To obtain the minimum processing time, we equate the finish times of the processors, as a consequence of which each of the α_j's $(j = 2,\ldots,m-1)$ can be expressed as

$$\alpha_j = \alpha_{j+1}r_i\tag{4.80}$$

and

$$\alpha_1 = \alpha_2 C\tag{4.81}$$

where

$$r_i = \frac{w_{eq}T_{cp} + zT_{cm}}{w_{eq}T_{cp}}\tag{4.82}$$

$$C = \frac{w_{eq}T_{cp} + zT_{cm}}{wT_{cp}}\tag{4.83}$$

Here, i is the level of the subtree within the original tree. Using the above, the load fractions can be expressed as functions of α_m as follows:

$$\alpha_1 = \alpha_m r_i^{m-2}C$$

$$\alpha_j = \alpha_m r_i^{m-j}, \quad j = 2, 3,\ldots,m-1\tag{4.84}$$

Using the normalization equation and Equation (4.84), α_m can be found as a function of r_i and C as

$$\alpha_m = \frac{r_i - 1}{(C+1)r_i^{m-1} - Cr_i^{m-2} - 1}\tag{4.85}$$

Now all other optimal values of α_j's can be computed using Equation (4.84). Since $\alpha_1 = \alpha_m r_i^{m-2}C$, α_1 can be expressed in terms of r_i and C as follows:

$$\alpha_1 = \frac{r_i^{m-1} - r_i^{m-2}}{r_i^{m-1} - r_i^{m-2} + \frac{1}{C}(r_i^{m-1} - 1)}\tag{4.86}$$

In order to find w_{eqi} (the overall equivalent speed parameter), we equate the finish time of the root processor to $w_{eqi}T_{cp}$. Here w_{eqi} is a constant that is inversely proportional to the speed of an *equivalent* processor that will replace all the processors in Figure 4.25c and preserve the characteristics of the original system.

$$w_{eqi} = w\alpha_1 \tag{4.87}$$

Substituting the value obtained for α_1 in the above equation, we find that:

$$w_{eqi} = w\left\{\frac{r_i^{m-1} - r_i^{m-2}}{r_i^{m-1} - r_i^{m-2} + \frac{1}{c}(r_i^{m-1} - 1)}\right\} \tag{4.88}$$

Starting at Level $N-1$, one can use Equation (4.77) to reduce the tree in Figure 4.25a by one level and then move up to Level $N - 2$. Starting from the subtrees where children are at Level $N - 2$ and up to the root processor, one uses Equation (4.88) to find $w_{eqtotal}$. Here $w_{eqtotal}$ is a constant that is inversely proportional to the speed of an "equivalent" processor that will replace the whole tree in Figure 4.25a while preserving the same characteristics as the original system. Computing $w_{eqtotal}$, the minimum finish time T_{ftnf} can be written as follows:

$$T_{ftnf} = T_{cp}w_{eqtotal} \tag{4.89}$$

4.6.2 Without-Front-End Processors

For this case, we follow the same steps as in the previous section. Here too, we have two cases. The timing diagram for the first case is the same as that for the bus network (without front end) as shown in Figure 4.21. From the timing diagram, equations similar to those for the bus network with front end can be easily derived and solved to yield the minimum processing time as

$$T(\alpha) = zT_{cm} + \left(\frac{r-1}{r^{m-1}+r-2}\right)(wT_{cp} - zT_{cm}) \tag{4.90}$$

where r is defined in Equation (4.76). While deriving the above equation, we implicitly assume that $wT_{cp} > zT_{cm}$ without any loss of generality. We now equate Equation (4.90) and $w_{eqt}T_{cp}$ to obtain

$$w_{eqt} = \frac{1}{T_{cp}}\left\{zT_{cm} + \left(\frac{r-1}{r^{m-1}+r-2}\right)(wT_{cp} - zT_{cm})\right\} \tag{4.91}$$

The timing diagram for the second case is also the same as in Figure 4.21 with $w_1 = w$ and $w_2 = \cdots = w_m = w_{eq}$. With this, we obtain the finish time expressions as

$$T_i = (\alpha_2 + \cdots + \alpha_i)zT_{cm} + \alpha_i w_{eq}T_{cp}, \quad i = 2, \ldots, m \tag{4.92}$$

and

$$T_1 = (1 - \alpha_1)zT_{cm} + \alpha_1 wT_{cp} \tag{4.93}$$

To obtain the minimum processing time, we equate the finish times of the processors, as a consequence of which each of the α_i ($i = 2, \ldots, m - 1$) can be expressed as

$$\alpha_i = \alpha_i r_i \tag{4.94}$$

$$\alpha_1 = \alpha_m c \tag{4.95}$$

where r_i is defined earlier and $c = w_{eq}/w$. The load fractions can be written in terms of α_m, r_i, and c as

$$\alpha_j = \alpha_m r^{m-j}, \quad j = 2, \ldots, m-1$$

$$\alpha_1 = \alpha_m c \tag{4.96}$$

Using the normalization equation and Equation (4.96), α_m can be written as a function of r_i and c as

$$\alpha_m = \frac{r_i - 1}{c(r_i - 1) + r_i^{m-1} - 1} \tag{4.97}$$

Now all other optimal values of α_j's can be computed using Equation (4.96). Since $\alpha_1 = \alpha_m c$, α_1 can be expressed in terms of r_i and c as

$$\alpha_1 = \frac{r_i - 1}{(r_i - 1) + \frac{1}{c}(r_i^{m-1} - 1)} \tag{4.98}$$

We now equate Equation (4.93) to $w_{eqi} T_{cp}$ in order to find w_{eqi}, a constant that is inversely proportional to the speed of an *equivalent* processor that will replace all processors in Figure 4.25c and preserve the same characteristics as the original system. Note again that for load sharing to produce a net saving we must have $w > z\delta$ in the equation

$$w_{eqi} = z\delta + \alpha_1(w - z\delta) \tag{4.99}$$

where $\delta = T_{cm}/T_{cp}$. Substituting the value obtained for α_1 in the above equation, we find that

$$w_{eqi} = z\delta + \left\{ \frac{r_i - 1}{(r_i - 1) + \frac{1}{c}(r_i^{m-1} - 1)} \right\} (w - z\delta) \tag{4.100}$$

Starting at Level $N-1$, one can use Equation (4.91) to reduce the tree in Figure 4.25a by one level. For the subtrees whose children are at Level $N-2$ and above, one uses Equation (4.100) until $w_{eqtotal}$ is obtained. Here, $w_{eqtotal}$ is a constant that is inversely proportional to the speed of an *equivalent* processor that will replace the whole tree in Figure 4.25a, while preserving the same characteristics as the original system. Computing $w_{eqtotal}$, the minimum finish time T_{ftnf} can be written as follows:

$$T_{ftnf} = T_{cp} w_{eqtotal} \tag{4.101}$$

4.7 PERFORMANCE LIMITS OF A BINARY TREE NETWORK

To illustrate the utility of the equivalent network concept, we consider an infinite binary tree network. Here, our aim is to solve for the ultimate finish time limit. A binary tree network is shown in Figure 4.26. We consider the with- and without-front-end cases separately.

4.7.1 With-Front-End Processors

To obtain the processing time for an infinite binary tree, that is, $m = \infty$, one collapses the tree into three processors as shown in Figure 4.27. The right side of the tree has

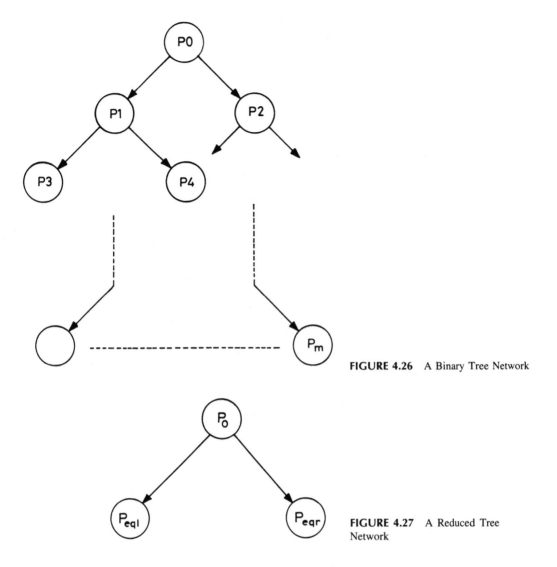

FIGURE 4.26 A Binary Tree Network

FIGURE 4.27 A Reduced Tree Network

been replaced by an equivalent processor with equivalent processing speed parameter w_{eq}^{∞}. The same is true for the left side of the tree, too. Naturally, as the left and right subtrees are infinite trees in their own right, an equivalent processor for either one of them has the same computational speed as one for the entire tree. The timing diagram for this equivalent system, which preserves the same characteristics of an infinite size binary tree, is shown in Figure 4.28. The load distribution equations are:

$$\alpha_0 w T_{cp} = \alpha_l z T_{cm} + \alpha_l w_{eq}^{\infty} T_{cp} \qquad (4.102)$$

$$\alpha_l w_{eq}^{\infty} T_{cp} = \alpha_r z T_{cm} + \alpha_r w_{eq}^{\infty} T_{cp} \qquad (4.103)$$

$$\alpha_0 w T_{cp} = w_{eq}^{\infty} T_{cp} \qquad (4.104)$$

Also, the normalizing equation is

$$\alpha_0 + \alpha_l + \alpha_r = 1 \qquad (4.105)$$

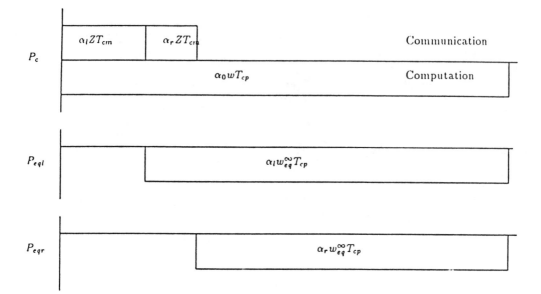

P_c

$\alpha_l Z T_{cm}$ $\alpha_r Z T_{cm}$ Communication

$\alpha_0 w T_{cp}$ Computation

P_{eql}

$\alpha_l w_{eq}^{\infty} T_{cp}$

P_{eqr}

$\alpha_r w_{eq}^{\infty} T_{cp}$

FIGURE 4.28   Timing Diagram: Reduced Network (with Front End)

These equations are nonlinear and w_{eq}^{∞} can be determined by solving iteratively the following equation:

$$w_{eq}^{\infty} = \frac{w(zT_{cm} + w_{eq}^{\infty} T_{cp})}{zT_{cm} + w_{eq}^{\infty} T_{cp} + wT_{cp} + \frac{ww_{eq}^{\infty} T_{cp}^2}{zT_{cm} + w_{eq}^{\infty} T_{cp}}} \tag{4.106}$$

It may be noted that from Equation (4.106) a closed-form expression for w_{eq}^{∞} can also be obtained by some algebraic manipulations, which results in a cubic equation. This in turn can be solved to obtain an expression for w_{eq}^{∞}. However, this is not our objective here. The minimum finish time for an infinite tree network with front-end processors $T_{fe}^{\infty}(\alpha)$ can now be computed by the following equation:

$$T_{fe}^{\infty}(\alpha) = w_{eq}^{\infty} T_{cp} \tag{4.107}$$

4.7.2 Without-Front-End Processors

Consider now the case where the processors in the network are not equipped with front end. In this case, as before, both the left and the right branch below the root processor are collapsed into one equivalent processor each. The timing diagram of the reduced tree is depicted in Figure 4.29, from which it can be seen that the ultimate finish time limit, $T_{nfe}^{\infty}(\alpha)$ can be computed in four different ways:

$$T_{nfe}^{\infty}(\alpha) = (\alpha_l + \alpha_r)zT_{cm} + \alpha_0 w T_{cp} \tag{4.108}$$

$$T_{nfe}^{\infty}(\alpha) = \alpha_l z T_{cm} + \alpha_l w_{eq}^{\infty} T_{cp} \tag{4.109}$$

$$T_{nfe}^{\infty}(\alpha) = (\alpha_l + \alpha_r)zT_{cm} + \alpha_r w_{eq}^{\infty} T_{cp} \tag{4.110}$$

$$T_{nfe}^{\infty}(\alpha) = w_{eq}^{\infty} T_{cp} \tag{4.111}$$

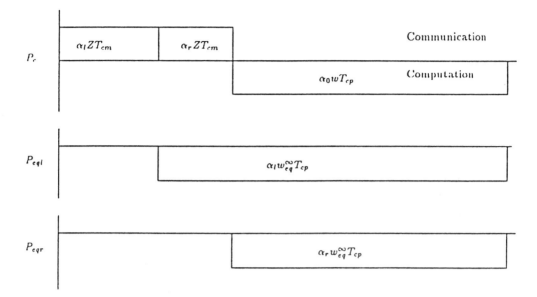

FIGURE 4.29   Timing Diagram: Reduced Network (without Front End)

Solving the above system of nonlinear equations with Equation (4.105), we can find the expression that enables us to determine the exact numerical value of w_{eq}^{∞} by iteration.

$$w_{eq}^{\infty} = \frac{w(zT_{cm} + w_{eq}^{\infty}T_{cp})^2}{(w_{eq}^{\infty}T_{cp})^2 + ww_{eq}^{\infty}T_{cp}^2 + wT_{cp}(zT_{cm} + w_{eq}^{\infty}T_{cp})} \qquad (4.112)$$

Again we stress the fact that solving Equation (4.112) and obtaining a closed-form expression is not our primary objective. Attempts to solve Equation (4.112) will result in a cubic equation in w_{eq}^{∞}, whose roots give the required closed-form expression. However, the ultimate finish time can be computed using Equation (4.111).

4.8 CONCLUDING REMARKS

The following are the highlights of this chapter:

- The basic load distribution equations for general tree networks with communication delays, processing an arbitrarily divisible load, were obtained for both with- and without-front-end cases.

- The recursive equations for optimal load distribution were obtained by making use of the optimality criterion that all the processors must stop computing at the same instant in time.

- Optimal load distribution equations were obtained for the case in which each processor is required to send back the results of its computation to the load originating processor through its parent processor.

- The above results were then applied to several bus-oriented architectures and analytical proof of the optimality criterion was obtained.
- The concept of equivalent processors in homogeneous tree networks was introduced and used to analyze the ultimate performance limits of large binary tree networks.
- A number of computational results were presented to illustrate various aspects of load distribution in tree networks.

In this chapter we have mainly presented the basic load distribution equations for general tree networks. We have also provided considerable insight into the load distribution process through analytical and computational results. In subsequent chapters we will present more general analytical results to support many of the observations made here.

BIBLIOGRAPHIC NOTES

Section 4.1–4.4   The load distribution equations for the general tree network were presented by Cheng and Robertazzi (1990). This paper examines various aspects of this problem.

Section 4.5   The problem of optimal load distribution in bus networks and the proof of the optimality criterion was given by Sohn and Robertazzi (1993a, 1996). The computational results on the position of processors in a bus network appeared in Bataineh and Robertazzi (1991 and 1992).

Section 4.6   The concept of processor equivalence was proposed by Bataineh et al. (1994), and used to obtain a closed-form solution to the minimum processing time for bus networks. This concept, in a slightly different sense, has also been used in the context of sharing divisible loads in hypercube and mesh networks by Blazewicz and Drozdowski (1994a, 1994b).

Section 4.7   The concept of processor equivalence was used to obtain the ultimate performance limits of infinite homogeneous binary tree networks in Bataineh and Robertazzi (1992).

CHAPTER 5

Optimality Conditions for Load Distribution

The computational results given in the previous chapters show that in order to achieve optimal processing time in a single-level tree or linear network, the processing load must be partitioned in such a way that all the processors stop computing their load fractions at the same instant in time. This is an intuitively appealing notion, since otherwise some of the processors have to remain idle while waiting for the other processors to complete their computation. In Chapter 4, we proved this assertion to be true in a fairly straightforward manner for bus networks. In this chapter, we provide a rigorous proof of the fact that this result is true only for a certain class of single-level tree networks. We show that this result is not true for the general class of single-level tree networks and obtain a condition by which the optimal load distribution is decided. More specifically, we show that in a general tree network it is not essential to utilize all the processors. Using these general results, a number of special cases (some of which were illustrated through examples in the previous chapters) are analytically derived. In Chapter 3, using the concept of processor equivalence, we gave a recursive proof for the optimality condition for linear networks. These results for linear networks are presented in this chapter in a more rigorous framework.

5.1 SINGLE-LEVEL TREE NETWORK

A single-level tree network with $(m + 1)$ processors and m links, denoted as Σ, is shown in Figure 5.1. The child processors $p_1, p_2, \ldots, p_m$ are connected to a root processor p_0 via links $l_1, l_2, \ldots, l_m$. The root processor divides the total processing load

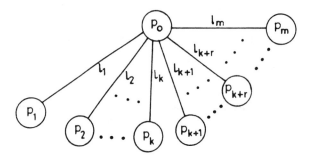

FIGURE 5.1   Single-Level Tree
Network Σ

into $(m + 1)$ parts, keeps its own share α_0, and distributes the remaining load fractions $\alpha_1, \alpha_2, \ldots, \alpha_m$ to the child processors $p_1, p_2, \ldots, p_m$ in the sequence $1, \ldots, m$. Each processor begins computing immediately upon receiving its load fraction and continues to do so until its load fraction is exhausted.

5.1.1 With-Front-End Processors

Since the root processor is equipped with a front end, the distribution of the load fractions is continuously done by the front end while the root processor (p_0) simultaneously computes its own fraction α_0. The timing diagram for a given load distribution $\alpha \in L$ is shown in Figure 5.2. Note that the timing diagram is drawn by assuming that all the $(m + 1)$ processors stop computing at the same instant in time. From this timing diagram the corresponding recursive load distribution equations are

$$\alpha_k w_k T_{cp} = \alpha_{k+1} z_{k+1} T_{cm} + \alpha_{k+1} w_{k+1} T_{cp}, \quad k = 0, \ldots, m - 1 \qquad (5.1)$$

and the normalizing equation is

$$\sum_{j=0}^{m} \alpha_j = 1 \qquad (5.2)$$

Rewriting Equation (5.1) as

$$\alpha_k = \alpha_{k+1} f_{k+1}, \quad k = 0, 1, \ldots, m - 1 \qquad (5.3)$$

where

$$f_{k+1} = \left(\frac{w_{k+1} + z_{k+1}\delta}{w_k} \right) \qquad (5.4)$$

and $\delta = T_{cm}/T_{cp}$ is as in Chapter 2. These recursive equations can be solved by expressing all the α_k ($k = 0, 1, \ldots, m - 1$) in terms of α_m as

$$\alpha_k = \left\{ \prod_{j=k+1}^{m} f_j \right\} \alpha_m \qquad (5.5)$$

From Equation (5.2), the value of α_m is obtained as

$$\alpha_m = \frac{1}{1 + \sum_{i=1}^{m} \prod_{j=i}^{m} f_j} \qquad (5.6)$$

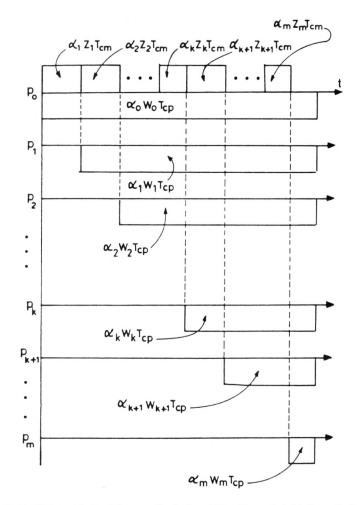

FIGURE 5.2   Timing Diagram: Single-Level Tree Network (with Front End)

Thus, the fraction of the processing load assigned to the kth processor is

$$\alpha_k = \frac{\displaystyle\prod_{j=k+1}^{m} f_j}{1 + \displaystyle\sum_{i=1}^{m} \prod_{j=i}^{m} f_j}, \quad k = 0, 1, \ldots, m-1 \tag{5.7}$$

From Figure 5.2, it can be seen that the processing time $T(\alpha)$ is also the finish time of the root processor given by $\alpha_0 w_0 T_{cp}$. Thus,

$$T(\alpha) = \left(\frac{\displaystyle\prod_{j=1}^{m} f_j}{1 + \displaystyle\sum_{i=1}^{m} \prod_{j=i}^{m} f_j} \right) w_0 T_{cp} \tag{5.8}$$

The above closed-form solution will be used to prove some important results on the minimization of processing time.

5.1.2 Without-Front-End Processors

In this case, since the root processor p_0 is not equipped with a front end, it first distributes the fraction of the processing loads $\alpha_1, \alpha_2, \ldots, \alpha_m$ to the processors $p_1, p_2, \ldots, p_m$, respectively, and then begins computing its own fraction of the load. The timing diagram for a given load distribution $\alpha \in L$ is shown in Figure 5.3. As

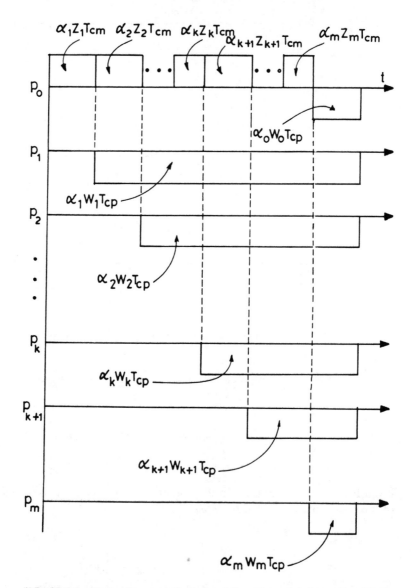

FIGURE 5.3   Timing Diagram: Single-Level Tree Network (without Front End)

in the with-front-end case, the timing diagram is obtained by assuming that all the $(m + 1)$ processors stop computing at the same instant in time. From this timing diagram the corresponding recursive load distribution equations are

$$\alpha_0 w_0 T_{cp} = \alpha_m w_m T_{cp},$$

$$\alpha_k w_k T_{cp} = \alpha_{k+1} z_{k+1} T_{cm} + \alpha_{k+1} z_{k+1} T_{cp}, \quad k = 1, 2, \ldots, m-1 \quad (5.9)$$

The normalizing equation is

$$\sum_{j=0}^{m} \alpha_j = 1 \quad (5.10)$$

Using Equation (5.4), the load fractions assigned to the processors are obtained as

$$\alpha_0 = \frac{\frac{w_m}{w_0}}{1 + \frac{w_m}{w_0} + \sum_{i=2}^{m} \prod_{j=i}^{m} f_j},$$

$$\alpha_k = \frac{\prod_{j=k+1}^{m} f_j}{1 + \frac{w_m}{w_0} + \sum_{i=2}^{m} \prod_{j=i}^{m} f_j}, \quad k = 1, 2, \ldots, m-1$$

$$\alpha_m = \frac{1}{1 + \frac{w_m}{w_0} + \sum_{i=2}^{m} \prod_{j=i}^{m} f_j} \quad (5.11)$$

Here the processing time $T(\alpha)$ is obtained from the timing diagram in Figure 5.3 and is given by

$$T(\alpha) = \left(\frac{\prod_{j=1}^{m} f_j}{1 + \frac{w_m}{w_0} + \sum_{i=2}^{m} \prod_{j=i}^{m} f_j} \right) w_0 T_{cp} \quad (5.12)$$

5.1.3 Concept of Equivalent Network

Given a distributed computing network dedicated to a certain application, the natural propensity is to use all the processors in the network to minimize the processing time. However, we shall now demonstrate through an example that by not making use of certain processor-link pairs in a single-level tree network, we can obtain a better time performance.

Example 5.1

Consider a single-level tree network with $m = 3$ and $w_0 = 2.0$, $w_1 = 3.0$, $w_2 = 1.0$, $w_3 = 2.0$, $z_1 = 2.0$, $z_2 = 0.5$, $z_3 = 5.0$, and $T_{cm} = T_{cp} = 1.0$. The root processor is assumed to be equipped with a front end. With these parameters, assuming that all the processors stop computing at the same time instant, the load distribution $\alpha \in L$ is given as $\alpha = \{0.4321, 0.1728, 0.3457, 0.0494\}$ and $T(\alpha) = 0.8642$. Note that these values are obtained from Equations (5.6) through (5.8). Let us redistribute α in such a way that the load fraction α_1 is assigned to p_2 in addition to its own load fraction α_2, and p_1 is not given any load. Then, the new load distribution is given by $\alpha' = \{0.4321, 0, 0.5185, 0.0494\}$. In this case we obtain the finish times as $T_2(\alpha') = 0.77775 < T(\alpha)$, and $T_3(\alpha') = 0.60505 < T(\alpha)$. However, the processing time contributed by the root processor remains unchanged. Now, suppose we use a load distribution such that all processors (other than p_1) stop computing at the same time instant. Then, using Equation (5.7), the new load distribution is obtained as $\alpha'' = \{0.3962, 0, 0.5283, 0.0755\}$ and $T(\alpha'') = 0.7924$, which is an improvement over $T(\alpha)$ and $T(\alpha')$.

From the above example, we see that it may be possible to actually improve performance by eliminating some processor-link pairs from a network, which is the same as assigning zero loads to these processor-link pairs. To identify such processor-link pairs, we shall now introduce the concept of an *equivalent network*, which is somewhat different from the equivalent processor defined in Chapters 3 and 4. However, before this, we define a reduced network obtained from a single-level tree network Σ as follows:

The *reduced network* obtained from a single-level tree network Σ is defined as a network obtained by eliminating some child processors and their corresponding links (that is, processor-link pairs) from Σ. By convention we assume that Σ itself is also a reduced network of Σ.

Consider the set of processors $p_{k+1}, \ldots, p_{k+r}$ in the single-level tree network shown in Figure 5.4, where $k \in \{1, \ldots, m\}$ and $r \in \{1, \ldots, m-k\}$. This set of processors can be replaced by a single equivalent processor denoted by $p(k+1, \ldots, k+r)$ with parameter $w(k+1, \ldots, k+r)$ connected to the root via the equivalent link denoted by $l(k+1, \ldots, k+r)$ with parameter $z(k+1, \ldots, k+r)$. The resulting network is called an *equivalent network*. There could be many such equivalent representations possible. However, for our requirements, we will define a specific representation that satisfies the following properties: If the initial load distribution $\alpha = (\alpha_0, \alpha_1, \ldots, \alpha_k, \alpha_{k+1}, \ldots, \alpha_{k+r}, \alpha_{k+r+1}, \ldots, \alpha_m) \in L$ is such that $T_i(\alpha) = T'$, for $i = k+1, \ldots, k+r$ (that is, the finish times of processors $p_{k+1}, \ldots, p_{k+r}$ are the same), then

(a) The finish time of the equivalent processor with the new load distribution $\alpha' = (\alpha_0, \alpha_1, \ldots, \alpha_k, \alpha_{k+1} + \cdots + \alpha_{k+r}, \alpha_{k+r+1}, \ldots, \alpha_m) \in L$ is also T'. Note that the load processed by the equivalent processor is now $\alpha_{k+1} + \cdots + \alpha_{k+r}$; and that the new load distribution α' is a $(m - r + 2)$tuple, since the equivalent network now has $(m - r + 1)$ child processors.

(b) The total delay in communicating the load fractions $\alpha_{k+1}, \ldots, \alpha_{k+r}$ in the original network is the same as the delay in communicating the load $\alpha_{k+1} + \cdots + \alpha_{k+r}$ in the equivalent network.

(c) The time taken by p_{k+r} to compute α_{k+r} in the original network is the same as the time taken by the equivalent processor to compute the load $\alpha_{k+1} + \cdots + \alpha_{k+r}$.

Note that processors other than $p_{k+1}, \ldots, p_{k+r}$ need not have their finish time as T' either in the original network or in the equivalent network, and that their finish times remain unchanged. Further, note that any two of the above properties together imply the third. From the above, we derive closed-form expressions for the equivalent processor and link parameters as follows: Consider the timing diagram in Figure 5.4. From this, we obtain the following recursive relation:

$$\alpha_{k+i} w_{k+i} T_{cp} = \alpha_{k+i+1} \left(w_{k+i+1} T_{cp} + z_{k+i+1} T_{cm} \right), \quad i = 1, \ldots, r-1 \qquad (5.13)$$

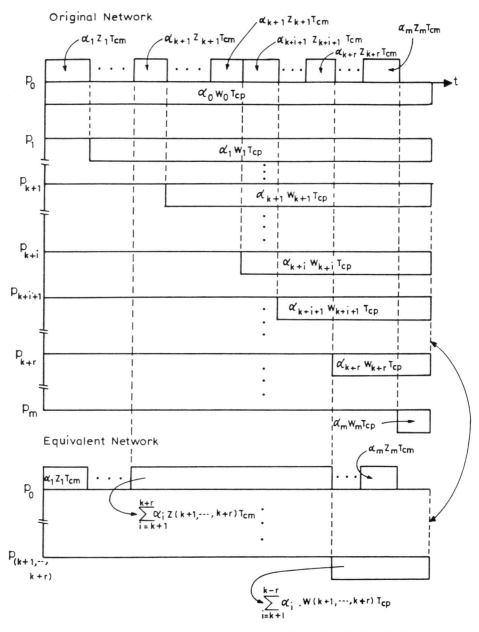

FIGURE 5.4 Timing Diagram for Equivalent Network (with Front End)

from which we obtain

$$\alpha_{k+i} = \alpha_{k+r} \left(\prod_{p=k+i+1}^{k+r} f_p \right), \quad i = 1, \ldots, r-1 \tag{5.14}$$

Let β be the total load assigned to processors $p_{k+1}, \ldots, p_{k+r}$. Then,

$$\beta = \sum_{i=1}^{r} \alpha_{k+i} \tag{5.15}$$

Substituting Equation (5.14) in Equation (5.15), we have

$$\alpha_{k+r} = \left(\frac{1}{1 + \sum\limits_{i=k+2}^{k+r} \prod\limits_{p=i}^{k+r} f_p} \right) \beta \tag{5.16}$$

Now applying property (c), shown in Figure 5.4, we obtain

$$\alpha_{k+r} w_{k+r} = \beta w\,(k+1, \ldots, k+r) \tag{5.17}$$

Substituting Equation (5.16) in Equation (5.17) we obtain the expression

$$w\,(k+1, \ldots, k+r) = \left(\frac{1}{1 + \sum\limits_{i=k+2}^{k+r} \prod\limits_{p=i}^{k+r} f_p} \right) w_{k+r} \tag{5.18}$$

Similarly, using property (b), shown in Figure 5.4, we have

$$\beta z\,(k+1, \ldots, k+r)\, T_{cm} = \sum_{i=k+1}^{k+r} \alpha_i z_i T_{cm} \tag{5.19}$$

Using Equations (5.14) through (5.16) in Equation (5.19) we obtain the expression

$$z\,(k+1, \ldots, k+r) = \frac{\sum\limits_{i=k+2}^{k+r} \left\{ \left(\prod\limits_{p=i}^{k+r} f_p \right) z_{i-1} \right\} + z_{k+r}}{1 + \sum\limits_{i=k+2}^{k+r} \prod\limits_{p=i}^{k+r} f_p} \tag{5.20}$$

In the above derivation, although we used the artifice of a specific initial load distribution to obtain the expressions for equivalent processor and link speed parameters, these expressions themselves are independent of the load distribution. Next we derive some expressions that will be used frequently later. From Equation (5.13) we obtain

$$\alpha_{k+i} = \left(\frac{1}{f_{k+i} f_{k+i-1} \cdots f_{k+2}} \right) \alpha_{k+1}, \quad i = 2, \ldots, r \tag{5.21}$$

We define a quantity Q_{k+i} as

$$Q_{k+i} = \frac{\alpha_{k+i}}{\sum\limits_{j=1}^{r} \alpha_{k+j}} = \left(\frac{1}{\beta} \right) \alpha_{k+1}, \quad i = 1, \ldots, r \tag{5.22}$$

The ratio Q_{k+i} defines the fraction of the load β, assigned to p_{k+i}, in the above load distribution. Substituting Equation (5.21) in Equation (5.22) we obtain

$$Q_{k+i} = \frac{\prod\limits_{p=i+1}^{r} f_{k+p}}{1 + \sum\limits_{p=2}^{r} \prod\limits_{q=p}^{r} f_{k+p}}, \quad i = 1, \ldots, r-1 \tag{5.23}$$

and

$$Q_{k+r} = \frac{1}{1 + \sum\limits_{p=2}^{r} \prod\limits_{q=p}^{r} f_{k+p}} \tag{5.24}$$

Obviously,

$$\sum_{i=1}^{r} Q_{k+i} = 1 \quad \text{and} \quad 0 < Q_{k+i} < 1 \tag{5.25}$$

Further, from Equation (5.23) and Equation (5.24) we observe that

$$Q_{k+i} = Q_{k+i+1} f_{k+i+1}, \quad i = 1, \ldots, r-1 \tag{5.26}$$

Using Equation (5.26) we can readily show that for all $j = 1, \ldots, r$ the following equality holds:

$$\sum_{i=1}^{j} Q_{k+i} z_{k+i} T_{cm} + Q_{k+j} w_{k+j} T_{cp} = \sum_{i=1}^{r} Q_{k+i} z_{k+i} T_{cm} + Q_{k+r} w_{k+r} T_{cp} \tag{5.27}$$

5.1.4 Rules for Optimal Load Distribution

In this section we state some specific rules to be satisfied by an optimal load distribution in a single-level tree network equipped with a front end. We shall later prove the optimality of these rules.

Rule A.   Given a single-level tree network Σ, define a set $E_A = \phi$, and a tree network $\Sigma^* \leftarrow \Sigma$. Then execute the following algorithm.

Step 1. Scan the processor-link pairs in Σ^* from right to left, that is, from the last processor-link pair to the first (see Figure 5.1). Let the link l_k be the first to violate the following condition for some $r \in \{1, \ldots, m - k\}$:

$$z_k T_{cm} < z(k+1, \ldots, k+r) T_{cm} + w(k+1, \ldots, k+r) T_{cp} \qquad (5.28)$$

which, upon substituting Equation (5.18) and Equation (5.20) and simplifying, can be rewritten as

$$z_k T_{cm} < \frac{(z_{k+1} T_{cm} + w_{k+1} T_{cp}) \prod\limits_{p=k+2}^{k+r} f_p}{1 + \sum\limits_{i=k+2}^{k+r} \prod\limits_{p=i}^{k+r} f_p} \qquad (5.29)$$

Obtain a reduced network Σ' by eliminating the processor-link pair (l_k, p_k) from Σ^* and putting its index (in the original network Σ) in the set E_A. If we suppose that Equation (5.28) is not violated by any link, then $\Sigma' = \Sigma^*$.

Step 2. If $\Sigma' \neq \Sigma^*$, then redefine $\Sigma^* \leftarrow \Sigma'$; let $m = m-1$; renumber the processor-link pairs in Σ^* from left to right; and go to Step 1. If $\Sigma' = \Sigma^*$, then go to Step 3.

Step 3. The root processor assigns a nonzero load fraction to a processor p_k via link l_k in Σ if and only if $k \notin E_A$.

Note that the indices in E_A refer to the original network Σ. From now onwards, if we mention that Equation (5.28) is violated by link l_k, then this means that $k \in E_A$. Similarly if we mention that Equation (5.28) is satisfied by a link l_k, then this means that $k \notin E_A$.

Rule B. All the processors receiving nonzero load fractions must stop computing at the same time instant.

Rule A needs some explanation. For this, consider the condition obtained from Equation (5.28) when $r = 1$:

$$z_k T_{cm} < z_{k+1} T_{cm} + w_{k+1} T_{cp} \qquad (5.30)$$

If Equation (5.30) is violated, that is, $z_k T_{cm} \geq z_{k+1} T_{cm} + w_{k+1} T_{cp}$, then the time taken by the front end to distribute a fraction of the load to p_k via l_k is greater than, or the same as, the time taken to distribute the same load fraction through l_{k+1} and process it at p_{k+1}. Hence, it is logical to send the load fraction α_k (in addition to α_{k+1}) to p_{k+1} rather than to p_k. Extending the same logic, Rule A implies that if Equation (5.28) is violated by a link l_k for some $r \geq 1$, then it is possible to redistribute the load fraction α_k among the set of processors $p_{k+1}, \ldots, p_{k+r}$, without increasing the processing time. In Example 5.1, it may be noted that the processor-link pair (l_1, p_1) was removed because it violated Equation (5.28) for $k = 1$ and $r = 1$, that is, we had $z_1 T_{cm} > (z_2 T_{cm} + w_2 T_{cp})$. Hence, according to Rule A, p_1 does not get any load. The following example clearly illustrates the significance of the above rules when Equation (5.28) is violated by more than one processor-link pair.

Example 5.2

Consider a single-level tree network with $m = 4$. The root processor is assumed to be equipped with a front end and the speed parameters are $w_0 = 2.0$, $w_1 = 2.0$, $w_2 = 7.0$, $w_3 = 3.0$, $w_4 = 1.0$, $z_1 = 6.0$, $z_2 = 2.0$, $z_3 = 4.0$, $z_4 = 0.5$, and $T_{cm} = T_{cp} = 1.0$. With these parameters, assuming that all the processors stop computing at the same time instant, the load distribution $\alpha \in L$ is given as $\alpha = \{0.6793, 0.1698, 0.0377, 0.0377, 0.0755\}$ and $T(\alpha) = 1.3586$. Here, Rule A is violated for $k = 1$ and $r = 2$, since $z(2, 3) = 3.0$, $w(2, 3) = 1.5$, and hence $z_1 T_{cm} > z(2, 3) T_{cm} + w(2, 3) T_{cp}$. Hence, applying Rule A, p_1 does not get any load. Let us redistribute α_1 equally between p_2 and p_3 and obtain a new load distribution as $\alpha' = \{0.6793, 0, 0.1226, 0.1226, 0.0755\}$. In this case the finish times are $T_2(\alpha') = T_3(\alpha') = 1.1034 < T(\alpha)$, $T_4(\alpha') = 0.84885 < T(\alpha)$. However, the processing time, contributed by the root processor, remains unchanged. Now, assuming that all processors (other than p_1) stop computing at the same time instant, the new load distribution is given by $\alpha'' = \{0.5294, 0, 0.11765, 0.11765, 0.2352\}$ and thus $T(\alpha'') = 1.0588$, which is an improvement over the time taken to process α.

The above Examples 5.1 and 5.2 illustrate that if Rule A is violated then the processing time is affected adversely if p_k is assigned a nonzero load. Moreover, by applying Rule B we obtain a marked improvement in the processing time. In fact, in the next section, we will formally prove this to be true for any general single-level tree network and any arbitrary load distribution. Note that an alternate form of Equation (5.29) is obtained by substituting Equations (5.17), (5.19) and (5.22) in the RHS of Equation (5.28):

$$z_k T_{cm} < \sum_{i=1}^{r} Q_{k+i} z_{k+i} T_{cm} + Q_{k+r} w_{k+r} T_{cp} \tag{5.31}$$

It is also important to note that Rule B has been used to derive the expressions for Q_{k+i} given in Equations (5.23) and (5.24).

5.1.5 Some Preliminary Results

In this section we shall justify the rules stated in the previous section. These results form the basis for optimal load distribution.

Lemma 5.1. In a single-level tree network, let l_k violate Equation (5.28) for some r and let l_{k+1} to l_m satisfy Equation (5.28). Further, let the initial load distribution be $\alpha = (\alpha_0, \alpha_1, \ldots, \alpha_{k-1}, \alpha_k, \alpha_{k+1}, \ldots, \alpha_{k+j}, \ldots, \alpha_{k+r}, \ldots, \alpha_m) \in L$ with $\alpha_k > 0$. Then there exists another load distribution $\alpha' = (\alpha_0, \alpha_1, \ldots, \alpha_{k-1}, 0, \alpha_{k+1} + \epsilon_{k+1}, \ldots, \alpha_{k+j} + \epsilon_{k+j}, \ldots, \alpha_{k+r} + \epsilon_{k+r}, \ldots, \alpha_m) \in L$, with $\epsilon_{k+i} = Q_{k+i} \alpha_k$ $(i = 1, \ldots, r)$ such that $T(\alpha') \leq T(\alpha)$.

Proof. Let us first assume that $\alpha_i > 0$ $(i = k + 1, \ldots, m)$. Since the load fractions α_i $(i = 0, \ldots, k - 1)$ remain unchanged for both the distributions α and α', we conclude that $T_i(\alpha') = T_i(\alpha)$ $(i = 0, \ldots, k - 1)$. For $i = k + 1, \ldots, k + r$, we proceed as follows: The finish times, for $j = 1, \ldots, r$, are

$$T_{k+j}(\alpha) = \sum_{i=1}^{k-1} \alpha_i z_i T_{cm} + \alpha_k z_k T_{cm} + \sum_{i=k+1}^{k+j} \alpha_i z_i T_{cm}$$
$$+ \alpha_{k+j} w_{k+j} T_{cp} \tag{5.32}$$

$$T_{k+j}\left(\alpha'\right) = \sum_{i=1}^{k-1} \alpha_i z_i T_{cm} + \sum_{i=k+1}^{k+j} (\alpha_i + \epsilon_i) z_i T_{cm} + \alpha_{k+j} w_{k+j} T_{cp}$$
$$+ \epsilon_{k+j} w_{k+j} T_{cp} \tag{5.33}$$

From Equations (5.32) and (5.33), for $j = 1, \ldots, r$, we get

$$T_{k+j}(\alpha) - T_{k+j}(\alpha') = \alpha_k z_k T_{cm} - \left\{ \sum_{i=k+1}^{k+j} \epsilon_i z_i T_{cm} + \epsilon_{k+j} w_{k+j} T_{cp} \right\} \tag{5.34}$$

Substituting $\epsilon_i = Q_i \alpha_k$ $(i = k+1, \ldots, k+r)$ in Equation (5.34) and using Equation (5.27), we obtain

$$T_{k+j}(\alpha) - T_{k+j}\left(\alpha'\right) = \alpha_k \left(z_k T_{cm} - K_1\right) \tag{5.35}$$

where K_1 is given by the RHS of Equation (5.31). Since Equation (5.28), and thus Equation (5.31), is violated by l_k, we conclude that $T_{k+j}(\alpha') \leq T_{k+j}(\alpha)$, for $j = 1, \ldots, r$. For $j = r+1, \ldots, m$,

$$T_{k+j}(\alpha) = \sum_{i=1}^{k+r} \alpha_i z_i T_{cm} + \sum_{i=k+r+1}^{k+j} \alpha_i z_i T_{cm} + \alpha_{k+j} w_{k+j} T_{cp} \tag{5.36}$$

$$T_{k+j}\left(\alpha'\right) = \sum_{i=1}^{k-1} \alpha_i z_i T_{cm} + \sum_{i=k+1}^{k+r} (\alpha_i + \epsilon_i) z_i T_{cm}$$
$$+ \sum_{i=k+r+1}^{k+j} \alpha_i z_i T_{cm} + \alpha_{k+j} w_{k+j} T_{cp} \tag{5.37}$$

From Equations (5.36) and (5.37), we obtain

$$T_{k+j}(\alpha) - T_{k+j}\left(\alpha'\right) = \alpha_k \left\{ z_k T_{cm} - \left(\sum_{i=1}^{r} Q_{k+i} z_i T_{cm} + \alpha_{k+r} w_{k+r} T_{cp} \right) \right\} \tag{5.38}$$

Since the first term in the RHS of Equation (5.38) reduces to the RHS of Equation (5.35), we have $T_{k+j}(\alpha') \leq T_{k+j}(\alpha)$ for $j = r+1, \ldots, m$. Hence, $T(\alpha') \leq T(\alpha)$.

If in the initial load distribution $\alpha_{k+j} = 0$, for some $j = p, \ldots, q$; $1 \leq p < q \leq m - k$; even then this result holds. However, in this case we need to show that $T_{k+j}(\alpha') \leq T_{k+p-1}(\alpha)$, only for $j = p, \ldots, q$. The proof follows the same steps as explained above. $\square$

This lemma justifies the examples given in the previous section. To prove the above lemma we redistributed α_k among $p_{k+1}, \ldots, p_{k+r}$, using a specific load distribution (given by the ratios Q_{k+i}). If Equation (5.28) is violated with a strict inequality, then there are infinitely many such redistributions possible, one of which is given in this lemma. However, if Equation (5.28) is violated with an equality then the redistribution given here is the only feasible redistribution. Hence, in a given network, if Equation (5.28) is violated by some processor-link pairs, then it is not necessary to assign any load to them. In other words, it is sufficient to consider a reduced network without these processor-link pairs. Such a network is called an *optimal reduced network*. Later in this chapter we will justify the *optimality* of this reduced network.

Lemma 5.2. In a single-level tree network, consider a load distribution in which some processors in E_A get nonzero loads. Then there exists another load distribution that does not degrade the time performance and in which all processors in E_A receive zero loads.

Proof. The set E_A contains the indices of all those processor-link pairs that do not satisfy Equation (5.28), in decreasing order. As we scan the elements of E_A in this order, let p_i, $i \in E_A$ be the first processor that has a nonzero load fraction. Then, according to Lemma 5.1, α_i can be redistributed among a bank of adjacent processors that do not contain any processors in E_A. This is apparent from the construction of E_A in Rule A. We successively apply the above argument to all p_j, $j \in E_A$, that receive a nonzero load, thus obtaining the desired redistribution.   □

Lemma 5.3. In a single-level tree network, let Equation (5.28) be satisfied by all links. Let the initial load distribution α be such that some of the child processors get zero load. Then there exists another load distribution α' such that all $\alpha_i' > 0$ ($i = 1, \ldots, m$) and $T(\alpha') \le T(\alpha)$.

Proof. We will first consider the following three cases.

Case i. $\alpha_{k-1} > 0$; and $\alpha_j = 0$ ($j = k+1, \ldots, m$), $k > 1$.
We will show that $T_k(\alpha') \le T_{k-1}(\alpha)$, where $\alpha' = (\alpha_0, \alpha_1, \ldots, \alpha_{k-1} - \epsilon,$ $\epsilon, 0, \ldots, 0) \in L$ is the new load distribution.

$$T_{k-1}(\alpha) = \sum_{p=1}^{k-1} \alpha_p z_p T_{cm} + \alpha_{k-1} w_{k-1} T_{cp} \qquad (5.39)$$

$$T_k(\alpha') = \sum_{p=1}^{k-2} \alpha_p z_p T_{cm} + (\alpha_{k-1} - \epsilon) z_{k-1} T_{cm}$$
$$+ \epsilon \left(z_k T_{cm} + w_k T_{cp} \right) \qquad (5.40)$$

From Equations (5.39) and (5.40), we obtain

$$T_k(\alpha') - T_{k-1}(\alpha) = \epsilon \left(z_k T_{cm} + w_k T_{cp} - z_{k-1} T_{cm} \right)$$
$$- \alpha_{k-1} w_{k-1} T_{cp} \qquad (5.41)$$

We can choose ϵ as $0 < \epsilon < \min\{\alpha_k, K_2\}$ where

$$K_2 = \frac{\alpha_{k-1} w_{k-1} T_{cp}}{z_k T_{cm} + w_k T_{cp} - z_{k-1} T_{cm}} \qquad (5.42)$$

such that $T_k(\alpha') \le T_{k-1}(\alpha)$.

Case ii. $\alpha_0 > 0, \alpha_j = 0$ ($j = 1, \ldots, m$).
The new load distribution is $\alpha' = (\alpha_0 - \epsilon, \epsilon, 0, \ldots, 0) \in L$. Then,

$$T_1(\alpha') - T_0(\alpha) = \epsilon \left(z_1 T_{cm} + w_1 T_{cp} \right) - \alpha_0 w_0 T_{cp} \qquad (5.43)$$

Then we can choose ϵ as $0 < \epsilon < \min\{\alpha_0, K_3\}$, where

$$K_3 = \frac{\alpha_0 w_0 T_{cp}}{z_1 T_{cm} + w_1 T_{cp}} \tag{5.44}$$

This ensures $T_i(\alpha') \leq T_0(\alpha) = T(\alpha)$ and $\alpha'_0 > 0$ and $\alpha'_1 > 0$.

Case iii.   Let $\alpha_k = 0, \quad k > 0; \quad \alpha_j > 0 \quad (j = k+1, \ldots, m)$.
The new load distribution is given by $\alpha' = (\alpha_0, \ldots, \alpha_{k-1}, \epsilon, \alpha_{k+1} - \epsilon_{k+1}, \alpha_m - \epsilon_m)$. The expressions for $T_j(\alpha)$ and $T_j(\alpha')$ $(j = k+1, \ldots, m)$ are given by

$$T_j(\alpha) = \sum_{p=1}^{k-1} \alpha_p z_p T_{cm} + \sum_{p=k+1}^{j} \alpha_p z_p T_{cm} + \alpha_j w_j T_{cp} \tag{5.45}$$

$$T_j(\alpha') = \sum_{p=1}^{k-1} \alpha_p z_p T_{cm} + \epsilon z_k T_{cm} + \sum_{p=k+1}^{j} (\alpha_p - \epsilon_p) z_p T_{cm} \\ + (\alpha_j - \epsilon_j) w_j T_{cp} \tag{5.46}$$

From Equations (5.45) and (5.46) we obtain

$$T_j(\alpha) - T_j(\alpha') = \epsilon_j w_j T_{cp} + \sum_{p=k+1}^{j} \epsilon_p z_p T_{cm} - \epsilon z_k T_{cm} \tag{5.47}$$

We choose ϵ_p as

$$\epsilon_p = Q_p \epsilon, \quad p = k+1, \ldots, m \tag{5.48}$$

where Q_p is given by Equations (5.23) and (5.24), with $r = m - k$. Then,

$$T_j(\alpha) - T_j(\alpha') = \alpha_j w_j T_{cp} \\ + \epsilon \left\{ Q_j w_j T_{cp} + \sum_{p=k+1}^{j} Q_p z_p T_{cm} - z_k T_{cm} \right\} \tag{5.49}$$

Since Equation (5.28), and hence Equation (5.31), is satisfied, using Equation (5.27) in Equation (5.49) we see that $T_j(\alpha') < T_j(\alpha)$, for $j = k+1, \ldots, m$. Note that the ϵ we choose must be such that $0 < \epsilon < K_4$, where

$$K_4 = \frac{T(\alpha) - \sum_{p=1}^{k-1} \alpha_p z_p T_{cm}}{z_k T_{cm} + w_k T_{cp}} \tag{5.50}$$

where $T(\alpha)$ is the processing time. This ensures that $T_k(\alpha') < T_k(\alpha)$. Further, let us define α_{min} as

$$\alpha_{min} = \min_{j \in \{k+1, \ldots, m\}} \alpha_j \tag{5.51}$$

Then we should choose $\epsilon > 0$ in such a way that

$$\epsilon < \alpha_{min} \tag{5.52}$$

Therefore, it is sufficient to choose ϵ as

$$0 < \epsilon < \min\{K_4, \alpha_{min}\} \tag{5.53}$$

This ensures that $T_j(\alpha') \leq T_j(\alpha)$, and α'_j $(j = k, \ldots, m)$.

Now, let us prove the lemma for an arbitrary load distribution $\alpha \in L$. Scanning the timing diagram sequentially from p_m to p_0 we notice that if there are any processor-link pairs with $\alpha_i = 0$, then it falls under one of the three cases mentioned above. Repeated application of the redistributions specified in these cases will ensure a final redistribution α' with $\alpha'_i > 0$ $(i = 1, \ldots, m)$ and $T(\alpha') \leq T(\alpha)$. This completes the proof. $\square$

Lemma 5.4.   Consider the collection I' of the indices of all the processor-link pairs in a single-level tree network that satisfy Equation (5.28). Let the initial load distribution $\alpha \in L$ be such that $\alpha_i = 0$ for some or all $i \in I'$. Then there exists another load distribution $\alpha' = (\alpha'_0, \ldots, \alpha'_m)$, $\alpha'_i > 0$ for all $i \in I'$, such that $T(\alpha') \leq T(\alpha)$.

Proof. To prove this lemma, we first apply Lemma 5.2 to obtain a redistribution such that all processors in E_A receive zero loads. According to Lemma 5.2 it is sufficient to consider only such load distributions. In other words, it is sufficient to consider a reduced network containing only processor-link pairs in I'. Then, applying Lemma 5.3 the proof of this lemma is immediate. $\square$

Lemma 5.5.   Consider a single-level tree network in which all the links satisfy Equation (5.28). Let the initial load distribution $\alpha = (\alpha_0, \ldots, \alpha_k, \ldots, \alpha_m) \in L$ be such that $\alpha_i > 0$ $(i = 0, \ldots, m)$. Let $T_j(\alpha) = T(\alpha)$ $(j = k+1, \ldots, k+r)$ for some $k \in \{0, \ldots, m-1\}$ and for some $r \in \{1, \ldots, m-k\}$. Also, let $T_k(\alpha) < T(\alpha)$, and $T_{k+r+j}(\alpha) < T(\alpha)$ $(j = 1, \ldots, m-(k+r))$, whenever $k+r < m$. Then there exists another load distribution $\alpha' = (\alpha_0, \ldots, \alpha_{k-1}, \alpha_k + \epsilon, \alpha_{k+1} - \epsilon_{k+1}, \ldots, \alpha_{k+r} - \epsilon_{k+r}, \alpha_{k+r+1}, \ldots, \alpha_m) \in L$, with $\epsilon = \epsilon_{k+1} + \cdots + \epsilon_{k+r}$, and $\epsilon_j > 0$ $(j = k+1, \ldots, k+r)$, such that $T_j(\alpha') < T(\alpha)$ $(j = k, \ldots, m)$.

Proof. We shall prove this lemma for the following two cases.

Case i. $k = 0$.
We can write $T_0(\alpha)$, and $T_j(\alpha)$ $(j = 1, \ldots, r)$, as

$$T_0(\alpha) = \alpha_0 w_0 T_{cp} \tag{5.54}$$

$$T_j(\alpha) = \sum_{i=1}^{j} \alpha_i z_i T_{cm} + \alpha_j w_j T_{cp} \tag{5.55}$$

Similarly, for the load distribution $\alpha' \in L$, for $j = 1, \ldots, r$, we write

$$T_0(\alpha') = (\alpha_0 + \epsilon) w_0 T_{cp} \tag{5.56}$$

$$T_j(\alpha') = \sum_{i=1}^{j} (\alpha_i - \epsilon_i) z_i T_{cm} + (\alpha_j - \epsilon_j) w_j T_{cp} \tag{5.57}$$

From Equations (5.55) and (5.56) we obtain, for $j = 1, \ldots, r$,

$$T_j(\alpha) - T_0(\alpha') = \sum_{i=1}^{j} \alpha_i z_i T_{cm} + \alpha_j w_j T_{cp}$$
$$- \alpha_0 w_0 T_{cp} - \epsilon w_0 T_{cp} \tag{5.58}$$

Suppose we choose an ϵ such that $0 < \epsilon < \min\{K_5, K_6\}$, where

$$K_5 = \frac{\sum_{i=1}^{j} \alpha_i z_i T_{cm} + \alpha_j w_j T_{cp} - \alpha_0 w_0 T_{cp}}{w_0 T_{cp}}, \tag{5.59}$$

$$K_6 = \min\{\alpha_1, \ldots, \alpha_r\} \tag{5.60}$$

then $T_0(\alpha') < T(\alpha)$. The fact that $T_0(\alpha) < T_j(\alpha) = T(\alpha)$ $(j = 1, \ldots, r)$ ensures that $K_5 > 0$. Now we shall prove that $T_j(\alpha') < T(\alpha)$ $(j = 1, \ldots, r)$. For this we need to specify the individual $\epsilon_j > 0$ $(j = 1, \ldots, r)$. From Equations (5.55) and (5.57) we obtain

$$T_j(\alpha') - T_j(\alpha) = \sum_{i=1}^{j} \epsilon_i z_i T_{cm} + \epsilon_j w_j T_{cp} \tag{5.61}$$

We choose $\epsilon_j > 0$ as

$$\epsilon_j = Q_j \epsilon, \quad j = 1, \ldots, r \tag{5.62}$$

where Q_j is given by Equations (5.23) and (5.24) with $k = 0$. These values of ϵ_j $(j = 1, \ldots, r)$ satisfy our requirements of $T_j(\alpha') < T(\alpha)$ $(j = 0, \ldots, m)$.

Case ii. $k \in \{1, \ldots, m - 1\}$.
The expressions for $T_{k+j}(\alpha)$, $T_k(\alpha)$, and $T_k(\alpha')$ can be written as

$$T_{k+j}(\alpha) = T(\alpha) = \sum_{i=1}^{k+j} \alpha_i z_i T_{cm} + \alpha_{k+j} w_{k+j} T_{cp},$$
$$j = 1, \ldots, r \tag{5.63}$$

$$T_k(\alpha) = \sum_{i=1}^{k} \alpha_i z_i T_{cm} + \alpha_k w_k T_{cp} \tag{5.64}$$

$$T_k(\alpha') = \sum_{i=1}^{k-1} \alpha_i z_i T_{cm} + (\alpha_k + \epsilon)(z_k T_{cm} + w_k T_{cp}) \tag{5.65}$$

From Equations (5.63) and (5.65) we obtain, for $j = 1, \ldots, r$,

$$T_{k+j}(\alpha) - T_k(\alpha') = \sum_{i=k+1}^{k+j} \alpha_i z_i T_{cm} + \alpha_{k+j} w_{k+j} T_{cp}$$
$$- \alpha_k w_k T_{cp} - \epsilon(z_k T_{cm} + w_k T_{cp}) \tag{5.66}$$

Suppose we choose an ϵ such that $0 < \epsilon < \min\{K_7, K_8, K_9\}$ where

$$K_7 = \frac{\sum_{i=k+1}^{k+j} \alpha_i z_i T_{cm} + \alpha_{k+j} w_{k+j} T_{cp} - \alpha_k w_k T_{cp}}{z_k T_{cm} + w_k T_{cp}} \tag{5.67}$$

$$K_8 = \min\{\alpha_{k+1}, \ldots, \alpha_{k+r}\} \tag{5.68}$$

Then, $T_k(\alpha') < T_{k+j}(\alpha) = T(\alpha)$ $(j = 1, \ldots, r)$. It can be verified from Equations (5.63) and (5.64) that $K_7 > 0$ is ensured by $T_{k+j}(\alpha) > T_k(\alpha)$ $(j = 1, \ldots, r)$. Now we shall prove that $T_{k+j}(\alpha') < T_{k+j}(\alpha)$ $(j = 1, \ldots, r)$. For this we need to specify the individual $\epsilon_{k+j} > 0$ $(j = 1, \ldots, r)$ and the bound K_9. The expression for $T_{k+j}(\alpha')$ can be written as

$$T_{k+j}(\alpha') = \sum_{i=1}^{k-1} \alpha_i z_i T_{cm} + (\alpha_k + \epsilon) z_k T_{cm} + \sum_{i=k+1}^{k+j} (\alpha_i - \epsilon_i) z_i T_{cm}$$
$$+ (\alpha_{k+j} - \epsilon_{k+j}) w_{k+j} T_{cp} \tag{5.69}$$

From Equations (5.63) and (5.69), we obtain

$$T_{k+j}(\alpha) - T_{k+j}(\alpha') = -\epsilon z_k T_{cm} + \sum_{i=k+1}^{k+j} \epsilon_i z_i T_{cm}$$
$$+ \epsilon_{k+j} w_{k+j} T_{cp} \tag{5.70}$$

Suppose we choose ϵ_{k+j} as

$$\epsilon_{k+j} = Q_{k+j}\epsilon, \quad j = 1, \ldots, r \tag{5.71}$$

where Q_{k+j} is given by Equations (5.23) and (5.24). Substituting Equation (5.71) in Equation (5.70) and using Equations (5.27) and (5.31), we see that $T_{k+j}(\alpha') < T_{k+j}(\alpha) = T(\alpha)$ $(j = 1, \ldots, r)$. Now, K_9 is obtained as follows: Whenever $(k + r) < m$, we define

$$d_{min} = \min_{j \in \{k+r+1, \ldots, m\}} \{T(\alpha) - T_j(\alpha)\} \tag{5.72}$$

It can easily be seen that when $z_k \le z(k + 1, \ldots, k + r)$, $T_{k+r+1}(\alpha') < T(\alpha)$ is automatically satisfied for the above choice of ϵ. In this case, we choose K_9 as ∞. However, when $z_k > z(k + 1, \ldots, k + r)$ we define K_9 as

$$K_9 = \frac{d_{min}}{\{z_k - z(k + 1, \ldots, k + r)\} T_{cm}} \tag{5.73}$$

This ensures that $T_j(\alpha') < T(\alpha)$, for $j = k, \ldots, m$. $\square$

The significance of the above lemma can be explained as follows: Consider an arbitrary load distribution in a network that satisfies Equation (5.28), and in which the processing time, $T(\alpha)$, is contributed by a set of adjacent child processors. Then, by transferring some loads from these processors to their immediate predecessor (whose finish time is less than $T(\alpha)$), it is possible to reduce the finish time of this set of child processors without increasing the finish time of their immediate predecessor beyond

$T(\alpha)$. In addition, if the finish times of the successors of this set of child processors are less than $T(\alpha)$, then they remain so. Note that if the immediate predecessor is the root processor, as in Case i of Lemma 5.5, then this transfer is possible regardless of whether Equation (5.28) is satisfied or not. Alternatively, when the immediate predecessor is a child processor, as in Case ii of Lemma 5.5, then this transfer is possible only if Equation (5.28) is satisfied by the immediate predecessor.

Lemma 5.6. Consider a single-level tree network that satisfies Equation (5.28). Let the initial load distribution $\alpha = (\alpha_0, \ldots, \alpha_m) \in L$ be such that $T_j(\alpha) = T(\alpha)$ $(j = 0, \ldots, r)$ for some $r \in \{0, \ldots, m-1\}$, and $T_k(\alpha) < T(\alpha)$ $(k = r+1, \ldots, m)$, where $T(\alpha)$ is the processing time. Then there exists a load distribution $\alpha' = (\alpha_0 - \epsilon_0, \ldots, \alpha_r - \epsilon_r, \alpha_{r+1} + \epsilon, \alpha_{r+2}, \ldots, \alpha_m) \in L$, with $\epsilon_j > 0$ $(j = 0, \ldots, r)$, and $\epsilon = \epsilon_0 + \cdots + \epsilon_r$, such that $T_j(\alpha') < T(\alpha)$ $(j = 0, \ldots, m)$.

Proof. Let us define d_{min} as in Equation (5.72) above. The expression for $T_{r+1}(\alpha')$ can be written as

$$T_{r+1}\left(\alpha'\right) = T_{r+1}(\alpha) - \sum_{i=1}^{r} \epsilon_i z_i T_{cm} + \epsilon \left(z_{r+1} T_{cm} + w_{r+1} T_{cp}\right) \qquad (5.74)$$

Then,

$$T(\alpha) - T_{r+1}(\alpha') = T(\alpha) - T_{r+1}(\alpha) + \sum_{i=1}^{r} \epsilon_i z_i T_{cm}$$
$$- \epsilon \left(z_{r+1} T_{cm} + w_{r+1} T_{cp}\right) \qquad (5.75)$$

We choose the value of ϵ such that

$$0 < \epsilon < \frac{d_{min}}{z_{r+1} T_{cm} + w_{r+1} T_{cp}} \qquad (5.76)$$

Since $\{T(\alpha) - T_{r+1}(\alpha)\} > d_{min}$, we see that $T_{r+1}(\alpha') < T(\alpha)$. Now we shall prove that $T_j(\alpha') < T(\alpha)$ $(j = r+2, \ldots, m)$. For $j = r+2, \ldots, m$,

$$T(\alpha) - T_j(\alpha') = T(\alpha) - T_j(\alpha) + \sum_{i=1}^{r} \epsilon_i z_i T_{cm} - \epsilon z_{r+1} T_{cm} \qquad (5.77)$$

We know that $\{T(\alpha) - T_j(\alpha)\} > d_{min}$. Using an ϵ that satisfies Equation (5.76), we see that $\epsilon z_{r+1} T_{cm} < d_{min}$. Hence, $T_j(\alpha') < T(\alpha)$ $(j = r+2, \ldots, m)$. Note that the load fraction ϵ_i $(i = 0, \ldots, r)$ must have the additional property that $0 \le \epsilon_i \le \alpha_i$ $(i = 0, \ldots, r)$. $\square$

The significance of this lemma can be explained as follows: Consider an arbitrary load distribution in which the time $T(\alpha)$ is contributed to only by a set of adjacent processors including the root. Then, by transferring some load from this set of processors to its immediate successor, which has a finish time less than $T(\alpha)$, it is possible to decrease the finish time of this set of processors while keeping the finish time of all the other processors at a value less than $T(\alpha)$.

Lemma 5.7. For a single-level tree network there exists an $\alpha^* \in L$ that satisfies

$$\alpha^* = \arg \min_{\alpha \in L} T(\alpha)$$

Proof. Let $I = \{0, \ldots, m\}$. Consider the following functions for an $\alpha \in L$:

$$T_0'(\alpha) = \alpha_0 w_0 T_{cp}$$

$$T_i'(\alpha) = \sum_{j=1}^{i} \alpha_j z_j T_{cm} + \alpha_i w_i T_{cp}, \quad i = 1, \ldots, m \tag{5.78}$$

Since the above functions are linear, bounded, and continuous over the compact set L, the function

$$T'(\alpha) = \max_{i \in I} \{T_i'(\alpha)\} \tag{5.79}$$

exists for every $\alpha \in L$ and is also continuous over L. Hence, there exists an α^* such that $T'(\alpha)$ has a minimum at α^*. Now, the actual finish time equations are given by

$$T_i(\alpha) = \begin{cases} T_i'(\alpha), & \alpha_i \neq 0 \\ 0, & \alpha_i = 0 \end{cases} \tag{5.80}$$

Define,

$$T(\alpha) = \max_{i \in I} \{T_i(\alpha)\} \tag{5.81}$$

We will show that $T(\alpha) = T'(\alpha)$. Note that $T(\alpha) = T'(\alpha)$ for $\alpha \in \text{int}(L)$. At the boundary we have some $\alpha_i = 0$. We define $I' = \{i \in I : \alpha_i = 0\}$. Obviously, by Equation (5.2), $I \setminus I' \neq \phi$. Then, at the boundary of L, we have

$$T(\alpha) = \max_{i \in I \setminus I'} \{T_i(\alpha)\} = \max_{i \in I \setminus I'} \{T_i'(\alpha)\} = \max_{i \in I} \{T_i'(\alpha)\} = T'(\alpha) \tag{5.82}$$

The third equality in Equation (5.82) is true since, from Equation (5.78), we see that for every $i \in I'$ there exists a $j \in I \setminus I'$ such that $T_j'(\alpha) > T_i'(\alpha)$. This proves that $T(\alpha) = T'(\alpha)$. Hence, $\alpha^* \in L$ is also a minimum for $T(\alpha)$. $\qquad\square$

5.1.6 Main Results

In this section, we state and prove some theorems to obtain optimal load distributions. But first we define a few terms, which will be used in the proofs.

Let $I = \{0, \ldots, m\}$ denote the ordered set of indices of the processors. Let I_{max} be an ordered subset of I for a given load distribution $\alpha \in L$, and be defined as

$$I_{max} = \{i \in I \ : \ T_i(\alpha) = T(\alpha)\} \tag{5.83}$$

We partition the set I_{max} into ordered subsets $S_1, \ldots, S_q$ such that

$$I_{max} = \bigcup_{k=1}^{q} S_k, \ \text{with} \ S_i \cap S_j = \phi, \ \text{for} \ i \neq j \tag{5.84}$$

Further, each subset S_k is a maximal set such that any two adjacent elements of S_k differ at most by one. The following example illustrates the above definitions. Let

$m = 20$. Thus, $I = \{0, \ldots, 20\}$. For a given load distribution $\alpha \in L$ let $I_{max} = \{0, 1, 7, 8, 10, 13, 14, 15, 19\}$. Then we have the partition of I_{max} as follows: $S_1 = \{0, 1\}$, $S_2 = \{7, 8\}$, $S_3 = \{10\}$, $S_4 = \{13, 14, 15\}$, $S_5 = \{19\}$.

Theorem 5.1. Optimal Solution and Uniqueness, with Front End In a single-level tree network let all links satisfy (5.28). Then the processing time is a minimum if and only if the load distribution satisfies Rule B. Further, this optimal load distribution is also unique.

Proof. Let us first prove that if the processing time is minimum then the load distribution satisfies Rule B. We will prove this by contradiction. Let us assume that Rule B is violated by a load distribution. Let all the processors in this load distribution get nonzero load. Then, we can form the set I_{max} and partition it into subsets $S_1, \ldots, S_q$. By applying first Lemma 5.5 (sequentially backwards from q to 1) and then Lemma 5.6, to all the subsets satisfying the conditions of Lemma 5.5 and Lemma 5.6, we can obtain a new load distribution for which the processing time is less. Suppose that in the initial load distribution, some of the processors have zero loads. Then by applying Lemma 5.4 we can obtain another load distribution in which all processors get nonzero loads without degrading the time performance. Again, repeating the steps given above, we can obtain a new load distribution with less processing time. This contradicts our initial assumption of minimum processing time, thus completing the first part of the proof.

Now we shall prove that if a load distribution satisfies Rule B then the processing time is minimum. We shall again prove this by contradiction. Let $\alpha = (\alpha_0, \ldots, \alpha_m) \in L$ be the initial load distribution such that Rule B is satisfied, but let us assume that the processing time is not a minimum. By the existence result (Lemma 5.7) we know that there exists a load distribution $\alpha^* \in L$ such that the minimum processing time is achieved. By the first part of this proof we also know that this load distribution α^* should satisfy Rule B. Then, by our assumption, $T_j(\alpha^*) < T_j(\alpha)$, $j = 0, \ldots, m$. From Equation (5.14), substituting $k = 0$ and $r = m$ and using the fact that the load distribution satisfies Rule B, we obtain

$$\alpha_i = \left(\prod_{j=i+1}^{m} f_j \right) \alpha_m, \quad i = 0, \ldots, m-1 \tag{5.85}$$

Similarly,

$$\alpha_i^* = \left(\prod_{j=i+1}^{m} f_j \right) \alpha_m^*, \quad i = 0, \ldots, m-1 \tag{5.86}$$

Since $T_j(\alpha^*) - T_j(\alpha) < 0$,

$$T_j(\alpha^*) - T_j(\alpha) = \sum_{i=1}^{j} (\alpha_i^* - \alpha_i) z_i T_{cm} + (\alpha_j^* - \alpha_j) w_j T_{cp} < 0 \tag{5.87}$$

Substituting Equations (5.85) and (5.86) in Equation (5.87) we obtain

$$T_j(\alpha^*) - T_j(\alpha) = (\alpha_m^* - \alpha_m) \left\{ \sum_{i=1}^{j} \left(\prod_{k=i+1}^{m} f_k \right) z_i T_{cm} + \left(\prod_{k=j+1}^{m} f_k \right) w_j T_{cp} \right\} < 0$$

$$\tag{5.88}$$

from which $\alpha_m^* < \alpha_m$. Thus, from Equations (5.85) and (5.86), $\alpha_i^* < \alpha_i$ ($i = 0, \ldots, m$). Hence,

$$\sum_{i=0}^{m} \alpha_i^* < \sum_{i=0}^{m} \alpha_i \qquad (5.89)$$

This leads to a contradiction since both α, $\alpha^* \in L$ and therefore their components should add up to one.

To prove uniqueness, consider two load distributions $\alpha, \alpha^* \in L$, which satisfy Rule B and hence both give minimum processing time, that is, $T(\alpha) = T(\alpha^*) = T^*$. Then, in Equation (5.88) the inequality sign should be replaced by an equality sign so that $\alpha_m = \alpha_m^*$. Using Equations (5.85) and (5.86) we immediately conclude that $\alpha = \alpha^*$. $\qquad \Box$

Theorem 5.2.   In a general single-level tree network, optimal time performance is obtained by applying Rules A and B together.

Proof. Consider a load distribution $\alpha \in L$ which violates Rule A. Then by Lemma 5.2, Lemma 5.4, or both, there exists another load distribution $\alpha' \in L$ satisfying Rule A, such that $T(\alpha') \leq T(\alpha)$. The load distribution α' assigns nonzero loads to those and only those links which satisfy Equation (5.28). Hence, it is sufficient to consider a reduced network containing only these processor-link pairs. Then, by Theorem 5.1, application of Rule B leads to an optimal time performance. $\qquad \Box$

Given a single-level tree network Σ, it is possible to obtain finitely many reduced networks each of which satisfies the property that none of their links violate Equation (5.28). Obviously, we can apply the result of Theorem 5.1 to each of these reduced networks to obtain optimal load distribution and minimum processing time. The optimal reduced network is the one for which we have the minimum of these minimum processing times.

In this section we will prove that this optimal reduced network is the one obtained from Σ by eliminating those and only those processor-link pairs that violate Equation (5.28). We will also prove the uniqueness of this reduced network in a restricted sense. For this, let S denote the set of all reduced networks obtained from the original network Σ. Let $C \subseteq S$ denote the set of all reduced networks all of whose links satisfy Equation (5.28). That the set C contains finitely many elements is obvious from the fact that it contains at least m elements, each of which consists of only one processor-link pair (l_k, p_k), $k \in I$, connected to p_0. Further, let Σ', $\Sigma'' \in S$. Then, $\Sigma' \subseteq \Sigma''$ means that Σ' is a reduced network obtained from Σ'', and $\Sigma' \backslash \Sigma''$ denotes the set of all processor-link pairs that are present in Σ', but not in Σ''. Further, we denote the processing time of a network Σ, with a load distribution $\alpha \in L$, as $T(\Sigma, \alpha)$ and the finish time of the processor p_k in the network Σ as $T_k(\Sigma, \alpha)$. The minimum processing time (achieved by using an optimal load distribution $\alpha^* \in L$) is represented as $T(\Sigma, \alpha^*) = T^*(\Sigma)$.

Note that if $\Sigma' \subseteq \Sigma$, then we can obtain Σ from Σ' by appending to Σ' the processor-link pairs in $\Sigma \backslash \Sigma'$. By the term *appending*, we mean that these processor-link pairs are placed back in the network Σ' in exactly the same positions as in the original network Σ. Interpreted in another way, we can think of the child processors being connected to the root via links having *switches* on them. *Appending* a processor-link pair implies *closing* the corresponding switch. Similarly, *eliminating* a processor-link pair implies *opening* the corresponding switch. A limited analogy can be drawn between a load distribution α and the above interpretation as follows. If in a given load distribution α there are some zeros, then this is equivalent to keeping the corresponding switches open. Before proving the main theorem we shall prove an important intermediate result first.

Lemma 5.8.   Let Σ' be a reduced network obtained from a network Σ'' by eliminating one of the processor-link pairs (l_k, p_k) that satisfies Equation (5.28). Then $T^*(\Sigma'') < T^*(\Sigma')$.

Proof. Let $\alpha^* \in L$ be the optimal load distribution in the network Σ'. Let us obtain Σ'' by appending the pair (l_k, p_k) to Σ'. According to Lemma 5.3 (Case ii), we can redistribute the load fractions assigned to the processors $k+1$ to m among the processors k to m and obtain a new load distribution α' such that $T_i(\Sigma'', \alpha') = T^*(\Sigma')$, $i \in I_1 = \{0, \ldots, k-1\}$ and $T_j(\Sigma'', \alpha') < T^*(\Sigma')$, $j \in I_2 = \{k, \ldots, m\}$. Hence, $T^*(\Sigma') = T(\Sigma'', \alpha')$. Suppose none of the links in Σ'' violate Equation (5.28). Then direct application of Theorem 5.1 yields $T^*(\Sigma'') < T^*(\Sigma')$. Suppose some of the links in Σ'' violate Equation (5.28) then these links must belong to I_1. Now, by Lemma 5.2, these links need not be assigned any load and a redistribution α'' is possible that ensures $T_i(\Sigma'', \alpha'') \le T_i(\Sigma'', \alpha') = T^*(\Sigma')$, $i \in I_1$, and $T_j(\Sigma'', \alpha'') \le T_j(\Sigma'', \alpha') < T^*(\Sigma')$, $j \in I_2$. Now, according to Theorem 5.1 (through Lemmas 5.5 and 5.6), there exists an optimal load distribution such that $T^*(\Sigma'') < T^*(\Sigma')$.   □

Note that Lemma 5.8 is a strengthened version of Lemma 5.4. Now we will prove the optimality of the reduced network in S, and its uniqueness in C.

Theorem 5.3.   Consider a reduced network Σ^* obtained from a general single-level tree network by eliminating those and only those links that violate Equation (5.28). Then Σ^* is an optimal reduced network and is also uniquely optimal in C.

Proof. Optimality of the reduced network is immediate from Theorem 5.2. In order to prove uniqueness, assume there are two different networks $\Sigma^*, \Sigma' \in C$ both of which give optimal time performance. Obviously, $\Sigma^* \not\subseteq \Sigma'$ since it will violate the condition imposed on $\Sigma' \in C$. Suppose $\Sigma' \subseteq \Sigma^*$. Then, by Lemma 5.8, we get $T^*(\Sigma^*) < T^*(\Sigma')$, which means that Σ' cannot be optimal. Suppose $\Sigma' \backslash \Sigma^* \ne \phi$ and $\Sigma^* \backslash \Sigma' \ne \phi$. Then let $\Sigma'' = \Sigma^* \bigcup (\Sigma' \backslash \Sigma^*)$, where '$\bigcup$' implies that the processor-link pairs in $\Sigma' \backslash \Sigma^*$ are appended to Σ^* to obtain Σ''. Obviously, $\Sigma'' \in S \backslash C$. Then, by Theorem 5.2, $T^*(\Sigma^*) = T^*(\Sigma'')$. Now, we obtain Σ' from Σ'' as $\Sigma' = \Sigma'' \backslash (\Sigma^* \backslash \Sigma')$. Note that $\Sigma^* \backslash \Sigma'$ contains processor-link pairs that do not violate Equation (5.28). Hence by Lemma 5.8, $T^*(\Sigma'') < T^*(\Sigma')$. Hence, $T^*(\Sigma^*) < T^*(\Sigma')$. Thus Σ' cannot be optimal in time performance. This proves the uniqueness of the optimal reduced network.   □

The following example illustrates the above results.

Example 5.3

Let $m = 3$ and $T_{cm} = T_{cp} = 1$. Let $w_0 = 1.0, w_1 = 0.5, w_2 = 0.2, w_3 = 0.5, z_1 = 1.2, z_2 = 1.1$, and $z_3 = 0.6$. With these parameters it can be verified that $z_1 T_{cm} > z(2,3)T_{cm} + w(2,3)T_{cp}$ and $z_2 T_{cm} = z_3 T_{cm} + w_3 T_{cp}$. From this network we can obtain

TABLE 5.1   Example 5.3

No.	Network	Optimal processing time
1	p_0	1.00000
2	$p_0, (l_1, p_1)$	0.62963
3	$p_0, (l_2, p_2)$	0.56522
4*	$p_0, (l_3, p_3)$	0.52380
5	$p_0, (l_1, p_1), (l_2, p_2)$	0.55112
6	$p_0, (l_2, p_2), (l_3, p_3)$	0.52380
7	$p_0, (l_1, p_1), (l_3, p_3)$	0.52380
8	$p_0, (l_1, p_1), (l_2, p_2), (l_3, p_3)$	0.52380

* Optimal reduced network.

eight reduced networks, whose optimal processing times are shown in Table 5.1. It can be seen that Networks 1 to 5 belong to C and Network 4 is the optimal reduced network which is unique in C.

We summarize the above results as follows. In order to obtain the optimal time performance in a given general single-level tree network, we first apply Rule A and eliminate all those and only those links that violate Equation (5.28). We then apply Rule B to obtain the optimal load distribution, which gives the minimum time performance. Note that to identify processor-link pairs that violate Equation (5.28), we can either scan the network from right to left (that is, from m to 1) or from left to right (that is, from 1 to m). However, it may be noted that if we scan from m to 1, then we require only one scan, whereas if we scan from 1 to m then one scan may not suffice. In the latter case the scanning process terminates when a scan fails to identify even a single processor-link pair that violates Equation (5.28).

5.1.7 Extensions: Without-Front-End Processors

In this section we extend the above results to the case when the root processor is not equipped with a front end. In this case the timing diagram for the child processors is exactly the same as in the case when it is equipped with a front end. But the root processor starts computing only after distributing all the load fractions. Here we need to append another rule (Rule A$'$) to the load distribution defined by the Rules A and B stated in Section 5.1.4.

Rule A$'$.   The root processor assigns a nonzero load fraction only to those child processors p_i for which the link l_i satisfies the following condition:

$$w_0 > z_i \delta, \quad i = 1, 2, \ldots, m \qquad (5.90)$$

This rule can be explained as follows. If $w_0 T_{cp} < z_i T_{cm}$, the time taken to process the load fraction at the root processor is less than or equal to the time delay in sending it to p_i via l_i. Hence, it is logical to process this load at the root processor itself. It should be noted that in the with-front-end case, the above condition does not play a role since the root processor does computation and communication simultaneously. We will assume that in the network Σ, when the root processor is not equipped with a front end, all the links satisfy Equation (5.90) and all the processors take part in the computation.

Analogous to Lemma 5.2 for Rule A′, it is straightforward to show that implementing Rule A′ does not degrade the time performance. We omit the details. Now, we will state the condition for optimal load distribution.

Theorem 5.4. Optimal Solution and Uniqueness, without Front End   In a single-level tree network Σ (when the root processor is not equipped with a front end), let all the links satisfy Equations (5.90) and (5.28). Then the processing time is minimum if and only if the load distribution satisfies Rule B. Further, this optimal load distribution is also unique.

Proof. The proof follows a similar approach as in Theorem 5.1. The processors are grouped according to the properties given in Equations (5.83) and (5.84). Results analogous to Lemma 5.5 and Lemma 5.6 can be used to complete the proof. However, note that to prove Lemma 5.6 it is necessary that Equation (5.90) should also be satisfied. $\qquad\square$

When p_0 is equipped with a front end, we could obtain the optimal reduced network by eliminating those links that did not satisfy Equation (5.28). However when p_0 is not equipped with a front end, we have two conditions to be accounted for (Equations (5.28) and (5.90)) and the sequence in which these conditions are used to eliminate the inefficient links has to be examined. Consider a sequence of operations in which we first eliminate those processor-link pairs that violate Equation (5.90) and then from the resultant reduced network we eliminate those processor-link pairs that violate Equation (5.28). We denote this operation by the symbol $A'A$. Similarly we can define AA'. Now let $E_{A'A}^{A'}$ denote the set of all processor-link pairs that get eliminated by the application of Equation (5.90) in the operation $A'A$, and let $E_{A'A}^{A}$ denote the set of all processor-link pairs that get eliminated by the application of Equation (5.28) in the same operation $A'A$. Then $E_{A'A} = E_{A'A}^{A'} \bigcup E_{A'A}^{A}$ denotes the set of all processor-link pairs that are eliminated in the operation $A'A$. Similarly we can define $E_{AA'}^{A}$, $E_{AA'}^{A'}$ and $E_{AA'}$. We shall now prove that $E_{A'A} \subseteq E_{AA'}$. For this we require the following result.

Lemma 5.9.   Let Σ be a single-level tree network in which (l_k, p_k) violates Equation (5.28) for some r, but satisfies Equation (5.90). Let Σ' be a network obtained by appending a processor-link pair (l_q, p_q) to Σ in any position between k and $k+r$. Further, let $w_0 T_{cp} \le z_q T_{cm}$ and $z_q T_{cm} < z(k+i, \ldots, k+r)T_{cm} + w(k+i, \ldots, k+r)T_{cp}$, for all $i \in \{1, \ldots, r\}$. Then (l_k, p_k) violates Equation (5.28) in Σ'.

Proof. Let (l_q, p_q) be appended immediately after the link l_{k+i} for some $i \in \{0, \ldots, r-1\}$. We adopt the following notations: For $i < r$, let $z_{eq}^1 = z(k+1, \ldots, k+i)$, $w_{eq}^1 = w(k+1, \ldots, k+i)$, $z_{eq}^2 = z(k+i+1, \ldots, k+r)$, and $w_{eq}^2 = w(k+i+1, \ldots, k+r)$. Further, $z_{eq} = z(k+1, \ldots, k+r)$ and $w_{eq} = w(k+1, \ldots, k+r)$.

Case i. $i = 0$.

According to the statement of the lemma we have the following conditions:

$$z_k T_{cm} \ge z_{eq} T_{cm} + w_{eq} T_{cp} \tag{5.91}$$

$$z_k T_{cm} < w_0 T_{cp} \tag{5.92}$$

$$z_q T_{cm} \geq w_0 T_{cp} \tag{5.93}$$

From these conditions, it is immediately apparent that $z_q T_{cm} > z_{eq} T_{cm} + w_{eq} T_{cp}$ and hence, while applying Rule A to the network, (l_q, p_q) gets eliminated. Thus (l_k, p_k) violates Equation (5.28) in the resultant reduced network.

Case ii. $i \in \{1, \dots, r-1\}$.

Here, in addition to the conditions set forth in Equations (5.91) through (5.93), we have the following condition:

$$z_q T_{cm} < z_{eq}^2 T_{cm} + w_{eq}^2 T_{cp} \tag{5.94}$$

Using the RHS of Equation (5.29) we rewrite Equation (5.91) as

$$z_k T_{cm} \geq \frac{P_1}{Q_1} \tag{5.95}$$

where

$$P_1 = \frac{\left(w_{eq}^2 T_{cp} + z_{eq}^2 T_{cm}\right)\left(w_{eq}^1 T_{cp} + z_{eq}^1 T_{cm}\right)}{w_{eq}^1 T_{cp}} \tag{5.96a}$$

$$Q_1 = 1 + \left(\frac{w_{eq}^2 T_{cp} + z_{eq}^2 T_{cm}}{w_{eq}^1 T_{cp}}\right) \tag{5.96b}$$

To prove that l_k violates Equation (5.28) in Σ', it is sufficient to show that

$$z_k T_{cm} \geq \frac{P_2}{Q_2} \tag{5.97}$$

where

$$P_2 = \frac{\left(w_{eq}^2 T_{cp} + z_{eq}^2 T_{cm}\right)\left(w_{eq}^1 T_{cp} + z_{eq}^1 T_{cm}\right)\left(w_q T_{cp} + z_q T_{cm}\right)}{w_q w_{eq}^1 T_{cp}^2} \tag{5.98}$$

$$Q_2 = 1 + \frac{\left(w_{eq}^2 T_{cp} + z_{eq}^2 T_{cm}\right)\left(w_q T_{cp} + z_q T_{cm}\right)}{w_{eq}^1 w_q T_{cp}^2}$$

$$+ \frac{\left(w_{eq}^2 T_{cp} + z_{eq}^2 T_{cm}\right)}{w_q T_{cp}} \tag{5.99}$$

where the RHS of Equation (5.97) is obtained by considering the equivalent representation of (z_{eq}^1, w_{eq}^1), (z_q, w_q) and (z_{eq}^2, w_{eq}^2). We will show that the RHS of Equation (5.95) is greater than the RHS of Equation (5.97). For this we multiply the numerator and the denominator of Equation (5.95) by $(w_q T_{cp} + z_q T_{cm})/w_{eq}^1 T_{cp}$ and then apply Equation (5.94). This completes the proof of the lemma.   □

Theorem 5.5.   In a single-level tree network, when the root processor p_0 is not equipped with a front end, $E_{A'A} \subseteq E_{AA'}$.

Proof. Let $k \in E_{A'A}$. This means that either $k \in E_{A'A}^{A'}$ or $k \in E_{A'A}^{A}$. If $k \in E_{A'A}^{A'}$ then it automatically implies that $k \in E_{AA'}$, since if (l_k, p_k) does not get eliminated by Equation (5.28) in the sequence AA' then it will definitely get eliminated by violating Equation (5.90). On the other hand, if $k \in E_{A'A}^{A}$, we proceed as follows. Let Σ' be the reduced network obtained from Σ by the operation A'. Suppose all the links eliminated by A' were either between 1 and k or between $k + r$ and m. Then, $k \in E_{AA'}^{A}$. Alternatively, if any of the links were between k and $k + r$ then by Lemma 5.9 we again would have $k \in E_{AA'}^{A}$. This completes the proof of the theorem.
□

From this theorem we see that the reduced network obtained by the sequence $A'A$ is the superset (not necessarily a proper one) of the network obtained by the sequence AA'. Combining this result with Theorem 5.4 and Lemma 5.4 (suitably modified for the without-front-end case) the network obtained by the sequence $A'A$ is the optimal reduced network. Hence, one should apply Rule A' first and then Rule A.

Now consider the following example, which illustrates the points made in the above theorem.

Example 5.4

Let $m = 3$ and $T_{cp} = T_{cm} = 1.0$. The speed parameters are $w_0 = 1.2, w_1 = 1.0, w_2 = 0.2, w_3 = 0.2, z_1 = 1.0, z_2 = 0.9$, and $z_3 = 1.5$. It can be verified that $z_1 T_{cm} > z(2, 3)T_{cm} + w(2, 3)T_{cp}$. Following the above notations, we then obtain $E_{AA'}^{A} = \{1\}$, $E_{AA'}^{A'} = \{3\}, E_{A'A}^{A'} = \{3\}$, and $E_{A'A}^{A} = \phi$, thus verifying the theorem. Further, the processing time for the resulting networks when we adopt the sequences $A'A$ and AA' are obtained as $T_{A'A} = 0.46610$ and $T_{AA'} = 0.57391$, respectively.

Theorem 5.6. In a general single-level tree network Σ, when p_0 is not equipped with a front end, the optimal time performance is obtained by assigning zero loads to all processor-link pairs in $E_{A'A}$, and nonzero loads, satisfying Rule B, to all processors in $\Sigma \backslash E_{A'A}$.

Proof. The proof follows an approach similar to that of Theorem 5.2 with the additional results obtained in Theorems 5.4 and 5.5.
□

Here, too, we can prove that $\Sigma \backslash E_{A'A}$ is the optimal reduced network and is also unique in the collection C of all reduced networks, all of whose links satisfy Equations (5.28) and (5.90).

Hence, in a single-level tree network, when the root processor is not equipped with a front end, the optimal time performance is achieved by first eliminating all those links that violate Equation (5.90) and then eliminating those links that violate Equation (5.28). All the remaining processors in the resultant reduced network can now be given nonzero loads. Finally by applying Rule B we obtain the optimal load distribution.

5.2 LINEAR NETWORK

A linear network of $(m + 1)$ processors connected via m communication links is shown in Figure 3.1a. The processing load is assumed to originate at p_0.

5.2.1 With-Front-End Processors

We denote the load fractions to the processors $p_0, \ldots, p_m$ as $\alpha_0, \ldots, \alpha_m$, respectively. The timing diagram for a load distribution $\alpha \in L$ is the same as in Figure 3.7. Note that this timing diagram is drawn by assuming that all the processors stop computing at the same instant in time. From this timing diagram the corresponding recursive equations are

$$
\begin{aligned}
\alpha_i w_i T_{cp} &= \left(1 - \sum_{p=0}^{i} \alpha_p \right) z_{i+1} T_{cm} + \alpha_{i+1} w_{i+1} T_{cp} \\
&= \left(\sum_{p=i+1}^{m} \alpha_p \right) z_{i+1} T_{cm} + \alpha_{i+1} w_{i+1} T_{cp}, \quad i = 0, \ldots, m-1
\end{aligned}
\tag{5.100}
$$

and the normalizing equation is

$$
\sum_{i=0}^{m} \alpha_i = 1
\tag{5.101}
$$

We now have $(m+1)$ linear equations with $(m+1)$ unknowns. Except for a homogeneous network, this set of equations does not have a straightforward closed-form solution. However, it is easy to prove that these equations have a solution in which each α_i $(i = 0, 1, \ldots, m-1)$ can be expressed in terms of α_m as

$$
\alpha_i = X_i \alpha_m
\tag{5.102}
$$

where $X_i > 0$ is a constant and is a function of the processor and link speed parameters. The proof for this can be obtained by induction as follows: We know that $X_m = 1$. From Equation (5.100) we obtain

$$
\alpha_{m-1} w_{m-1} T_{cp} = \alpha_m \left(w_m T_{cp} + z_m T_{cm} \right)
\tag{5.103}
$$

Hence,

$$
\alpha_{m-1} = X_{m-1} \alpha_m
\tag{5.104}
$$

Obviously,

$$
X_{m-1} = \left(\frac{w_m T_{cp} + z_m T_{cm}}{w_{m-1}} \right) > 0
\tag{5.105}
$$

Now assume that

$$
\alpha_j = X_j \alpha_m, \qquad j = i, \ldots, m-1
\tag{5.106}
$$

with $X_j > 0$. Now we will show that $\alpha_{i-1} = X_{i-1} \alpha_m$ and $X_{i-1} > 0$. From Equation (5.100) we obtain

$$
\alpha_{i-1} w_{i-1} T_{cp} = \alpha_i w_i T_{cp} + \left(\sum_{j=i}^{m} \alpha_j \right) z_i T_{cm}
\tag{5.107}
$$

Using Equation (5.106), this can be rewritten as

$$
\alpha_{i-1} w_{i-1} T_{cp} = X_i \alpha_m w_i T_{cp} + \left(\sum_{j=i}^{m} X_j \right) \alpha_m z_i T_{cm}
\tag{5.108}
$$

Hence, we can write

$$\alpha_{i-1} = X_{i-1}\alpha_m \tag{5.109}$$

where

$$X_{i-1} = X_i \left(\frac{w_i T_{cp} + z_i T_{cm}}{w_{i-1} T_{cp}} \right) + \left(\sum_{j=i+1}^{m} X_j \right) \left(\frac{z_i T_{cm}}{w_{i-1} T_{cp}} \right) \tag{5.110}$$

Clearly, $X_{i-1} > 0$ since $X_j > 0$ $(j = i, \ldots, m)$. Hence the proof.

5.2.2 Without-Front-End Processors

The timing diagram for this case is the same as in Figure 3.9. As in the with-front-end case, here the timing diagram is drawn by assuming that all the $(m + 1)$ processors stop computing at the same instant in time. From the timing diagram the corresponding recursive equations are

$$\alpha_i w_i T_{cp} = \left(1 - \sum_{p=0}^{i+1} \alpha_p \right) z_{i+2} T_{cm} + \alpha_{i+1} w_{i+1} T_{cp}$$

$$= \left(\sum_{p=i+2}^{m} \alpha_p \right) z_{i+2} T_{cm} + \alpha_{i+1} w_{i+1} T_{cp}, \quad i = 0, \ldots, m - 2,$$

$$\alpha_{m-1} w_{m-1} T_{cp} = \alpha_m w_m T_{cp} \tag{5.111}$$

The normalizing equation is the same as Equation (5.101). Now we have $(m + 1)$ equations with $(m + 1)$ unknowns. As in the with-front-end case, these equations do not have a straightforward closed-form solution, but it is again possible to prove that each α_i $(i = 0, \ldots, m - 1)$ can be expressed as in Equation (5.102). The processing time is given by

$$T(\alpha) = \alpha_0 w_0 T_{cp} + (1 - \alpha_0) z_1 T_{cm} \tag{5.112}$$

5.2.3 Rules for Optimal Load Distribution

In the case of single-level tree networks we stated rules for obtaining the optimal load distribution. Here, the rule for the with-front-end case is the same as Rule B in Section 5.1.4.

Rule B. All the processors receiving nonzero load fractions must stop computing at the same time instant.

It may be noted that in linear networks, a rule analogous to Rule A does not exist. Later we shall prove that Rule B is a necessary and sufficient condition for a load distribution to be optimal in the with-front-end case. Before that, in the next section, we will derive some intermediate results.

5.2.4 Some Preliminary Results

Lemma 5.10. In a linear network of processors equipped with front ends, for some $k \in \{0, \ldots, m-1\}$, let $T_{k-1}(\alpha) = T(\alpha)$ and $T_j(\alpha) < T_{k-1}(\alpha)$ $(j = k, \ldots, m)$, where $\alpha = (\alpha_0, \ldots, \alpha_{k-1}, \alpha_k, \alpha_{k+1}, \ldots, \alpha_m) \in L$ is the initial load distribution. Then there exists another load distribution $\alpha' = (\alpha_0, \ldots, \alpha_{k-1} - \epsilon, \alpha_k + \epsilon, \alpha_{k+1}, \ldots, \alpha_m) \in L$ such that $T_j(\alpha') < T_{k-1}(\alpha) = T(\alpha)(j = k-1, \ldots, m)$.

Proof. The expressions for $T_{k-1}(\alpha)$ and $T_k(\alpha')$ can be written as

$$T_{k-1}(\alpha) = \sum_{i=1}^{k-1} \sum_{p=i}^{m} \alpha_p z_i T_{cm} + \alpha_{k-1} w_{k-1} T_{cp} \tag{5.113}$$

$$T_k(\alpha') = \sum_{i=1}^{k} \sum_{p=i}^{m} \alpha_p z_i T_{cm} + \epsilon z_k T_{cm} + (\alpha_k + \epsilon) w_k T_{cp} \tag{5.114}$$

From Equations (5.113) and (5.114) we obtain

$$T_k(\alpha') - T_{k-1}(\alpha) = \sum_{p=k}^{m} \alpha_p z_k T_{cm} + \epsilon z_k T_{cm}$$
$$+ (\alpha_k + \epsilon) w_k T_{cp} - \alpha_{k-1} w_{k-1} T_{cp} \tag{5.115}$$

Suppose we choose ϵ as $0 < \epsilon < \min\{K_{10}, d_{min}\}$, where

$$K_{10} = \frac{\alpha_{k-1} w_{k-1} T_{cp} - \left\{ \sum_{p=k}^{m} \alpha_p z_k T_{cm} + \alpha_k w_k T_{cp} \right\}}{(z_k T_{cm} + w_k T_{cp})} \tag{5.116}$$

$$d_{min} = \min_{k \leq i \leq m} \left\{ \frac{T(\alpha) - T_i(\alpha)}{z_k T_{cm}} \right\} \tag{5.117}$$

Then, $T_k(\alpha') < T_{k-1}(\alpha)$. Note that the numerator of Equation (5.116) is a positive quantity since $T_k(\alpha) < T_{k-1}(\alpha)$. It can easily be verified that $T_k(\alpha') < T_{k-1}(\alpha)$ since $\epsilon > 0$. Now we will show that $T_j(\alpha') < T_{k-1}(\alpha)$ for all $j = k+1, \ldots, m$. The expression for $T_j(\alpha')$ is

$$T_j(\alpha') = \sum_{i=1}^{k} \sum_{p=i}^{m} \alpha_p z_i T_{cm} + \sum_{i=k+1}^{j} \sum_{p=i}^{m} \alpha_p z_i T_{cm}$$
$$+ \epsilon z_k T_{cm} + \alpha_j w_j T_{cp} \tag{5.118}$$

From Equations (5.113) and (5.118) we obtain

$$T_j(\alpha') - T_{k-1}(\alpha) = \sum_{i=k}^{j} \sum_{p=i}^{m} \alpha_p z_i T_{cm} + \epsilon z_k T_{cm}$$
$$+ \alpha_j w_j T_{cp} - \alpha_{k-1} w_{k-1} T_{cp} \tag{5.119}$$

which is less than zero by our previous choice of ϵ, thus proving the lemma.   □

The significance of this lemma can be explained as follows. Consider a processor whose finish time is also the processing time of the network and let all its successors have their finish times strictly less. Then, it is possible to transfer a load ϵ from this processor to its immediate successor without degrading the time performance.

Lemma 5.11. In a linear network of processors equipped with front ends, let for some $k \in \{1, \ldots, m\}$, $T_k(\alpha) = T(\alpha)$ and $T_{k-1}(\alpha) < T_k(\alpha)$, where $\alpha = (\alpha_0, \ldots, \alpha_{k-2}, \alpha_{k-1}, \alpha_k, \alpha_{k+1}, \ldots, \alpha_m) \in L$ is the initial load distribution. Then there exists another load distribution $\alpha' = (\alpha_0, \ldots, \alpha_{k-2}, \alpha_{k-1} + \epsilon, \alpha_k - \epsilon, \alpha_{k+1}, \ldots, \alpha_m) \in L$ such that $T_j(\alpha') < T_k(\alpha) = T(\alpha)(j = k - 1, \ldots, m)$.

Proof. The expressions for $T_k(\alpha)$ and $T_{k-1}(\alpha')$ can be written as

$$T_k(\alpha) = \sum_{i=1}^{k} \sum_{p=i}^{m} \alpha_p z_i T_{cm} + \alpha_k w_k T_{cp} \qquad (5.120)$$

$$T_{k-1}(\alpha') = \sum_{i=1}^{k-1} \sum_{p=i}^{m} \alpha_p z_i T_{cm} + (\alpha_{k-1} + \epsilon) w_{k-1} T_{cp} \qquad (5.121)$$

From Equations (5.120) and (5.121) we obtain

$$T_{k-1}(\alpha') - T_k(\alpha) = (\alpha_{k-1} + \epsilon) w_{k-1} T_{cp} - \sum_{p=k}^{m} \alpha_p z_k T_{cm} - \alpha_k w_k T_{cp} \qquad (5.122)$$

Suppose we choose ϵ as $0 < \epsilon < K_{11}$, where

$$K_{11} = \frac{\left(\alpha_k w_k T_{cp} + \sum_{p=k}^{m} \alpha_p z_k T_{cm} \right) - \alpha_{k-1} w_{k-1} T_{cp}}{w_{k-1} T_{cp}} \qquad (5.123)$$

Then, $T_{k-1}(\alpha') < T_k(\alpha)$. Note that the numerator of Equation (5.123) is a positive quantity since $T_{k-1}(\alpha) < T_k(\alpha)$. It can easily be verified that $T_k(\alpha') < T_k(\alpha)$, as $\epsilon > 0$. Now we will show that $T_j(\alpha') < T_k(\alpha)$ $(j = k + 1, \ldots, m)$. The expression for $T_j(\alpha')$ is

$$T_j(\alpha') = \sum_{i=1}^{k} \sum_{p=i}^{m} \alpha_p z_i T_{cm} - \epsilon z_k T_{cm}$$

$$+ \sum_{i=k+1}^{j} \sum_{p=i}^{m} \alpha_p z_i T_{cm} + \alpha_j w_j T_{cp} \qquad (5.124)$$

From Equations (5.120) and (5.124) we obtain

$$T_j(\alpha') - T_k(\alpha) = \sum_{i=k+1}^{j} \sum_{p=i}^{m} \alpha_p z_i T_{cm} + \alpha_j w_j T_{cp} - \epsilon z_k T_{cm} - \alpha_k w_k T_{cp} \qquad (5.125)$$

Clearly, $T_j(\alpha') < T_k(\alpha)$, since, $T_j(\alpha) \le T_k(\alpha)(j = k + 1, \ldots, m)$ and $\epsilon > 0$, thus completing the proof of the lemma.   □

The significance of this lemma is as follows. Consider a processor whose finish time is also the processing time of the network and let its predecessor have a finish time strictly less than this value. Then, it is possible to transfer a load ϵ from this processor to its immediate predecessor in such a way that all its successors (and also its immediate predecessor) have their finish times strictly less than the processing time.

Lemma 5.12. For a linear network, there exists an $\alpha^* \in L$ that satisfies

$$\alpha^* = \arg\min_{\alpha \in L} T(\alpha)$$

Proof. Let $I = \{0, \ldots, m\}$. Consider the following functions for an $\alpha \in L$:

$$T_0'(\alpha) = \alpha_0 w_0 T_{cp} \tag{5.126a}$$

$$T_i'(\alpha) = \sum_{j=1}^{i} \sum_{p=j}^{m} \alpha_p z_j T_{cm} + \alpha_i w_i T_{cp} \quad i = 1, \ldots, m \tag{5.126b}$$

However, the actual finish time equations are given by

$$T_i(\alpha) = \begin{cases} T_i'(\alpha), & \alpha_i \neq 0 \\ 0, & \alpha_i = 0 \end{cases} \tag{5.127}$$

Following the same arguments as in Lemma 5.7, the proof is immediate. $\qquad\square$

5.2.5 Main Result

In this section we will state and prove the necessary and sufficient condition for optimal load distribution.

Theorem 5.7. Optimal Solution and Uniqueness, with Front End In a linear network of $(m + 1)$ processors equipped with front ends and connected via m links, the processing time is a minimum if and only if the load distribution satisfies Rule B. Moreover this optimal load distribution is unique.

Proof. First we will prove that if the processing time is a minimum then the load distribution satisfies Rule B. We prove this by contradiction. Suppose the given load distribution $\alpha \in L$ does not satisfy Rule B. Then, we can form a set I_{max}, as defined in Equation (5.83), and partition it into subsets $S_1, \ldots, S_q$ as defined in Equation (5.84). Then, for each of the subsets S_k $(1 \leq k \leq q)$, other than the subset containing the root, starting sequentially backwards from q to 1, we apply Lemma 5.11 to the first processor of each subset. Then we apply Lemma 5.10 to the subset containing the root, starting from the last processor in that subset. By this, we can obtain a load distribution for which the processing time is less. This contradicts our initial assumption of minimum processing time, thus completing the first part of the proof.

Now assume that the load distribution $\alpha \in L$ satisfies Rule B. We will prove that the processing time is a minimum. We again prove this by contradiction. Suppose the processing time is not a minimum. By the existence result (Lemma 5.12) we know that there exists an $\alpha^* \in L$ such that the minimum processing time is achieved. Also, we know from the first part of the proof of the present theorem that this α^* must be such that it satisfies Rule B. Then $T_j(\alpha^*) < T_j(\alpha)$ $(j = 0, \ldots, m)$. This means

$$T_j\left(\alpha^*\right) - T_j\left(\alpha\right) = \sum_{i=1}^{j} \sum_{p=i}^{m} \left(\alpha_p^* - \alpha_p\right) z_i T_{cm} + \left(\alpha_j^* - \alpha_j\right) w_j T_{cp} < 0 \tag{5.128}$$

In Section 5.2.1 we have shown that each α_i can be expressed in terms of α_m as $\alpha_i = X_i \alpha_m$, where $X_i > 0$ is a constant and is a function of processor and link speed parameters alone. Substituting for each of the α_i's in terms of α_m we obtain

$$T_j\left(\alpha^*\right) - T_j\left(\alpha\right) = \left(\alpha_m^* - \alpha_m\right)\left\{ \sum_{i=1}^{j} \sum_{p-i}^{m} X_p z_i T_{cm} + X_j w_j T_{cp} \right\} < 0 \qquad (5.129)$$

This means that $\alpha_m^* < \alpha_m$. Further, since Equation (5.109) is satisfied, we see that $\alpha_i^* < \alpha_i$, for all $i = 0, \ldots, m-1$. Hence,

$$\sum_{i=0}^{m} \alpha_i^* < \sum_{i=0}^{m} \alpha_i \qquad (5.130)$$

This contradicts the fact that all the load fractions must add up to one. Hence, for the load distribution $\alpha \in L$, the processing time is a minimum.

To prove uniqueness, we need to consider α and $\alpha^* \in L$ that satisfy Rule B and give minimum processing time, that is, $T(\alpha) = T(\alpha^*) = T^*$. Then in Equation (5.128) the inequality must be replaced with an equality sign. This shows that $\alpha_m = \alpha_m^*$. Again, from Equation (5.109), we immediately conclude that $\alpha = \alpha^*$. □

5.2.6 Extensions: Without-Front-End Processors

In this section we extend the above results to the case when the processors are not equipped with front ends. Here we need to append another rule (Rule Ã) to Rule B, stated in Section 5.2.3.

Rule Ã.   A processor p_k communicates the load to the processor p_{k+1} via the link l_{k+1} if and only if

$$z_{k+1} T_{cm} < w_k T_{cp} \qquad (5.131)$$

This can be explained as follows. If the condition given in Equation (5.131) is violated, then the time taken to process the load at p_k is less than or equal to the time delay in sending the same load to p_{k+1} via l_{k+1}. Hence it is logical to process the load at p_k itself. Thus, if for some link l_k this condition is violated, then the linear network is assumed to be truncated at p_k. In other words, none of the processors beyond p_k receive any load. It may be noted that this condition has the same form as Equation (5.90) except that on the RHS, instead of the root processor, we have the processor p_k. This is because of the fact that in a single-level tree network, the root and every child processor constitute a two processor linear network. Results analogous to Lemmas 5.10, 5.11, and 5.12 can easily be derived. However, in this case we also need the following additional result.

Lemma 5.13.   Let $\alpha \in L$ be a load distribution in a linear network of $(m+1)$ processors without front ends. Further, let l_{k+1} violate the condition given in Equation (5.131) and let the initial load distribution be $\alpha = (\alpha_0, \ldots, \alpha_{k-1}, \alpha_k, \alpha_{k+1}, \ldots, \alpha_m) \in L$. Then, there exists another load distribution $\alpha' = (\alpha_0, \ldots, \alpha_{k-1}, \alpha_k + \cdots + \alpha_m, 0, \ldots, 0) \in L$ such that the processing time will not degrade.

Proof. Since Equation (5.131) is violated, we have $z_{k+1}T_{cm} \geq w_k T_{cp}$. We obtain the expressions for $T_k(\alpha)$ and $T_k(\alpha')$ as

$$T_k(\alpha) = \sum_{i=1}^{k+1} \sum_{p=i}^{m} \alpha_p z_i T_{cm} + \alpha_k w_k T_{cp} \tag{5.132}$$

$$T_k(\alpha') = \sum_{i=1}^{k} \sum_{p=i}^{m} \alpha_p z_i T_{cm} + \sum_{i=k}^{m} \alpha_i w_k T_{cp} \tag{5.133}$$

From Equations (5.132) and (5.133) we obtain

$$T_k(\alpha) - T_k(\alpha') = (z_{k+1}T_{cm} - w_k T_{cp}) \left(\sum_{i=k+1}^{m} \alpha_i \right) \tag{5.134}$$

and $T_k(\alpha) \geq T_k(\alpha')$ since $w_k T_{cp} \leq z_{k+1}T_{cm}$. □

This lemma shows that given a linear network (without front end) in which a link violates the condition given in Equation (5.131), we may truncate the network at this point, without causing a degradation in time performance.

Now we state the necessary and sufficient condition for optimal load distribution for the without-front-end case.

Theorem 5.8. Optimal Solution and Uniqueness, without Front End   In a linear network of $(m + 1)$ processors without front ends connected via m communication links, let all the links satisfy Equation (5.131). Then the processing time is a minimum if and only if the load distribution satisfies Rule B. This load distribution is also unique.

Proof. The first part of the proof follows a similar approach to that used in Theorem 5.7, by using results analogous to Lemmas 5.10 through 5.12, respectively. To prove the theorem for a general network, consider a load distribution α that violates Rule Ã. Then by Lemma 5.13, we truncate the network at the point l_k where Equation (5.131) is violated for the smallest value of k, $k \in \{1, \ldots, m\}$, and obtain a load distribution $\alpha' \in L$ satisfying Rule Ã such that $T(\alpha') \leq T(\alpha)$. Then by the first part of this theorem, application of Rule B leads to an optimal time performance. Uniqueness is proved in a manner similar to the proof for Theorem 5.7. □

5.3 EFFECT OF INACCURATE MODELING

In this section we will justify the mathematical model adopted in this book by comparing it with a more accurate model. As we pointed out in Chapter 2, the mathematical model adopted in this book neglects all delays other than the transmission delay. For an exact model all the delays must be included. However, we will now show through an example that in a single-level tree network processing time does not show a significant deviation from our model even after including all the communication delays stated in Chapter 2. Moreover, we show that the condition shown by Equation (5.28) is sufficient for identifying the processor-link pairs that need not be assigned any computational load.

Example 5.5

Consider a single-level tree network Σ with two child processors. We assume that the root processor is equipped with a front end. Let us denote the sum of all the communication delays, except the transmission delay, as Δ_i for the links l_i $(i = 1, 2)$. This is known as *communication latency* in the literature. The timing diagram, with these communication delays, is shown in Figure 5.5a. The processors are assumed to stop computing at the same instant in time. From the timing diagram we obtain the recursive equations as follows:

$$T_0(\alpha) = \alpha_0 w_0 T_{cp} \tag{5.135}$$

$$T_1(\alpha) = \Delta_1 + \alpha_1(z_1 T_{cm} + w_1 T_{cp}) \tag{5.136}$$

$$T_2(\alpha) = \Delta_1 + \alpha_1 z_1 T_{cm} + \Delta_2 + \alpha_2(z_2 T_{cm} + w_1 T_{cp}) \tag{5.137}$$

Following the same procedure as in Section 5.1.1, the closed-form expression for the processing time is obtained as

$$T(\alpha') = \alpha_0 w_0 T_{cp}$$

$$= \left\{ \left(\frac{1 - X}{D} \right) f_2 f_1 + \frac{\Delta_2 f_1}{w_1 T_{cp}} + \frac{\Delta_1}{w_0 T_{cp}} \right\} w_0 T_{cp} \tag{5.138}$$

where

$$X = \frac{\Delta_2(1 + f_1)}{w_1 T_{cp}} + \frac{\Delta_1}{w_0 T_{cp}} \tag{5.139}$$

$$D = 1 + f_1 f_2 + f_2 \tag{5.140}$$

Now, let the speed parameters of the processors and the links be as follows: $w_0 = 2.0$, $w_1 = 3.0$, $w_2 = 0.5$, $z_1 = 2.0$, $z_2 = 1.0$, and $T_{cm} = T_{cp} = 1.0$. We assume the communication latency in the links to be equal, and consider $\Delta_1 = \Delta_2 = 1.7 \times 10^{-3}$ secs as in an Intel iPSC system. Using these speed parameters of the processors and the links, the load distribution α given by Equation (5.7) is $\alpha = (0.4545, 0.1819, 0.3636) \in L$. Now, we consider the communication latency due to the

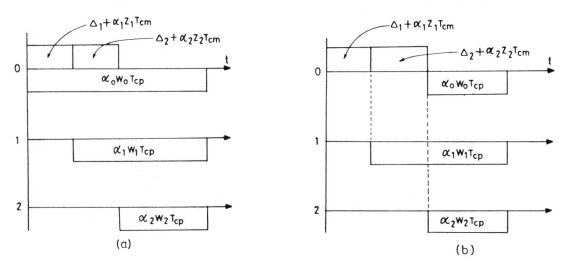

FIGURE 5.5   (a) Timing Diagram: With Front End (b) Timing Diagram: Without Front End

links to be nonzero and distribute α. In this case, the processing time is $T(\alpha) = 0.9126$. On the other hand, the processing time given by Equation (5.135) is $T(\alpha') = 0.9110$, where $\alpha' = (0.4544, 0.1830, 0.3626) \in L$. It may be noted that the above two values of the processing time do not differ significantly.

Now let us derive the condition analogous to that shown in Equation (5.28) when the communication delays are included. From the timing diagram it may be noted that the root processor assigns the load to p_1 if and only if

$$\Delta_2 + (\alpha_2 + \alpha_1)(z_2 T_{cm} + w_2 T_{cp}) > \Delta_1 + \alpha_1 z_1 T_{cm} + \Delta_2 \qquad (5.141)$$
$$+ \alpha_2 (z_2 T_{cm} + w_2 T_{cp})$$

where the RHS is the processing time of p_2, which is also equal to the processing time of p_1. The LHS of the above inequality is the processing time of p_2 when α_1 is assigned to it in addition to α_2. Simplifying the above inequality, we obtain

$$z_1 T_{cm} < (z_2 T_{cm} + w_2 T_{cp}) - \frac{\Delta_1}{\frac{(1-X)}{D} f_2 + \frac{\Delta_2}{w_1 T_{cp}}} \qquad (5.142)$$

This clearly shows that violation of Equation (5.28) also implies violation of Equation (5.142). It may be noted that Equation (5.142) is a modified form of Equation (5.28) as stated in this chapter. With the speed parameters given above, it can be seen that the LHS of Equation (5.28) for $k = 1$ is equal to 2.0 and the RHS is equal to 1.5. On the other hand, from Equation (5.142), we see that the RHS is equal to 1.4981 and the LHS is equal to 2.0. Hence, from the above discussion we see that the processor-link pair that violates Equation (5.28) continues to do so even after including the communication delays.

Now, as an extension, we will show, for a network in which if all the processor-link pairs satisfy Equation (5.28), that by considering the communication latency in the model, some processor-link pairs may violate Equation (5.142). For this, consider the following network speed parameters: $m = 2$, $w_0 = 2.0$, $w_1 = 3.0$, $w_2 = 1.0$, $z_1 = 1.49999$, $z_2 = 0.5$ and $T_{cm} = T_{cp} = 1.0$. Let $\Delta_1 = \Delta_2 = 1.7 \times 10^{-3}$ seconds. Using these speed parameters, the load distribution α given by Equation (5.7) is $\alpha = (0.4286, 0.1905, 0.3809)$. Now, we consider the communication latency in the links to be nonzero and distribute the above load α. We obtain the processing time as $T(\alpha) = 0.8605$. It can be easily verified that the processor-link pair (l_1, p_1) satisfies Equation (5.28) but violates Equation (5.142) and hence we redistribute the total load in such a way that the processor p_1 gets zero load. Further, we make the processors p_0 and p_2 stop computing at the same time instant. In this case, the processing time is given by $T(\alpha'') = 0.8581$, where $\alpha'' = (0.4291, 0, 0.5709) \in L$.

The above example clearly illustrates a situation in which violation of Equation (5.142) need not imply violation of Equation (5.28). However, we see that the results, with the simplified model described in Chapter 2, are reasonably accurate in comparison with results obtained from the more accurate model described here.

Similarly, for the without-front-end case, following the same procedure adopted in this section to derive Equation (5.142), an equivalent and more accurate condition including the communication latency can be derived in place of Equation (5.90). For a two-processor system, when the communication latency is considered, the root processor will assign a nonzero load to, say, p_1 if and only if

$$\alpha_1 z_1 T_{cm} + \Delta_1 < \alpha_1 w_0 T_{cp} \qquad (5.143)$$

From the timing diagram shown in Figure 5.5b, the recursive equations can be obtained. Following the same procedure as given for the with-front-end case, we may substitute for α_1 and rewrite Equation (5.143) as

$$z_1 T_{cm} < w_0 T_{cp} - \frac{\Delta_1}{\left(\frac{1-X}{1+f_2+w_2/w_0}\right) f_2 + \frac{\Delta_2}{w_1 T_{cp}}} \qquad (5.144)$$

where

$$X = 1 - \frac{\Delta_2}{w_1 T_{cp}} \qquad (5.145)$$

Thus the modified form of Equation (5.90) is given by Equation (5.144). Here, too, it may be readily seen that violation of Equation (5.90) also implies violation of Equation (5.144).

5.4 CONCLUDING REMARKS

The following are the highlights of this chapter, in which we have considered two types of network architectures, namely, single-level tree and star networks, and linear networks.

- Closed-form expressions for the processing time in a single-level tree network were derived for the situation in which the root processor is equipped with a front end and also for that in which it is not.
- The concept of an equivalent network for a single-level tree network was defined and closed-form expressions for the equivalent processor and link speed parameters were obtained. This concept of equivalent network was used to obtain a condition (Rule A) which identifies those processor-link pairs that can be removed from the network, that is, that need not be given any computational load.
- In the case of a single-level tree network without front ends, an additional condition between the root processor and the links (Rule A′) was stated to identify those processor-link pairs that can be removed from the network. It was also proved that Rule A′ has precedence over Rule A.
- In the case of linear networks without front ends, a similar condition (Rule Ã) was obtained. Using this condition it was proved that by truncating the network at the point where this condition is violated, the time performance does not degrade.
- It was proved that all the processors that get nonzero loads must stop computing at the same instant in time (Rule B).
- The necessity and the sufficiency of the previous condition was proved for optimal load distribution.
- In the case of single-level tree networks, the idea of reduced network was defined. It was shown that the network obtained by applying Rule A is the optimal reduced network and is unique in a restricted class of reduced networks.

- Finally, the inaccuracies in the adopted model were considered by comparing the results from the adopted model with those for a more accurate model through an example.

In all subsequent chapters, the optimality conditions obtained here will be used to get optimal load distribution. In the next chapter, we will obtain closed-form solutions for homogeneous linear networks and prove some important results analytically. Further, in this chapter, while deriving the results for single-level tree networks, we implicitly assumed that the sequence of load distribution by the root processor was fixed, that is, from p_1 to p_m. Since there are $m!$ possible ways of distributing the load fractions, it would be natural to ask whether one of them gives a better time performance than the others. We may also consider a physical rearrangement of the links and the processors. If such a physical rearrangement is allowed, then it would be of interest to explore the best possible way in which the processors and links are to be connected so that we obtain the best time performance. These two problems are addressed in Chapter 7.

BIBLIOGRAPHIC NOTES

Most of the material presented in this chapter is from Bharadwaj et al. (1992b). Some of the proofs are worked out more elaborately here.

Section 5.1 Cheng and Robertazzi (1990) had conjectured that given certain conditions on the network parameter values it might be necessary to send load fractions to only some of the processors. Rule A, stated in the present chapter, precisely identifies those processors that should not get any load fraction. The standard continuity-compactness argument [Royden (1988)] is used to prove the existence of an optimal load distribution in Lemma 5.7. The results on optimal sequence of applying Rules A and A' given here are new.

Section 5.2 The optimality conditions for linear networks were proved earlier through a recursive technique by Robertazzi (1993) and is given in Chapter 3. The proof given in this chapter is more elaborate.

Section 5.3 The effect of communication latency is explained well in Reed and Grunwald (1987). The data used in Example 3.5 is also taken from this source.

CHAPTER 6

Analytical Results
for Linear Networks

In Chapter 3 we derived recursive equations for the determination of optimal load fractions assigned to each processor in a linear network and presented a technique to numerically solve these equations. In this chapter, we obtain closed-form expressions for optimal load fractions assigned to each processor in a *homogeneous* linear network. The advantage of having a closed-form solution is that analytical techniques can be brought to bear upon them to get results that otherwise would require considerable computational effort. These closed-form expressions are used to prove the important result that in a given linear network, when the processing load originates at the interior of the network, the minimum processing time is independent of the sequence in which the root processor shares the processing load with its left and right neighbors.

As in the previous chapters, here we have organized the material in terms of the cases being considered (boundary/interior, with/without front ends).

6.1 DEFINITION AND SOME REMARKS

The linear network of $(m + 1)$ processors $p_0, p_1, \ldots, p_m$ connected via communication links $l_1, l_2, \ldots, l_m$ is as shown in Figure 3.1a. The processing load is assumed to originate at p_0 *(boundary case)*. For the interior case, shown in Figure 3.1b, the processors and links on either side of the load origination processor p_0 are denoted as $p_1^l, p_2^l, \ldots, p_L^l$ and $l_1^l, l_2^l, \ldots, l_L^l$ for the left hand side and $p_1^r, p_2^r, \ldots, p_R^r$

and $l_1^r, l_2^r, \ldots, l_R^r$ for the right hand side such that $(R + L + 1)$ is the total number of processors in the network. We shall now define a few useful terms:

(i) *Sequence*: In the interior case, p_0 may first distribute load to the processors on the left hand side and then distribute load to the processors on the right hand side, or *vice versa*. Thus, there are two sequences of load distribution.

(ii) *Optimal Load Sequence*: In the interior case, this is defined as that sequence (of the two possible sequences given in (i) above) of load distribution for which the processing time is minimum.

For a linear network, the *load distribution strategy* used in Chapter 3 is formally defined through the following rules:

(i) The root processor keeps its own fraction α_0 and sends the remaining $(1 - \alpha_0)$ to the processor p_1. Processor p_1 keeps the fraction α_1 of the total processing load and transmits the remaining load $(1 - \alpha_0 - \alpha_1)$ to p_2. Similarly, the ith processor keeps its fraction α_i (of the processing load) and transmits the remaining $(1 - \alpha_0 - \alpha_1 - \cdots - \alpha_i)$ to the $(i + 1)$th processor. The last processor, upon receiving the processing load, performs only computation.

(ii) All the processors must perform computation continuously.

(iii) A processor starts computing its load fraction as soon as its front end finishes receiving it. When the processor is not equipped with a front end, the processor starts computing its load fraction as soon as it completes communicating the remaining fractions to the next processor.

It may be noted that for optimality it is both necessary and sufficient that the load distribution should be such that all processors must stop computing at the same instant in time. This fact has been proved in Chapter 5. It was also shown in Chapter 5 that for the without-front-end case the time taken by any processor to send a load fraction to its immediate successor should be less than the time required by the processor itself to process this fraction. If any processor p_i and the link following it violates this condition then we assume that all processors after p_i get zero load, that is, for all practical purposes one can assume that the linear network is truncated after p_i.

Since in this chapter we consider only a homogeneous network with processor speed parameter w and link speed parameter z, we assume that in the without-front-end case the relation $wT_{cp} > zT_{cm}$ holds.

6.2 LOAD ORIGINATION AT THE BOUNDARY

First we consider the boundary case for processors with and without front ends.

6.2.1 Load Distribution Equations: With Front End

Using the rules mentioned in the above section for a homogeneous system of $(m + 1)$ processors, the timing diagram obtained is the same as in Figure 3.7, but with $w_i = w$

and $z_i = z$ for all i. From this timing diagram, we can write the following load distribution equations:

$$\alpha_i w T_{cp} = (1 - \alpha_0 - \cdots - \alpha_i) z T_{cm} + \alpha_{i+1} w T_{cp}, \quad i = 0, 1, \ldots, m - 1 \quad (6.1)$$

We also have the normalizing equation as

$$\alpha_0 + \alpha_1 + \cdots + \alpha_m = 1 \quad (6.2)$$

From Equations (6.1) and (6.2), we can see that there are $(m+1)$ linear equations that can be solved numerically, using the method given in Chapter 3, to yield the optimal load fractions processed by individual processors.

6.2.2 Closed-Form Solution: With Front End

In this case, Equation (6.1) can be rewritten as

$$\alpha_i = (1 - \alpha_0 - \cdots - \alpha_i)\sigma + \alpha_{i+1}, \quad i = 0, \ldots, m - 1 \quad (6.3)$$

where $\sigma = z T_{cm} / w T_{cp}$ and is defined as the network parameter in Chapter 2. Equations (6.3) and (6.2) together provide $(m + 1)$ equations in $(m + 1)$ unknowns. These can be solved in the closed form by using the following relabeling transformation:

$$\beta_i = \alpha_{m-i}, \quad i = 0, \ldots, m \quad (6.4)$$

that is, we renumber the load fractions from the last processor to the root in that order. Using this transformation, Equation (6.3) can be rewritten as

$$\beta_i = (\beta_0 + \beta_1 + \cdots + \beta_{i-1})\sigma + \beta_{i-1}, \quad i = 1, \ldots, m \quad (6.5)$$

We can write each β_i $(i = 1, \ldots, m)$ as a function of β_0 and σ. Denoting $\beta_0 = \epsilon$, this relation can be expressed as

$$\beta_i = f_i(\sigma)\epsilon \quad (6.6)$$

where

$$f_i(\sigma) = c(i, 0)\sigma^0 + c(i, 1)\sigma^1 + \cdots + c(i, i)\sigma^i \quad (6.7)$$

The function $f_i(\sigma)$ is an ith degree polynomial in σ and $c(i, j)$ represents the coefficient of σ^j in the function $f_i(\sigma)$ and is expressed as

$$c(i, j) = \frac{(i + j)!}{(2j)!(i - j)!}, \quad j \le i \quad (6.8)$$

We can derive the above expression as follows: From Equation (6.5),

$$\beta_{i-1} = (\beta_0 + \beta_1 + \cdots + \beta_{i-2})\sigma + \beta_{i-2} \quad (6.9)$$

But Equation (6.5) itself can be rewritten as

$$\beta_i = (\beta_0 + \beta_1 + \cdots + \beta_{i-2})\sigma + \beta_{i-2} - \beta_{i-2} + \beta_{i-1}\sigma + \beta_{i-1}$$

$$= \beta_{i-1} - \beta_{i-2} + \beta_{i-1}\sigma + \beta_{i-1}$$

$$= (2 + \sigma)\beta_{i-1} - \beta_{i-2} \quad (6.10)$$

But note that this recursive equation is valid only for $i = 2, \ldots, m$. Hence, Equation (6.5) along with appropriate initial conditions yields the following recursive equations:

$$\beta_0 = \epsilon$$

$$\beta_1 = (1 + \sigma)\beta_0$$

$$\beta_i = (2 + \sigma)\beta_{i-1} - \beta_{i-2}, \quad i = 2, 3, \ldots, m \tag{6.11}$$

Substituting Equation (6.7) in Equation (6.11) and collecting the coefficients of different powers of σ on both sides we get

$$
\begin{aligned}
c(i,0)\sigma^0 + c(i,1)\sigma^1 + \cdots + c(i,i)\sigma^i &= \{2c(i-1,0) - c(i-2,0)\}\sigma^0 \\
&+ \{2c(i-1,1) + c(i-1,0) - c(i-2,1)\}\sigma^1 \\
&+ \{2c(i-1,2) + c(i-1,1) - c(i-2,2)\}\sigma^2 + \cdots \\
&+ \{2c(i-1,i-2) + c(i-1,i-3) - c(i-2,i-2)\}\sigma^{i-2} \\
&+ \{2c(i-1,i-1) + c(i-1,i-2)\}\sigma^{i-1} \\
&+ \{c(i-1,i-1)\}\sigma^i
\end{aligned}
\tag{6.12}
$$

Equating the coefficients of the powers of σ on both sides we get

$$
\begin{aligned}
c(i,0) &= 2c(i-1,0) - c(i-2,0) \\
c(i,j) &= 2c(i-1,j) + c(i-1,j-1) - c(i-2,j), \quad j = 1, \ldots, i-2 \\
c(i,i-1) &= 2c(i-1,i-1) + c(i-1,i-2) \\
c(i,i) &= c(i-1,i-1)
\end{aligned}
\tag{6.13}
$$

with boundary conditions

$$c(0,0) = c(1,0) = 1 \tag{6.14}$$

The boundary conditions are obtained by making use of the expressions for β_0 and β_1 in Equation (6.11). It is easily verified that Equation (6.8) is the solution to Equation (6.13) with the boundary conditions shown in Equation (6.14). Thus, the general expression for β_i can be written as

$$\beta_i = \epsilon \sum_{j=0}^{i} c(i,j)\sigma^j \tag{6.15}$$

From the normalizing equation (6.2) the value of $\beta_0 = \epsilon$ can be obtained as

$$\epsilon = \frac{1}{\sum_{i=0}^{m} f_i(\sigma)} \tag{6.16}$$

Substituting Equations (6.7) and (6.8) in Equation (6.16) and collecting the coefficients of the various powers of σ, we obtain

$$\epsilon = \frac{1}{\sum_{j=0}^{m} \left[\sigma^j \left\{ \sum_{i=j}^{m} \frac{(i+j)!}{(2j)!(i-j)!} \right\} \right]} \tag{6.17}$$

TABLE 6.1 Matrix C

	$j=0$	1	2	3	4	5	6	7	8	9
$i=0$	1	0	0	0	0	0	0	0	0	.
1	1	1	0	0	0	0	0	0	0	.
2	1	3	1	0	0	0	0	0	0	.
3	1	6	5	1	0	0	0	0	0	.
4	1	10	15	7	1	0	0	0	0	.
5	1	15	35	28	9	1	0	0	0	.
6	1	21	70	84	45	11	1	0	0	.
7	1	28	126	210	165	66	13	1	0	.
8	.	.	.	.	.	.	.	.	.	.

Later, we will discuss a simple procedure to compute the value of ϵ without using the summation in the denominator of Equation (6.17). An easy way to represent the closed-form solution is to write the coefficients $c(i, j)$ in the form of a matrix C as shown in Table 6.1. The columns indexed by j represent the powers of σ and the rows indexed by i represent the processor number. The nonzero entries in the matrix are given by Equation (6.8). Note that for the ith processor the coefficients $c(i, j)$ are nonzero only up to $i = j$. It can also be seen that the entries in this table can be generated independently of m. The matrix C has an interesting relationship with the famous Pascal's triangle. It can be observed that the nonzero entries in each column of matrix C are the same as the elements of alternate diagonals of Pascal's triangle. Here, each column in the C matrix starts at a point one entry below the previous column.

The fraction of the total load shared by the ith processor (when there are $m+1$ processors) is given by the ratio of the polynomial in σ formed by the ith row to the sum of the polynomials formed by each row up to the mth row, that is,

$$\beta_i = \frac{f_i(\sigma)}{\sum_{i=0}^{m} f_i(\sigma)}, \quad i = 0, \ldots, m \tag{6.18}$$

The processing time (denoted here by T) is given by

$$T = \frac{f_m(\sigma)}{\sum_{i=0}^{m} f_i(\sigma)} \tag{6.19}$$

The denominator of Equation (6.18) can easily be found by rewriting Equation (6.5) as

$$\beta_0 + \beta_1 + \cdots + \beta_{i-1} = \frac{\beta_i - \beta_{i-1}}{\sigma} \tag{6.20}$$

Letting $i = m + 1$, and substituting Equation (6.6), we get

$$\sum_{i=0}^{m} f_i(\sigma) = \frac{f_{m+1}(\sigma) - f_m(\sigma)}{\sigma} \tag{6.21}$$

Here, $f_{m+1}(\sigma)$ is obtained by generating the elements of the $(m+1)$th row in matrix C using the same recursive relation Equation (6.13). This polynomial can be considered to be for a fictitious processor p_{m+1}. An alternative is to rewrite Equation (6.20) as

$$(\beta_0 + \beta_1 + \cdots + \beta_{i-2}) + \beta_{i-1} = \frac{\beta_{i-1} - \beta_{i-2}}{\sigma} + \beta_{i-1} \tag{6.22}$$

from which, by letting $i = m + 1$ and substituting Equation (6.6), we directly get

$$\sum_{i=0}^{m} f_i(\sigma) = f_m(\sigma) + \frac{f_m(\sigma) - f_{m-1}(\sigma)}{\sigma} \tag{6.23}$$

From Equation (6.23) we can easily compute the value of ϵ without going through the process of summing up all the polynomials used in Equations (6.16) and (6.17).

Example 6.1

Consider a linear network of 5 processors ($m = 4$). The processing load on each processor is obtained from Table 6.1 as follows:

$$\sum_{i=0}^{4} f_i(\sigma) = \frac{f_5(\sigma) - f_4(\sigma)}{\sigma}$$

$$= 5 + 20\sigma + 21\sigma^2 + 8\sigma^3 + \sigma^4$$

$$= K$$

Then,

$$\beta_0 = \frac{1}{K} \qquad \text{(load on processor } p_4\text{)}$$

$$\beta_1 = \frac{1 + \sigma}{K} \qquad \text{(load on processor } p_3\text{)}$$

$$\beta_2 = \frac{1 + 3\sigma + \sigma^2}{K} \qquad \text{(load on processor } p_2\text{)}$$

$$\beta_3 = \frac{1 + 6\sigma + 5\sigma^2 + \sigma^3}{K} \qquad \text{(load on processor } p_1\text{)}$$

$$\beta_4 = \frac{1 + 10\sigma + 15\sigma^2 + 7\sigma^3 + \sigma^4}{K} \qquad \text{(load on processor } p_0\text{)}$$

where $\sigma = z T_{cm}/w T_{cp}$ is the network parameter defined in Chapter 2. The processing time is given by $\beta_4 w T_{cp}$.

6.2.3 Load Distribution Equations: Without Front End

The load distribution process and the timing diagram are the same as in Figure 3.9 with $w_i = w$ and $z_i = z$, for all i. From this timing diagram, we can write the following equations:

$$\alpha_i w T_{cp} = (1 - \alpha_0 - \cdots - \alpha_{i+1}) z T_{cm} + \alpha_{i+1} w T_{cp}, \quad i = 0, \ldots, m - 2 \tag{6.24}$$

$$\alpha_{m-1} w T_{cp} = \alpha_m w T_{cp} \tag{6.25}$$

and the normalizing equation is given by Equation (6.2).

6.2.4 Closed-Form Solution: Without Front End

In this case, Equations (6.24) and (6.25) can be written as

$$\alpha_i = (1 - \alpha_0 - \alpha_1 - \cdots - \alpha_{i+1})\sigma + \alpha_{i+1}, \quad i = 0, \ldots, m - 1 \tag{6.26}$$

$$\alpha_{m-1} = \alpha_m \tag{6.27}$$

Here, by the condition $wT_{cp} > zT_{cm}$, we have $\sigma < 1$. Equations (6.26) and (6.27), along with the normalizing equation, are of the same type as discussed in the with-front-end case. We again follow the relabeling transformation given by Equation (6.4) and rewrite Equations (6.26) and (6.27) as follows:

$$\beta_1 = \beta_0$$
$$\beta_i = (\beta_0 + \beta_1 + \cdots + \beta_{i-2})\sigma + \beta_{i-1}, \quad i = 2, \ldots, m \tag{6.28}$$

Now we can get a closed-form solution for Equation (6.28) coupled with the normalizing equation. For this purpose, we follow the same procedure as in the with-front-end case above. By denoting $\beta_0 = \beta_1 = \epsilon$, each β_i $(i = 2, \ldots, m)$ can be expressed as

$$\beta_i = g_i(\sigma)\epsilon \tag{6.29}$$

where $g_i(\sigma)$ is a qth degree polynomial in σ defined by

$$g_i(\sigma) = d(i, 0)\sigma^0 + d(i, 1)\sigma^1 + \cdots + d(i, q)\sigma^q \tag{6.30}$$

where $q = \lfloor \frac{i}{2} \rfloor$ and $d(i, j)$ represents the coefficient of σ^j in the polynomial $g_i(\sigma)$ and is given as

$$d(i, j) = \frac{i!}{(2j)!(i - 2j)!}, \quad j \le \left\lfloor \frac{i}{2} \right\rfloor \tag{6.31}$$

We can derive the above expression as follows: From Equation (6.28),

$$\beta_{i-1} = (\beta_0 + \beta_1 + \cdots + \beta_{i-3})\sigma + \beta_{i-2} \tag{6.32}$$

Thus, Equation (6.28) can be rewritten as

$$\beta_0 = \beta_1 = \epsilon$$
$$\beta_i = 2\,\beta_{i-1} - (1 - \sigma)\beta_{i-2} \tag{6.33}$$

which is valid for $i = 2, \ldots, m$. Substituting Equation (6.30) in Equation (6.33) we get

$$
d(i, 0)\sigma^0 + d(i, 1)\sigma^1 + \cdots + d\left(i, \left\lfloor \frac{i}{2} \right\rfloor - 1\right)\sigma^{\lfloor \frac{i}{2} \rfloor - 1} + d\left(i, \left\lfloor \frac{i}{2} \right\rfloor\right)\sigma^{\lfloor \frac{i}{2} \rfloor}
$$
$$
= 2\left\{ d(i-1, 0)\sigma^0 + d(i-1, 1)\sigma^1 + \cdots + d\left(i-1, \left\lfloor \frac{i-1}{2} \right\rfloor\right)\sigma^{\lfloor \frac{i-1}{2} \rfloor} \right\}
$$
$$
- \left\{ d(i-2, 0)\sigma^0 + d(i-2, 1)\sigma^1 + \cdots + d\left(i-2, \left\lfloor \frac{i}{2} \right\rfloor - 1\right)\sigma^{\lfloor \frac{i}{2} \rfloor - 1} \right\}
$$
$$
+ \left\{ d(i-2, 0)\sigma^1 + d(i-2, 1)\sigma^2 + \cdots + d\left(i-2, \left\lfloor \frac{i}{2} \right\rfloor - 1\right)\sigma^{\lfloor \frac{i}{2} \rfloor} \right\}
$$
$$\tag{6.34}$$

Now, collecting all the coefficients of the different powers of σ, we obtain the following recursive equations:

$$d(i, 0) = 2d(i - 1, 0) - d(i - 2, 0)$$

$$d(i, j) = 2d(i - 1, j) - d(i - 2, j) + d(i - 2, j - 1), \quad j = 1, \ldots, \left\lfloor \frac{i}{2} \right\rfloor - 1$$

$$d\left(i, \left\lfloor \frac{i}{2} \right\rfloor\right) = \begin{cases} d\left(i - 2, \left\lfloor \frac{i}{2} \right\rfloor - 1\right), & \text{if } i \text{ is even} \\ 2d\left(i - 1, \left\lfloor \frac{i}{2} \right\rfloor\right) + d\left(i - 2, \left\lfloor \frac{i}{2} \right\rfloor - 1\right), & \text{if } i \text{ is odd} \end{cases} \tag{6.35}$$

with the boundary conditions

$$d(0, 0) = d(1, 0) = 1 \tag{6.36}$$

The boundary conditions are obtained by making use of the fact that $\beta_0 = \beta_1 = \epsilon$. It can be easily verified that Equation (6.31) is the solution to the above recursive equations.

Thus, the general expression for β_i is given as

$$\beta_i = \epsilon \sum_{j=0}^{q} d(i, j) \sigma^j \tag{6.37}$$

Using the normalizing equation, the value of ϵ can be obtained as

$$\epsilon = \cfrac{1}{\sum_{j=0}^{\lfloor \frac{m}{2} \rfloor} \left\{ \sigma^j \left(\sum_{i=2j}^{m} \frac{i!}{(2j)!(i-2j)!} \right) \right\}} \tag{6.38}$$

The coefficients $d(i, j)$ can be written in the form of a matrix D as shown in Table 6.2. The matrix D also has a relationship with Pascal's triangle similar to that of matrix C, except for the fact that each successive column starts from a point two entries below the previous column. Once this matrix is generated, the solution procedure is the same as discussed in the with-front-end case. Thus,

$$\beta_i = \frac{g_i(\sigma)}{\sum_{i=0}^{m} g_i(\sigma)} \tag{6.39}$$

The denominator of Equation (6.39) can be easily obtained by using Equation (6.28) which can be rewritten as

$$\beta_0 + \beta_1 + \cdots + \beta_{i-2} = \frac{\beta_i - \beta_{i-1}}{\sigma} \tag{6.40}$$

Letting $i = m + 2$ and substituting Equation (6.29), we get

$$\sum_{i=0}^{m} g_i(\sigma) = \frac{g_{m+2}(\sigma) - g_{m+1}(\sigma)}{\sigma} \tag{6.41}$$

here, too, $g_{m+1}(\sigma)$ and $g_{m+2}(\sigma)$ are obtained by generating the elements of the $(m+1)$th and $(m+2)$th rows in matrix D using the recursive relations Equation (6.34). These polynomials may be considered to belong to two fictitious processors p_{m+1} and p_{m+2}. Alternatively, we can rewrite Equation (6.40) as

$$(\beta_0 + \beta_1 + \cdots + \beta_{i-4}) + \beta_{i-3} + \beta_{i-2} = \frac{\beta_{i-2} - \beta_{i-3}}{\sigma} + \beta_{i-3} + \beta_{i-2} \tag{6.42}$$

TABLE 6.2 Matrix D

	$j = 0$	1	2	3	4	5	6	7	8
$i = 0$	1	0	0	0	0	0	0	0	.
1	1	0	0	0	0	0	0	0	.
2	1	1	0	0	0	0	0	0	.
3	1	3	0	0	0	0	0	0	.
4	1	6	1	0	0	0	0	0	.
5	1	10	5	0	0	0	0	0	.
6	1	15	15	1	0	0	0	0	.
7	1	21	35	7	0	0	0	0	.
8	1	28	70	28	1	0	0	0	.
9	1	36	126	84	9	0	0	0	.
10	.		.		.	.	.	.	.

Letting $i = m + 2$ and substituting Equation (6.29) we get

$$\sum_{i=0}^{m} g_i(\sigma) = \frac{g_m(\sigma) - g_{m-1}(\sigma)}{\sigma} + g_{m-1}(\sigma) + g_m(\sigma)$$

$$= \left(1 + \frac{1}{\sigma}\right) g_m(\sigma) + \left(1 - \frac{1}{\sigma}\right) g_{m-1}(\sigma) \tag{6.43}$$

The processing time (denoted here by T) is given by

$$T = \beta_m w T_{cp} + (1 - \beta_m) z T_{cm}$$
$$= \{\beta_m + (1 - \beta_m)\sigma\} w T_{cp}$$
$$= \left\{ \frac{g_m(\sigma) + \{1 - g_m(\sigma)\}\sigma}{\sum_{i=0}^{m} g_i(\sigma)} \right\} w T_{cp} \tag{6.44}$$

From Equation (6.40),

$$1 = \beta_0 + \beta_1 + \cdots + \beta_{m-1} + \beta_m$$
$$= \frac{\beta_{m+1} - \beta_m}{\sigma} + \beta_m \tag{6.45}$$

Hence,

$$(1 - \beta_m)\sigma + \beta_m = \beta_{m+1} \tag{6.46}$$

that is,

$$\{1 - g_m(\sigma)\}\sigma + g_m(\sigma) = g_{m+1}(\sigma) \tag{6.47}$$

Hence,

$$T = \left\{ \frac{g_{m+1}(\sigma)}{\sum_{i=0}^{m} g_i(\sigma)} \right\} w T_{cp} \tag{6.48}$$

Example 6.2

Consider the network given in Example 6.1, with the modification that the processors are not equipped with-front-ends. Here we have

$$\sum_{i=0}^{4} g_i(\sigma) = \frac{g_6(\sigma) - g_5(\sigma)}{\sigma}$$

$$= 5 + 10\sigma + \sigma^2$$

$$= K$$

$$\beta_0 = \beta_1 = \frac{1}{K} \qquad \text{(load on processors } p_4 \text{ and } p_3)$$

$$\beta_2 = \frac{1+\sigma}{K} \qquad \text{(load on processor } p_2)$$

Then,

$$\beta_3 = \frac{1+3\sigma}{K} \qquad \text{(load on processor } p_1)$$

$$\beta_4 = \frac{1+6\sigma+\sigma^2}{K} \qquad \text{(load on processor } p_0)$$

The processing time is

$$\beta_4 w T_{cp} + (1-\beta_4)z T_{cm} = \{\beta_4 + (1-\beta_4)\sigma\}w T_{cp}$$

$$= \left\{ \frac{1+10\sigma+5\sigma^2}{K} \right\} w T_{cp}$$

6.3 LOAD ORIGINATION AT THE INTERIOR

In this section, we analyze the case where a processor in the interior of the network, instead of the one at the boundary, receives the full processing load. There are L processors to its left and R processors to its right (as shown in Figure 3.1b). The processor that receives the full load (root processor) has to share the processing load in an optimal manner.

6.3.1 Load Distribution Equations: With Front End

The root processor first transmits a fraction α^l of the total processing load to its left immediate neighbor, then transmits a fraction α^r to its right immediate neighbor, and keeps the remaining fraction $(1-\alpha^l-\alpha^r = \alpha_0)$ for itself to compute. Upon receiving the α^l load the processor on the left shares it with its neighbor in the manner described in the boundary case. The processor on the right performs a similar operation with α^r of the processing load. The timing diagram for this case is the same as in Figure 3.11 but with $\beta_l = \alpha^l$, $\beta_r = \alpha^r$; and $w_i^r = w_i^l = w$, $z_i^r = z_i^l = z$, for all i. Note that the sequence of load distribution is such that first the fraction α^l is sent to the left and then the fraction α^r is sent to the right. The governing equations are written separately for the left and right sides as follows:

Left side:

$$\alpha_0 w T_{cp} = \alpha^l z T_{cm} + \alpha_1^l w T_{cp} \tag{6.49}$$

$$\alpha_i^l w T_{cp} = (\alpha^l - \alpha_1^l - \cdots - \alpha_i^l) z T_{cm} + \alpha_{i+1}^l w T_{cp}, \quad i = 1, \ldots, L-1 \tag{6.50}$$

Right side:

$$\alpha_0 w T_{cp} = (\alpha^l + \alpha^r) z T_{cm} + \alpha_1^r w T_{cp} \tag{6.51}$$

$$\alpha_i^r w T_{cp} = (\alpha^r - \alpha_1^r - \cdots - \alpha_i^r) z T_{cm} + \alpha_{i+1}^r w T_{cp}, \quad i = 1, \ldots, R-1 \tag{6.52}$$

In the above equations, the superscripts identify the direction and the subscripts identify the processor number. The number assigned to the root processor is zero. Also note that Equations (6.50) and (6.52) are similar to the governing equations of the boundary case, but the summation of α_i^l ($i = 1, \ldots, L$) is equal to α^l and the summation of α_i^r ($i = 1, \ldots, R$) is equal to α^r. Equations (6.49) and (6.51) connect the load distribution equations for the processors on the left and right sides. The normalization equation is

$$\alpha_0 + \alpha_1^l + \alpha_2^l + \cdots + \alpha_L^l + \alpha_1^r + \cdots + \alpha_R^r = 1 \tag{6.53}$$

Note that Equations (6.49) through (6.52) form a system of $(R + L + 1)$ linear equations with $(R + L + 1)$ unknowns. They can be solved computationally using the method given in Chapter 3. However, here we shall exploit the homogeneity of the network to obtain a closed-form solution to the optimal load distribution problem.

6.3.2 Closed-Form Solution: With Front End

We will use the following transformation

$$\beta_0 = \alpha_0$$
$$\beta_i^l = \alpha_{L-i}^l, \quad i = 0, \ldots, L-1$$
$$\beta_i^r = \alpha_{R-i}^r, \quad i = 0, \ldots, R-1 \tag{6.54}$$

and rewrite Equations (6.49) through (6.52) as follows:

Left side:

$$\beta_0 = (\beta_0^l + \beta_1^l + \cdots + \beta_{L-1}^l)\sigma + \beta_{L-1}^l \tag{6.55}$$

$$\beta_i^l = (\beta_0^l + \beta_1^l + \cdots + \beta_{i-1}^l)\sigma + \beta_{i-1}^l, \quad i = 1, \ldots, L-1 \tag{6.56}$$

Right side:

$$\beta_0 = (\beta_0^l + \cdots + \beta_{L-1}^l + \beta_0^r + \cdots + \beta_{R-1}^r)\sigma + \beta_{R-1}^r \tag{6.57}$$

$$\beta_i^r = (\beta_0^r + \cdots + \beta_{i-1}^r)\sigma + \beta_{i-1}^r, \quad i = 1, \ldots, R-1 \tag{6.58}$$

The normalizing equation is given by

$$\beta_0 + \beta_0^l + \cdots + \beta_{L-1}^l + \beta_0^r + \cdots + \beta_{R-1}^r = 1 \tag{6.59}$$

Exactly as in the boundary case with front end, we assume

$$\beta_0^l = \epsilon^l$$
$$\beta_0^r = \epsilon^r \tag{6.60}$$

and thus

$$\beta_i^l = f_i(\sigma)\epsilon^l, \quad i = 1, 2, \ldots, L-1$$
$$\beta_i^r = f_i(\sigma)\epsilon^r, \quad i = 1, 2, \ldots, R-1$$
$$\beta_0 = f_L(\sigma)\epsilon^l \tag{6.61}$$

where $f_i(\sigma)$ is defined as in the boundary case and its coefficients can be obtained from Table 6.1. Note that, with the transformation, the processing loads on the left and right are expressed as functions of β_0^l and β_0^r respectively. Also β_0^l and β_0^r corresponds to α_L^l and α_R^r. Now equating Equations (6.55) and (6.57) we obtain

$$\beta_{L-1}^l = (\beta_0^r + \cdots + \beta_{R-1}^r)\sigma + \beta_{R-1}^r \tag{6.62}$$

Substituting Equation (6.61) we obtain

$$f_{L-1}(\sigma)\epsilon^l = [\{f_0(\sigma) + \cdots + f_{R-1}(\sigma)\}\sigma + f_{R-1}(\sigma)]\epsilon^r$$
$$= f_R(\sigma)\epsilon^r \tag{6.63}$$

Hence,

$$\epsilon^l = \left\{ \frac{f_R(\sigma)}{f_{L-1}(\sigma)} \right\} \epsilon^r \tag{6.64}$$

Using Equation (6.64), we can rewrite Equations (6.55) through (6.58) as

$$\beta_0 = f_L(\sigma)\epsilon^l$$
$$= \left\{ \frac{f_L(\sigma) f_R(\sigma)}{f_{L-1}(\sigma)} \right\} \epsilon^r$$
$$\beta_i^l = f_i(\sigma)\epsilon^l$$
$$= \left\{ \frac{f_i(\sigma) f_R(\sigma)}{f_{L-1}(\sigma)} \right\} \epsilon^r, \quad i = 0, 1, \ldots, L-1$$
$$\beta_i^r = f_i(\sigma)\epsilon^r, \quad i = 0, \ldots, R-1 \tag{6.65}$$

Substituting Equation (6.65) in the normalizing equation (6.59), the value of $\epsilon^r = \beta_1^r$ can be obtained as

$$\epsilon^r = \frac{1}{\sum_{i=0}^{R-1} f_i(\sigma) + \frac{f_R(\sigma)}{f_{L-1}(\sigma)} \sum_{i=0}^{L} f_i(\sigma)} \tag{6.66}$$

Note that $f_R(\sigma)$ and $f_L(\sigma)$ are the polynomials generated by the Lth and Rth rows of matrix C in Table 6.1 and may be considered to be associated with some fictitious processors. However, it should also be noted that $f_L(\sigma)\epsilon^l$ is also the load on the root processor and that the processing time is given by

$$T = \beta_0 w T_{cp}$$

$$= \left\{ \frac{f_L(\sigma) f_R(\sigma)}{f_{L-1}(\sigma) \sum_{i=0}^{R-1} f_i(\sigma) + f_R(\sigma) \sum_{i=0}^{L} f_i(\sigma)} \right\} w T_{cp} \qquad (6.67)$$

As mentioned earlier, the root processor follows the sequence of first sending the fraction of the load α^l to the left and then sending the fraction of the load α^r to the right. Now, we prove that the processing time remains the same, even if the sequence is reversed (that is, when the root processor first sends a processing load to the right and then sends a processing load to the left).

It can be seen that the following two situations are equivalent:

Case i. There are L processors on the left and R processors on the right of the root processor. The load is first sent to the right.

Case ii. There are R processors on the left and L processors on the right of the root processor. The load is first sent to the left.

Thus processing time in Case i above can be found by obtaining the same for Case ii. This can be done easily by interchanging L and R in Equation (6.67). This gives the processing time corresponding to Case ii as

$$T' = \left\{ \frac{f_R(\sigma) f_L(\sigma)}{f_{R-1}(\sigma) \sum_{i=0}^{L-1} f_i(\sigma) + f_L(\sigma) \sum_{i=0}^{R} f_i(\sigma)} \right\} w T_{cp} \qquad (6.68)$$

We will now prove that $T = T'$. In T and T' the numerators are the same. Thus, we have to prove that the denominators are also the same. In other words, we have to prove the following:

$$f_{L-1}(\sigma) \sum_{i=0}^{R-1} f_i(\sigma) + f_R(\sigma) \sum_{i=0}^{L} f_i(\sigma) - f_{R-1}(\sigma) \sum_{i=0}^{L-1} f_i(\sigma) - f_L(\sigma) \sum_{i=0}^{R} f_i(\sigma) = 0$$

$$(6.69)$$

We know that

$$\sum_{i=1}^{m} f_i(\sigma) = \sum_{i=1}^{m-1} f_i(\sigma) + f_m(\sigma) \qquad (6.70)$$

Using Equation (6.70), the LHS of Equation (6.69) reduces to

$$f_{L-1}(\sigma) \sum_{i=0}^{R-1} f_i(\sigma) + f_R(\sigma) \sum_{i=0}^{L-1} f_i(\sigma) - f_{R-1}(\sigma) \sum_{i=0}^{L-1} f_i(\sigma) - f_L(\sigma) \sum_{i=0}^{R-1} f_i(\sigma) \quad (6.71)$$

Collecting the appropriate terms in Expression (6.71), we have

$$\left\{ \sum_{i=0}^{L-1} f_i(\sigma) \right\} \{ f_R(\sigma) - f_{R-1}(\sigma) \} - \left\{ \sum_{i=0}^{R-1} f_i(\sigma) \right\} \{ f_L(\sigma) - f_{L-1}(\sigma) \} \qquad (6.72)$$

In Equation (6.21), putting $m = R - 1$ and then $m = L - 1$, and substituting the resultant expressions, Expression (6.72) reduces to zero.

Hence the minimum processing time is independent of the sequence of load distribution by the root processor. However, the loads on individual processors do depend on the sequence of load distribution.

Alternatively, note that by using Equation (6.21) the expression for processing time, shown in Equation (6.67), can itself be simplified to

$$T = \left\{ \frac{\sigma f_L(\sigma) f_R(\sigma)}{(1 + \sigma) f_L(\sigma) f_R(\sigma) - f_{L-1}(\sigma) f_{R-1}(\sigma)} \right\} w T_{cp} \tag{6.73}$$

which has the property that it is symmetrical with respect to L and R. Hence the processing time is independent of the sequence of load distribution.

6.3.3 Load Distribution Equations: Without Front End

In this section, we study the interior case in a linear network in which none of the processors are equipped with front ends. Each processor first communicates the processing load to its neighbor and then starts its own computation. The timing diagram for this case is the same as in Figure 3.13 but with $\beta_l = \alpha^l$, $\beta_r = \alpha^r$; and $w_i^r = w_i^l = w$, $z_i^r = z_i^l = z$, for all i. Note that the root processor follows the sequence of first sending the load to the left and then sending the load to the right. The governing equations for the left and right side are as follows:

Left side:

$$\alpha_0 w T_{cp} = (\alpha^l - \alpha_1^l) z T_{cm} + \alpha_1^l w T_{cp} - \alpha^r z T_{cm} \tag{6.74}$$

$$\alpha_i^l w T_{cp} = (\alpha^l - \alpha_1^l - \cdots - \alpha_{i+1}^l) z T_{cm} + \alpha_{i+1}^l w T_{cp} \quad i = 1, \ldots, L - 1 \tag{6.75}$$

Right side:

$$\alpha_0 w T_{cp} = (\alpha^r - \alpha_1^r) z T_{cm} + \alpha_1^r w T_{cp} \tag{6.76}$$

$$\alpha_i^r w T_{cp} = (\alpha^r - \alpha_1^r - \cdots - \alpha_{i+1}^r) z T_{cm} + \alpha_{i+1}^r w T_{cp} \quad i = 1, \ldots, R - 1 \tag{6.77}$$

The normalizing equation is given by Equation (6.53).

6.3.4 Closed-Form Solution: Without Front End

We follow the same relabeling transformation used in the with-front-end case and rewrite the above equations.

Left side:

$$\beta_1^l = \beta_0^l \tag{6.78}$$

$$\beta_i^l = (\beta_0^l + \cdots + \beta_{i-2}^l)\sigma + \beta_{i-1}^l, \quad i = 2, \ldots, L - 1 \tag{6.79}$$

$$\beta_0 = (\beta^l - \beta^r - \beta_{L-1}^l)\sigma + \beta_{L-1}^l \tag{6.80}$$

Right side:

$$\beta_1^r = \beta_0^r \tag{6.81}$$

$$\beta_i^r = (\beta_0^r + \cdots + \beta_{i-2}^r)\sigma + \beta_{i-1}^r, \quad i = 2, \ldots, R-1 \tag{6.82}$$

$$\beta_0 = (\beta^r - \beta_{R-1}^r)\sigma + \beta_{R-1}^r \tag{6.83}$$

The normalization equation is

$$\beta_0 + \beta_0^l + \cdots + \beta_{L-1}^l + \beta_0^r + \cdots + \beta_{R-1}^r = 1 \tag{6.84}$$

We again define

$$\beta_0^l = \epsilon^l, \beta_0^r = \epsilon^r \tag{6.85}$$

Using the same technique as in the boundary case, we have

$$\beta_0 = g_R(\sigma)\epsilon^r \tag{6.86}$$

$$\beta_i^r = g_i(\sigma)\epsilon^r, \quad i = 0, \ldots, R-1 \tag{6.87}$$

$$\beta_i^l = g_i(\sigma)\epsilon^l, \quad i = 0, \ldots, L-1 \tag{6.88}$$

with $g_0(\sigma) = 1$. The polynomial $g_i(\sigma)$ is defined earlier and its coefficients are given in Table 6.2. Now equating Equations (6.80) and (6.83), and substituting Equations (6.87) and (6.88), we get the relationship between ϵ^l and ϵ^r as

$$\epsilon^l = X\epsilon^r \tag{6.89}$$

where

$$X = \frac{(1-\sigma)g_{R-1}(\sigma) + 2\sigma \sum_{i=0}^{R-1} g_i(\sigma)}{(1-\sigma)g_{L-1}(\sigma) + \sigma \sum_{i=0}^{L-1} g_i(\sigma)} \tag{6.90}$$

Using this relation along with the normalization equation, ϵ^r is obtained as

$$\epsilon^r = \frac{1}{\sum_{i=0}^{R} g_i(\sigma) + X \sum_{i=0}^{L-1} g_i(\sigma)} \tag{6.91}$$

Once the value of ϵ^r is known all the β_j's can be computed. The processing time is given by

$$T = \beta_0 w T_{cp} + \beta^l z T_{cm} + \beta^r z T_{cm}$$

$$= \{\beta_0 + (\beta^l + \beta^r)\sigma\} w T_{cp} \tag{6.92}$$

Substituting appropriate expressions for β_0, β^l, and β^r, we get

$$T = \left\{ \frac{g_R(\sigma) + \sigma\{X \sum_{i=0}^{L-1} g_i(\sigma) + \sum_{i=0}^{R-1} g_i(\sigma)\}}{g_R(\sigma) + X \sum_{i=0}^{L-1} g_i(\sigma) + \sum_{i=0}^{R-1} g_i(\sigma)} \right\} w T_{cp} \tag{6.93}$$

which, upon substituting the expression for X and simplifying, yields the following expression. We omit the argument σ for simplicity.

$$T = \left(\frac{X_1}{X_2}\right) w T_{cp} \tag{6.94}$$

where

$$X_1 = (1-\sigma)g_R g_{L-1} + \sigma g_R \sum_{i=0}^{L-1} g_i + \sigma(1-\sigma)\left\{g_{R-1}\sum_{i=0}^{L-1} g_i + g_{L-1}\sum_{i=0}^{R-1} g_i\right\}$$

$$+ 3\sigma^2 \left(\sum_{i=0}^{R-1} g_i\right)\left(\sum_{i=0}^{L-1} g_i\right)$$

$$X_2 = (1-\sigma)g_R g_{L-1} + \sigma g_R \sum_{i=0}^{L-1} g_i + (1-\sigma)\left\{g_{R-1}\sum_{i=0}^{L-1} g_i + g_{L-1}\sum_{i=0}^{R-1} g_i\right\}$$

$$+ 3\sigma \left(\sum_{i=0}^{R-1} g_i\right)\left(\sum_{i=0}^{L-1} g_i\right)$$

From (6.79), we obtain

$$\sum_{i=0}^{L-2} g_i = \frac{g_L - g_{L-1}}{\sigma} \tag{6.95}$$

Using this in the second term of both the numerator and denominator of Equation (6.94) we obtain

$$T =$$

$$\left\{\frac{g_R g_L + \sigma(1-\sigma)\left\{g_{R-1}\sum_{i=0}^{L-1} g_i + g_{L-1}\sum_{i=0}^{R-1} g_i\right\} + 3\sigma^2\left(\sum_{i=0}^{R-1} g_i\right)\left(\sum_{i=0}^{L-1} g_i\right)}{g_R g_L + (1-\sigma)\left\{g_{R-1}\sum_{i=0}^{L-1} g_i + g_{L-1}\sum_{i=0}^{R-1} g_i\right\} + 3\sigma\left(\sum_{i=0}^{R-1} g_i\right)\left(\sum_{i=0}^{L-1} g_i\right)}\right\} w T_{cp} \tag{6.96}$$

As mentioned earlier, the root processor follows the sequence of first sending the fraction α^l to the left and then sending the fraction α^r to the right. It is easy to see that the processing time remains the same even when the sequence is reversed. For this we follow the procedure outlined in the with-front-end case and note that both the numerator and the denominator of Equation (6.96) are symmetrical with respect to L and R, that is, the expression for T does not change even when L and R are interchanged.

Based on the above results, we can state the following theorem, which is true for both the with- and without-front-end cases.

Theorem 6.1.   In a given linear homogeneous network of communicating processors, when the processing load originates at the interior of the network, the minimum processing time is independent of the sequence of load distribution by the root processor.

6.4 CONCLUDING REMARKS

Following are the highlights of this chapter:

- Closed-form expressions for minimum processing time in a linear network were derived for the following cases:
  - **(i)** Load origination at the boundary: with-front-end processors
  - **(ii)** Load origination at the boundary: without-front-end processors
  - **(iii)** Load origination at the interior: with-front-end processors
  - **(iv)** Load origination at the interior: without-front-end processors

- It was proved that minimum processing time is independent of the sequence of load distribution by the root processor when the load originates at the interior of the network.

In Chapter 8, we will use the above closed-form solutions to obtain the asymptotic performance of linear networks. In Chapter 9, we will analyze another load distribution strategy for linear networks which will further reduce the processing time while utilizing the front ends efficiently.

BIBLIOGRAPHIC NOTES

Most of the material presented in this chapter is from Mani and Ghose (1994). Some of the proofs are worked out more elaborately here. Pascal's triangle is a useful concept in many computer science applications and can be found in many textbooks.

CHAPTER 7

Optimal Sequencing and Arrangement in Single-Level Tree Networks

In most of Chapter 4, it was assumed that the root processor p_0 distributes the load fractions sequentially from p_1 to p_m. In Table 4.1, we presented some performance results which showed that by keeping the fastest processor at the root it was possible to improve performance in the with-front-end case. We also observed that by changing the sequence of load distribution among the child processors in a bus network the time performance does not change. In this chapter, we show analytically that in a general single-level tree network the time performance does depend on the sequence of load distribution among the child processors. If there are m child processors in the network, then there are $m!$ different load distribution sequences possible. It is of interest to identify that particular sequence (out of all possible sequences) which yields the minimum processing time. This is the first of the two main objectives of this chapter. The second objective is to show that it is possible to reduce the processing time further through a physical rearrangement of the processors and links without actually disturbing the single-level tree topology. We derive analytical results to obtain the optimal sequence of load distribution and the optimal arrangement of links and processors in a single-level tree network for both with- and without-front-end cases. We also obtain results for some special cases, such as bus networks. These analytical results justify the numerical results presented in Chapter 4.

7.1 DEFINITIONS AND SOME REMARKS

The single-level tree network configuration shown in Figure 5.1 can be represented as an ordered set as follows:

$$\Sigma = \{p_0, (l_1, p_1), \ldots, (l_k, p_k), \ldots, (l_m, p_m)\} \qquad (7.1)$$

where (l_k, p_k) represents the kth processor (p_k) connected to the root (p_0) via a link (l_k). This ordered set Σ gives the *arrangement* of $(m+1)$ processors and m links. The order represents the *sequence* in which the root processor distributes load fractions to the child processors (that is, from processors p_1 to p_m through links l_1 to l_m). Note that this order need not represent any physical order in which the processors are arranged. However, for convenience, and without loss of generality, we also assume that the sequence of load distribution is from left to right in Figure 5.1. Thus, a change in the sequence of load distribution is equivalent to a corresponding change in the order shown in the ordered set Σ in Equation (7.1) or in Figure 5.1. Similarly, the architectural arrangement refers to the connections between links and the processors, that is, it describes the formation of each processor-link pair in a network. Now, for notational convenience, we redenote the processing time of the network (denoted as $T(\alpha)$ in Chapter 5) as $T(\Sigma, \alpha)$. To clarify these notations consider the example given below.

Example 7.1

Consider the following networks, represented as

$$\Sigma_1 = \{p_0, (l_1, p_1), (l_2, p_2), (l_3, p_3), (l_4, p_4)\}$$
$$\Sigma_2 = \{p_0, (l_1, p_1), (l_3, p_3), (l_2, p_2), (l_4, p_4)\}$$
$$\Sigma_3 = \{p_0, (l_1, p_1), (l_2, p_3), (l_3, p_2), (l_4, p_4)\}$$
$$\Sigma_4 = \{p_0, (l_1, p_1), (l_3, p_2), (l_2, p_3), (l_4, p_4)\}$$

The network Σ_1 is the same as in Equation (7.1) and is used as the reference in the following discussion. In Σ_2, the processor-link pairs (l_2, p_2) and (l_3, p_3) are interchanged. Therefore, the load is first distributed to p_3 via l_3 and then to p_2 via l_2. On the other hand, in Σ_3 the processors p_2 and p_3 alone are physically interchanged. Thus, the load is first distributed to p_3 via l_2 and then to p_2 via l_3. In the case of Σ_4, the links l_2 and l_3 alone are physically interchanged, and the load is distributed first to p_2 via l_3 and then to p_3 via l_2. Thus, the difference between Σ_1 and Σ_2 lies in the sequence of load distribution, while the architectural arrangement remains undisturbed. The difference between Σ_1 and Σ_3 lies in the architectural arrangement. The difference between Σ_1 and Σ_4 lies in both the sequence of load distribution and the architectural arrangement. It may be noted that Σ_3 and Σ_4 have the same architectural arrangement but a different sequence of load distribution.

Based on the above definitions we define the following terms:

(i) *Optimal Sequence*: This is defined as that sequence of optimal load distribution for a given arrangement for which $T(\Sigma, \alpha)$ is a minimum.

(ii) *Optimal Arrangement*: This is defined as that architectural arrangement of processors and links for which $T(\Sigma, \alpha)$ is a minimum, provided that optimal sequence and optimal load distribution is followed.

In the following sections we will derive results regarding the optimal sequence of load distribution and the optimal architectural arrangement for a general single-level tree network. We will show that the time performance of such a network can be improved through a hierarchical two-step strategy, the first of which involves the identification of an optimal load distribution sequence and the next an optimal architectural rearrangement.

7.2 WITH-FRONT-END PROCESSORS

In this section, we use the closed-form solutions given in Section 5.1.1 to obtain the optimal sequence of load distribution and optimal architectural arrangement of a single-level tree network. We first prove some intermediate results based on the effect of change in sequence of load distribution and arrangement among two adjacent processor-link pairs k and $(k+1)$. For this, we rewrite the closed-form solution in such a way that only the terms corresponding to the kth and $(k+1)$th processor and link are present explicitly in the expression for processing time $T(\Sigma, \alpha)$. The other terms are absorbed in the constants defined below. It should be noted that this closed-form solution was derived by assuming that all the processor-link pairs satisfy the condition shown in Equation (5.28). Hence, all the processors get nonzero loads, and stop computing at the same instant in time.

In the following equations we use $f_k = (w_k + z_k\delta)/w_{k-1}$, which has been defined in Chapter 5 and will be used in this chapter, too.

$$T(\Sigma, \alpha) = \frac{C(k)(w_{k+2} + z_{k+2}\delta)(w_{k+1} + z_{k+1}\delta)(w_k + z_k\delta)w_0 T_{cp}/(w_{k+1}w_k w_{k-1})}{\left[\begin{array}{l} K_1(k) + K_2(k)(w_{k+2} + z_{k+2}\delta)\{1 + (w_{k+1} + z_{k+1}\delta)/w_k\}/w_{k+1} \\ + K_3(k)(w_{k+2} + z_{k+2}\delta)(w_{k+1} + z_{k+1}\delta)(w_k + z_k\delta)/(w_{k+1}w_k w_{k-1}) \end{array}\right]}$$
$$k = 1, \ldots, m-3 \tag{7.2}$$

where

$$C(k) = f_1 \cdots f_{k-1} f_{k+3} \cdots f_m$$
$$= \prod_{\substack{j=1 \\ j \neq k, k+1, k+2}}^{m} f_j \tag{7.3}$$

$$K_1(k) = 1 + (f_{k+3} \cdots f_m) + (f_{k+4} \cdots f_m) + \cdots + (f_{m-1}f_m) + f_m$$
$$= 1 + \sum_{i=k+3}^{m} \prod_{j=i}^{m} f_j \tag{7.4}$$

$$K_2(k) = f_{k+3} \cdots f_m$$
$$= \prod_{j=k+3}^{m} f_j \tag{7.5}$$

$$K_3(k) = (f_1 \cdots f_{k-1} f_{k+3} \cdots f_m)$$
$$+ (f_2 \cdots f_{k-1} f_{k+3} \cdots f_m)$$
$$+ \cdots + (f_{k-1} f_{k+3} \cdots f_m) + (f_{k+3} \cdots f_m) + \cdots$$
$$+ (f_{m-1} f_m) + f_m \tag{7.6}$$

$$= \sum_{i=1}^{m} \prod_{\substack{j=i \\ j \neq k, k+1, k+2}}^{m} f_j$$

The above expressions and constants are valid for $k = 1, \ldots, m - 3$. These have to be redefined for the right extreme end of the tree.

$$T(\Sigma, \alpha) = \left\{ \frac{D(k) \, f_k f_{k+1} \cdots f_m}{1 + K_4(k) f_k \cdots f_m + f_{k+1} \cdots f_m + \cdots + f_m} \right\} w_0 T_{cp}, \tag{7.7}$$
$$k = m - 2, \, m - 1$$

where

$$D(k) = f_1 \cdots f_{k-1}$$
$$= \prod_{j=1}^{k-1} f_j \tag{7.8}$$

$$K_4(k) = 1 + (f_1 \cdots f_{k-1}) + (f_2 \cdots f_{k-1}) + \cdots$$
$$+ (f_{k-2} f_{k-1}) + f_{k-1}$$

$$= \left(1 + \sum_{i=1}^{k-1} \prod_{j=i}^{k-1} f_j \right) \tag{7.9}$$

7.2.1 Optimal Sequence

Now we present some intermediate results necessary to identify the optimal sequence of load distribution. Note that an interchange of processor-link pairs (l_k, p_k) and (l_{k+1}, p_{k+1}) implies only a change in the sequence of load distribution and does not involve any architectural rearrangement.

Lemma 7.1. Consider a single-level tree network Σ in which the condition (5.28) is satisfied by all the processor-link pairs. In Σ, if $z_{k+1} \leq z_k$ for any two adjacent processor-link pairs, then the processing time will decrease or remain the same when (l_k, p_k) and (l_{k+1}, p_{k+1}) are interchanged.

Proof. When the pairs (l_k, p_k) and (l_{k+1}, p_{k+1}) are interchanged, the resulting arrangement Σ_A is

$$\Sigma_A = \{p_0, (l_1, p_1), (l_2, p_2), \ldots, (l_{k+1}, p_{k+1}), (l_k, p_k), \ldots (l_m, p_m)\} \tag{7.10}$$

First let us assume that Equation (5.28) is satisfied by all the links and processors in Σ_A, and thus all the m child processors take part in the computation process. Let α and α_A be the optimal load distributions (according to Theorem 5.1) for the networks

Σ and Σ_A, respectively. We have to prove that $T(\Sigma_A, \alpha_A) < T(\Sigma, \alpha)$ if $z_{k+1} < z_k$. Using the constants defined earlier, and assuming $z_{k+1} = \tau z_k$, $\tau \leq 1$, the processing times $T(\Sigma, \alpha)$ and $T(\Sigma_A, \alpha_A)$ are obtained from Equation (7.2) as follows:

$$T(\Sigma, \alpha) = \frac{C(k)(w_{k+2} + z_{k+2}\delta)(w_{k+1} + \tau z_k \delta)(w_k + z_k \delta)w_0 T_{cp}/(w_{k+1} w_k w_{k-1})}{\begin{bmatrix} K_1(k) + K_2(k)(w_{k+2} + z_{k+2}\delta)\{1 + (w_{k+1} + \tau z_k \delta)/w_k\}/w_{k+1} \\ + K_3(k)(w_{k+2} + z_{k+2}\delta)(w_{k+1} + \tau z_k \delta)(w_k + z_k \delta)/(w_{k+1} w_k w_{k-1}) \end{bmatrix}}$$
$$k = 1, \ldots, m - 3 \qquad (7.11)$$

$$T(\Sigma_A, \alpha_A) = \frac{C(k)(w_{k+2} + z_{k+2}\delta)(w_k + z_k \delta)(w_{k+1} + \tau z_k \delta)w_0 T_{cp}/(w_k w_{k+1} w_{k-1})}{\begin{bmatrix} K_1(k) + K_2(k)(w_{k+2} + z_{k+2}\delta)\{1 + (w_k + z_k \delta)/w_{k+l}\}/w_k \\ + K_3(k)(w_{k+2} + z_{k+2}\delta)(w_k + z_k \delta)(w_{k+1} + \tau z_k \delta)/(w_k w_{k+1} w_{k-1}) \end{bmatrix}}$$
$$k = 1, \ldots, m - 3 \qquad (7.12)$$

Let us denote the numerators of Equations (7.11) and (7.12) as N_1 and N_2, and the respective denominators as D_1 and D_2. Since $N_1 = N_2$, we calculate the value of $D_1 - D_2$.

$$D_1 - D_2 = \left\{ \frac{C(k)K_2(k)(w_{k+2} + z_{k+2}\delta)^2}{(w_{k-1} w_k^2 w_{k+1}^2)} \right\}$$
$$\times (w_k + z_k \delta)(w_{k+1} + \tau z_k \delta)\,(1 - \tau)\,z_k \delta w_0 T_{cp} \qquad (7.13)$$

Thus, in Equation (7.13) the $RHS \geq 0$ when $\tau \leq 1$, which proves the lemma. Also note that when $\tau < 1$, $RHS > 0$, implying a definite decrease in the processing time, while the $RHS = 0$ only when $\tau = 1$, that is, $z_k = z_{k+1}$.

Now suppose that Equation (5.28) is not satisfied in the network Σ_A by some processor-link pairs. Then, in the optimal load distribution these processors should not get any load. By applying Theorem 5.1 to Σ_A, we immediately conclude that the optimal processing time is less than $T(\Sigma_A, \alpha_A)$ given in Equation (7.12).   □

The lemma is proved above only for $k = 1, 2, \ldots, m - 3$. For $k = m - 2$ and $m - 1$, a similar proof can be obtained using Equations (7.7) through (7.9).

An immediate consequence of this result is the following theorem.

Theorem 7.1. Optimal Sequence   In a single-level tree network Σ, in order to achieve minimum processing time, the sequence of load distribution by the root processor p_0 should follow the order in which the link speeds decrease.

Proof. We will prove this by contradiction. In a network Σ, let the condition given in the theorem be violated by at least one processor-link pair. We will show that this sequence of load distribution cannot yield the minimum processing time. For this, we first obtain the reduced network Σ' by eliminating all processor-link pairs that violate Equation (5.28). Let the set E contain the collection of all these processor-link pairs eliminated from Σ. Now we can have one of the following two cases:

Case i. $E = \phi$. Then $\Sigma' = \Sigma$. In this case, we can directly apply Lemma 7.1 and obtain a strict improvement in time performance.

Case ii. $E \neq \phi$. Then $\Sigma' \subset \Sigma$. By Theorem 5.1, we have $T(\Sigma', \alpha') = T(\Sigma, \alpha)$, where α' and α are the optimal load distributions for Σ' and Σ, respectively. Now we can have two cases:

Case ii(a).   Let all the processor-link pairs in Σ' satisfy the condition stated in this theorem. This implies that the links are arranged in order of decreasing speed. Then we can append all the processor-link pairs in E to Σ' one at a time in such a way that the resultant network at each step does not violate Equation (5.28). One way to do this would be to append these processor-link pairs in appropriate positions such that the links continue to be arranged in order of decreasing speed. By Lemma 5.8, each such operation of appending the processor-link pairs causes a definite improvement in time performance.

Case ii(b).   Let at least one processor-link pair in Σ' violate the condition stated in this theorem. Then we can immediately apply Lemma 7.1 to get a definite improvement in the time performance.

The above arguments contradict our initial assumption that the original load distribution sequence is optimal.   □

The above theorem essentially provides a necessary and sufficient condition for a sequence of load distribution to be optimal. According to this condition, the load should be distributed first through the fastest link, then through the next fastest link, and so on until the slowest link is assigned the last load fraction. The optimal sequence theorem has a wider applicability than is apparent from above. In a general DCS, the load originating at a processor site may be distributed to several processors that are free to take up a new task. The load originating processor can estimate the total delay (communication delay plus the delay in the intermediate processors) to each of the available processors and then use the optimal sequence result to distribute the load. If a large number of processors is available and we must choose only a subset of them, then again the optimal sequence theorem can be used to make this choice. Thus the optimal sequence theorem is applicable in a variety of situations to a general DCS and is not necessarily restricted to a single-level tree network.

Note that the optimal sequence of load distribution can be achieved without effecting any architectural rearrangement. However, if architectural rearrangement is permitted then it may be possible to improve the time performance of a network further. We will explore this possibility in the next section.

7.2.2 Optimal Arrangement

Note that an interchange of processors p_k and p_{k+1} implies an architectural rearrangement, as it requires existing processor-link pairs to be broken and new pairs to be formed.

Lemma 7.2.   Consider a single-level tree network Σ, in which all the processor-link pairs satisfy $z_{k+1} \geq z_k$, for all $k = 1, 2, \ldots, m - 1$. Suppose for two adjacent processors p_k and p_{k+1} we have $w_k \geq w_{k+1}$. Then the processing time will decrease or remain the same when only the processors p_k and p_{k+1} are interchanged.

Proof. Since the links are arranged in decreasing order of speeds the network satisfies Equation (5.28) initially and continues to do so subsequently even when processors are interchanged. Let the processors p_k and p_{k+1} be interchanged, resulting in an arrangement given by

$$\Sigma_B = \{p_0, (l_1, p_1), (l_2, p_2), \ldots, (l_k, p_{k+1}), (l_{k+1}, p_k), \ldots, (l_m, p_m)\} \tag{7.14}$$

Let α and α_B be the optimal load distributions for Σ and Σ_B, respectively. Using the constants defined earlier, in Equations (7.3) through (7.6), and assuming $w_{k+1} = \beta w_k$, $\beta \leq 1$, and $z_{k+1} = \tau z_k$, $\tau \geq 1$, the processing times for the above two cases are obtained from Equation (7.2) as follows:

$$T(\Sigma, \alpha) = \frac{C(k)(w_{k+2} + z_{k+2}\delta)(\beta w_k + \tau z_k\delta)(w_k + z_k\delta)w_0 T_{cp}/(\beta w_k^2 w_{k-1})}{\begin{bmatrix} K_1(k) + K_2(k)(w_{k+2} + z_{k+2}\delta)\{1 + (\beta w_k + \tau z_k\delta)/w_k\}/(\beta w_k) \\ + K_3(k)(w_{k+2} + z_{k+2}\delta)(\beta w_k + \tau z_k\delta)(w_k + z_k\delta)/(\beta w_k^2 w_{k-1}) \end{bmatrix}}$$

$$k = 1, \ldots, m - 3 \tag{7.15}$$

$$T(\Sigma_B, \alpha_B) = \frac{C(k)(w_{k+2} + z_{k+2}\delta)(w_k + \tau z_k\delta)(\beta w_k + z_k\delta)w_0 T_{cp}/(\beta w_k^2 w_{k-1})}{\begin{bmatrix} K_1(k) + K_2(k)(w_{k+2} + z_{k+2}\delta)\{1 + (w_k + \tau z_k\delta)/(\beta w_k)\}/w_k \\ + K_3(k)(w_{k+2} + z_{k+2}\delta)(w_k + \tau z_k\delta)(\beta w_k + z_k\delta)/(\beta w_k^2 w_{k-1}) \end{bmatrix}}$$

$$k = 1, \ldots, m - 3 \tag{7.16}$$

Let N_1 and N_2 be the numerators and D_1 and D_2 be the denominators of Equations (7.15) and (7.16), respectively. Then,

$$N_1 D_2 - N_2 D_1 =$$

$$C(k)(w_{k+2} + z_{k+2}\delta) \left\{ K_1(k) + \frac{K_2(k)(w_{k+2} + z_{k+2}\delta)(\beta w_k + w_k + \tau z_k\delta)}{(\beta w_k^2)} \right\}$$

$$\times \frac{\{(1 - \tau)\,(\beta - 1)\,w_k z_k \delta w_0 T_{cp}\}}{(w_{k-1}\beta w_k^2)} \tag{7.17}$$

The $RHS \geq 0$ when $\beta \leq 1$, given that $\tau \geq 1$, thus proving the lemma. $\square$

In the above, the lemma was proved for $k = 1, 2, \ldots, m - 3$. It can be similarly proved for $k = m - 2$ and $m - 1$ using Equations (7.7) through (7.9).

An immediate consequence of the above lemma is the following theorem:

Theorem 7.2. In a single-level tree network Σ, if all the links are identical, that is, $z_i = z$ $(i = 1, 2, \ldots, m)$, then the processing time is independent of the order in which the processors are arranged.

Proof. Suppose the processing time is dependent on the order of arrangement of the processors. Then, since there are only a finite number of possible arrangements ($< m!$), there exists at least one optimal arrangement that yields the minimum processing time. Now consider the fact that any arbitrary arrangement of processors can be obtained from the optimal arrangement by a finite number of interchanges between two adjacent processors. But according to Equation (7.17) in Lemma 7.2, the RHS of this equation is equal to zero when $\tau = 1$ regardless of the value of β. Thus, each such interchange does not affect the processing time. Hence all the arrangements must have the same processing time. This completes the proof of the theorem.   □

The single-level tree network with identical links considered in Theorem 7.2 also serves as a model for a bus network in which a single processor (the root) connected to a bus distributes the load to the other processors (the child processors) connected onto the same bus. Hence, in a bus network the positions of the processors other than the root are immaterial. In fact, this theorem was shown to be true in Chapter 4.

Theorem 7.3.   In a single-level tree network Σ, in order to achieve minimum processing time, the processors and links should be arranged in such a way that $w_{k+1} \geq w_k$ and $z_{k+1} \geq z_k$, for all $k = 1, 2, \ldots, m - 1$.

Proof. We shall prove this theorem by contradiction. Consider a network in which the arrangement of links and processors is such that the conditions stated in the theorem are violated. Assume that this network yields the minimum processing time. By applying Theorem 7.1, we can obtain a network Σ' in which all the links are arranged in order of decreasing speed and gives a better time performance than Σ. We then apply Lemma 7.2 to the network Σ', and obtain a network Σ'', which gives a still better time performance. This contradicts our initial assumption, thus proving the theorem.   □

Theorem 7.3 proposes a method by which minimum processing time can be achieved, provided an architectural rearrangement of links and processors, connected to the root processor, is possible. However, until now we have not included the root processor in the architectural rearrangement. The following lemma deals with this aspect of the problem. Here, we assume that either all the processors are equipped with front ends or that only the root is equipped with a front end and that the front end remains at the root while exchanging the root with a child processor.

Lemma 7.3.   Consider in a single level tree network Σ, in which $w_{k+1} \geq w_k$ and $z_{k+1} \geq z_k$ $(k = 1, 2, \ldots, m - 1)$. If $w_1 \leq w_0$, then the processing time will decrease or remain the same if p_0 and p_1 are interchanged.

Proof. Since the processors and links are arranged so that $w_{k+1} \geq w_k$ and $z_{k+1} \geq z_k$, the fastest link-processor pair will be in the first left position, that is, (l_1, p_1). Suppose we interchange the root processor p_0 with the processor p_1. The resulting arrangement will be as follows:

$$\Sigma_C = \{p_1, (l_1, p_0), (l_2, p_2), \ldots, (l_m, p_m)\} \tag{7.18}$$

Let α and α_C be the optimal load distributions for Σ and Σ_C, respectively. We have to prove that $T(\Sigma_C, \alpha_C) \leq T(\Sigma, \alpha)$ if $w_1 \leq w_0$. For this we use the constants $K_1(k)$ and $K_2(k)$ defined in Equations (7.4) and (7.5) with $k = 0$. Letting $w_0 = \beta w_1, \beta \geq 1$, the processing times $T(\Sigma, \alpha)$ and $T(\Sigma_C, \alpha_C)$ are obtained as follows:

$$T(\Sigma, \alpha) = \frac{K_2(0)(w_2 + z_2\delta)(w_1 + z_1\delta)\beta w_1 T_{cp}/(\beta w_1^2)}{\left[K_1(0) + K_2(0)(w_2 + z_2\delta)\{1 + (w_1 + z_1\delta)/\beta w_1\}w_1\right]} \tag{7.19}$$

$$T(\Sigma_C, \alpha_C) = \frac{K_2(0)(w_2 + z_2\delta)(\beta w_1 + z_1\delta)w_1 T_{cp}/(\beta w_1^2)}{\left[K_1(0) + K_2(0)(w_2 + z_2\delta)\{1 + (\beta w_1 + z_1\delta)/w_1\}/\beta w_1\right]} \quad (7.20)$$

Denoting the numerators as N_1 and N_2 and denominators as D_1 and D_2, respectively, the value of $N_1 D_2 - N_2 D_1$ is obtained as follows:

$$N_1 D_2 - N_2 D_1 = \left\{\frac{K_2(0)K_1(0)(w_2 + z_2\delta)}{(\beta w_1^2)}\right\}$$

$$\times \left[z_1\delta + (w_2 + z_2\delta)\left\{\frac{z_1\delta}{w_1} + \frac{(w_1 + z_1\delta)(\beta w_1 + z_1\delta)}{\beta w_1^2}\right\}\right]$$

$$(\beta - 1)w_1 T_{cp} \quad (7.21)$$

In Equation (7.21), the $RHS \geq 0$ since $\beta \geq 1$, thus proving the Lemma.   □

Note that in Equation (7.21), if $\beta > 1$, then the RHS > 0, implying a strict decrease in the processing time. Using all the above results we state the following theorem:

Theorem 7.4. Optimal Arrangement   Given a set of $(m + 1)$ processors and m links to be arranged in a single-level tree architecture, the processing time will be minimum if the processors and links are arranged in such a way that $w_0 \leq w_1$, $w_{k+1} \geq w_k$, and $z_{k+1} \geq z_k$, $k = 1, 2, \ldots, m - 1$.

Proof.   Proof is immediate from Theorem 7.3 and Lemma 7.3.   □

Theorem 7.4 shows that if it is possible to include the root processor in the rearrangement scheme, then the best performance can be achieved by putting the fastest processor at the root.

In the next section we will show that the results in Lemmas 7.1 and 7.2, and Theorems 7.1 through 7.4, are also valid when the root is not equipped with a front end, though Lemma 7.3 and Theorem 7.4 need not hold true in a general case.

7.3 WITHOUT-FRONT-END PROCESSORS

In this section, as in our discussion of the with-front-end case, we use the closed-form expression derived in Section 5.1.2 to obtain the optimal sequence of load distribution and optimal architectural rearrangement for the without-front-end case. We first prove some intermediate results. For this we use a closed-form solution that was derived by assuming that all the processor-link pairs satisfy the conditions set forth in Equations (5.28) and (5.90). Hence all the processors get nonzero loads, and stop computing at the same instant in time. The closed-form solution $T(\Sigma, \alpha)$ is given by

$$T(\Sigma, \alpha) = \frac{C(k)(w_{k+2} + z_{k+2}\delta)(w_{k+1} + z_{k+1}\delta)(w_k + z_k\delta)w_0 T_{cp}/(w_{k+1}w_k w_{k-1})}{\left[\begin{array}{c} M_1(k) + K_2(k)(w_{k+2} + z_{k+2}\delta)\{1 + (w_{k+1} + z_{k+1}\delta)/w_k\}/w_{k+1} \\ + M_2(k)(w_{k+2} + z_{k+2}\delta)(w_{k+1} + z_{k+1}\delta)(w_k + z_k\delta)/(w_{k+1}w_k w_{k-1}) \end{array}\right]}$$

$$k = 2, \ldots, m - 3 \quad (7.22)$$

where

$$M_1(k) = K_1(k) + \frac{w_m}{w_0} \qquad (7.23)$$

$$M_2(k) = \sum_{i=1}^{k-1} \prod_{\substack{j=i+1 \\ j \neq k, k+1, k+2}}^{m} f_j \qquad (7.24)$$

These constants are valid for $k = 2, 3, \ldots, m-2$. As in the with- front-end case, the processing time for the left and right extremes of the tree are as follows: For $k = 1$,

$$T(\Sigma, \alpha) = \left\{ \frac{K_2(1) f_3 f_2 f_1}{M_1(1) + K_2(1) f_2 f_3 + K_2(1) f_3} \right\} w_0 T_{cp} \qquad (7.25)$$

and for $k = m - 2, m - 1$,

$$T(\Sigma, \alpha) = \left\{ \frac{D(k) f_k f_{k+1} \cdots f_m}{1 + (w_m/w_0) + K_5(k) f_k \cdots f_m + f_{k+1} \cdots f_m + \cdots + f_m} \right\} w_0 T_{cp} \qquad (7.26)$$

where

$$K_5(k) = 1 + \sum_{i=2}^{k-1} \prod_{j=i}^{k-1} f_j \qquad (7.27)$$

It may be noted that Equations (7.2) and (7.22) have the same structure except for some of the constants. Hence, in the without-front-end case, Lemmas 7.1 and 7.2, and Theorems 7.1, 7.2, and 7.3, are still valid. While proving these lemmas the condition set forth in Equation (5.90) continues to be satisfied for all the processor-link pairs. These observations imply that even when the root processor is not equipped with a front end, the optimal sequence of load distribution, and the optimal arrangement of links and child processors, remains the same as in the with-front-end case, that is, the optimal sequence of load distribution follows the order in which the link speeds decrease (Theorem 7.1), and the optimal architectural rearrangement follows the order in which both the link speeds and the child processor speeds decrease (Theorem 7.3). Moreover, when the links are identical, the arrangement of the child processors does not affect the processing time (Theorem 7.2). When the root processor is also considered during the architectural rearrangement, the results obtained in the with-front-end case are valid for the without-front-end case only when the links are identical. However, this result requires a slightly different proof.

Lemma 7.4.   Consider in a single-level tree network Σ, with $w_{k+1} \geq w_k$ ($k = 1, 2, \ldots, m-1$) and $z_k = z$ ($k = 1, 2, \ldots, m$). If $w_1 \leq w_0$ then the minimum processing time will decrease or remain the same by interchanging the root processor p_0 with the first left-hand side processor p_1.

Proof. Interchanging p_1 and p_0, we get the following configuration:

$$\Sigma_D = \{p_1, (l_1, p_0), (l_2, p_2), \ldots, (l_m, p_m)\} \qquad (7.28)$$

Let α and α_D be the optimal load distributions for Σ and Σ_D, respectively. We have to prove that $T(\Sigma_D, \alpha_D) \leq T(\Sigma, \alpha)$ if $w_1 \leq w_0$. We define the following constants:

$$N = (w_2 + z_2\delta)K_2(0) \tag{7.29}$$

$$X = 1 + \sum_{i=2}^{m-1} \prod_{j=i+1}^{m} f_j \tag{7.30}$$

Using this, the closed-form expression for $T(\Sigma, \alpha)$ can now be written as

$$T(\Sigma, \alpha) = \frac{\left(\frac{N}{w_1}\right)\left(\frac{w_1+z\delta}{w_0}\right)w_0 T_{cp}}{X + \frac{w_m}{w_0} + \frac{N}{w_1}} \tag{7.31}$$

As mentioned earlier, so far we have assumed that Equations (5.28) and (5.90) are satisfied for the initial arrangement Σ. However, when p_1 and p_0 are interchanged Equation (5.90) may no longer be valid. Thus we have two cases.

Case i. $w_1 > z\delta$. Then, the expression for $T(\Sigma_D, \alpha_D)$ is

$$T(\Sigma_D, \alpha_D) = \frac{\left(\frac{N}{w_0}\right)\left(\frac{w_0+z\delta}{w_1}\right)w_1 T_{cp}}{X + \frac{w_m}{w_1} + \frac{N}{w_0}} \tag{7.32}$$

Let us denote the numerators of Equations (7.31) and (7.32) as N_1 and N_2, and the denominators as D_1 and D_2, respectively.

$$N_1 D_2 - N_2 D_1 = \left(\frac{N}{(w_1 w_0)}\right)\left[z\delta X + w_m\left\{1 + z\delta\left(\frac{w_0+w_1}{w_1 w_0}\right)\right\} - N\right](w_0 - w_1) \tag{7.33}$$

which can be further reduced to

$$N_1 D_2 - N_2 D_1 = \left(\frac{N}{w_0 w_1}\right)\left\{z\delta + w_m z\delta\left(\frac{w_0+w_1}{w_0 w_1}\right)\right\}(w_0 - w_1) \tag{7.34}$$

In Equation (7.34), the RHS ≥ 0 if $w_0 \geq w_1$, which proves the lemma.

Case ii. $w_1 \leq z\delta$. The processing time is

$$T(\Sigma_D, \alpha_D) = w_1 T_{cp} \tag{7.35}$$

This happens because $w_1 \leq z\delta$, which violates Equation (5.90). Thus, the root does not distribute any load to the child processors. We have to prove that $T(\Sigma_D, \alpha_D) \leq T(\Sigma, \alpha)$, if $w_1 \leq w_0$. From Equations (7.31) and (7.35), we get

$$T(\Sigma, \alpha) - T(\Sigma_D, \alpha_D) = \left(\frac{N}{w_1}\right)\left(1 - \frac{w_1}{z\delta}\right)(w_1 + z\delta) - w_1 w_m\left(\frac{1}{w_0} - \frac{1}{z\delta}\right) \tag{7.36}$$

In Equation (7.36) the $RHS \geq 0$ if $w_1 \leq z\delta$ and $w_0 \geq z\delta$, thus proving the lemma. □

It may be observed that in the above proof, since all the link speeds are equal, Equation (5.28) is automatically satisfied. The natural extension of this lemma is the following theorem.

Theorem 7.5. Optimal Arrangement for Equal Link Speeds   Given a set of $(m + 1)$ processors with arbitrary speeds and m links with equal speeds, to be arranged in a single-level tree architecture, the processing time will be minimum if the fastest processor is at the root.

Proof. The proof follows immediately from Lemma 7.4.   □

Note that the result in Theorem 7.5 is valid even for the with-front-end case since it is a special case of Theorem 7.4. Also, when the conditions of Theorem 7.5 are satisfied, the best performance is achieved, irrespective of the arrangement of child processors, so long as the root processor is the fastest.

Unlike the with-front-end case, when the link speeds are different, the fastest processor need not be the root processor in order to achieve minimum processing time. This is shown with an example in the ensuing section. It is not possible to arrive at a simple condition (as in Theorem 7.4) to determine the root processor in the without-front-end case. Therefore, we propose the following algorithm to achieve an optimal arrangement in this case.

Algorithm 7.1.   Let there be $(m + 1)$ processors and m links with different speeds. We denote the root processor as p_r and its corresponding speed parameter as w_r.

Step 0.   Arrange the processors and links such that $w_0 \leq w_1$, $w_k \leq w_{k+1}$, $z_k \leq z_{k+1}$, for $k = 1, 2, \ldots, m - 1$, where w_0 is the speed parameter of the root processor in this initial arrangement.

Step 1.   Set $w_r = w_0$.
Delete all links l_i for which $w_r \leq z_i \delta$. Denote the new network as Σ_0.
Compute $T(\Sigma_0, \alpha^0)$, where α^0 is the optimal load distribution for Σ_0.
Restore the deleted links.
Set $k = 1$.

Step 2.   Interchange p_k and p_r.
Set $w_r = w_k$.
Delete all links l_i for which $w_r \leq z_i \delta$. Denote this network as Σ_k.
Compute $T(\Sigma_k, \alpha^k)$, where α^k is the optimal load distribution for Σ_k.
Restore the deleted links.
$k = k + 1$.
If $k \leq m$ go to Step 2.

Step 3.   Find $j = \arg \min_{0 \leq k \leq m} T(\Sigma_k, \alpha^k)$
The configuration Σ_j is the optimal arrangement.

It should be noted that this algorithm starts with a network in which all the links and child processors are arranged in order of decreasing speed, and this condition continues to hold throughout the execution of the algorithm. Hence, Equation (5.28) is always satisfied by all the processor-link pairs.

7.4 ILLUSTRATIVE EXAMPLES

In this section we present some illustrative numerical examples for the results proved in the previous sections.

Example 7.2   (*With Front End*)

The processor and link speed parameters for several single-level tree networks and the corresponding processing times are shown in Table 7.1. Case I shows the initial arrangement of processors and links. In Case II, we interchange the links l_1 and l_2, and p_1 and p_2, simultaneously (Lemma 7.1). The processing time in Case II is less than that in Case I. Now, if architectural rearrangement is not possible, then Case II also gives the optimal sequence in which the load should be distributed by the root processor (Theorem 7.1). Next, if architectural rearrangement is possible, then by applying Lemma 7.2, we see (in Case III) that by interchanging the processors p_1 and p_2 we get a further decrease in the processing time. In fact this is the best performance that can be obtained if the processor at the root is not disturbed (Theorem 7.3). Cases IV through VI in Table 7.1 demonstrate the repeated application of Lemmas 7.2 and 7.3 to obtain an optimal arrangement of processors and links as prescribed by Theorem 7.4.

TABLE 7.1   Root Processor with Front End

Case	w_0	w_1	w_2	w_3	z_1	z_2	z_3	$T(\Sigma, \alpha)$
			$T_{cm} = 1.0$, $T_{cp} = 2.0$, $\delta = 0.5$					
I	0.6	0.2	0.3	0.5	0.2	0.1	0.3	0.256941
II	0.6	0.3	0.2	0.5	0.1	0.2	0.3	0.242128
III	0.6	0.2	0.3	0.5	0.1	0.2	0.3	0.232835
IV	0.2	0.6	0.3	0.5	0.1	0.2	0.3	0.201791
V	0.2	0.3	0.6	0.5	0.1	0.2	0.3	0.195849
VI	0.2	0.3	0.5	0.6	0.1	0.2	0.3	0.195348

Example 7.3   (*Without Front End*)

The same network as in the previous example, but without front ends, is considered here. The results are shown in Table 7.2. The discussions for Cases I through III in the table are identical to those for the case in which the root processor is equipped with a front end. Case IV considers the network in which all the links have the same speed. Case V, in which the processor arrangement is as prescribed by Theorem 7.5, yields

TABLE 7.2   Root Processor Without-Front-End

Case	w_0	w_1	w_2	w_3	z_1	z_2	z_3	$T(\Sigma, \alpha)$
			$T_{cm} = 1.0$, $T_{cp} = 2.0$, $\delta = 0.5$					
I	0.6	0.2	0.3	0.5	0.2	0.1	0.3	0.291978
II	0.6	0.3	0.2	0.5	0.1	0.2	0.3	0.273000
III	0.6	0.2	0.3	0.5	0.1	0.2	0.3	0.260000
IV	0.6	0.2	0.3	0.5	0.1	0.1	0.1	0.233333
V	0.2	0.3	0.5	0.6	0.1	0.2	0.3	0.217136

the minimum processing time. Note that in these examples the condition set forth in Equation (5.90) is satisfied for all i ($i = 1, 2, 3$).

Earlier we stated that, in the without-front-end case, when all the links have different speeds, the root processor need not be the fastest of all the processors in order to achieve the minimum processing time. The example that follows clearly demonstrates this fact.

Example 7.4 (*Without Front End*)

This example illustrates all the steps of the algorithm proposed in Section 7.3 and the results are shown in Table 7.3. Here, initially the processors and the links have been arranged in order of decreasing speed, with the root as the fastest processor. For $k = 1$ and 2, Step 2 of the algorithm is carried out. Finally, in Step 3 we choose the arrangement that gives the minimum processing time (given by $k = 1$). Note that the processing time is minimum for a case in which the root processor is not the fastest.

TABLE 7.3   Optimal Arrangement for Without-Front-End Case

	$T_{cm} = 0.2$, $T_{cp} = 2.0$, $\delta = 0.1$					
k	w_0	w_1	w_2	z_1	z_2	$\Gamma(T(p_k))$
0	1.0	1.5	3.0	1.0	8.0	1.240816
1	1.5	1.0	3.0	1.0	8.0	1.229411
2	3.0	1.0	1.5	1.0	8.0	1.331578

7.5 CONCLUDING REMARKS

The following are the highlights of this chapter:

- Analytical proofs were presented for several numerical results obtained in Chapter 4.

- It was proved that when architectural rearrangement is not possible the best performance is obtained when the load distribution follows the sequence in which the link speeds decrease.

- It was shown that when all the link speeds are identical (bus network), the processing time is independent of the order in which the processors are arranged.

- It was shown that if architectural rearrangement of processors and links is allowed, then in the with-front-end case, the best time performance is obtained when all the processors and links are arranged in the order of decreasing speeds, and the fastest processor is at the root. However, in the without-front-end case, the arrangement of child processors follows a decreasing order of processor and link speeds, but the root processor need not be the fastest.

- An algorithm was proposed to obtain the best architectural rearrangement for the without-front-end case.

In the next chapter we will explore the ultimate performance limits of single-level tree and linear networks, using the load distribution strategy discussed in all the previous chapters, with respect to the network parameters and the number of processors.

BIBLIOGRAPHIC NOTES

Section 7.2   Rigorous proofs for the results given in this chapter are from Bharadwaj et al. (1992a, 1994). The optimal sequence theorem has also been proved by Kim et al. (1996), but in a restricted sense. Their proof implicitly assumes that Equation (5.28) is always satisfied by all the processor-link pairs in the network while interchanging any two links. Moreover, their proof is valid only for the with-front-end case. Some numerical results to substantiate the statement of Theorem 7.2 were given by Bataineh and Robertazzi (1991). They also proved this result for a three processor bus network. The optimal arrangement result (without including the root processor) was obtained only for the with-front-end case by Kim et al. (1993), but again with the assumption that Equation (5.28) is always satisfied. A point worth mentioning here is that interchange arguments similar to the ones used in this chapter are also commonly used to prove many optimality results in classical scheduling theory [Stankovic et al. (1995)].

Section 7.3   The results for the without-front-end case are also mainly from Bharadwaj et al. (1992a, 1994). However, in the special case of a bus network, these results were observed in the numerical simulations by Bataineh and Robertazzi (1991). They had conjectured that in such architectures the fastest processor should be at the root to achieve minimum processing time.

CHAPTER **8**

Asymptotic Performance Analysis: Linear and Tree Networks

In earlier chapters, we derived optimality conditions and closed-form expressions for the determination of the optimal load fractions in linear and tree networks. In Chapters 3 and 4, the numerical results showed that increasing the number of processors beyond a certain limit did not improve the performance of the network significantly. This was due to the deleterious effect of communication delay. These results could be obtained only after a considerable amount of computation. A certain amount of analytical support for the results on ultimate performance limits of processors was also obtained through the concept of processor equivalence in linear and tree networks. In this chapter, we carry out an elaborate analysis of the load distribution process and obtain these and many other important results through a formal asymptotic analysis of the load distribution equations. This asymptotic performance analysis also provides definitive answers to the following questions:

(i) By how much does the processing time reduce if an existing network is augmented by a specific number of additional processors?

(ii) How does the network performance change if the speed of all the processors and/or links are varied?

Further, the asymptotic performance analysis is useful in obtaining the cost-benefit analysis and trade-off relationships between the cost of enhancing the capability of each individual element in an existing network and the corresponding reduction in processing time.

As in the previous chapters, here we have organized the material in terms of the cases being considered (linear/tree, with/without front ends).

8.1 DEFINITIONS AND SOME REMARKS

We consider a network of m processors attached to the root in a linear and tree configuration as described in earlier chapters. All the processors in the network are identical and all the links are also identical (that is, we consider a homogeneous network). A system of m processors or an m-processor system essentially means a root processor to which m processors are attached in a linear fashion (for a linear network) or m child processors are attached in a single-level tree configuration (for a tree network). Thus, essentially, an m-processor network contains a total of $(m + 1)$ processors. In this chapter, we will denote the processing time of an m-processor system as $T(m)$. Note that the processing time referred to here is the optimal processing time obtained by applying the optimality conditions given in Chapter 5. Below we define some additional terms that will be used to denote measures of system performance.

(i) *Speedup*: Let $S(m, m + m_1)$ denote the speedup achieved by adding m_1 processors to an existing m processor system. Then the speedup is defined as

$$S(m, m + m_1) = \frac{T(m)}{T(m + m_1)} \tag{8.1}$$

(ii) *Fractional Saving in Computation Time*: Another useful measure of performance is the fractional saving in computation time when m_1 additional processors are added to the existing m-processor system. The fractional saving in computation time, denoted by $P(m, m + m_1)$, is defined as

$$P(m, m + m_1) = \frac{T(m) - T(m + m_1)}{T(m)} \tag{8.2}$$

One may also define another quantity called the *Percentage saving in computation time*, which can be obtained by multiplying the fractional saving in computation time by 100. Equation (8.1) can also be written as

$$S(m, m + m_1) = \frac{\left\{ \frac{T(0)}{T(m+m_1)} \right\}}{\left\{ \frac{T(0)}{T(m)} \right\}} \tag{8.3}$$

Hence

$$S(m, m + m_1) = \frac{S(0, m + m_1)}{S(0, m)} \tag{8.4}$$

with $S(0, 0) = 1$. Using Equations (8.1) and (8.4), the fractional saving can be expressed as

$$P(m, m + m_1) = 1 - \left\{ \frac{S(0, m)}{S(0, m + m_1)} \right\} \tag{8.5}$$

The performance measure $S(m, m + m_1)$ is important in the case of networks that process large quantities of load arriving at frequent intervals. Here, $S(m, m+m_1)$

denotes the factor of increase in the amount of load that can be processed by the network in a given interval of time. The performance measure $P(m, m + m_1)$ is important in those networks whose computational output is required elsewhere for further processing. Here, $P(m, m + m_1)$ denotes the factor of time saved in providing the required output.

In the next sections, we derive the load distribution equations for linear and tree networks (for processors equipped with and without front ends) with the assumptions that the optimality conditions derived in Chapter 5 hold and all the processors stop computing at the same time instant.

8.2 LINEAR NETWORKS WITH FRONT ENDS

In this section, we will consider linear networks in which all processors are equipped with front ends.

8.2.1 Closed-Form Expressions

The timing diagram for this case is the same as Figure 3.7 with $z_i = z$ and $w_i = w$, for all i. The governing equations are:

$$\alpha_i w T_{cp} = (1 - \alpha_0 - \alpha_1 - \cdots - \alpha_i) z T_{cm} + \alpha_{i+1} w T_{cp}, \quad i = 0, 1, \ldots, m - 1 \quad (8.6)$$

The normalizing equation is

$$\alpha_0 + \alpha_1 + \cdots + \alpha_m = 1 \quad (8.7)$$

Equation (8.6) can be rewritten as

$$\alpha_i = (1 - \alpha_0 - \alpha_1 - \cdots - \alpha_i)\sigma + \alpha_{i+1}, \quad i = 0, 1, \ldots, m - 1 \quad (8.8)$$

where

$$\sigma = \frac{z T_{cm}}{w T_{cp}} \quad (8.9)$$

is the network parameter defined in Chapter 2. Equations (8.7) and (8.8) can be solved recursively by expressing all α_i ($i = 0, 1, \ldots, m - 1$) in terms of α_m and substituting in Equation (8.7). This operation yields the closed-form solution (Chapter 6),

$$\alpha_i = \frac{f_i(m, \sigma)}{\sum_{i=0}^{m} f_i(m, \sigma)} \quad (8.10)$$

where

$$f_i(m, \sigma) = c(i, 0)\sigma^0 + c(i, 1)\sigma^1 + \cdots + c(i, j)\sigma^j + \cdots + c(i, m - i)\sigma^{m-i} \quad (8.11)$$

The function $f_i(m, \sigma)$ is a polynomial of $(m - i)$th degree and the coefficient of σ^i in the function $f_i(m, \sigma)$ is given by

$$c(i, j) = \frac{(m - i + j)!}{(2j)!(m - i - j)!}, \quad i = 0, \ldots, m \text{ and } j \leq (m - i) \quad (8.12)$$

Note that the $f_i(m, \sigma)$ defined here is the same as the $f_{m-i}(\sigma)$ defined in Chapter 6. This equivalence arises from the fact that in Chapter 6 the processors were numbered from the last to the root (after transformation from α to β), whereas here the original sequence of numbering is preserved. Equations (8.10) through (8.12) are sufficient to obtain the optimal load distribution in an m-processor linear network. However, we will not make an explicit use of the closed-form expression in the ensuing analysis. From the timing diagram shown in Figure 3.7, the time taken to complete a *unit* computational load assigned to a network with m processors connected to the root in a linear array is given by

$$
\begin{aligned}
T(m) &= \alpha_0 w T_{cp} \\
&= \left\{ \frac{f_0(m, \sigma)}{\sum_{i=0}^{m} f_i(m, \sigma)} \right\} w T_{cp}
\end{aligned}
\tag{8.13}
$$

Note that $T(0) = w T_{cp}$ is the time taken by the root processor alone to process the entire load. Thus, the speedup achieved by using m extra processors along with the root processor is given by

$$
S(0, m) = \frac{\sum_{i=0}^{m} f_i(m, \sigma)}{f_0(m, \sigma)}
\tag{8.14}
$$

8.2.2 Asymptotic Analysis

Here we examine the behavior of $S(m, m + m_1)$ and $P(m, m + m_1)$ as $m_1 \to \infty$. Consider a linear network with m processors connected to the root. Substituting $i = 0$ in Equation (8.8) we obtain,

$$
\alpha_0 = (1 - \alpha_0)\sigma + \alpha_1
\tag{8.15}
$$

Substituting Equation (8.10), the above expression can be rewritten as

$$
\sum_{i=0}^{m} f_i(m, \sigma) = f_0(m, \sigma) + \left(\frac{1}{\sigma} \right) \{ f_0(m, \sigma) - f_1(m, \sigma) \}
\tag{8.16}
$$

Using the above, $S(0, m)$ from Equation (8.14) can be rewritten as

$$
S(0, m) = 1 + \left(\frac{1}{\sigma} \right) \left\{ 1 - \frac{f_1(m, \sigma)}{f_0(m, \sigma)} \right\}
\tag{8.17}
$$

Thus,

$$
\lim_{m \to \infty} S(0, m) = 1 + \left(\frac{1}{\sigma} \right) \left\{ 1 - \lim_{m \to \infty} \frac{f_1(m, \sigma)}{f_0(m, \sigma)} \right\}
\tag{8.18}
$$

and is denoted by $S(0, \infty)$. Now, substituting $i = k$ and $i = k + 1$ in Equation (8.8), using Equation (8.10), and performing some simple algebraic manipulations we obtain the following recursive relationship:

$$
\frac{f_{k+1}(m, \sigma)}{f_k(m, \sigma)} = \frac{1}{\left\{ (2 + \sigma) - \frac{f_{k+2}(m, \sigma)}{f_{k+1}(m, \sigma)} \right\}}
\tag{8.19}
$$

Now substituting $k = 0, 1, 2, \ldots$ and so on successively in Equation (8.19) we obtain the following expression which extends to infinity provided that $m \to \infty$. Thus,

$$\lim_{m \to \infty} \frac{f_1(m, \sigma)}{f_0(m, \sigma)} = \cfrac{1}{(2 + \sigma) - \cfrac{1}{(2 + \sigma) - \cfrac{1}{(2 + \sigma) - \cdots}}} \tag{8.20}$$

which is in the form of a continued fraction and can be easily solved to yield

$$\lim_{m \to \infty} \frac{f_1(m, \sigma)}{f_0(m, \sigma)} = 1 + \left(\frac{1}{2}\right) \left\{\sigma - \sqrt{\sigma(\sigma + 4)}\right\} \tag{8.21}$$

from which

$$S(0, \infty) = \left(\frac{1}{2}\right) \left\{1 + \sqrt{1 + \frac{4}{\sigma}}\right\} \tag{8.22}$$

The variation in $S(0, m)$ with m can be obtained from the following recursive relationship, which can be obtained by substituting Equation (8.19) into Equation (8.17) and noting that $f_1(m, \sigma) = f_0(m - 1, \sigma)$ and $f_2(m, \sigma) = f_1(m - 1, \sigma)$:

$$S(0, m) = \frac{1 + (\sigma + 1)S(0, m - 1)}{1 + \sigma S(0, m - 1)} \tag{8.23}$$

with $S(0, 0) = 1$. From Equation (8.4),

$$\lim_{m_1 \to \infty} S(m, m + m_1) = \left\{\frac{1}{S(0, m)}\right\} \lim_{m_1 \to \infty} S(0, m + m_1) \tag{8.24}$$

we define

$$\lim_{m_1 \to \infty} S(m, m + m_1) = S(m, \infty) \tag{8.25}$$

and rewrite Equation (8.24) as

$$S(m, \infty) = \frac{S(0, \infty)}{S(0, m)} \tag{8.26}$$

where $S(0, m)$ can be calculated using Equation (8.23). Similarly, denoting

$$\lim_{m_1 \to \infty} P(m, m + m_1) = P(m, \infty) \tag{8.27}$$

we get

$$P(m, \infty) = 1 - \frac{S(0, m)}{S(0, \infty)} \tag{8.28}$$

from which we obtain

$$P(0, \infty) = 1 + \left(\frac{\sigma}{2}\right) \left\{1 - \sqrt{1 + \frac{4}{\sigma}}\right\} \tag{8.29}$$

Using Equation (8.23) we can also derive the recursive relation

$$P(0, m) = \frac{1}{(2 + \sigma) - P(0, m - 1)} \tag{8.30}$$

Let α_i^m denote the computational load assigned to the ith processor when there are m processors connected to the root. Let us denote

$$\lim_{m \to \infty} \alpha_i^m = \alpha_i^\infty \tag{8.31}$$

Then,

$$\alpha_i^\infty = \lim_{m \to \infty} \left\{ \frac{f_i(m, \sigma)}{\sum_{i=0}^m f_i(m, \sigma)} \right\} \tag{8.32}$$

which can also be written as

$$
\begin{aligned}
\alpha_i^\infty &= \lim_{m \to \infty} \left[\left\{ \frac{f_{i-1}(m, \sigma)}{\sum_{i=0}^m f_i(m, \sigma)} \right\} \left\{ \frac{f_i(m, \sigma)}{f_{i-1}(m, \sigma)} \right\} \right] \\
&= \lim_{m \to \infty} \left\{ \frac{f_{i-1}(m, \sigma)}{\sum_{i=0}^m f_i(m, \sigma)} \right\} \lim_{m \to \infty} \left\{ \frac{f_i(m, \sigma)}{f_{i-1}(m, \sigma)} \right\} \\
&= \alpha_{i-1}^\infty \lim_{m \to \infty} \left\{ \frac{f_i(m, \sigma)}{f_{i-1}(m, \sigma)} \right\}
\end{aligned}
\tag{8.33}
$$

From Equation (8.19) we again obtain the same continued fraction, which can be solved to yield

$$\lim_{m \to \infty} \left\{ \frac{f_i(m, \sigma)}{f_{i-1}(m, \sigma)} \right\} = 1 + \left(\frac{1}{2} \right) \left\{ \sigma - \sqrt{\sigma(\sigma + 4)} \right\} \tag{8.34}$$

Equation (8.34) can now be restated as

$$\alpha_i^\infty = \alpha_{i-1}^\infty \left\{ 1 + \frac{\left\{ \sigma - \sqrt{\sigma(\sigma + 4)} \right\}}{2} \right\} \tag{8.35}$$

where

$$\alpha_0^\infty = \frac{1}{S(0, \infty)} = \frac{1}{\frac{1}{2} \left\{ 1 + \sqrt{1 + (4/\sigma)} \right\}} \tag{8.36}$$

Thus,

$$\alpha_i^\infty = \frac{\left[1 + \left\{ \sigma - \sqrt{\sigma(\sigma + 4)} \right\}/2 \right]^i}{\left\{ 1 + \sqrt{1 + (4/\sigma)} \right\} / 2} \tag{8.37}$$

which can be further simplified to yield

$$\alpha_i^\infty = \frac{\left\{ 1 - \frac{1}{S(0, \infty)} \right\}^i}{S(0, \infty)} \tag{8.38}$$

Equation (8.38) gives the optimal load distribution to the ith processor as $m \to \infty$. Thus, the load assigned to the ith processor asymptotically approaches the value α_i^∞ as the number of processors increases in the linear network.

8.2.3 Analysis of the Results

The results obtained above in the asymptotic analysis are significant in many ways. The parameter σ defined in Equation (8.9) has the following interpretation. It is the ratio of the time delay in transmitting the entire load through one communication channel and the time taken to process the same load in one processor. Figure 8.1 shows that the speedup is higher for low values of σ but quickly levels off to a value given by Equation (8.22). Thus, the best speedup can be achieved by adding just a few processors to the root. For example, for $\sigma = 0.1$, about four or five processors are enough to obtain more than 90 percent of the maximum speedup possible.

In view of the above, in an existing linear network having a sufficient number of processors attached to the root, it might be wiser to invest in obtaining better communication channels (that is, lowering the value of z and hence σ) rather than investing in more processors. Letting

$$\sigma = \frac{1}{2^q} \tag{8.39}$$

we can obtain a relationship between $S(0, m)$ and q, which would show the variation in speedup achieved, by adding m processors to the root with improved communication channel performance. This can be obtained recursively by using Equation (8.23):

$$S(0, m) = \frac{1 + (1 + 1/2^q)S(0, m - 1)}{1 + (1/2^q)S(0, m - 1)} \tag{8.40}$$

with $S(0, 0) = 1$. It can be easily seen that

$$\lim_{q \to \infty} S(0, m) = m + 1 \tag{8.41}$$

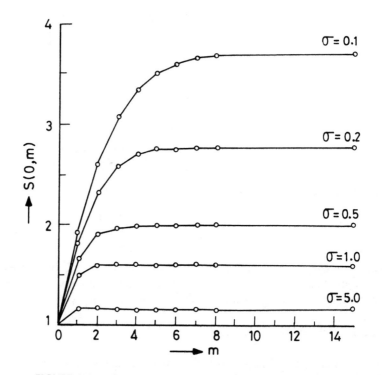

FIGURE 8.1 $S(0, m)$ and m for a Linear Network (with Front End)

This demonstrates the obvious result that when the communication delay approaches zero, the processing load is shared equally by all processors. Hence, the maximum achievable speedup possible by using $m+1$ processors is $m+1$. From Equation (8.22), we have

$$S(0, \infty) = \frac{1}{2} \left\{ 1 + \sqrt{1 + 2^{q+2}} \right\} \qquad (8.42)$$

Thus as $q \to \infty$, $S(0, \infty) \to \infty$. For high values of $q > 0$, it is easy to see that

$$S(0, \infty) \approx 2^{q/2} = \frac{1}{\sqrt{\sigma}} \qquad (8.43)$$

The above equation implies that for large values of m and q, when the communication delay is halved, the speedup achieved increases by a factor of about $\sqrt{2}$. Figure 8.2 shows the variation in $S(0, m)$ with q for various values of m. The load distribution to individual processors as $m \to \infty$ can be found from Equations (8.37) and (8.39). For $\sigma = 0.25$, we have $\alpha_0^\infty = 39.6\%$, $\alpha_1^\infty = 23.8\%$, $\alpha_2^\infty = 14.5\%$, $\alpha_3^\infty = 8.84\%$, and $\alpha_4^\infty = 5.38\%$. This accounts for more than 90% of the load. For higher values of σ an even lesser number of processors share a large portion of the load. Thus, when there is a large number of processors, the processors after the first few are not utilized efficiently.

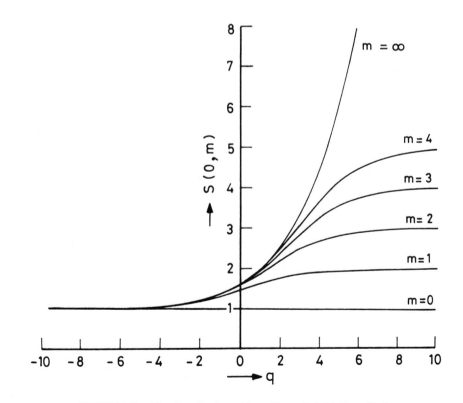

FIGURE 8.2 $S(0, m)$ and q for a Linear Network (with Front End)

8.3 LINEAR NETWORKS WITHOUT FRONT ENDS

In this section we will consider a linear network in which the processors are not equipped with front ends.

8.3.1 Closed-Form Expressions

The timing diagram for this case is as shown in Figure 3.9 with $z_i = z$ and $w_i = w$, for all i. In this model we have the additional assumption that

$$\sigma < 1 \tag{8.44}$$

is satisfied by the network parameter. This assumption is needed here; otherwise a processor need not send the load to its immediate successor (see Chapter 5). The load distribution equations are as follows:

$$\alpha_i = (1 - \alpha_0 - \alpha_1 - \cdots - \alpha_{i+1})\sigma + \alpha_{i+1}, \quad i = 0, \ldots, m-1 \tag{8.45}$$

As before, Equation (8.45) along with the normalizing equation can be solved in the closed form by expressing all α_i $(i = 0, 1, \ldots, m-1)$ in terms of α_m. This operation yields

$$\alpha_i = \frac{g_i(m, \sigma)}{\sum_{i=0}^m g_i(m, \sigma)}, \quad i = 0, 1, \ldots, m \tag{8.46}$$

where

$$g_i(m, \sigma) = d(i, 0)\sigma^0 + d(i, 1)\sigma^1 + \cdots + d(i, b)\sigma^b \tag{8.47}$$

with

$$b = (m - i) \text{ div } 2 \tag{8.48}$$

and

$$d(i, j) = \frac{(m - i)!}{(2j)!(m - i - 2j)!} \tag{8.49}$$

These equations were derived in Chapter 6 and can be used to obtain optimal load distribution among the $(m + 1)$ processors in a given linear network of processors without front ends. However, we will not make explicit use of this closed-form expression in the subsequent analysis. The time taken to complete a computational task assigned to a linear network of m processors attached to the root can be obtained as

$$
\begin{aligned}
T(m) &= (1 - \alpha_0)zT_{cm} + \alpha_0 wT_{cp} \\
&= zT_{cm} + \alpha_0(wT_{cp} - zT_{cm}) \\
&= \{\sigma + (1 - \sigma)\alpha_0\}wT_{cp} \\
&= \left\{\sigma + \frac{(1 - \sigma)g_0(m, \sigma)}{\sum_{i=0}^m g_i(m, \sigma)}\right\} wT_{cp}
\end{aligned}
\tag{8.50}
$$

Here, $T(0) = wT_{cp}$ is the time taken by the root processor alone to process the entire load. The speedup achieved by connecting m_1 additional processors to an existing

m-processor linear network is $S(m, m + m_1)$, and is given by Equation (8.1). Thus,

$$S(0, m) = \cfrac{1}{\left\{\sigma + (1 - \sigma)\cfrac{g_0(m, \sigma)}{\sum_{i=0}^{m} g_i(m, \sigma)}\right\}} \tag{8.51}$$

From Equation (8.51) one may also derive $P(m, m + m_1)$, given in Equation (8.2).

8.3.2 Asymptotic Analysis

We will examine the behavior of $S(m, m + m_1)$ and $P(m, m + m_1)$ as $m_1 \to \infty$. Again, consider a linear network with m processors attached to the root. Substituting $i = 0$ in Equation (8.45), we get

$$\alpha_0 = (1 - \alpha_0 - \alpha_1)\sigma + \alpha_1 \tag{8.52}$$

Substituting Equation (8.46) we obtain

$$\frac{\sum_{i=0}^{m} g_i(m, \sigma)}{g_0(m, \sigma)} = \left(1 + \frac{1}{\sigma}\right) + \left(1 - \frac{1}{\sigma}\right)\left\{\frac{g_1(m, \sigma)}{g_0(m, \sigma)}\right\} \tag{8.53}$$

Now, substituting $i = k$ and $k + 1$ in Equation (8.45) and performing some simple algebraic manipulations, we obtain the following recursive relationship:

$$\frac{g_{k+1}(m, \sigma)}{g_k(m, \sigma)} = \cfrac{1}{2 - (1 - \sigma)\left\{\frac{g_{k+2}(m, \sigma)}{g_{k+1}(m, \sigma)}\right\}} \tag{8.54}$$

Thus, using the same argument as in the with-front-end case and substituting $k = 0, 1, 2, \ldots$ and so on successively, we get

$$\lim_{m \to \infty} \frac{g_1(m, \sigma)}{g_0(m, \sigma)} = \cfrac{1}{2 - (1 - \sigma)\cfrac{1}{2 - (1 - \sigma)\cfrac{1}{2 - \cdots}}} \tag{8.55}$$

which is a continued fraction and can be solved to yield

$$\lim_{m \to \infty} \frac{g_1(m, \sigma)}{g_0(m, \sigma)} = \frac{1}{1 + \sqrt{\sigma}} \tag{8.56}$$

From this, using Equation (8.53), we get

$$\lim_{m \to \infty} \frac{\sum_{i=0}^{m} g_i(m, \sigma)}{g_0(m, \sigma)} = \left(1 + \frac{1}{\sigma}\right) + \left(1 - \frac{1}{\sigma}\right)\lim_{m \to \infty}\left\{\frac{g_1(m, \sigma)}{g_0(m, \sigma)}\right\}$$

$$= 1 + \frac{1}{\sqrt{\sigma}} \tag{8.57}$$

and therefore, from Equation (8.51),

$$\lim_{m \to \infty} S(0, m) = S(0, \infty) = \frac{1}{\sqrt{\sigma}} \tag{8.58}$$

The variation of $S(0, m)$ with m is obtained as

$$S(0, m) = \frac{1 + S(0, m - 1)}{1 + \sigma S(0, m - 1)} \qquad (8.59)$$

with $S(0, 0) = 1$. Therefore,

$$\lim_{m_1 \to \infty} S(m, m + m_1) = \frac{(1/\sqrt{\sigma})}{S(0, m)} \qquad (8.60)$$

where $S(0, m)$ can be calculated using Equation (8.59). We also obtain

$$P(0, \infty) = 1 - \sqrt{\sigma} \qquad (8.61)$$

Using Equation (8.59) we can derive the following recursive relationship:

$$P(0, m) = \frac{(1 - \sigma)}{2 - P(0, m - 1)} \qquad (8.62)$$

If α_i^m denotes the computational load assigned to the ith processor when there are m processors connected to the root, then

$$\alpha_i^\infty = \lim_{m \to \infty} \alpha_i^m = \lim_{m \to \infty} \left\{ \frac{g_i(m, \sigma)}{\sum_{i=0}^{m} g_i(m, \sigma)} \right\} \qquad (8.63)$$

which can be written as

$$\begin{aligned}
\alpha_i^\infty &= \lim_{m \to \infty} \left[\left\{ \frac{g_{i-1}(m, \sigma)}{\sum_{i=0}^{m} g_i(m, \sigma)} \right\} \left\{ \frac{g_i(m, \sigma)}{g_{i-1}(m, \sigma)} \right\} \right] \\
&= \lim_{m \to \infty} \left\{ \frac{g_{i-1}(m, \sigma)}{\sum_{i=0}^{m} g_i(m, \sigma)} \right\} \lim_{m \to \infty} \left\{ \frac{g_i(m, \sigma)}{g_{i-1}(m, \sigma)} \right\}
\end{aligned} \qquad (8.64)$$

However, from Equation (8.56),

$$\lim_{m \to \infty} \frac{g_i(m, \sigma)}{g_{i-1}(m, \sigma)} = \frac{1}{1 + \sqrt{\sigma}} \qquad (8.65)$$

which implies that

$$\alpha_i^\infty = \frac{\alpha_{i-1}^\infty}{1 + \sqrt{\sigma}} \qquad (8.66)$$

where, from Equation (8.57),

$$\alpha_0^\infty = \frac{\sqrt{\sigma}}{1 + \sqrt{\sigma}} \qquad (8.67)$$

Thus,

$$\alpha_i^\infty = \frac{\sqrt{\sigma}}{(1 + \sqrt{\sigma})^{i+1}} \qquad (8.68)$$

The above relation gives the optimal load fraction assigned to the ith processor as $m \to \infty$. Thus, the load assigned to the ith processor asymptotically approaches the value α_i^∞ as the number of processors increases in a linear network.

8.3.3 Analysis of the Results

Figure 8.3 shows that the speedup is higher for low values of σ but is almost insignificant for higher values. As expected, for a given value of σ, the speedup is less than in the with-front-end case. Here, too, there is no significant benefit in adding more than a few processors to the root. Now, let σ be defined as in Equation (8.39). Then, from Equation (8.59),

$$\lim_{q \to \infty} S(0, m) = m + 1 \tag{8.69}$$

This is the maximum achievable speedup and is the same as in the with-front-end case. In fact, we can see that when σ is small the adverse effect of the absence of front ends is much less than when σ is high. From Equation (8.58),

$$S(0, \infty) = 2^{q/2} = \frac{1}{\sqrt{\sigma}} \tag{8.70}$$

Hence, when the communication delay is halved the speedup approximately increases by a factor of $\sqrt{2}$. This is true for all values of $\sigma < 1$, and for reasonably large values of m (for example, $m \geq 3$ when $\sigma = 0.4$ or $m \geq 5$ when $\sigma = 0.2$). Figure 8.4 shows the variation in $S(0, m)$ with q for various values of m. Values of $q > 0$ only are considered since $\sigma < 1$. For low values of q (that is, high values of σ) the speedup achieved is substantially less compared to the with-front-end case. However, for high values of q the speedup in both cases is almost the same.

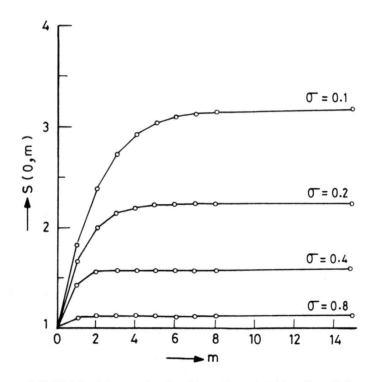

FIGURE 8.3 $S(0, m)$ and m for a Linear Network (without Front End)

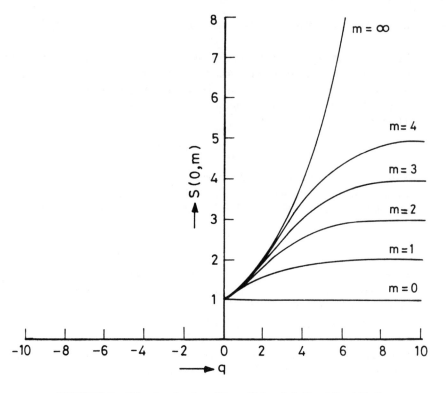

FIGURE 8.4 $S(0, m)$ and q for a Linear Network (without Front End)

8.4 SINGLE-LEVEL TREE NETWORKS WITH FRONT ENDS

In this section we consider a single-level tree network or a star network in which the root processor is equipped with a front-end processor.

8.4.1 Closed-Form Expressions

The timing diagram for this case is the same as shown in Figure 5.2, but with $z_i = z$ and $w_i = w$, for all i. The load distribution equations are as follows:

$$\alpha_i = (1 + \sigma)\alpha_{i+1}, \quad i = 0, 1, \ldots, m - 1 \tag{8.71}$$

and the normalizing equation is

$$\alpha_0 + \alpha_1 + \cdots + \alpha_m = 1 \tag{8.72}$$

These equations are easily solved in the closed form by expressing all α_i ($i = 0, 1, \ldots, m - 1$) in terms of α_m and substituting in Equation (8.72). As shown in Chapter 5, this yields

$$\alpha_i = \frac{\sigma(1 + \sigma)^{m-i}}{(1 + \sigma)^{m+1} - 1}, \quad i = 0, 1, \ldots, m. \tag{8.73}$$

The above equation can be used to obtain the optimal load distribution among the $m + 1$ processors. The time taken to complete a computational task assigned to a single-level tree network of m processors attached to the root is given by

$$T(m) = \left\{ \frac{\sigma(1+\sigma)^m}{(1+\sigma)^{m+1} - 1} \right\} wT_{cp} \tag{8.74}$$

Here, $T(0) = wT_{cp}$ is the time taken by the root processor alone to process the entire load. The speedup achieved by connecting m_1 additional processors to the existing m processors is given by $S(m, m + m_1)$, which satisfies Equation (8.1). Here,

$$S(0, m) = \frac{(1+\sigma)^{m+1} - 1}{\sigma(1+\sigma)^m} \tag{8.75}$$

from which

$$S(m, m + m_1) = \frac{(1+\sigma)^{m+m_1+1} - 1}{(1+\sigma)^{m_1} \left\{ (1+\sigma)^{m+1} - 1 \right\}} \tag{8.76}$$

The factor $P(m, m + m_1)$ can be defined through Equation (8.2).

8.4.2 Asymptotic Analysis

Here,

$$S(0, \infty) = \lim_{m \to \infty} S(0, m) = 1 + \frac{1}{\sigma} \tag{8.77}$$

Using Equation (8.76), we have

$$\lim_{m_1 \to \infty} S(m, m + m_1) = \frac{(1+\sigma)^{m+1}}{(1+\sigma)^{m+1} - 1} \tag{8.78}$$

The variation of $S(0, m)$ with m can also be obtained through the recursive relationship

$$S(0, m) = \frac{1}{(1+\sigma)^m} + S(0, m - 1) \tag{8.79}$$

with $S(0, 0) = 1$. We also obtain

$$P(0, \infty) = \frac{1}{(1+\sigma)} \tag{8.80}$$

and, from Equation (8.4),

$$P(0, m) = \frac{(1+\sigma)^m - 1}{(1+\sigma)^{m+1} - 1} \tag{8.81}$$

If α_i^m denotes the computational load assigned to the ith processor when there are m processors connected to the root, then from Equation (8.73),

$$\alpha_i^\infty = \lim_{m \to \infty} \alpha_i^m = \frac{\sigma}{(1+\sigma)^{i+1}}, \quad i = 0, 1, \ldots, m \tag{8.82}$$

This relation gives the optimal load distribution to the ith processor as $m \to \infty$. Thus, the load assigned to the ith processor asymptotically approaches the value α_i^∞ as the number of processors increases in a single-level tree network.

8.4.3 Analysis of the Results

Figure 8.5 shows that for low values of σ the speedup saturates after a larger number of processors than in the case of a linear network. It implies that when the communication speed is high, connecting additional processors in a single-level tree network is more beneficial than in a linear network. However, for high values of σ this is not true. We also note that the speedup saturation level is higher for a tree network than for a linear network.

If σ is defined as in Equation (8.39), then

$$\lim_{q \to \infty} S(0, m) = \lim_{\sigma \to 0} \left\{ \frac{(1 + \sigma)^{m+1} - 1}{\sigma (1 + \sigma)^m} \right\} = m + 1 \tag{8.83}$$

From Equation (8.77),

$$S(0, \infty) \approx 2^q \tag{8.84}$$

for large values of q. This implies that the speedup increases almost by a factor of 2 when the communication delay is halved. This shows better performance than in case of linear networks. Figure 8.6 shows the variation of $S(0, m)$ with q for various values of m. We note that for low values of q (that is, high values of σ or

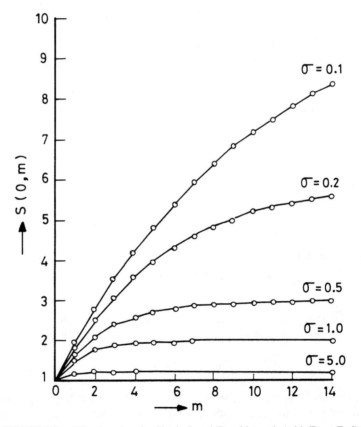

FIGURE 8.5 $S(0, m)$ and m for Single-Level Tree Network (with Front End)

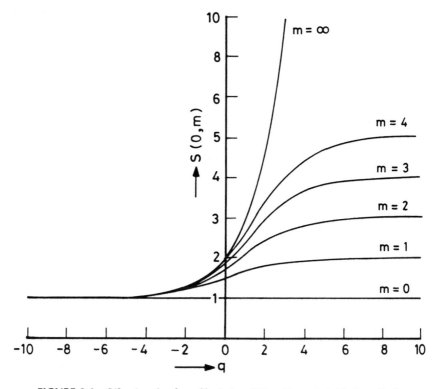

FIGURE 8.6 $S(0, m)$ and q for a Single-Level Tree Network (with Front End)

slow communication channels) the performance of tree networks is better than linear networks, whereas for high values of q, the performance of both networks is almost the same.

8.5 SINGLE-LEVEL TREE NETWORKS WITHOUT FRONT ENDS

In this section we consider a single-level tree network in which the root processor is not equipped with a front end.

8.5.1 Closed-Form Expressions

The timing diagram for this case is the same as in Figure 5.3, but with $z_i = z$ and $w_i = w$, for all i. Here, too, we assume that $\sigma < 1$ for reasons given in Chapter 5. The load distribution equations are as follows:

$$\alpha_i = (1 + \sigma)\alpha_{i+1}, \quad i = 1, 2, \ldots, m - 1 \tag{8.85}$$

$$\alpha_m = \alpha_0 \tag{8.86}$$

The normalizing equation is

$$\alpha_0 + \alpha_1 + \cdots + \alpha_m = 1 \tag{8.87}$$

These equations can also be solved in the closed form by expressing all α_i ($i = 0, 1, \ldots, m - 1$) in terms of α_m and then using Equation (8.87). This yields

$$\alpha_0 = \alpha_m \tag{8.88}$$

$$\alpha_i = \frac{\sigma(1 + \sigma)^{m-i}}{(1 + \sigma)^m + \sigma - 1}, \quad i = 1, \ldots, m \tag{8.89}$$

The processing time is given by

$$
\begin{aligned}
T(m) &= \left(\sum_{i=1}^{m} \alpha_i \right) z T_{cm} + \alpha_0 w T_{cp} \\
&= \left\{ \left(\sum_{i=1}^{m} \alpha_i \right) \sigma + \alpha_0 \right\} w T_{cp} \\
&= \left\{ \frac{\sigma^2 \sum_{i=1}^{m}(1 + \sigma)^{m-i} + \sigma}{(1 + \sigma)^m + \sigma - 1} \right\} w T_{cp} \\
&= \left\{ \frac{\sigma(1 + \sigma)^m}{(1 + \sigma)^m + \sigma - 1} \right\} w T_{cp}
\end{aligned}
\tag{8.90}
$$

The above equations are valid for $m \geq 1$, and $T(0) = w T_{cp}$ is the time taken by the root processor alone to process the entire load.

The speedup achieved by connecting m_1 additional processors to the existing m processors is given by $S(m, m + m_1)$, which satisfies Equation (8.4). Here,

$$S(0, m) = \frac{(1 + \sigma)^m + \sigma - 1}{\sigma(1 + \sigma)^m} \tag{8.91}$$

from which

$$S(m, m + m_1) = \frac{(1 + \sigma)^{m+m_1} + \sigma - 1}{\{(1 + \sigma)^m + \sigma - 1\}(1 + \sigma)^{m_1}} \tag{8.92}$$

The factor $P(m, m + m_1)$ can be defined through Equation (8.5).

8.5.2 Asymptotic Analysis

We have

$$S(0, \infty) = \lim_{m \to \infty} S(0, m) = \frac{1}{\sigma} \tag{8.93}$$

Using Equation (8.92), we have

$$\lim_{m_1 \to \infty} S(m, m + m_1) = \frac{(1 + \sigma)^m}{(1 + \sigma)^m + \sigma - 1} \tag{8.94}$$

The variation of $S(0, m)$ with m can also be obtained through the recursive relationship

$$S(0, m) = \left\{ \frac{(1 - \sigma)}{(1 + \sigma)^m} \right\} + S(0, m - 1) \tag{8.95}$$

with $S(0, 0) = 1$. We can also obtain, from Equation (8.5),

$$P(0, m) = (1 - \sigma) \left\{ \frac{(1 + \sigma)^m - 1}{(1 + \sigma)^m + \sigma - 1} \right\} \tag{8.96}$$

and

$$P(0, \infty) = 1 - \sigma \tag{8.97}$$

Also, from Equation (8.89),

$$\alpha_i^\infty = \lim_{m \to \infty} \alpha_i^m = \frac{\sigma}{(1 + \sigma)^i}, \quad i = 1, 2, \ldots, m \tag{8.98}$$

$$\alpha_0^\infty = \alpha_m^\infty \tag{8.99}$$

Hence, the load assigned to the ith processor asymptotically approaches the value α_i^∞, as the number of processors increase in the single-level tree network.

8.5.3 Analysis of the Results

Figure 8.7 shows a phenomenon similar to one discussed earlier. If σ is defined as in Equation (8.39), then

$$\lim_{q \to \infty} S(0, m) = \lim_{\sigma \to \infty} \left\{ \frac{(1 + \sigma)^m + \sigma - 1}{\sigma (1 + \sigma)^m} \right\} = m + 1 \tag{8.100}$$

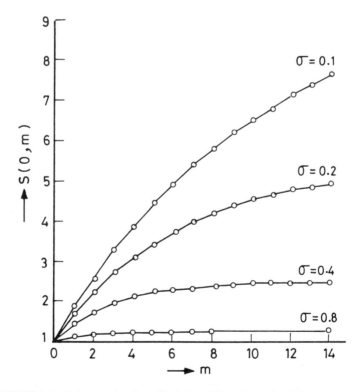

FIGURE 8.7 $S(0, m)$ and m for a Single-Level Tree Network (without Front End)

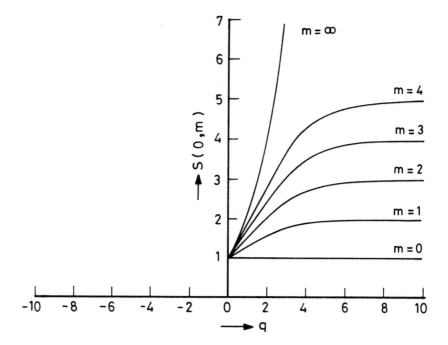

FIGURE 8.8 $S(0, m)$ and q for a Single-Level Tree Network (without Front End)

From Equation (8.93),

$$S(0, \infty) = 2^q \qquad (8.101)$$

Hence, the speedup increases almost by a factor of 2 when the communication delay is halved, in cases where m is reasonably large. Figure 8.8 shows the variation in $S(0, m)$ with q for various values of m.

8.6 CONCLUDING REMARKS

Following are the highlights of this chapter:

- Asymptotic performance analysis was carried out to obtain the bounds on speedup and fractional saving in computation time for the following cases:
  (i) Linear network: with-front-end processors
  (ii) Linear network: without-front-end processors
  (iii) Tree network: with-front-end processors
  (iv) Tree network: without-front-end processors
- We observed that, just as the sequential portion of an algorithm limits the speedup in parallel computing (Amdahl's law), communication delay has a similar effect in distributed computing systems.
- We also showed that in both linear and single-level tree networks, significant performance enhancement is achieved by utilizing only the first few processors. Sharing the load with more processors leads to underutilization of these

additional processors without causing any significant improvement in the over-all performance. We also showed the dependence of this phenomena on the communication delay.

- Closed-form expressions were derived for speedup and fractional saving in processing time. These expressions were used to obtain analytical results that otherwise would have required extensive computation.

Here we have provided an asymptotic performance analysis for a certain load distribution strategy. Similar analyses for other load distribution strategies will be carried out in subsequent chapters.

BIBLIOGRAPHIC NOTES

Most of the results obtained in this chapter are from Ghose and Mani (1994). A definition of Amdahl's law can be found in Quinn (1987). Some of the results given here were also obtained by Robertazzi (1993) using the processor equivalence concept and were presented in Chapters 3 and 4. An interesting asymptotic analysis for a hypercube and mesh network with respect to the dimension, and to the number of layers used, is available for a broadcast type of communication strategy in Blazewicz and Drozdowski (1994a, 1994b). However, the load distribution strategy used is somewhat different from the one used in this chapter.

CHAPTER 9

Efficient Utilization of Front Ends in Linear Networks

In this chapter, we present a technique of utilizing the front ends of the processors in a linear network in an efficient manner. Earlier studies on linear networks, given in Chapters 3, 5, 6, and 8, employ a particular kind of load distribution strategy in which each processor in the network begins computing its load fraction only after its front end has received all the load that passes through it. But if each processor begins computing immediately upon receiving its own load fraction without waiting for the entire load to be received by the front end, then we can further optimize time performance. This chapter presents an analysis of this new strategy for the case when the processing load originates at the boundary (*boundary case*) and for that when the processing load originates at the interior of the network (*interior case*). In the latter case, we also present some results related to the optimal sequence of load distribution and the optimal load origination point. More specifically, we show that, unlike in Chapter 6, the time performance of this strategy does depend on the sequence of load distribution.

9.1 MOTIVATION AND SOME REMARKS

We first provide a motivation for the new load distribution strategy through a simple example.

Example 9.1

Consider a linear network of three processors p_0, p_1, and p_2, all equipped with front ends and connected via communication links l_1, l_2. The processing load originates at the processor p_0. The timing diagram given in Figure 9.1a is obtained using the load

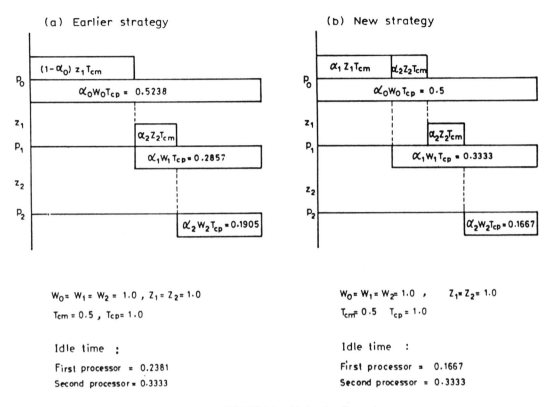

FIGURE 9.1 Motivating Example

distribution strategy given in earlier chapters. Figure 9.1b shows the timing diagram for the new strategy in which the processor p_0 distributes the load fractions to the processors p_1 and p_2 one at a time. Processor p_1 begins computing as soon as it has received its own load fraction α_1, while the front end of p_1 receives and then transmits the load fraction α_2 to p_2. It can be seen that an overall reduction of 4.76 percent in the processing time over the earlier strategy is achieved.

Consider the linear network of processors shown in Figure 3.1a and 3.1b. For the boundary case, the processing time is defined as

$$T(m) = \max(T_0, T_1, \ldots, T_m) \qquad (9.1)$$

But for the interior case the processing time is defined as

$$T(R, L) = \max\left(T_0, T_1^l, \ldots, T_L^l, T_1^r, \ldots, T_R^r\right) \qquad (9.2)$$

with T_k^l and T_k^r are the finish times of the p_kth processor on the left and right side of the root processor, respectively. The definition of *sequence* of load distribution and the *optimal load sequence* used in this chapter are the same as in Section 6.1.

In a linear network, the new load distribution strategy is formally defined through the following rules:

(i) The front end of the root processor divides the total load into a number of fractions (the number being equal to the number of processors); keeps its own fraction for computation; and sends the other fractions one at a time in a proper sequence.

(ii) All the processors must perform computation continuously until the end.

(iii) A processor begins computing its load fraction as soon as its front end finishes receiving it.

(iv) A front end begins transmitting as soon as it has received the load from its predecessor and the front end of its successor is free.

(v) At any given instant in time, a front end can either receive or transmit the processing load, but not both.

It may be noted that in Chapter 5, we have proved that in a linear network, for the load distribution to be optimal, it is both necessary and sufficient that all the processors must stop computing at the same instant in time, provided that the condition $w_i T_{cp} \geq z_{i+1} T_{cm}$, holds for all i in the network. It is easy to show that this result holds even here.

9.2 LOAD ORIGINATION AT THE BOUNDARY

In this section, we use the above-mentioned rules to obtain the timing diagram for load distribution in the boundary case. We also obtain the recursive equations and their closed-form solution. Next, using this closed-form expression, an asymptotic analysis on the performance of the network is carried out.

9.2.1 Closed-Form Solution

In this case, the root processor p_0 divides the total load into $(m + 1)$ parts, namely $\alpha_0, \alpha_1, \ldots, \alpha_m$. The root processor keeps the fraction α_0 for itself. It first transmits the fraction α_1 to p_1 via l_1. Next it transmits the load fractions $\alpha_2, \ldots, \alpha_m$, one at a time, through the front ends of p_1 to p_{m-1} via the links l_1 to l_m. The timing diagram for this strategy is shown in Figure 9.2. The load distribution equations are

$$\alpha_i w_i T_{cp} = \alpha_{i+1}(w_{i+1} T_{cp} + z_{i+1} T_{cm} + z_i T_{cm} + z_{i-1} T_{cm}),$$
$$i = 0, 1, \ldots, m - 1 \tag{9.3}$$

subject to

$$\alpha_i z_j \leq \alpha_{i-1} z_{j+2}, \quad i = 4, 5, \ldots m \text{ and } j = 1, \ldots, i - 3 \tag{9.4}$$

The constraints shown in Equation (9.4) are sufficient to ensure that a front end does not receive and transmit loads simultaneously. When $i = 3$, α_2 is processed at p_2 and is not transmitted via link l_3, and hence no constraints are required. These constraints play a crucial role only from $i = 4$ onwards. Further, from Equation (9.3) we see that when $i = 0$ and 1, the terms z_0 and z_{-1} do not signify anything and

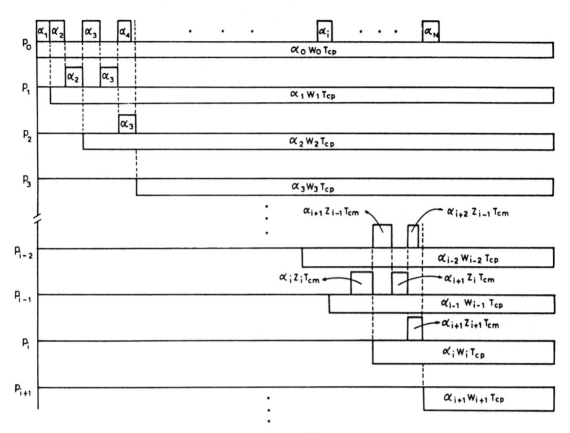

FIGURE 9.2   Timing Diagram: Boundary Case

hence we assume that $z_0 = z_{-1} = 0$. For $i = 0$ and 1, the first two terms on the RHS of Equation (9.3) alone contribute. Further, we have the normalizing equation

$$\sum_{i=0}^{m} \alpha_i = 1 , \quad 0 \le \alpha_i \le 1 \tag{9.5}$$

Equations (9.3) and (9.5) constitute a system of $(m+1)$ linear equations with $(m+1)$ unknowns, yielding a unique solution. This would be a feasible solution if and only if it lies in the feasible region defined by Equation (9.4). However, for a general case of arbitrarily chosen processor speeds and link speeds this feasibility condition may not be satisfied. Hence we shall make some assumptions on the processor and link speeds that will ensure the existence of a feasible solution. For this we first solve Equations (9.3) and (9.5). We can rewrite all $(m + 1)$ equations given in Equations (9.3) in terms of α_m. Thus, the load fraction to the kth processor can be written as

$$\alpha_k = \alpha_m \left\{ \prod_{j=k}^{m-1} f_j \right\} , \quad k = 0, 1, \ldots, m - 1 \tag{9.6}$$

where

$$f_j = \frac{w_{j+1} + \sum_{k=j-1}^{j+1} z_k \delta}{w_j} \tag{9.7}$$

where δ is as defined in Chapter 2. Using Equation (9.5), the value of α_m is obtained as

$$\alpha_m = \frac{1}{\left(1 + \sum_{i=0}^{m-1} \prod_{j=i}^{m-1} f_j\right)} \tag{9.8}$$

Thus, the fraction of the load assigned to the kth processor is

$$\alpha_k = \frac{\left(\prod_{j=k}^{m-1} f_j\right)}{\left(1 + \sum_{i=0}^{m-1} \prod_{j=i}^{m-1} f_j\right)} \tag{9.9}$$

From Figure 9.2, it can be seen that the processing time $T(m)$ is given by $\alpha_0 w_0 T_{cp}$. Hence,

$$T(m) = \left\{ \frac{\prod_{j=0}^{m-1} f_j}{1 + \sum_{i=0}^{m-1} \prod_{j=i}^{m-1} f_j} \right\} w_0 T_{cp} \tag{9.10}$$

where f_j is as given in Equation (9.7). It can be seen that $f_j > 1$ for all j if $w_{j+1} \geq w_j$ for all j. From Equation (9.9) this implies, that $\alpha_{k+1} < \alpha_k$ for all k. Now suppose that $z_{k+1} \geq z_k$ for all k, then the inequalities in Equation (9.4) are automatically satisfied. Thus we assume that the processors and the links in the network are arranged in the decreasing order of speeds, that is,

$$w_k \leq w_{k+1}, \quad z_k \leq z_{k+1}, \text{ for all } k \tag{9.11}$$

These assumptions are not as restrictive as they may appear to be, as they also include all homogeneous linear networks that have identical processors and identical links. Hence, whenever Equation (9.11) is satisfied, the solution to the load distribution problem is obtained by solving Equations (9.3) and (9.5). When Equation (9.11) is not satisfied, though the solution obtained is not feasible in an optimal sense, the new strategy of load distribution can still be employed to improve the performance of a linear network. We will demonstrate this with an example in Section 9.4.

9.2.2 Asymptotic Analysis

We use the above closed-form solution to obtain the ultimate performance limits of the network with respect to the number of processors. For this we consider a homogeneous network in which all the processors are identical and all the links are identical. In other words $w_i = w$ $(i = 0, 1, \ldots, m)$ and $z_j = z$ $(j = 1 \ldots, m)$. In this case, the closed-form solution given in Equation (9.10) can be written as

$$T(m) = \left\{ \frac{3\sigma f_0 f_1 f^{m-2}}{3\sigma (f_0 + 1) f_1 f^{m-2} + f^{m-1} - 1} \right\} wT_{cp} \qquad m \geq 2 \qquad (9.12)$$

where

$$f_0 = 1 + \sigma, \quad f_1 = 1 + 2\sigma, \quad f = 1 + 3\sigma \qquad (9.13)$$

Hence,

$$T(\infty) = \lim_{m \to \infty} T(m) = \left\{ \frac{P}{P + Q} \right\} wT_{cp} \qquad (9.14)$$

where

$$P = 3\sigma f_0 f_1 \qquad (9.15)$$

$$Q = 6\sigma^2 + 6\sigma + 1 \qquad (9.16)$$

A comparison with the strategy proposed in earlier chapters reveals the following interesting issues. From Chapter 8, we obtain $T'(\infty)$ for the earlier strategy as

$$T'(\infty) = \left\{ \frac{2}{\left(1 + \sqrt{1 + 4/\sigma}\right)} \right\} wT_{cp} \qquad (9.17)$$

Comparing Equations (9.14) and (9.17) it can be easily proved that $T(\infty) \leq T'(\infty)$ for all σ. The proof is as follows: From Equations (9.15) and (9.16) we get

$$T(\infty) = \frac{3\sigma f_0 f_1}{3\sigma f_0 f_1 + (6\sigma^2 + 6\sigma + 1)}$$

By substituting the values of f_0 and f_1, and doing some algebraic manipulations, we get

$$T'(\infty) = T(\infty) + (1 + 6\sigma + 21\sigma^2 + 33\sigma^3 + 18\sigma^4)$$

Hence, the processing time for the new load distribution strategy is always less than the earlier strategy.

In Figure 9.3 we plot the processing time against the number of processors for $\sigma = 0.1$ and $\sigma = 1.0$. These performance curves are bounded by an upper limit of $T(m) = 1$ (as $\sigma \to \infty$) and a lower limit of $T(m) = \frac{1}{(m+1)}$ (as $\sigma \to 0$). These limits are the same for both strategies. When there are only two processors in the network both strategies give identical time performance. As the number of processors increases, the time performance of the new strategy becomes better compared to the earlier one. In Figure 9.4 we plot $T(\infty)$ vs $\ln(\sigma)$ and show that the performance of the new strategy is always superior to the earlier strategy though they converge to the same performance as $\sigma \to 0$ and $\sigma \to \infty$.

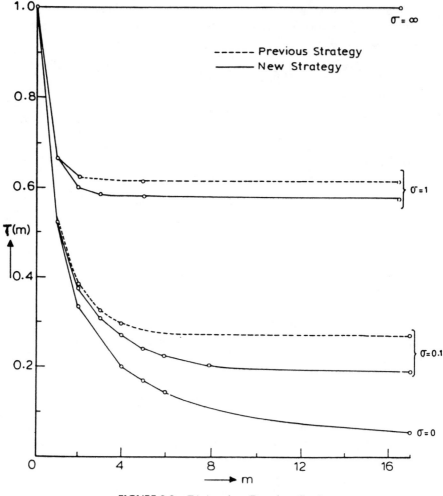

FIGURE 9.3 $T(m)$ and m (Boundary Case)

9.3 LOAD ORIGINATION AT THE INTERIOR OF THE NETWORK

In this section, using the rules stated in Section 9.1, we obtain the timing diagram
for load distribution, the recursive equations, and their closed-form solution for the
case when the load originates at the interior of the network. Using this closed-form
solution, we perform an asymptotic analysis and prove two important results on
optimal sequencing and optimal load origination point in such a network.

9.3.1 Closed-Form Solution

The timing diagram for this case is shown in Figure 9.5. The load is assumed to
be distributed first to the right hand side and then to the left hand side. Note that
Figure 9.5 shows the load distribution for only two processors on both sides of the
root. The load distribution for the remaining processors follows the same pattern as

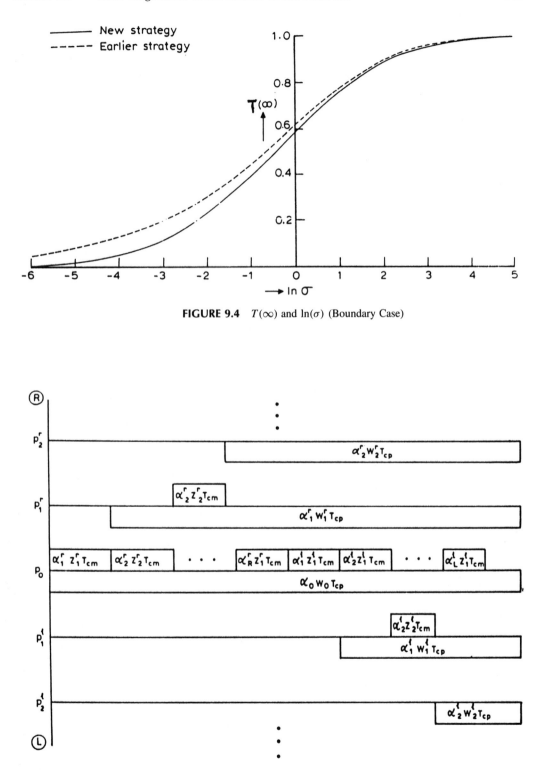

FIGURE 9.4 $T(\infty)$ and $\ln(\sigma)$ (Boundary Case)

FIGURE 9.5   Timing Diagram: Interior Case

shown in Figure 9.2 for the boundary case. From Figure 9.5, the following recursive equations can be obtained:

$$\alpha_i^r w_i^r T_{cp} = \alpha_{i+1}^r (w_{i+1}^r T_{cp} + z_{i+1}^r T_{cm} + z_1^r T_{cm} + z_{i-1}^r T_{cm}),$$

$$i = 0, 1, \ldots, R - 1 \tag{9.18}$$

$$\alpha_i^l w_i^l T_{cp} = \alpha_{i+1}^l (w_{i+1}^l T_{cp} + z_{i+1}^l T_{cm} + z_1^l T_{cm} + z_{i-1}^l T_{cm}),$$

$$i = 1, 2, \ldots, L - 1. \tag{9.19}$$

$$\alpha_0 w_0 T_{cp} = \alpha_1^l (w_1^l T_{cp} + z_1^l T_{cm}) + \left(\sum_{i=1}^R \alpha_i^r \right) z_1^r T_{cm}$$

$$+ \left(\sum_{i=2}^{R-1} \alpha_i^r z_2^r T_{cm} \right) \tag{9.20}$$

As in the boundary case, here we need to assume $z_0^l = z_{-1}^l = z_0^r = z_{-1}^r = 0$. Also, we have $\alpha_0^r = \alpha_0$. The normalizing equation is given by

$$\alpha_0 + \sum_{i=1}^R \alpha_i^r + \sum_{i=1}^L \alpha_i^l = 1 \tag{9.21}$$

As in the boundary case, the following constraints have to be satisfied:

$$\alpha_i^l z_j^l \le \alpha_{i-1}^l z_{j+2}^l, \ i = 4, 5, \ldots, L, \ j = 1, 2, \ldots, i - 3 \tag{9.22}$$

$$\alpha_i^r z_j^r \le \alpha_{i-1}^r z_{j+2}^r, \ i = 4, 5, \ldots, R, \ j = 1, 2, \ldots, i - 3 \tag{9.23}$$

Following arguments similar to those given in the previous section, we may solve the above set of Equations (9.18) through (9.21) to yield a unique solution. Each fraction of load α_i^r ($i = 0, 1, \ldots, R - 1$) can be expressed in terms of α_R^r. Hence the load fraction α_i^r to the ith processor p_i^r is given by

$$\alpha_i^r = \alpha_R^r \mu^r(i, R - 1), \qquad i = 0, 1, \ldots, R - 1 \tag{9.24}$$

where

$$\mu^r(x, y) = \prod_{j=x}^y f_j^r \tag{9.25}$$

and

$$f_j^r = \left(\frac{w_{j+1}^r + \sum_{k=j-1}^{j+1} z_k^r \delta}{w_j^r} \right) \tag{9.26}$$

Similarly, for the left hand side the load fraction for the ith processor p_i^l is given by

$$\alpha_i^l = \alpha_L^l \mu^l(i, L - 1), \ i = 1, 2, \ldots, L - 1 \tag{9.27}$$

where $\mu^l(i, L - 1)$ and f_j^l are defined as in Equations (9.25) and (9.26) with the superscript 'r' replaced by 'l'. Furthermore, from Equation (9.20), α_0 is also given by

$$\alpha_0 = \alpha_L^l \mu^l(0, L-1) + \alpha_R^r \left[\{\mu^r(1, R-1) + 1\} \left(\frac{z_1^r \delta}{w_0} \right) \right.$$
$$\left. + \theta^r(2, R-1)(z_1^r + z_2^r) \left(\frac{\delta}{w_0} \right) \right] \tag{9.28}$$

where

$$\theta^r(x, y) = \sum_{i=x}^{y} \prod_{j=i}^{y} f_j^r \tag{9.29}$$

Equating Equation (9.24) with $i = 0$ and Equation (9.28) we obtain a relationship between α_R^r and α_L^l as

$$\left(\frac{\alpha_R^r}{\alpha_L^l} \right) = \frac{\{w_0 \mu^l(0, L-1)\}}{\{\mu^r(1, R-1)w_1^r - \theta^r(2, R-1)(z_1^r + z_2^r)\delta - z_1^r \delta\}} \tag{9.30}$$

In the normalizing equation Equation (9.21), using Equation (9.30), α_j^l is expressed in terms of α_R^r, for all $j = 1, 2, \ldots, L$. From this equation, the value of α_R^r is obtained as

$$\alpha_R^r = \frac{1}{\phi} \tag{9.31}$$

where

$$\phi = 1 + \theta^r(2, R-1) + (1 + f_0^r)\mu^r(1, R-1) + \left(\frac{G^r}{G^l} \right) K \tag{9.32}$$

and

$$K = 1 + \theta^l(2, L-1) + \mu^l(1, L-1) \tag{9.33}$$

$$G^r = \left\{ \frac{f_1^r w_1^r \{\mu^r(2, R-1)\} - \{(z_1^r + z_2^r)\delta\} \{\theta^r(2, R-1)\} - z_1^r \delta}{w_0} \right\} \tag{9.34}$$

$$G^l = \mu^l(0, L-1) \tag{9.35}$$

Let us denote the processing time for the entire load as $T(x, y)$, where the arguments (x, y) form an ordered pair, meaning that the load is first sent to the right hand side with x processors and then to the left hand side with y processors. From Figure 9.5, the processing time for the entire load is given by

$$T(R, L) = \alpha_0 w_0 T_{cp} \tag{9.36}$$

where α_0 is given by

$$\alpha_0 = \frac{\mu^r(0, R-1)}{\phi} \tag{9.37}$$

Thus the processing time is given by

$$T(R, L) = \left\{ \frac{\mu^r(0, R-1)}{\phi} \right\} w_0 T_{cp} \tag{9.38}$$

From Equation (9.26) it can be seen that when $w^l_{j+1} \geq w^l_j$ we have $f^l_j > 1$; this implies that $\alpha^l_{i+1} \leq \alpha^l_i$ for all i. Now if $z^l_{i+1} \geq z^l_i$ for all i, then the inequalities in Equation (9.23) are automatically satisfied. Similar arguments hold for the right hand side, too. Hence we assume that the links and processors are arranged in order of decreasing speed, as in the boundary case, on both sides. Thus, for all k

$$w^l_k \leq w^l_{k+1}$$

$$z^l_k \leq z^l_{k+1}$$

$$w^r_k \leq w^r_{k+1}$$

$$z^r_k \leq z^r_{k+1}$$

(9.39)

The closed-form expression given by Equation (9.38) is valid only when $R > 2$ and $L > 2$. By following a similar procedure, we can get the closed-form expressions when $R < 2$ or $L < 2$. These are given below.

(i) $T(1,1) = \left\{ \dfrac{f^r_0 f^l_0}{f^l_0(1 + f^r_0) + (w^r_1/w_0)} \right\} w_0 T_{cp}$

(9.40)

(ii) $T(1,2) = \left\{ \dfrac{f^r_0 f^l_0 f^l_1}{\{f^l_0 f^l_1(1 + f^r_0)\} + (1 + f^l_1)\{f^r_0 - (z^r_1 \delta/w_0)\}} \right\} w_0 T_{cp}$

(9.41)

(iii) $T(2,1) = \left\{ \dfrac{f^r_0 f^r_1}{1 + f^r_1(1 + f^r_0) + \{(f^r_0 f^r_1 - (1 + f^r_1)z^r_1 \delta/w_0)\}/f^l_0} \right\} w_0 T_{cp}$

(9.42)

(iv) $T(2,2) = \left\{ \dfrac{f^r_1 f^r_0}{1 + f^r_1(1 + f^r_0) + \dfrac{(f^r_1 w^r_1 - z^r_1 \delta)(1 + f^l_1)}{(f^l_0 f^l_1 w_0)}} \right\} w_0 T_{cp}$

(9.43)

(v) $T(x,1) = \left\{ \dfrac{\mu^r(0, x-1)}{\phi_1} \right\} w_0 T_{cp}, \quad \text{for } x > 2$

(9.44)

where,

$$\phi_1 = 1 + (1 + f^r_0)\mu^r(1, x-1) + \theta^r(2, x-1) + \dfrac{G^r_1}{G^l_1}$$

(9.45)

$$G^r_1 = \left[z^r_1 \delta \{1 + \theta^r(2, x-1) + \mu^r(1, x-1)\} \right.$$
$$\left. + z^r_2 \delta \theta^r(2, x-1) - w_0 f^r_0 f^r_1 \mu^r(2, x-1) \right]/w_0$$

(9.46)

$$G^l_1 = f^l_1$$

(9.47)

(vi) $T(1,x) = \left(\dfrac{f^r_1}{\phi_2} \right) w_0 T_{cp}, \quad \text{for } x > 2$

(9.48)

where

$$\phi_2 = 1 + f^r_1 + \left(\dfrac{G^r_2}{G^l_2} \right) \{f^l_1 + \theta^l(2, x-1) + \mu^l(1, x-1)\}$$

(9.49)

$$G_2^r = \left(\frac{w_1^r}{w_0} \right) \tag{9.50}$$

$$G_2^l = \mu^l(0, x - 1) \tag{9.51}$$

(vii) $T(2, x) = \left(\dfrac{f_0^r f_1^r}{\phi_3} \right) w_0 T_{cp}, \quad$ for $x > 2 \tag{9.52}$

where

$$\phi_3 = 1 + f_1^r (1 + f_0^r)$$
$$+ \left(\frac{G_3^r}{G_3^l} \right) \{ 1 + \theta^l(2, x - 1) + \mu^l(1, x - 1) \} \tag{9.53}$$

$$G_3^r = f_0^r f_1^r - \left\{ \frac{z_1^r \delta(1 + f_1^r)}{w_0} \right\} \tag{9.54}$$

$$G_3^l = \mu^l(0, x - 1) \tag{9.55}$$

(viii) $T(x, 2) = \left\{ \dfrac{\mu^r(0, x - 1)}{\phi_4} \right\} w_0 T_{cp}, \quad$ for $x > 2 \tag{9.56}$

where

$$\phi_4 = 1 + \theta^r(2, x - 1) + (1 + f_0^r)\mu^r(1, x - 1) + \left(\frac{G_4^r}{G_4^l} \right)(1 + f_1^l) \tag{9.57}$$

$$G_4^r = \left[z_1^r \delta \{ 1 + \theta^r(2, x - 1) + \mu^r (1, x - 1) \} \right.$$
$$\left. + z_2^r \delta \theta^r (2, x - 1) - w_0 \mu^r(0, x - 1) \right] / w_0 \tag{9.58}$$

$$G_4^l = f_0^l f_1^l \tag{9.59}$$

It may be noted that the expression shown in Equation (9.40) is identical to $T(1, 1)$ in the strategy given in Chapter 6 since, with only one processor on both sides, the present strategy gives the same load distribution as the earlier one.

9.3.2 Asymptotic Analysis

We use the above closed-form solution to obtain the ultimate performance limits of the system with respect to the number of processors. For this we consider a homogeneous network in which $w_i^l = w_i^r = w$ and $z_i^l = z_i^r = z$ for all i. In this case, the closed-form expressions given above for $R > 2$ and $L > 2$ reduce to

$$T(1, L) = \left\{ \frac{3 \sigma f_0^2 f_1 f^{L-2}}{f^{L-2} \{ 3\sigma f_0 f_1 (1 + f_0) + 3\sigma f_1 + f \} - 1} \right\} w T_{cp} \tag{9.60}$$

$$T(R, 1) = \left\{ \frac{3 \sigma f_0^2 f_1 f^{R-2}}{f^{R-2} \{ 3\sigma f_0 f_1 (2 + f_0) + f(f_0 - 2\sigma) - 3\sigma^2 f_1 \} + (\sigma f - 1)} \right\} w T_{cp} \tag{9.61}$$

$$T(2, L) = \left\{ \frac{3\sigma f_0 f_1^2 f^{L-2}}{f^{L-2} \{3\sigma(1 + f_1)(1 + f_0 f_1) + 3\sigma f_0 f_1 + 1\} - 1} \right\} wT_{cp} \qquad (9.62)$$

$$T(R, 2) = \left\{ \frac{3\sigma f_0 f_1^2 f^{R-2}}{f^{R-2} \{3\sigma f_1^2(1 + f_0) + f_1 f + 2\sigma\} + (2\sigma f - 1)} \right\} wT_{cp} \qquad (9.63)$$

$$T(R, L) = \left\{ \frac{9\sigma^2 f_0^2 f_1^2 f^{R+L-4}}{K_1 f^{R+L-4} - \sigma f^{R-2} + K_2 f^{L-2} + (3\sigma^2 - 2\sigma f)} \right\} wT_{cp} \qquad (9.64)$$

where

$$K_1 = 3\sigma f_0 f_1 f + 9\sigma^2 f_0 f_1^2(1 + f_0) + \sigma(f + 3\sigma f_1) \qquad (9.65)$$

$$K_2 = (2\sigma f - 3\sigma^2)(f + 3\sigma f_1) - 3\sigma f_0 f_1 \qquad (9.66)$$

with f_0, f_1 and f as defined in Equation (9.13). Now by letting R and L tend to infinity individually and jointly in Equations (9.60) through (9.64), we obtain the following expressions.

$$T(1, \infty) = \lim_{L \to \infty} T(1, L) = \left(\frac{A}{B} \right) wT_{cp} \qquad (9.67)$$

$$T(\infty, 1) = \lim_{R \to \infty} T(R, 1) = \left(\frac{A}{C} \right) wT_{cp} \qquad (9.68)$$

$$T(2, \infty) = \lim_{L \to \infty} T(2, L) = \left(\frac{Af_1}{Df_0} \right) wT_{cp} \qquad (9.69)$$

$$T(\infty, 2) = \lim_{R \to \infty} T(R, 2) = \left(\frac{Af_1}{E} \right) wT_{cp} \qquad (9.70)$$

$$T(\infty, L) = \lim_{R \to \infty} T(R, L) = \left(\frac{3\sigma f_1 A f^{L-2}}{K_1 f^{L-2} - \sigma} \right) wT_{cp}, \qquad L > 2 \qquad (9.71)$$

$$T(R, \infty) = \lim_{L \to \infty} T(R, L) = \left(\frac{3\sigma f_1 A f^{R-2}}{K_1 f^{R-2} + K_2} \right) wT_{cp}, \qquad R > 2 \qquad (9.72)$$

$$T(\infty, \infty) = \lim_{\substack{R \to \infty \\ L \to \infty}} T(R, L) = \left(\frac{3\sigma f_1 A}{K_1} \right) wT_{cp} \qquad (9.73)$$

where

$$A = 3\sigma f_0^2 f_1 \qquad (9.74)$$

$$B = 3\sigma f_0 f_1(1 + f_0) + 3\sigma f_1 + f \qquad (9.75)$$

$$C = 3\sigma f_0 f_1(2 + f_0) + f(f_0 - 2\sigma) - 3\sigma^2 f_1 \qquad (9.76)$$

$$D = 3\sigma(1 + f_1)(1 + f_0 f_1) + 3\sigma f_0 f_1 + 1 \qquad (9.77)$$

$$E = 3\sigma f_0 f_1^2(1 + f_0) + f_0 f_1 f + 2\sigma f_0 \qquad (9.78)$$

It should be noted that $T(\infty, L)$ and $T(R, \infty)$ are not equal even when $R = L$. This indicates that the sequence of load distribution affects the processing time. We shall analyze this further in the next section.

In Chapter 3, the value of $T(\infty, \infty)$ for the earlier strategy was given in Equation (3.129). Comparing this with the present value we note that there is considerable improvement in the processing time. This can be seen by substituting different values of σ in both expressions (that is, Equations (3.129) and (9.73)).

9.3.3 Optimal Load Sequence

Now we state and prove an important result regarding the sequence of load distribution for the interior case.

Theorem 9.1.   In the interior case, having identical processors and identical links, with x processors on the right and y processors on the left, the processing time will be a minimum if the sequence of load distribution by the root processor goes first to the side with the lesser number of processors.

Proof. From Equations (9.41) and (9.42) it can be verified that $T(1, 2)$ and $T(2, 1)$ have the same closed-form expressions. Hence, it remains to be proved that

(i) $T(1, x) < T(x, 1)$, for $x > 2$
(ii) $T(2, x) < T(x, 2)$, for $x > 2$
(iii) $T(x, y) < T(y, x)$, for $x > 2$, $y > 2$, if $x < y$

Cases (i) and (ii) can be easily proved using Equations (9.60) through (9.63). To prove case (iii), consider Equation (9.64). It can be observed that the expression $T(x, y)$ can be obtained from Equation (9.64) by putting $R = x$ and $L = y$, and $T(y, x)$ can be obtained by interchanging x and y in the resulting expression. Thus,

$$T(y, x) = \left\{ \frac{9\sigma^2 f_0^2 f_1^2 f^{x+y-4}}{f^{x+y-4}K_1 - \sigma f^{y-2} + f^{x-2}K_2 + (3\sigma^2 - 2\sigma f)} \right\} w T_{cp} \qquad (9.79)$$

where K_1 and K_2 are given by Equations (9.65) and (9.66), respectively. Note that with $R = x$, $L = y$, the numerators of Equations (9.64) and (9.79) are identical. Denoting the denominators of Equations (9.64) and (9.79) as D_1 and D_2, respectively, the value of $(D_1 - D_2)$ is obtained as

$$D_1 - D_2 = \sigma^2(f^{y-2} - f^{x-2})(18\sigma^2 + 24\sigma + 24) \qquad (9.80)$$

From Equation (9.80) it can be seen that $(D_1 - D_2) > 0$ since $\sigma > 0$, $f > 1$. Thus it proves that $T(x, y) < T(y, x)$, if $x < y$. This completes the proof of the theorem.
□

In Chapter 6 it was shown that for the earlier proposed strategy for load distribution, processing time was independent of the sequence of load distribution. In this new strategy, this is not true.

9.3.4 Optimal Load Origination

In this section we prove an important theorem regarding the optimal load origination point in a homogeneous linear network. For notational simplicity, we redenote the processors as $p_0, p_1, p_2, \ldots, p_m$ from the right hand side. We assume that the load originates at a processor at the interior of the network. We also assume that the load is first distributed to the right hand side processors and then to the left hand side processors. Hence, when the load originates at the ith processor, there will be i processors on the right hand side and $(m - i)$ processors on the left hand side. The processing time is denoted by $T(i, m - i)$. Now the problem is to find an $i = i^*$, the optimal load origination point, such that $T(i^*, m - i^*)$ is a minimum, that is,

$$i^* = \arg\min_{i \in \{0,1,...,m\}} \{T(i, m - i)\} \tag{9.81}$$

To find this i^*, we use the following preliminary results.

Lemma 9.1.   For $m = 2$, $T(1, 1) < T(0, 2)$.

Proof. We obtain $T(1, 1)$ and $T(0, 2)$ from Equations (9.40) and (9.12) as

$$T(1, 1) = \left\{ \frac{f_0^2}{1 + f_0(1 + f_0)} \right\} wT_{cp} \tag{9.82}$$

$$T(0, 2) = \left\{ \frac{f_1}{f_1 + 2} \right\} wT_{cp} \tag{9.83}$$

Using the above expressions, the lemma is proved easily.

Lemma 9.2.   For $m = 3$, $T(1, 2) < T(0, 3)$.

Proof. We obtain $T(1, 2)$ and $T(0, 3)$ from Equations (9.41) and (9.12) as

$$T(1, 2) = \left\{ \frac{f_0 f_1}{f_1(1 + f_0) + 2} \right\} wT_{cp} \tag{9.84}$$

$$T(0, 3) = \left\{ \frac{f_0 f_1 f}{f_1 f(1 + f_0) + f + 1} \right\} wT_{cp} \tag{9.85}$$

Using Equations (9.84) and (9.85), the lemma can be proved easily.   □

Lemma 9.3.   For $m = 4$,
(i) $T(1, 3) < T(0, 4)$
(ii) $T(1, 3) > T(2, 2)$

Proof
(i) We obtain $T(0, 4)$ and $T(1, 3)$ from Equations (9.12) and (9.60) as

$$T(0, 4) = \left\{ \frac{3\sigma f_0 f_1 f^2}{f^2(3\sigma f_1 + 3\sigma f_0 f_1 + f) - 1} \right\} wT_{cp} \tag{9.86}$$

$$T(1, 3) = \left\{ \frac{3\sigma f_0^2 f_1 f}{f\{3\sigma f_0 f_1(1 + f_0) + 3\sigma f_1 + f\} - 1} \right\} wT_{cp} \tag{9.87}$$

From Equations (9.86) and (9.87) we can prove that $T(1, 3) < T(0, 4)$.

(ii) We obtain $T(2, 2)$ from Equation (9.43) as

$$T(2, 2) = \left\{ \frac{f_0 f_1^2}{f_1(1 + f_0 f_1 + f_1) + (1 + f_1)} \right\} w T_{cp} \qquad (9.88)$$

From Equations (9.87) and (9.88) we can prove that $T(1, 3) > T(2, 2)$.   □

Lemma 9.4. For $m = 5$,
(i) $T(1, 4) < T(0, 5)$
(ii) $T(2, 3) < T(1, 4)$.

Proof
(i) We obtain $T(1, 4)$ and $T(0, 5)$ from Equations (9.60) and (9.12) as

$$T(1, 4) = \left\{ \frac{3\sigma f_0^2 f_1 f^2}{f^2(3\sigma f_0 f_1 + 3\sigma f_0^2 f_1 + 3\sigma f_1 + f) - 1} \right\} w T_{cp} \qquad (9.89)$$

$$T(0, 5) = \left\{ \frac{3\sigma f_0 f_1 f^3}{f^3(3\sigma f_1 + 3\sigma f_0 f_1 + f) - 1} \right\} w T_{cp} \qquad (9.90)$$

With suitable algebraic manipulations it can be easily proved that $T(1, 4) < T(0, 5)$.
(ii) We obtain $T(2, 3)$ from Equation (9.62) as

$$T(2, 3) = \left\{ \frac{3\sigma f_0 f_1^2 f}{f\{3\sigma(1 + f_1)(1 + f_0 f_1) + 3\sigma f_0 f_1 + 1\} - 1} \right\} w T_{cp} \qquad (9.91)$$

Similarly it can be proved that $T(2, 3) < T(1, 4)$.   □

Lemma 9.5. For $m > 5$
(i) $T(1, m - 1) < T(0, m)$
(ii) $T(2, m - 2) < T(1, m - 1)$
(iii) For $i \in \{2, 3, \ldots, \lfloor m/2 \rfloor\}$,
 $T(i + 1, m - i - 1) \leq T(i, m - i)$ if $f^{m-2i-1} g(\sigma) + 1 < 0$
 $T(i + 1, m - i - 1) \geq T(i, m - i)$ if $f^{m-2i-1} g(\sigma) + 1 \geq 0$
 where
 $g(\sigma) = 18\sigma^3 + 24\sigma^2 + 6\sigma - 1$

Proof
(i) We obtain $T(1, m - 1)$ and $T(0, m)$ from Equations (9.60) and (9.12) as

$$T(1, m - 1) = \left\{ \frac{3\sigma f_0^2 f_1 f^{m-3}}{f^{m-3}(3\sigma f_0 f_1 + 3\sigma f_0^2 f_1 + 3\sigma f_1 + f) - 1} \right\} w T_{cp} \qquad (9.92)$$

$$T(0, m) = \left\{ \frac{3\sigma f_0 f_1 f^{m-2}}{f^{m-2}(3\sigma f_1 + 3\sigma f_0 f_1 + f) - 1} \right\} w T_{cp} \qquad (9.93)$$

Using this it can be proved that $T(1, m - 1) < T(0, m)$.

(ii) We obtain $T(1, m-1)$ and $T(2, m-2)$ from Equations (9.60) and (9.62) as

$$T(1, m-1) = \left\{ \frac{3\sigma f_0^2 f_1 f^{m-3}}{f^{m-3}(3\sigma f_0 f_1 + 3\sigma f_0^2 f_1 + 3\sigma f_1 + f) - 1} \right\} w T_{cp} \quad (9.94)$$

$$T(2, m-2) = \left\{ \frac{3\sigma f_0 f_1^2 f^{m-4}}{f^{m-4}\{3\sigma(1 + f_1)(1 + f_0 f_1) + 3\sigma f_0 f_1 + 1\} - 1} \right\} w T_{cp}$$

$$(9.95)$$

Similarly, from Equations (9.94) and (9.95) it can be shown that $T(2, m-2) < T(1, m-1)$.

(iii) First we shall consider the case when $i = 2$. The expression for $T(3, m-3)$ can be obtained from (9.64) as

$$T(3, m-3) = \left\{ \frac{9\sigma^2 f_0^2 f_1^2 f^{m-4}}{K_1 f^{m-4} - \sigma f + K_2 f^{m-5} + (3\sigma^2 - 2\sigma f)} \right\} w T_{cp} \quad (9.96)$$

where K_1 and K_2 are as defined in Equations (9.65) and (9.66). The expression for $T(2, m-2)$ is given in Equation (9.95). Multiplying the numerator and denominator of Equation (9.95) by $3\sigma f_0$, the numerators of Equations (9.95) and (9.96) will be identical. Denoting the new denominators as D_2 and D_3, respectively, the value of $D_2 - D_3$ is obtained as

$$D_2 - D_3 = 3\sigma^2 \{f^{m-5} g(\sigma) + 1\} \quad (9.97)$$

where

$$g(\sigma) = \{18\sigma^3 + 24\sigma^2 + 6\sigma - 1\} \quad (9.98)$$

Thus, from Equation (9.97) it can be seen that $(D_2 - D_3) < 0$ if $f^{m-5} g(\sigma) + 1 < 0$ and hence $T(3, m-3) < T(2, m-2)$. Similarly $T(3, m-3) > T(2, m-2)$, if $f^{m-5} g(\sigma) + 1 > 0$.

Now consider the general case $i > 2$. The expressions for $T(i, m-i)$ and $T(i+1, m-i-1)$ can be obtained from Equation (9.64) as

$$T(i, m-i) = \left\{ \frac{9\sigma^2 f_0^2 f_1^2 f^{m-4}}{K_1 f^{m-4} - \sigma f^{i-2} + K_2 f^{m-2-i} + (3\sigma^2 - 2\sigma f)} \right\} w T_{cp}$$

$$(9.99)$$

$$T(i+1, m-i) = \left\{ \frac{9\sigma^2 f_0^2 f_1^2 f^{m-4}}{K_1 f^{m-4} - \sigma f^{i-1} + K_2 f^{m-i-3} + (3\sigma^2 - 2\sigma f)} \right\} w T_{cp}$$

$$(9.100)$$

Since the numerators of Equations (9.99) and (9.100) are identical, we find the difference in their denominators. Denoting the respective denominators as D_i and D_{i+1}, the value of $D_i - D_{i+1}$ is obtained as

$$D_i - D_{i+1} = \sigma f^{i-3} \{g(\sigma) f^{m-2i-1} + 1\} \quad (9.101)$$

where $g(\sigma)$ is given by Equation (9.98). Thus, from Equation (9.101), it can be seen that $(D_i - D_{i+1}) < 0$, if $f^{m-2i-1} g(\sigma) + 1 < 0$, which means that $T(i+$

$1, m - i - 1) < T(i, m - i)$. Similarly, $T(i + 1, m - i - 1) \geq T(i, m - i)$ if $f^{m-2i-1}g(\sigma) + 1 \geq 0$. This proves the lemma.   □

Now we state the optimal load origination theorem based on the above lemmas.

Theorem 9.2.   In a linear network consisting of $(m + 1)$ identical processors denoted as $p_0, p_1, \ldots, p_m$, let the sequence of load distribution be first towards p_0. Then the processing time will be a minimum if the load originates at the processor p_{i^*}, where i^* is given as follows:

  (I) when $m = 0$, $i^* = 0$
 (II) when $m = 1$, $i^* = 0$ or 1
(III) when $m = 2$, $i^* = 1$
(IV) when $m = 3$, $i^* = 1$ or 2
 (V) when $m = 4$ or 5, $i^* = 2$
(VI) when $m > 5$,
      (a) if $\{f^{m-5}g(\sigma) + 1\} > 0$, then $i^* = 2$
      (b) if $\{f^{m-5}g(\sigma) + 1\} = 0$, then $i^* = 2$ or 3
      (c) if $\{f^{m-5}g(\sigma) + 1\} < 0$, then
         (i) if $h(\sigma) = \lceil h(\sigma) \rceil$,
            then $i^* = h(\sigma)$ or $h(\sigma) + 1$
        (ii) if $h(\sigma) \neq \lceil h(\sigma) \rceil$,
            then $i^* = \lceil h(\sigma) \rceil$
      where

$$h(\sigma) = \left\lceil \frac{(m - 1) + \left(\dfrac{\ln(-g(\sigma))}{\ln(f)}\right)}{2} \right\rceil$$

Here $g(\sigma)$ is given by equation (9.98).

Proof. The proofs for (I) and (II) are trivial.

(III) When $m = 2$, from Lemma 9.1, it can be seen that $i^* = 1$.
(IV) When $m = 3$, it has been shown in Theorem 9.1 that $T(1, 2) = T(2, 1)$. Further, using Lemma 9.2, we see that $i^* = 1$ or 2.
 (V) When $m = 4$, using Theorem 9.1, $T(1, 3) < T(3, 1)$. From Lemma 9.3, we see that $T(1, 3) < T(0, 4)$ and $T(1, 3) > T(2, 2)$. Therefore, $i^* = 2$ for $m = 4$. When $m = 5$, using Theorem 9.1, we see that $T(1, 4) < T(4, 1)$ and $T(2, 3) < T(3, 2)$. Further, from Lemma 9.4, it can be seen that $T(1, 4) < T(0, 5)$ and $T(2, 3) < T(1, 4)$, which implies that $i^* = 2$.
(VI) (a) From Lemma 9.5, it can be seen that, when $f^{m-5}g(\sigma) + 1 > 0$, $T(2, m - 2) < T(3, m - 3)$. Further, it is easily proved that $f^{m-2i-1}g(\sigma) + 1 > 0$, for $i \in \{3, 4, \ldots, \lfloor m/2 \rfloor\}$ and hence $T(i + 1, m - i - 1) > T(i, m - i)$, $i \in \{3, 4, \ldots, \lfloor m/2 \rfloor\}$. This proves that $i^* = 2$.
    (b) If $f^{m-5}g(\sigma) + 1 = 0$ then, similarly, $f^{m-2i-1}g(\sigma) + 1 > 0$ for $i \in \{3, \ldots, \lfloor m/2 \rfloor\}$ and therefore $i^* = 2$ or 3.
    (c) For $i \in \{2, 3, \ldots, \lfloor m/2 \rfloor\}$, if $f^{m-5}g(\sigma) + 1 < 0$, then from Lemma 9.5, $T(i+1, m-i-1) < T(i, m-i)$. Since $f > 1$, the inequality $f^{m-2i-1}g(\sigma) +$

$1 < 0$ implies that $g(\sigma) < 0$. Now consider the minimum $i^* \in \{3, \ldots, \lfloor m/2 \rfloor\}$ such that $T(i^*, m - i^*) \leq T(i^* + 1, m - i^* - 1)$. From Theorem 9.1 such an i^* must exist. Now consider the two possible cases:

(i) $T(i^*, m - i^*) = T(i^* + 1, m - i^* - 1)$. This implies that $f^{m-2i-1}g(\sigma) + 1 = 0$. From which $i^* = h(\sigma)$ or $h(\sigma) + 1$.

(ii) $T(i^*, m - i^*) < T(i^* + 1, m - i^*)$ This implies that $f^{m-2i-1}g(\sigma) + 1 > 0$. From which $i^* = \lceil h(\sigma) \rceil$.

It can be easily verified that $T(i, m - i) < T(i + 1, m - i - 1)$ for $i > i^* + 1$ in Case i and $i > i^*$ in Case ii. From this we get the optimal load origination point for the case $m > 5$. This proves the theorem. □

The concept of optimal load origination point has a significant application in a ring network, too. If the load originates at a specific node in a ring network, having a given number of processors, then the results of the above theorem can be used to determine the optimal number of processors on the left and right hand sides of the load originating processor to which load has to be distributed. Note that in this case the last processors on the left and right sides do not communicate.

9.4 UTILITY OF THE INFEASIBLE SOLUTION

In Section 9.2.1, we have assumed that the processors and links should be arranged in order of decreasing speed. This assumption is sufficient to obtain a set of linear equations with a feasible solution. For an arbitrary arrangement of processors and links the set of equations will not yield a feasible solution. However, given the infeasible load distribution, the basic concept behind the new strategy can still be employed to show an improvement in time performance over the earlier strategy given in Chapters 3 and 6. The example that follows illustrates this. Consider the linear network shown in Figure 9.6 with $T_{cm} = 1.0$ and $T_{cp} = 2.0$. The inequalities shown in Equation (9.11) are violated here. But the system of Equations (9.3) and (9.5) can still be solved to yield $\alpha_0 = 0.4711, \alpha_1 = 0.3768, \alpha_2 = 0.1077, \alpha_3 = 0.0154, \alpha_4 = 0.0154$, and $\alpha_5 = 0.0136$. Note that with these values the inequalities in Equation (9.4) are violated. Hence the timing diagram given in Figure 9.2 is no longer valid. However, we can still use the rules of load distribution given in Section 9.1 to distribute these load fractions as shown in the timing diagram in Figure 9.6. From the figure, it can be observed that all the processors do not stop at the same time instant, and processing time is given by the processor p_5 as 1.926. When the earlier strategy is adopted for this linear network, the processing time obtained is 2.055. Thus, even in the case of arbitrary arrangement, the new strategy shows an improvement in time performance.

9.5 CONCLUDING REMARKS

The highlights of this chapter are as follows:

- An efficient way of utilizing the front ends of the processors in a linear network was proposed.

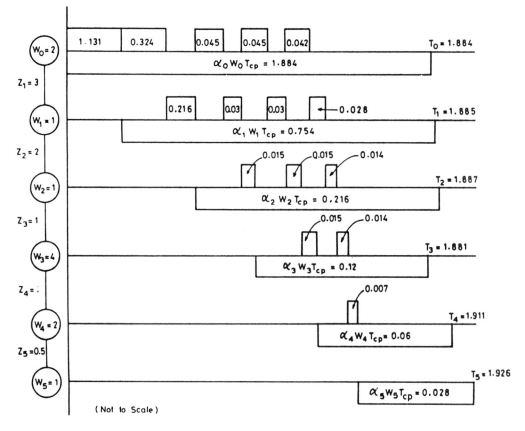

FIGURE 9.6   Example for Arbitrary Arrangeme⌐

- For heterogeneous networks, in which the processors and the links are arranged in order of decreasing speed, we derived closed-form expressions for processing time, for the case in which the processing load originates at the boundary and for that in which it originates at a point at the interior of the network.

- Using these closed-form expressions for a homogeneous network, we carried out an asymptotic analysis for both the cases to obtain the bounds on time performance.

- We proved that in a linear network, when the processing load originates at the interior, the processing time will be optimal if the load is distributed first to the side with a lesser number of processors.

- For the interior case, we obtained an optimal load origination point in a homogeneous network.

BIBLIOGRAPHIC NOTES

Most of the material presented in this chapter is from Bharadwaj et al. (1995a).

CHAPTER 10

Multi-Installment Load Distribution in Single-Level Tree Networks

In all the previous chapters, we assumed that a processor receives its load fraction in a single installment. While this strategy is easy to implement, it gives rise to considerable idle time for almost all the processors since a processor can start computing only after receiving the entire load fraction assigned to it. One way to reduce these idle times is to send the load fractions in more than one installment so that a processor can begin its computation earlier in time. In this chapter we further exploit the arbitrarily divisible nature of the processing load to devise a multi-installment load distribution strategy for single-level tree networks. From a practical perspective, this strategy is more difficult to implement than the previous one since the root processor or its front end has to perform a larger number of operations to prepare the data for transmission (see Chapter 2). However, we show that the increase in complexity is rewarded by a considerable improvement in time performance.

The multi-installment strategy is also advantageous when the processors in the network have a limited memory or buffer size and the data file to be processed is very large. In this situation, the load fraction assigned to a processor in the single installment strategy may be too large to be accommodated in its memory. In this chapter, we show that in a multi-installment strategy, the size of the load fractions assigned to a processor in each installment can be controlled by choosing a sufficiently large number of installments. Thus, this strategy helps to avoid the problem of buffer overflow, which might occur in the single installment strategy.

10.1 MOTIVATION AND PRELIMINARY REMARKS

We first show that the processing time can be decreased by distributing the load in two installments rather than in one.

Example 10.1

Consider a single-level tree network, consisting of one root processor and one child processor, both equipped with front ends. The total processing load has to be shared in an optimal manner such that the processing time is minimized. In the timing diagram for load distribution given in Figure 10.1, it can be seen that a child processor has to be idle for a certain amount of time before it actually starts computing. Hence, if by some means this idle time can be reduced so that the child processor can start computing at an earlier point in time, then we can further reduce the processing time. One way of reducing the waiting time is to send the processing load in more than one installment. Figure 10.1 shows the case in which the load is sent in one installment and Figure 10.2 shows the case in which the same load is sent in two installments. We choose the installments in both cases in such a way that both processors stop computing at the same time instant. From Figures 10.1 and 10.2, we can see that the processing time is reduced by 9.6 percent by sending the load in two installments.

Now we consider the general case of a single-level tree network consisting of one root processor (p_0) and m child processors $p_1, \ldots, p_m$, connected to p_0. Further, we assume that in the with-front-end case, all the processor-link pairs satisfy Equation (5.28) and in the without-front-end case they satisfy Equations (5.90) and (5.28). The root processor distributes the load assigned to each child processor in n installments. We redenote the processing time, defined in Chapter 2, as $T(m, n)$ to make it an explicit function of both the number of child processors (m) and the number of installments (n). Further, here, unlike in previous chapters, when we consider the with-front-end case we assume that all the child processors, in addition to the root processor, are equipped with front ends.
The load distribution in installments is assumed to follow the rules given below.

(i) The root processor p_0 keeps a fraction of the total processing load for itself to compute and distributes the rest to the child processors.

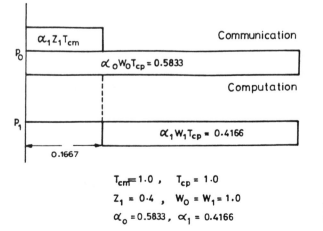

$$T_{cm} = 1.0 \ , \quad T_{cp} = 1.0$$
$$Z_1 = 0.4 \ , \quad W_0 = W_1 = 1.0$$
$$\alpha_0 = 0.5833 \ , \quad \alpha_1 = 0.4166$$

FIGURE 10.1 Load Distribution in One Installment

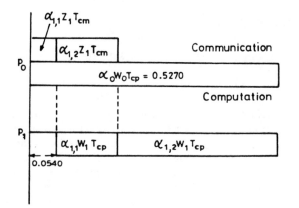

$$T_{cm} = 1.0 \quad , \quad T_{cp} = 1.0$$
$$Z_1 = 0.4 \quad , \quad W_0 = W_1 = 1.0$$
$$\alpha_0 = 0.5270, \ \alpha_{1,1} = 0.135, \ \alpha_{1,2} = 0.338$$

FIGURE 10.2 Load Distribution in Two Installments

(ii) The root processor distributes the load fractions of the first installment to all the child processors following a given fixed sequence, and then the load fractions of the second installment in the same sequence, and so on, until the last installment. Note that when the processors are equipped with front ends, the load distribution is actually done by the front ends.

(iii) The front end of the root processor (or the root processor itself when there is no front end) is continuously engaged in distributing the load until all the installments have been communicated.

(iv) When the processors are equipped with front ends, they must be engaged continuously in computation, once they start computing, from the first installment until the end of the last installment. On the other hand, when the processors are not equipped with front ends, a processor first receives a load fraction and then computes it. This process repeats itself continuously until all the installments assigned to it are exhausted.

(v) A processor starts computing a given installment the moment its front end finishes receiving it.

In Chapter 5 it was shown that the time performance of the single installment strategy is optimal when all the processors stop computing at the same instant in time. Although we do not provide a rigorous proof for this assumption in the case of a multi-installment strategy, it is indeed true even here. An intuitive argument, similar to the one in Chapters 4, is sufficient to justify this assertion.

10.2 GENERAL LOAD DISTRIBUTION EQUATIONS

The single-level tree network architecture Σ consists of one root processor and m child processors as shown in Figure 10.3. For analytical ease, we redenote the processors as $p_m, p_{m-1}, \ldots, p_1$ and the communication links as $l_m, l_{m-1}, \ldots, l_1$. This

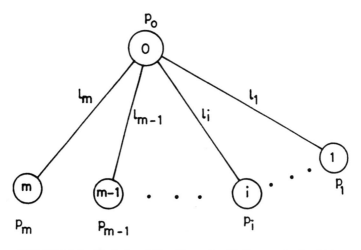

FIGURE 10.3   Single-Level Tree Network with Communication Links

tree configuration can be represented as an ordered set as follows:

$$\Sigma = \{p_0, (l_m, p_m), (l_{m-1}, p_{m-1}), \ldots, (l_i, p_i), \ldots, (l_1, p_1)\} \qquad (10.1)$$

where (l_i, p_i) represents the fact that the ith processor p_i is connected to p_0 via link l_i. The load distribution is done sequentially from the left end of the tree to the right end of the tree, which is also the order given in Equation (10.1). Note that here the links and processors are renumbered in a reverse order in contrast to the numbering followed in the previous chapters. Further, the installments are also numbered in a reverse order. This notation is adopted for ease in obtaining the load distribution equations and their solution (either computationally or analytically) for a general case of an arbitrary number of processors and installments. Thus, for example, in this notation, in a system with one root and three child processors ($m = 3$) and with three installments ($n = 3$) we have the load distribution as follows:

α_0: Load fraction to the root processor

$\alpha_{3,3}$: First installment to p_3

$\alpha_{2,3}$: First installment to p_2

$\alpha_{1,3}$: First installment to p_1

$\alpha_{3,2}$: Second installment to p_3

$\alpha_{2,2}$: Second installment to p_2

$\alpha_{1,2}$: Second installment to p_1

$\alpha_{3,1}$: Third installment to p_3

$\alpha_{2,1}$: Third installment to p_2

$\alpha_{1,1}$: Third installment to p_1

Note that the first installment is actually numbered as 3, the second installment as 2, and the third installment as 1. Hence, in general, we define $\alpha_{i,j}$ as the load fraction assigned to p_i in the $(n - j + 1)$th installment.

10.2.1 Load Distribution Equations: With Front End

Consider a system of $(m + 1)$ processors in which the load is distributed in n installments using the rules mentioned above. The installments are such that all the processors stop computing at the same time instant. The timing diagram is shown in Figure 10.4, from which we write the following recursive equations.

$$\alpha_{i,1} w_i T_{cp} = \alpha_{i-1,1}(z_{i-1}T_{cm} + w_{i-1}T_{cp}), \quad i = 2, 3, \ldots, m \tag{10.2}$$

$$\alpha_{i,j} = \left\{ \sum_{k=1}^{i-1} \alpha_{k,j} z_k + \sum_{k=i}^{m} \alpha_{k,j-1} z_k \right\} \left\{ \frac{\delta}{w_i} \right\},$$
$$i = 1, \ldots, m; \quad \text{and} \quad j = 2, \ldots, n \tag{10.3}$$

where $\delta = T_{cm}/T_{cp}$ is as defined in Chapter 2. From Equation (10.2) we have

$$\alpha_{i,1} = \alpha_{1,1} \left\{ \prod_{k=1}^{i-1} \frac{w_k + z_k \delta}{w_{k+1}} \right\} \tag{10.4}$$

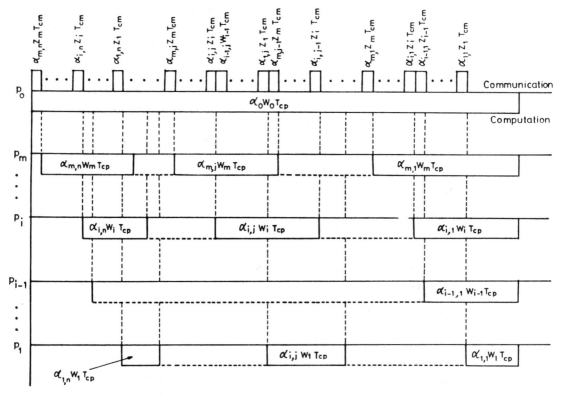

FIGURE 10.4   Timing Diagram: Single-Level Tree Network (with Front End)

and hence the load on the root processor is

$$\alpha_0 = \left\{\sum_{i=1}^{m}\sum_{j=1}^{n}\alpha_{i,j}z_i\right\}\left\{\frac{\delta}{w_0}\right\} + \alpha_{1,1}\left\{\frac{w_1}{w_0}\right\} \tag{10.5}$$

The normalizing equation is given by

$$\alpha_0 + \alpha_{1,1} + \ldots + \alpha_{m,n} = 1 \tag{10.6}$$

Note that in Equation (10.3) the first summation in the RHS vanishes when $i = 1$. Thus, we have in total $(mn + 1)$ linear equations and $(mn + 1)$ unknowns. These equations can be solved recursively by using Equation (10.4) to obtain $\alpha_{i,1}$ ($i = 2, 3, \ldots, m$) as a function of $\alpha_{1,1}$. The remaining $\alpha_{i,j}$ are then obtained using Equation (10.3). Then the value of α_0 is obtained as a function of $\alpha_{1,1}$ using Equation (10.5). Using the normalizing Equation (10.6) the exact value of $\alpha_{1,1}$ is computed. The remaining $\alpha_{i,j}$'s and α_0 can then be computed. The processing time is the same as that of the root and is given by $\alpha_0 w_0 T_{cp}$ (see Figure 10.4).

10.2.2 Load Distribution Equations: Without Front End

When the processors are not equipped with front ends, in the case when $m = 1$, it can be verified that the performance is independent of the number of installments. This happens because the root processor can start computing only after distributing all the installments to its child processors. Since there is only one child processor, any multi-installment strategy is identical to the single installment strategy. Hence, the model considered is only valid for $m \geq 2$. The corresponding timing diagram is shown in Figure 10.5, from which the following recursive equations can be obtained:

$$\alpha_{i,1}w_i T_{cp} = \alpha_{i-1,1}\left(w_{i-1}T_{cp} + z_{i-1}T_{cm}\right), \quad i = 2, \ldots, m \tag{10.7}$$

$$\alpha_{i,j} = \left\{\sum_{k=1}^{i-1}\alpha_{k,j}z_k + \sum_{k=i+1}^{m}\alpha_{k,j-1}z_k\right\}\left\{\frac{\delta}{w_i}\right\},$$
$$i = 1, \ldots, m \text{ and } j = 2, \ldots, n. \tag{10.8}$$

From Equation (10.7), we have

$$\alpha_{i,1} = \alpha_{1,1}\left\{\prod_{k=1}^{i-1}\frac{w_k + z_k\delta}{w_{k+1}}\right\} \tag{10.9}$$

and the load on the root processor is

$$\alpha_0 = \alpha_{1,1}\left\{\frac{w_1}{w_0}\right\} \tag{10.10}$$

The normalizing equation is given by Equation (10.6). Note that, as in the previous case, the first summation in the RHS of Equation (10.8) vanishes when $i = 1$ and the second summation vanishes when $i = m$. Following the procedure described in the earlier case, these recursive equations can be used to compute the individual load fractions to the processors in each installment. The processing time is computed by adding the computation time of the root processor to the communication delays incurred by the root processor in communicating all the installments (see Figure 10.5).

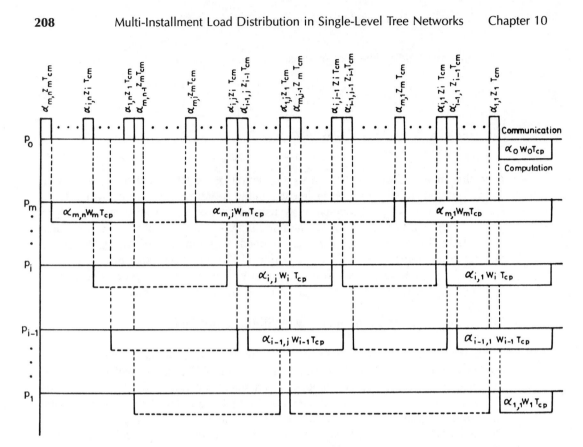

FIGURE 10.5   Timing Diagram: Single-Level Tree Network (without Front End)

Since the closed-form solution for the processing time in a general case (with and without front ends) is difficult to derive, in the next section we give closed-form solutions for a homogeneous network (that is, $z_i = z$ for $i = 1, 2, \ldots, m$ and $w_i = w$ for $i = 0, 1, \ldots, m$).

10.3 CLOSED-FORM SOLUTIONS: WITH FRONT END

For a homogeneous network, Equations (10.4), (10.3), and (10.5) can be rewritten as

$$\alpha_{i,1} = \alpha_{1,1}(1 + \sigma)^{i-1}, \qquad i = 2, \ldots, m \tag{10.11}$$

$$\alpha_{i,j} = \left\{ \sum_{k=1}^{i-1} \alpha_{k,j} + \sum_{k=i}^{m} \alpha_{k,j-1} \right\} \sigma, \tag{10.12}$$

$$i = 1, \ldots, m; \quad j = 2, \ldots, n$$

$$\alpha_0 = \left\{ \sum_{i=1}^{m} \sum_{j=1}^{n} \alpha_{i,j} \right\} \sigma + \alpha_{1,1} \tag{10.13}$$

For further simplification we use the following notation:

$$\alpha_{i,j} = \alpha_{1,1} X_k, \quad i = 1, \ldots, m; \quad j = 1, \ldots, n \tag{10.14}$$

where

$$k = (i - 1) + (j - 1)m \tag{10.15}$$

Then, from Equations (10.11), (10.12), and (10.13) we obtain

$$X_k = (1 + \sigma)^k, \quad k = 0, 1, \ldots, m - 1 \tag{10.16}$$

$$X_k = (X_{k-1} + X_{k-2} + \cdots + X_{k-m})\sigma,$$

$$k = m, m + 1, \ldots, mn - 1 \tag{10.17}$$

Therefore,

$$\alpha_0 = \alpha_{1,1}(\sigma X + 1) \tag{10.18}$$

where

$$X = \sum_{i=0}^{mn-1} X_i \tag{10.19}$$

Using the normalizing equation (10.6) we have

$$\alpha_{1,1} = \frac{1}{1 + (1 + \sigma)X} \tag{10.20}$$

Thus, the processing time $T(m, n)$ is obtained as

$$T(m, n) = \left\{ \frac{\sigma X + 1}{(1 + \sigma)X + 1} \right\} w T_{cp} \tag{10.21}$$

Hence, once the value of X is known, the processing time $T(m, n)$ can be obtained. In order to obtain X, we have to obtain the expressions for X_i $(i = 0, 1, \ldots, mn-1)$. This can be done by using the generating functions technique. The generating function should have X_i $(i = 1, \ldots, mn - 1)$ as its coefficients, in the form of polynomials in σ, generated by the recursive equations given in Equation (10.17) with initial conditions as in Equation (10.16). The generating function is given as

$$G(s) = X_0 + X_1 s + \cdots + X_j s^j + \cdots \tag{10.22}$$

Note that the index of the coefficients in the generating function is not limited to $mn-1$ but goes to infinity. These coefficients are also given by the recursive equations with its index extended beyond $mn - 1$. However, for the purpose of computing $T(m, n)$, we need to consider terms from X_0 to X_{mn-1} only.

Following the standard procedure for obtaining closed-form expressions for the coefficients in the generating function, we obtain

$$G(s) = \frac{1 + s + \cdots + s^{m-1}}{1 - \sigma s(1 + s + \cdots + s^{m-1})} \tag{10.23}$$

This can now be expanded into a power series in which the coefficients of s^j is X_j. The expansion into power series can be done in two ways. The first method is by using the rational expansion theorem and the other is by using binomial expansion of the numerator and the denominator of Equation (10.23). We will show that both methods lead to the same closed-form solution.

10.3.1 Solution Using Rational Expansion Theorem

We state the rational expansion theorem as follows:

Theorem 10.1. If $G(s) = P(s)/Q(s)$, and $Q(s)$ has only distinct roots given by $1/\mu_1, 1/\mu_2, \ldots, 1/\mu_m$ then we can express X_k as

$$X_k = a_1(\mu_1)^k + a_2(\mu_2)^k + \cdots + a_m(\mu_m)^k, \quad k = 0, 1, \ldots, mn - 1 \tag{10.24}$$

where

$$a_j = -\mu_j P(1/\mu_j)/Q'(1/\mu_j), \quad j = 1, \ldots, m \tag{10.25}$$

and $Q'(1/\mu_j)$ is the first order derivative of $Q(s)$ evaluated at $(1/\mu_j)$.

Applying this theorem to Equation (10.23), the numerator $P(s)$ and the denominator $Q(s)$ of $G(s)$ are given as

$$P(s) = 1 + s + \cdots + s^{m-1} \tag{10.26}$$

$$Q(s) = 1 - \sigma s P(s) \tag{10.27}$$

From Equations (10.24) through (10.27), we have

$$X_k = \left(\frac{1}{\sigma}\right) \sum_{i=1}^{m} \frac{(\mu_i)^{k+1}(\mu_i - 1)\{(\mu_i)^m - 1\}}{\mu_i\{(\mu_i)^m - 1\} - m(\mu_i - 1)} \tag{10.28}$$

Equation (10.28) above shows that X_k can be expressed in terms of the roots of $Q(s)$ alone. Substituting in Equation (10.19) we have

$$X = \left(\frac{1}{\sigma}\right) \sum_{k=0}^{mn-1} \sum_{i=1}^{m} \frac{(\mu_i)^{k+1}(\mu_i - 1)\{(\mu_i)^m - 1\}}{\mu_i\{(\mu_i)^m - 1\} - m(\mu_i - 1)} \tag{10.29}$$

which, when substituted in Equation (10.21), gives the closed-form solution for the processing time. Note that the function $Q(s)$ may have imaginary roots. However, the imaginary part gets canceled when the summation in Equation (10.28) is performed. It can be verified that $Q(s)$ has distinct roots. However, in cases where $Q(s)$ has repeated roots, one can use the general expansion theorem for rational generating functions and obtain closed-form expressions for X_j as functions of the roots of $Q(s)$. Following is an example that demonstrates the procedure explained above.

Example 10.2

Consider a single-level tree network consisting of a root and two child processors, equipped with front ends, in which load distribution is performed in three installments, that is, $m = 2$ and $n = 3$. Using Equation (10.23) the generating function $G(s)$ is obtained as

$$G(s) = \frac{1 + s}{1 - \sigma s(1 + s)}$$

so that

$$P(s) = 1 + s$$

$$Q(s) = 1 - \sigma s(1 + s)$$

The roots of the equation $Q(s)$ are given by

$$(1/\mu_1) = \frac{\left(-1 + \sqrt{1 + 4/\sigma}\right)}{2}$$

$$(1/\mu_2) = \frac{\left(-1 - \sqrt{1 + 4/\sigma}\right)}{2}$$

Using Equation (10.25),

$$a_1 = \frac{(c_1 + c_2)}{(c_1 - c_2)(c_1 c_2)}$$

$$a_2 = -\frac{(c_1 - c_2)}{(c_1 + c_2)(c_1 c_2)}$$

where

$$c_1 = \sqrt{4 + \sigma}, \quad c_2 = \sqrt{\sigma}$$

Using Equation (10.24), we have, for different values of k,

$$X_0 = 1, \ X_1 = 1 + \sigma, \ X_2 = 2\sigma + \sigma^2$$

$$X_3 = \sigma + 3\sigma^2 + \sigma^3, \ X_4 = 3\sigma^2 + 4\sigma^3 + \sigma^4, \ X_5 = \sigma^2 + 6\sigma^3 + 5\sigma^4 + \sigma^5$$

$$T(2, 3) = \left\{ \frac{1 + 2\sigma + 4\sigma^2 + 8\sigma^3 + 11\sigma^4 + 6\sigma^5 + \sigma^6}{3 + 6\sigma + 12\sigma^2 + 19\sigma^3 + 17\sigma^4 + 7\sigma^5 + \sigma^6} \right\} w T_{cp}$$

where $T(2, 3)$ is the processing time obtained from Equation (10.21).

Note that in order to compute X_i's using this procedure one has to obtain the roots of a polynomial of high degree when the value of m is large. This is a tedious procedure. But once the roots are obtained, the computation of X_i is easy.

10.3.2 Solution Using Binomial Expansion

Consider the generating function $G(s)$ in the form given in Equation (10.23). This can be written as

$$G(s) = \frac{(1 - s^m)}{1 - (1 + \sigma)s + \sigma s^{m+1}} \tag{10.30}$$

Defining

$$y = as(1 + bs^m) \tag{10.31}$$

where

$$a = (1 + \sigma) \tag{10.32}$$

and

$$b = -\left(\frac{\sigma}{a}\right) \tag{10.33}$$

we have

$$G(s) = (1 - s^m)(1 - y)^{-1} \tag{10.34}$$

Expanding Equation (10.34), $G(s)$ can be written as the difference of two series denoted by G_1 and G_2 (that is, $G(s) = G_1 - G_2$) where

$$G_1 = 1 + y + y^2 + \cdots \tag{10.35}$$

$$G_2 = s^m + s^m y + s^m y^2 + \cdots \tag{10.36}$$

From Equation (10.31) y^j can be written, using binomial expansion, as

$$y^j = a^j s^j \left\{ \binom{j}{0} (bs^m)^0 + \binom{j}{1} (bs^m)^1 + \cdots + \binom{j}{j} (bs^m)^j \right\} \tag{10.37}$$

Thus, X_p, the coefficient of s^p in Equation (10.34), is obtained as the difference of the coefficients of s^p in Equations (10.35) and (10.36), denoted by X_{p1} and X_{p2}, respectively. Thus,

$$X_p = X_{p1} - X_{p2} \tag{10.38}$$

where

$$X_{p1} = \sum_{k=0}^{L(p)} a^{p-km} b^k \binom{p - km}{k} \tag{10.39}$$

where

$$L(p) = \left\lfloor \frac{p}{m + 1} \right\rfloor \tag{10.40}$$

and

$$X_{p2} = \sum_{k=0}^{M(p)} a^{p-(k+1)m} b^k \binom{p - (k + 1)m}{k} \tag{10.41}$$

where

$$M(p) = \left\lfloor \frac{p - m}{m + 1} \right\rfloor \tag{10.42}$$

Note that Equations (10.39) and (10.41) can be further simplified to

$$X_{p1} = \sum_{k=0}^{L(p)} (-1)^k \sigma^k (1 + \sigma)^{p-(m+1)k} \binom{p - km}{k} \tag{10.43}$$

$$X_{p2} = \sum_{k=0}^{M(p)} (-1)^k \sigma^k (1 + \sigma)^{(p-m)-(m+1)k} \binom{p - (k + 1)m}{k} \tag{10.44}$$

Thus, X_p can be obtained from Equation (10.38) using Equations (10.43) and (10.44). Substituting this into Equation (10.19) we obtain X and subsequently, using Equation (10.21), we get the processing time. The following example demonstrates the above procedure.

Example 10.3

We consider the network in Example 10.2. For this system, the generating function $G(s)$ is given by

$$G(s) = \frac{1 + s}{1 - \sigma s(1 + s)}$$

This can be rewritten in the form of Equation (10.34) as

$$G(s) = \frac{1 - s^2}{1 - (1 + \sigma)s + \sigma s^3}$$

Thus,

$$y = as(1 + bs^2)$$

where a and b are as defined in Equations (10.32) and (10.33), respectively. Now, using Equations (10.43) and (10.44) together with Equations (10.40) and (10.42), we obtain

$$X_{01} = 1; \quad X_{02} = 0; \quad X_0 = 1$$
$$X_{11} = 1 + \sigma; \quad X_{12} = 0; \quad X_1 = 1 + \sigma$$
$$X_{21} = (1 + \sigma)^2; \quad X_{22} = 1; \quad X_2 = 2\sigma + \sigma^2$$
$$X_{31} = (1 + \sigma)^3 - \sigma; \quad X_{32} = 1 + \sigma; \quad X_3 = \sigma + 3\sigma^2 + \sigma^3$$
$$X_{41} = (1 + \sigma)^4 - 2\sigma(1 + \sigma); \quad X_{42} = (1 + \sigma)^2; \quad X_4 = 3\sigma^2 + 4\sigma^3 + \sigma^4$$
$$X_{51} = (1 + \sigma)^5 - 3\sigma(1 + \sigma)^2; \quad X_{52} = (1 + \sigma)^3 - \sigma; \quad X_5 = \sigma^2 + 6\sigma^3 + 5\sigma^4 + \sigma^5$$

Using the above in Equations (10.19) and (10.21) we obtain the processing time as

$$T(2, 3) = \left\{ \frac{1 + 2\sigma + 4\sigma^2 + 8\sigma^3 + 11\sigma^4 + 6\sigma^5 + \sigma^6}{3 + 6\sigma + 12\sigma^2 + 19\sigma^3 + 17\sigma^4 + 7\sigma^5 + \sigma^6} \right\} w T_{cp}$$

As expected, this is identical to the result obtained in Example 10.2.

This approach does not require the computation of the roots of a higher degree polynomial. This is an advantage over the previous method when m is large. However, here the computation of X_i involves the evaluation of factorials of fairly large numbers when n is large.

10.4 CLOSED-FORM SOLUTIONS: WITHOUT FRONT END

For a homogeneous network, Equations (10.8), (10.9), and (10.10) can be rewritten as

$$\alpha_{i,1} = \alpha_{1,1} (1 + \sigma)^{i-1}, \quad 1 = 2, \dots, m \qquad (10.45)$$

$$\alpha_{i,j} = \left\{ \sum_{k=1}^{i-1} \alpha_{k,j} + \sum_{k=i+1}^{m} \alpha_{k,j-1} \right\} \sigma, \qquad (10.46)$$

$$i = 1, \dots, m ; \quad j = 2, \dots, n$$

$$\alpha_0 = \alpha_{1,1} \qquad (10.47)$$

Following the procedure adopted in the previous section, we use Equations (10.14) and (10.15) in Equations (10.45) and (10.46) to obtain

$$X_k = (1 + \sigma)^k, \quad k = 0, 1, \ldots, m - 1 \tag{10.48}$$

$$X_k = (X_{k-1} + X_{k-2} + \cdots + X_{k-m+1}) \sigma,$$
$$k = m, m + 1, \ldots, mn - 1 \tag{10.49}$$

Using the normalizing Equation (10.6),

$$\alpha_{1,1} = \frac{1}{(1 + X)} \tag{10.50}$$

where X is given by Equation (10.19). The processing time $T(m, n)$ is obtained as

$$T(m, n) = \left(\frac{\sigma X + 1}{X + 1}\right) w T_{cp} \tag{10.51}$$

Here also X can be obtained using generating functions. The corresponding generating function for the recursive equations (10.49) with initial conditions as shown in Equation (10.48), with the index of recursion taken to infinity, is given by

$$G(s) = \frac{1 + s + \cdots s^{m-1}}{1 - \sigma(s + \cdots + s^{m-1})} \tag{10.52}$$

This can be expanded into a power series to obtain X_j as the coefficient of s^j. As mentioned in the previous section this can be done in two ways, as given below.

10.4.1 Solution Using Rational Expansion Theorem

Since the degree of the numerator and denominator polynomials of Equation (10.52) are same, we write $G(s)$ as

$$G(s) = -\left(\frac{1}{\sigma}\right) + \frac{P(s)}{Q(s)} \tag{10.53}$$

where

$$P(s) = 1 + \frac{1}{\sigma} \tag{10.54}$$

$$Q(s) = 1 - \sigma(s + s^2 + \cdots + s^{m-1}) \tag{10.55}$$

Let the roots of the polynomial $Q(s)$ be $1/\mu_1, 1/\mu_2, \ldots, 1/\mu_{m-1}$. Then we can express X_k as

$$X_0 = -\left(\frac{1}{\sigma}\right) + a_1 + a_2 + \cdots + a_{m-1} \tag{10.56}$$

$$X_k = a_1(\mu_1)^k + a_2(\mu_2)^k + \cdots + a_{m-1}(\mu_{m-1})^k,$$
$$k = 1, 2, \ldots, mn - 1 \tag{10.57}$$

where

$$a_j = \frac{-\mu_j P(1/\mu_j)}{Q'_j(1/\mu_j)}, \quad j = 1, \ldots, m - 1 \tag{10.58}$$

From this,

$$X_k = \left(\frac{1+\sigma}{\sigma^2}\right) \sum_{i=1}^{m-1} \frac{(\mu_i)^{m+k-1} (\mu_i - 1)^2}{(\mu_i)^m - 1 - m(\mu_i - 1)},$$ (10.59)

$$k = 1, \ldots, mn - 1$$

Thus, substituting in Equation (10.19) we obtain

$$X = \left(\frac{1+\sigma}{\sigma^2}\right) \sum_{k=0}^{mn-1} \sum_{i=1}^{m-1} \left[\frac{(\mu_i)^{m+k-1} (\mu_i - 1)^2}{\mu_i^m - 1 - m(\mu_i - 1)}\right] - \left(\frac{1}{\sigma}\right)$$ (10.60)

which, when substituted in Equation (10.51), yields the processing time.

Example 10.4

We again consider the same network as in the previous example. But now we assume that the processors are not equipped with front ends. Using Equation (10.53), the generating function $G(s)$ can be written as

$$G(s) = -\left(\frac{1}{\sigma}\right) + \frac{P(s)}{Q(s)}$$

where

$$P(s) = 1 + \frac{1}{\sigma}$$

$$Q(s) = 1 - s\sigma$$

The root of the equation $Q(s)$ is given by

$$(1/\mu_1) = \frac{1}{\sigma}$$

Using Equation (10.58) we obtain

$$a_1 = 1 + \frac{1}{\sigma}$$

Now using Equations (10.56) and (10.59) we obtain the values of X_k ($k = 0, \ldots, 5$) as

$$X_0 = 1, \ X_1 = 1 + \sigma, \ X_2 = \sigma + \sigma^2$$
$$X_3 = \sigma^2 + \sigma^3, \ X_4 = \sigma^3 + \sigma^4 X_5 = \sigma^4 + \sigma^5$$

These X_k's are substituted in Equation (10.60) to obtain the value of X as

$$X = 2 + 2\sigma + 2\sigma^2 + 2\sigma^3 + 2\sigma^4 + \sigma^5$$ (10.61)

Substituting this value of X in Equation (10.51), we obtain

$$T(2, 3) = \left\{\frac{1 + 2\sigma + 2\sigma^2 + 2\sigma^3 + 2\sigma^4 + 2\sigma^5 + \sigma^6}{3 + 2\sigma + 2\sigma^2 + 2\sigma^3 + 2\sigma^4 + \sigma^5}\right\} w T_{cp}$$

10.4.2 Solution Using Binomial Expansion

Consider the generating function $G(s)$ in the form given in Equation (10.52). This can be rewritten as

$$G(s) = \frac{1 - s^m}{1 + \sigma s^m - s(1 + \sigma)} \tag{10.62}$$

Define

$$r = as(1 + bs^{m-1}) \tag{10.63}$$

where a and b are as defined as in Equations (10.32) and (10.33). Then,

$$G(s) = (1 - s^m)(1 - r)^{-1} \tag{10.64}$$

Expanding the RHS of this expression, $G(s)$ can be written as the difference of two series denoted as G_1 and G_2 (that is, $G(s) = G_1 - G_2$) where

$$G_1 = 1 + r + r^2 + \cdots \tag{10.65}$$

$$G_2 = s^m + s^m r + s^m r^2 + \cdots \tag{10.66}$$

From Equation (10.63) r^j can be written, using binomial expansion, as

$$r^j = a^j s^j \left\{ \binom{j}{0} (bs^{m-1})^0 + \binom{j}{1} (bs^{m-1})^1 + \cdots + \binom{j}{j} (bs^{m-1})^j \right\} \tag{10.67}$$

Since our main aim is to find the coefficient of s^p, namely X_p, in Equation (10.64), we collect the coefficients corresponding to s^p from Equations (10.65) and (10.66), as X_{p1} and X_{p2}, respectively. Then

$$X_p = X_{p1} - X_{p2} \tag{10.68}$$

where

$$X_{p1} = \sum_{k=0}^{L(p)} a^{p-k(m-1)} b^k \binom{p - k(m-1)}{k} \tag{10.69}$$

where

$$L(p) = \left\lfloor \frac{p}{m} \right\rfloor \tag{10.70}$$

and where

$$X_{p2} = \sum_{k=0}^{M(p)} a^{p-m(k+1)+k} b^k \binom{p - m(k+1) + k}{k} \tag{10.71}$$

where

$$M(p) = \left\lfloor \frac{p}{m} \right\rfloor - 1 \tag{10.72}$$

Note that Equations (10.69) and (10.71) can be further simplified to

$$X_{p1} = \sum_{k=0}^{L(p)} (-1)^k \sigma^k (1 + \sigma)^{p-km} \binom{p - k(m-1)}{k} \tag{10.73}$$

$$X_{p2} = \sum_{k=0}^{M(p)} (-1)^k \sigma^k (1 + \sigma)^{p-m(k+1)} \binom{p - m(k+1) + k}{k} \tag{10.74}$$

Thus, X_p can be obtained from Equations (10.73), (10.74), and (10.68). Substituting X_p into Equation (10.19) we obtain X and subsequently, using Equation (10.51), we obtain the closed-form solution for the processing time.

Example 10.5

We consider the same network as in Example 10.4. For this system, the generating function $G(s)$ is given by Equation (10.61) and can be written as

$$G(s) = \frac{1 - s^2}{1 + \sigma s^2 - s(1 + \sigma)}$$

so that

$$r = as(1 + bs)$$

where a and b are as defined in Equations (10.32) and (10.33), respectively. Now, using Equations (10.72) and (10.73) with Equations (10.69) and (10.71), we obtain

$$X_{01} = 1; \quad X_{02} = 0; \quad X_0 = 1$$

$$X_{11} = 1 + \sigma; \quad X_{12} = 0; \quad X_1 = 1 + \sigma$$

$$X_{21} = (1 + \sigma)^2 - \sigma; \quad X_{22} = -\sigma; \quad X_2 = \sigma + \sigma^2$$

$$X_{31} = (1 + \sigma)^3 - 2\sigma(1 + \sigma); \quad X_{32} = 1 + \sigma; \quad X_3 = \sigma^2 + \sigma^3$$

$$X_{41} = (1 + \sigma)^4 - 3\sigma(1 + \sigma)^2 + \sigma^2; \quad X_{42} = (1 + \sigma)^2 - \sigma; \quad X_4 = \sigma^3 + \sigma^4$$

$$X_{51} = (1 + \sigma)^5 - 4\sigma(1 + \sigma)^3 + 3\sigma^2(1 + \sigma); \quad X_{52} = (1 + \sigma)^3 - 2\sigma(1 + \sigma);$$

$$X_5 = \sigma^4 + \sigma^5$$

Using these, the processing time $T(2, 3)$ is found to be the same as in Example 10.4.

10.5 ASYMPTOTIC PERFORMANCE ANALYSIS

In Chapters 4 and 8 an asymptotic performance analysis for the single installment strategy was carried out with respect to the number of processors and the network parameters, and several interesting results were obtained. We perform a similar analysis here, but with respect to the number of installments and the number of processors. Moreover, we shall use only the processing time as a performance measure.

In the previous sections we have obtained closed-form solutions for the processing time when there are m child processors and the processing load is distributed in n installments. It can be seen that the time performance gets better as m, or n, or both, increase. It is natural to examine the limit of performance enhancement that can be achieved by increasing m and n. In other words, we want to obtain the following expressions:

$$T(m, \infty) = \lim_{n \to \infty} T(m, n) \tag{10.75}$$

$$T(\infty, n) = \lim_{m \to \infty} T(m, n) \tag{10.76}$$

In the following sections, we evaluate Equations (10.75) and (10.76) for both with- and without-front-end cases.

10.5.1 With-Front-End Processors

Let $Y(i, j)$ be the coefficient of σ^j in X_i. Now consider Equations (10.16) and (10.17) in Section 10.3. These equations can then be rewritten as

$$Y(i, 0) = 1, \quad i = 0, 1, \ldots, m - 1 \tag{10.77}$$

$$Y(i, 0) = 0, \quad i = m, m + 1, \ldots, mn - 1 \tag{10.78}$$

$$Y(k, j) = 0, \quad k < 0 \tag{10.79}$$

$$Y(i, j) = Y(i - 1, j - 1) + Y(i - 2, j - 1) + \cdots + Y(i - m, j - 1),$$
$$i = 0, 1, \ldots, mn - 1 \quad \text{and} \quad j = 1, 2, \ldots, mn - 1 \tag{10.80}$$

Then using Equations (10.78) through (10.80), we can rewrite Equation (10.19) as

$$X = \sum_{i=0}^{mn-1} Y(i, 0) + \sigma \sum_{i=0}^{mn-1} Y(i, 1) + \cdots + \sigma^{mn-1} \sum_{i=0}^{mn-1} Y(i, mn - 1) \tag{10.81}$$

which can be written as

$$X = \sum_{j=0}^{mn-1} P(j)\sigma^j \tag{10.82}$$

where

$$P(j) = \sum_{i=0}^{mn-1} Y(i, j) \tag{10.83}$$

and is defined as the coefficient of σ^j in X. In order to evaluate Equation (10.75) we require

$$\lim_{n \to \infty} X = \sum_{j=0}^{\infty} \{\sigma^j \lim_{n \to \infty} P(j)\} \tag{10.84}$$

From Equation (10.80),

$$\lim_{n \to \infty} P(j) = \sum_{i=0}^{\infty} Y(i - 1, j - 1) + \cdots + \sum_{i=0}^{\infty} Y(i - m, j - 1) \tag{10.85}$$

which, upon using Equations (10.77) through (10.79), reduces to

$$\lim_{n \to \infty} P(j) = m \lim_{n \to \infty} \{P(j - 1)\} \tag{10.86}$$

However, from Equation (10.77) we know that

$$P(0) = m \tag{10.87}$$

Hence,

$$\lim_{n \to \infty} X = m + m^2\sigma + m^3\sigma^2 + \cdots \tag{10.88}$$

This equation can be further simplified depending on the condition we impose on the factor $m\sigma$. The following are the two different cases which may arise.

Case i. $m\sigma < 1$

For this case, it can be readily seen that Equation (10.88) can be written as

$$\lim_{n \to \infty} X = \frac{m}{(1 - m\sigma)} \tag{10.89}$$

Thus, the processing time is given by

$$T(m, \infty) = \left\{ \frac{1}{1 + m} \right\} w T_{cp} \tag{10.90}$$

Case ii. $m\sigma \geq 1$

For this case, it is obvious that Equation (10.88) will not converge to a finite value. Thus, it can be seen that the processing time is given by

$$T(m, \infty) = \left\{ \frac{\sigma}{1 + \sigma} \right\} w T_{cp} \tag{10.91}$$

Now we shall evaluate Equation (10.76). From Equations (10.77) through (10.80), we observe that as $m \to \infty$ (that is, when the number of processors tends to infinity) X also tends to infinity. This means

$$T(\infty, n) = \left\{ \frac{\sigma}{1 + \sigma} \right\} w T_{cp} \tag{10.92}$$

Summarizing the results, for the with-front-end case, we have

$$T(m, \infty) = \left\{ \frac{1}{1 + m} \right\} w T_{cp}, \quad \text{if } m\sigma < 1$$

$$T(m, \infty) = \left\{ \frac{\sigma}{1 + \sigma} \right\} w T_{cp}, \quad \text{if } m\sigma \geq 1$$

$$T(\infty, n) = \left\{ \frac{\sigma}{1 + \sigma} \right\} w T_{cp} \tag{10.93}$$

10.5.2 Without-Front-End Processors

As before, let $Y(i, j)$ be the coefficient of σ^j in X_i. Now consider Equations (10.48) and (10.49) in Section 10.4. These equations can then be rewritten as

$$Y(i, 0) = 1, \; i = 0, 1, \dots, m - 1 \tag{10.94}$$

$$Y(i, 0) = 0, \; i = m, m + 1, \dots, mn - 1 \tag{10.95}$$

$$Y(k, j) = 0, \quad k < 0 \tag{10.96}$$

$$Y(i, j) = Y(i - 1, j - 1) + Y(i - 2, j - 1) + \cdots + Y(i - m, j - 1),$$
$$i = 0, 1, \dots, mn - 1, \quad \text{and} \quad j = 1, 2, \dots mn - 1 \tag{10.97}$$

Using the same procedure as in the previous section,

$$\lim_{n \to \infty} P(j) = \sum_{i=0}^{\infty} Y(i - 1, j - 1) + \cdots + \sum_{i=0}^{\infty} Y(i - m + 1, j - 1) \tag{10.98}$$

which upon using Equations (10.94) through (10.96), reduces to

$$\lim_{n\to\infty} P(j) = (m-1) \lim_{n\to\infty} \{P(j-1)\} \tag{10.99}$$

Here, from Equation (10.94),

$$P(0) = m \tag{10.100}$$

Thus,

$$\lim_{n\to\infty} X = \sum_{i=0}^{\infty} X_i = m\{1 + (m-1)\sigma + (m-1)^2\sigma^2 + \cdots\} \tag{10.101}$$

Hence, depending on the factor $(m-1)\sigma$, we have the following cases.

Case i. $(m-1)\sigma < 1$
In this case, it can be seen that Equation (10.101) can be written as

$$\lim_{n\to\infty} X = \frac{m}{1 - (m-1)\sigma} \tag{10.102}$$

Thus, the processing time is given by

$$T(m, \infty) = \left\{ \frac{(1+\sigma)}{(m+1) - \sigma(m-1)} \right\} wT_{cp} \tag{10.103}$$

Case ii. $(m-1)\sigma \geq 1$
Here, Equation (10.101) will not converge to a finite value and hence we have

$$T(m, \infty) = \sigma wT_{cp} \tag{10.104}$$

Now, we shall evaluate Equation (10.76). This turns out to be

$$\lim_{m\to\infty} T(m, n) = \sigma wT_{cp} \tag{10.105}$$

Thus, summarizing the results, we have

$$T(m, \infty) = \left\{ \frac{(1+\sigma)}{(m+1) - \sigma(m-1)} \right\} wT_{cp}, \quad \text{if } (m-1)\sigma < 1$$

$$T(m, \infty) = \sigma wT_{cp}, \quad \text{if } (m-1)\sigma \geq 1$$

$$T(\infty, n) = \sigma wT_{cp} \tag{10.106}$$

10.6 DISCUSSION OF THE RESULTS

Figure 10.6a and 10.6b shows $T(m, n)$ and n for a given value of σ and different values of m. The values of $T(m, n)$ for $n=1$ are the processing times obtained by using the strategy described in Chapter 5. When the number of installments increases, the processing time reduces. But the reduction is not too significant after the first few installments. In fact, the processing time saturates to the value given by $T(m, \infty)$ in Equations (10.93) and (10.106). This appears to be true regardless of whether the processors are equipped with front ends or not. It also shows that, for the same values of m and n, the performance is always better when the processors are equipped with front ends than when they are not.

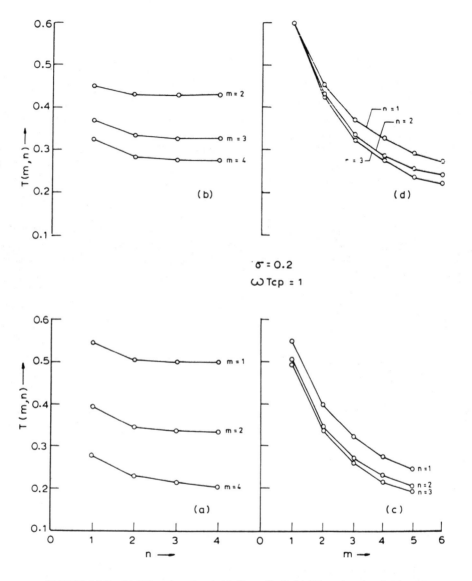

FIGURE 10.6   (a) $T(m, n)$ and n (with Front End) (b) $T(m, n)$ and n (without Front End) (c) $T(m, n)$ and m (with Front End) (d) $T(m, n)$ and m (without Front End)

In Figure 10.6c and 10.6d, $T(m, n)$ and m for a given σ and different values of n are shown. As predicted by Equations (10.93) and (10.106), as the number of processors increases, the processing time converges to the same value regardless of the value of n. Note that the results for $n = 1$ are the same as those obtained in Chapter 8.

The plots shown in Figure 10.6 reveal an interesting trade-off relationship between the number of installments and the number of processors. When the number of child processors are small, adding a new processor enhances performance more than increasing the number of installments does. However, when the number of child processors is large, increasing the number of installments will be more beneficial than adding a new processor. Further, as Figure 10.6 also shows, when the number of child processors is large it is possible for a network without front ends, using a large number of installments, to perform comparably to a network with front ends using a single installment strategy.

Figure 10.7 shows the ultimate performance limit $T(m, \infty)$ and m for different values of σ. It shows that as long as $m\sigma < 1$, in the with-front-end case $((m-1)\sigma < 1$ in the without-front-end case), the value of $T(m, \infty)$ decreases with increasing m and then levels off to the value given by Equation (10.91) (Equation (10.103) in the without-front-end case). The lower envelope of these curves in the case of processors equipped with front ends is independent of σ, unlike the without-front-end case. This is also evident from Figure 10.8, which shows $T(m, \infty)$ and σ.

The plots given in Figure 10.7 also reveal the following information. If the number of child processors is large, and a large number of installments are used, then the performance achieved remains almost unchanged even when some processors are removed from the network. It implies that, in a single-level tree network, for a given

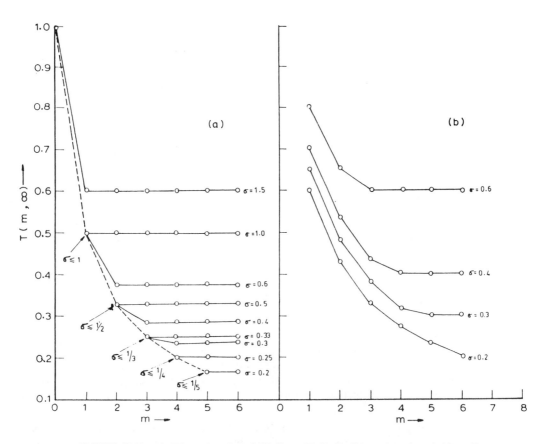

FIGURE 10.7   (a) $T(m, \infty)$ and m (with Front End) (b) $T(m, \infty)$ and m (without Front End)

value of σ, the processors beyond a certain number are redundant if sufficiently large number of installments are used.

From Figure 10.8, we observe that when processors are equipped with front ends, it is possible, by using a sufficiently large number of installments, to achieve almost full utilization of the processors when $m\sigma < 1$. In fact, the processing time $T(m, n)$ is independent of the value of σ so long as this condition is met. This is, however, not true when the processors are not equipped with front ends.

The above results provide some interesting insights into the multi-installment load distribution strategy. Given a network with one root processor and m child processors equipped with front ends, the processing time performance can be improved further by either adding more processors (which is not a cost-effective solution) or by sending the load in installments as proposed in this chapter. When $m\sigma < 1$, by increasing the number of installments one can ensure almost full utilization of all processors. When $m\sigma \geq 1$, then by increasing the number of installments one can reach a limit that is the same as the limit reached by using a large number of processors. Also, note that the multi-installment strategy helps in avoiding the buffer overflow

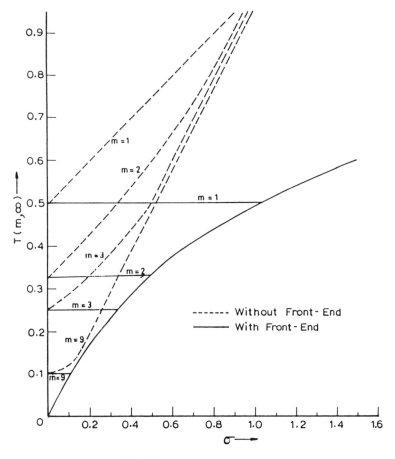

FIGURE 10.8 $T(m, \infty)$ and σ

problem, since the size of the load fractions in each installment can be controlled by selecting a suitable number of installments. Similar arguments hold true for the case in which the processors are not equipped with front ends.

All the above analysis is valid when there is no communication overhead associated with each installment. However, when this is not the case, we expect the total communication overhead to increase with the number of installments. In the single installment case, this overhead was neglected because the total number of load fractions communicated was limited to the number of processors. More specifically, in Chapter 2 it was mentioned that the constant part of the communication delay is neglected because the size of the load being processed is large and consequently the proportional part of the communication delay is much larger than the constant part. This assumption continues to hold in the single installment case. However, in the multi-installment case, for large values of n, each installment may be quite small. Hence, for these cases the above assumption may not be realistic. On the other hand, from the results obtained in this chapter, we observe that the time performance does not improve significantly beyond the first few installments (two or three). Thus, in a practical scenario, it would not be beneficial to use large number of installments. This argument, in a way, justifies the utility of the multi-installment strategy.

10.7 CONCLUDING REMARKS

The following are the highlights of this chapter:

- A multi-installment strategy for load distribution in a single-level tree network was proposed.
- Basic recursive equations to obtain individual load fractions for all the installments for heterogeneous networks were derived.
- Closed-form solutions were derived for individual load fractions for all the installments, and also for the processing time, for a homogeneous network. This was done using two different techniques: (i) rational expansion theorem, and (ii) binomial expansion.
- An asymptotic analysis was performed to explore the ultimate performance limits of the system.
- Some practical issues regarding the trade-off relationship between the number of processors and the number of installments were discussed.

Now that we have seen the time performance of the multi-installment strategy on single-level tree networks, it will be of interest to study the time performance of linear networks under this strategy. We will do so in the next chapter.

BIBLIOGRAPHIC NOTES

Section.10.1   The concept of sending the load in more than one installment to reduce communication overheads was proposed in Bharadwaj et al. (1992a, 1995b).

Section 10.3 and Section 10.4   An excellent treatment of the generating functions approach to solve recursive equations of the kind presented here is available in Graham et al. (1989).

Section 10.5   The asymptotic analysis and the results regarding the trade-off relationships between the number of processors and the number of installments can be found in Bharadwaj et al. (1992a, 1995b).

CHAPTER 11

Multi-Installment
Load Distribution
in Linear Networks

In this chapter, we study the performance of a linear network under the multi-installment load distribution strategy, described in the previous chapter. Unlike in the case of single-level tree networks, here we obtain a partial closed-form solution. In the absence of a complete closed-form solution, we carry out an asymptotic analysis to obtain some bounds on the performance limits of the network. For some network parameter values, we obtain exact performance limits computationally. The analysis and the computational results together bring out the important features of the multi-installment strategy. Note that the arguments in favor of the multi-installment strategy given in the previous chapter hold even here.

11.1 MOTIVATION AND SOME REMARKS

We first provide a motivation for the multi-installment strategy in linear networks through the following simple example.

Example 11.1

Consider a linear network of three processors p_0, p_1, and p_2 connected via the links l_0 and l_1. The processing load is assumed to originate at the processor p_0. Figure 11.1a shows the timing diagram for the case when the load distribution follows the earlier single-installment strategy and Figure 11.1b shows the timing diagram for the multi-installment strategy with the load distributed in two installments. Figure 11.1b shows that sending the same load to p_1 and p_2 in two installments reduces the overall processing time. Comparing Figures 11.1a and 11.1b we see that the processing time is reduced by 5.88 percent. This example motivates the study of multi-installment strategy in linear networks.

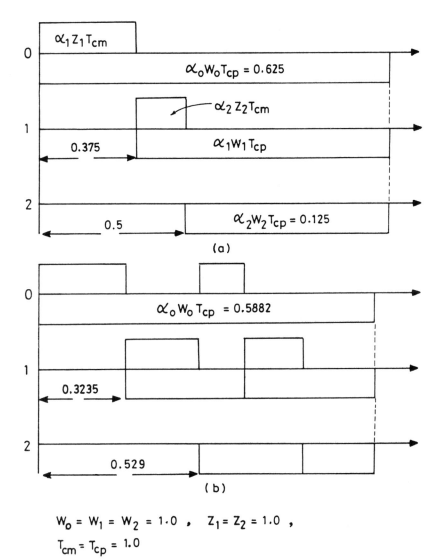

$$W_o = W_1 = W_2 = 1.0 \; , \quad Z_1 = Z_2 = 1.0 \; ,$$

$$T_{cm} = T_{cp} = 1.0$$

FIGURE 11.1   (a) Load Distribution in One Installment (b) Load Distribution in Two Installments

Now we consider a general case of a linear network of $(m + 1)$ processors $p_0, p_1, \ldots, p_m$ connected via the links $l_0, l_1, \ldots, l_{m-1}$ as shown in Figure 11.2a. Throughout this chapter it is assumed that the processing load originates at the processor p_m. We denote the load fractions assigned to processor p_i as α_i, given by

$$\alpha_i = \alpha_{i,(n-1)} + \alpha_{i,(n-2)} + \cdots + \alpha_{i,k} + \cdots + \alpha_{i,0} \tag{11.1}$$

where $\alpha_{i,k}$ is the load fraction assigned to p_i in the $(n - k)$th installment. Note that the number of installments (n) are numbered from $k = 0, \ldots, n - 1$, where $k = 0$ denotes the last (that is, nth) installment and $k = n - 1$ denotes the first installment. This reversal of notation is adopted for analytical ease.

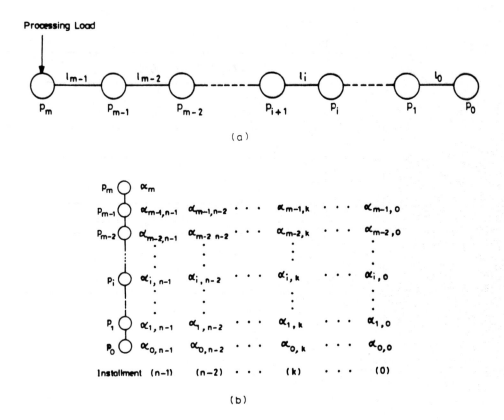

FIGURE 11.2   (a) Linear Network with Communication Links (b) Assignment of Load Fractions to the Processors

The multi-installment load distribution strategy follows the rules given below:

(i) A processor keeps its own fraction of the current installment for computing and distributes the rest of the installment to its immediate successor.

(ii) The load originating processor p_m will transmit a new installment to its successor p_{m-1} only at the time instant at which the processor p_1 finishes transmitting the load fraction of the previous installment to p_0.

(iii) Processors that are equipped with front ends are continuously engaged in the computing process from the time instant at which they receive their first installment.

(iv) A processor that is not equipped with a front end is continuously engaged in the computing process only in the time interval between the instant at which it finishes transmitting the rest of the load in a given installment to its immediate successor and the instant of its reception of the next installment from its immediate predecessor. The processor p_m computes in the time interval between successive installments and p_0 computes until the time instant at which it starts receiving its next installment.

Following the above rules (i) through (iii) (and (iv) for without-front-end) we state the necessary and sufficient condition for optimal load distribution as follows:

In a linear network of $(m+1)$ processors connected via m communication links, a load distribution that follows the rules (i) through (iv) is said to be optimal if and only if all the processors in the network stop computing at the same instant in time.

In Chapter 5 we proved the above optimality condition for the single installment case. Although we do not provide a rigorous proof for this assumption in the case of a multi-installment strategy, it is indeed true even here. An intuitive argument, similar to the ones in Chapters 3 and 4, is sufficient to justify this assertion.

11.2 ANALYSIS FOR WITH-FRONT-END PROCESSORS

In this section, we develop recursive equations for a heterogeneous network and, for certain cases, we obtain partial closed-form expressions for homogeneous networks. But first we shall consider the special case of a linear network with two processors ($m = 1$) and obtain a closed-form expression for the processing time.

11.2.1 Closed-Form Expression for $m = 1$

The timing diagram for this case is shown in Figure 11.3, from which we can write the following recursive equations:

$$\alpha_{0,k} w_0 T_{cp} = \alpha_{0,k-1} z_0 T_{cm}, \quad \text{for } k = 1, 2, \ldots, n-1 \tag{11.2}$$

The total load assigned to p_1 is denoted by α_1 and can be written from the timing diagram as

$$\alpha_1 = \frac{\left(\sum_{i=0}^{n-1} \alpha_{0,i}\right) w_0 T_{cp} + \alpha_{0,n-1} z_0 T_{cm}}{w_1 T_{cm}} \tag{11.3}$$

The normalizing equation is given by

$$\alpha_1 + \sum_{k=0}^{n-1} \alpha_{0,k} = 1 \tag{11.4}$$

Thus, we have $(n+1)$ linear equations with $(n+1)$ unknowns. This set of equations can be recursively solved by expressing each of the $\alpha_{0,i}$ ($i = 1, \ldots, n-1$) given by Equation (11.2) in terms of $\alpha_{0,0}$ as

$$\alpha_{0,k} = \alpha_{0,0} \left(\frac{z_0}{w_0}\right)^k \delta^k, \quad k = 1, 2, \ldots, n-1 \tag{11.5}$$

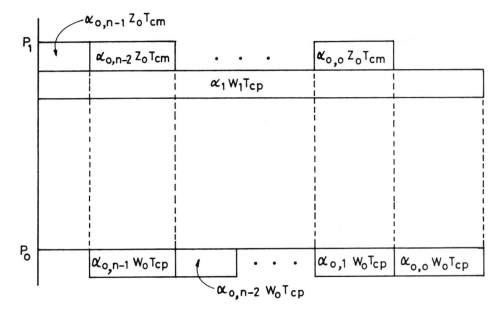

FIGURE 11.3   Timing Diagram: With Front End ($m = 1$)

where $\delta = T_{cm}/T_{cp}$. Further, substituting Equation (11.5) in Equation (11.3) we obtain

$$
\alpha_1 = \alpha_{0,0} \left\{ \frac{w_0}{w_1} + \left(\sum_{i=1}^{n-1} \left(\frac{z_0}{w_0} \right)^i \delta^i \right) \frac{w_0}{w_1} \right.
$$
$$
\left. + \left(\frac{z_0}{w_0} \right)^{n-1} \left(\frac{z_0}{w_1} \right) \delta^n \right\}
$$
(11.6)

Substituting Equations (11.5) and (11.6) in Equation (11.4) we obtain $\alpha_{0,0}$ as

$$
\alpha_{0,0} = \frac{1}{X}
$$
(11.7)

where

$$
X = \left\{ 1 + \frac{w_0}{w_1} + \left(\sum_{i=1}^{n-1} \left(\frac{z_0}{w_0} \right)^i \delta^i \right) \left(1 + \frac{w_0}{w_1} \right) \right.
$$
$$
\left. + \left(\frac{z_0}{w_0} \right)^{n-1} \left(\frac{z_0}{w_1} \right) \delta^n \right\}
$$
(11.8)

From the timing diagram, the processing time is given by

$$
T(1, n) = \alpha_1 w_1 T_{cp}
$$
(11.9)

Using Equation (11.7) in Equation (11.6) the value of α_1 can be immediately obtained. Now, let us derive the closed-form expression for homogeneous networks with $w_1 =$

$w_0 = w$ and $z_0 = z$. We rewrite Equation (11.9) as

$$T(1, n) = \left\{ \frac{\sum_{i=0}^{n} \sigma^i}{\sigma^n + 2\sum_{i=0}^{n-1} \sigma^i} \right\} w T_{cp} \qquad (11.10)$$

where $\sigma = z T_{cm}/w T_{cp}$ is the network parameter.

11.2.2 Load Distribution Equations for $m \geq 2$

For the ease of developing the recursive equations we denote the load fractions as $Y_0, \ldots, Y_{m-1}, Y_m, \ldots, Y_{2m-1}, \ldots, Y_{km}, \ldots, Y_{km+i}, \ldots, Y_{km+m-1}, Y_{km+m}, \ldots, Y_{mn-1}$, where the index k refers to installments and the index i refers to processors. Figure 11.2b explains the notation adopted. For example, in the case of three processors, that is, $m = 2$, with number of installments $n = 3$, we have $i \in \{0, 1\}$ and $k \in \{0, 1, 2\}$. We denote the load fractions as follows:

$\alpha_2 \rightarrow p_2$,
$Y_5 \rightarrow p_1 \quad Y_4 \rightarrow p_0$ (first installment; $k = 2$)
$Y_3 \rightarrow p_1 \quad Y_2 \rightarrow p_0$ (second installment; $k = 1$)
$Y_1 \rightarrow p_1 \quad Y_0 \rightarrow p_0$ (third installment; $k = 0$)

In other words, the first installment is denoted as $k = n - 1$, the second installment as $k = n - 2, \ldots$, and so on until the last installment, which is denoted as $k = 0$. Adopting the rules (i) through (iii) and the optimality condition stated in Section 11.1, the timing diagram for a network of $(m + 1)$ processors and m links is shown in Figure 11.4. From this timing diagram we write the following recursive equations:

$$Y_i w_i T_{cp} = Y_{i-1} w_{i-1} T_{cp} + \sum_{j=0}^{i-1} Y_j z_{i-1} T_{cm},$$

$$\text{for } i = 1, 2, \ldots, m-1 \qquad (11.11)$$

$$Y_{km} w_0 T_{cp} = \sum_{p=1}^{m} \sum_{j=(k-1)m}^{km-p} Y_j z_{m-p} T_{cm},$$

$$\text{for } k = 1, \ldots, n-1 \qquad (11.12)$$

$$Y_{km+i} w_i T_{cp} = Y_{km+i-1} w_{i-1} T_{cp} - \sum_{j=(k-1)m}^{km-(m-i+1)} Y_j z_{i-1} T_{cm} + \sum_{j=km}^{km+i-1} Y_j z_{i-1} T_{cm},$$

$$\text{for } i = 1, \ldots, m-1 \text{ and } k = 1, \ldots, n-1 \qquad (11.13)$$

The load fraction on the processor p_m is given by

$$\alpha_m = \left(\frac{1}{w_m T_{cp}}\right) \left(Y_0 w_0 T_{cp} + \sum_{k=1}^{n} \sum_{p=1}^{m} \sum_{i=(k-1)m}^{km-p} Y_i z_{m-p} T_{cm}\right) \qquad (11.14)$$

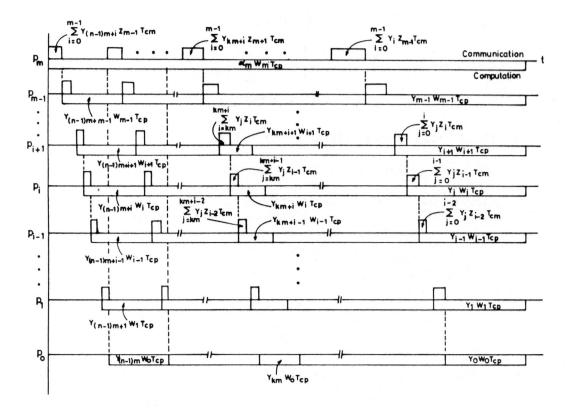

FIGURE 11.4   Timing Diagram: With Front End

The normalizing equation is given by

$$\alpha_m + \sum_{i=0}^{mn-1} Y_i = 1 \tag{11.15}$$

Thus, we have $(mn + 1)$ linear equations with $(mn + 1)$ unknowns. This set of equations can be recursively solved by expressing each of the Y_i $(i = 1, \dots, mn-1)$ given by Equations (11.11) and (11.12) in terms of Y_0. Then, substituting these values of Y_i $(i = 0, \dots, mn-1)$ in Equation (11.15), we obtain Y_0. Hence, the processing time can be computed from the timing diagram as shown in Figure 11.4 as

$$T(m, n) = \alpha_m w_m T_{cp} \tag{11.16}$$

where α_m is given by Equation (11.14).

11.2.3 Closed-Form Expression for $m \geq 2$

In this section we derive a closed-form solution for the special case of homogeneous networks with $w_i = w$ and $z_i = z$, for all i. Following the procedure explained for solving the recursive equations (11.11) through (11.15), we obtain the values of α_m and Y_i $(i = 0, 1, \dots, mn-1)$. The processing time $T(m, n)$, as given by Equation (11.16) can then be obtained from the timing diagram shown in Figure 11.4

as

$$T(m, n) = Y_0 w T_{cp} + \left\{ \sum_{j=0}^{m-1} \sum_{k=0}^{n-1} (m-j) Y_{km+j} \right\} z T_{cm} \qquad (11.17)$$

Hence, once the values of Y_i ($i = 0, 1, \ldots, mn - 1$) are known, the processing time can be computed. In order to obtain these Y_i's, we transform Equations (11.11) through (11.13) in such a way that we obtain a new set of recursive equations together with some initial conditions. Once these modified recursive equations are obtained we adopt the generating functions approach to solve them. It may be recalled that in Chapter 10 we used this approach for single-level tree networks. Here, too, the generating function should have as its coefficients the values generated by the recursive equations together with some initial conditions as follows:

$$Y_i = Y_{i-1} + \left(\sum_{j=0}^{i-1} Y_j \right) \sigma \qquad (11.18)$$

$$\text{for } i = 1, 2, \ldots, m - 1$$

$$Y_{km+i} = \left\{ \sum_{p=0}^{i} (m-i) Y_{(k-1)m+p} + \sum_{p=i+1}^{m-1} (m-p) Y_{(k-1)m+p} \right.$$

$$\left. + \sum_{p=m}^{m+i-1} (m+i-p) Y_{(k-1)m+p} \right\} \sigma \qquad (11.19)$$

$$\text{for } i = 0, 1, \ldots, m - 1 \text{ and } k = 1, 2, \ldots, n - 1$$

In order to obtain the load fractions Y_i's given by Equations (11.18) and (11.19), let us denote the recurrence relation for each i in Equations (11.18) and (11.19) as U_k^i ($i = 0, 1, \ldots, m - 1$), that is, $U_k^i = Y_{km+i}$. Then,

$$U_0^i = Y_i, \quad i = 0, 1, \ldots, m - 1 \qquad (11.20)$$

$$U_k^i = \left\{ \sum_{q=0}^{i} (m-i) U_{k-1}^q + \sum_{q=i+1}^{m-1} (m-q) U_{k-1}^q \right.$$

$$\left. + \sum_{q=m}^{m+i-1} (m+i-q) U_k^{q-m} \right\} \sigma, \qquad (11.21)$$

$$\text{for all } i = 0, 1, \ldots, m - 1$$

The above Equation (11.21) gives m recurrence relations with the initial conditions shown in Equation (11.20). These equations yield the generating function $U^i(s)$, which generates an infinite number of terms. But for our purposes, we need to consider terms until $(mn - 1)$ only, since we have load fractions from Y_0 to Y_{mn-1}.

We obtain the generating function $U^i(s)$ from Equations (11.20) and (11.21) as

$$U^i(s) = \left\{ \sum_{q=0}^{i}(m-i)U^i(s) + \sum_{q=i+1}^{m-1}(m-q)U^q(s) \right\} s\sigma$$
$$+ \left\{ \sum_{q=m}^{m+i-1}(m+i-q)U^{q-m}(s) \right\}\sigma + 1, \tag{11.22}$$

$$\text{for all } i = 0, 1, \ldots, m-1$$

Solving these m equations given in Equation (11.22), the m unknowns $U^i(s)$ ($i = 0, 1, \ldots, m-1$), can be obtained. To each of these relations, we apply the rational expansion theorem and suitably choose the required coefficients. This procedure is clearly demonstrated in the following example:

Example 11.2

Consider the case $m = 2$ and $n = 3$. Using Equations (11.18) and (11.19) we have, for $i = 0, 1$,

$$Y_{2k} = \left(2Y_{2(k-1)} + Y_{2(k-1)+1}\right)\sigma \tag{11.23}$$

$$Y_{2k+1} = \left(Y_{2(k-1)} + Y_{2(k-1)+1} + Y_{2(k-1)+2}\right)\sigma \tag{11.24}$$

From Equations (11.20) and (11.21) we have, for $i = 0, 1$, and $p = 1, 2$.

$$U_p^0 = \left(2U_{p-1}^0 + U_{p-1}^1\right)\sigma, \quad U_0^0 = Y_0 \tag{11.25}$$

$$U_p^1 = \left(U_{p-1}^0 + U_{p-1}^1 + U_p^0\right)\sigma, \quad U_0^1 = Y_1 \tag{11.26}$$

Thus, we have two recurrence relations with initial conditions. Using Equation (11.22) we write the above Equations (11.25) and (11.26) as

$$U^0(s) = 2s\sigma U^0(s) + s\sigma U^1(s) + 1 \tag{11.27}$$

$$U^1(s) = (s+1)\sigma U^0(s) + s\sigma U^1(s) + 1 \tag{11.28}$$

Solving Equations (11.27) and (11.28) we obtain

$$U^0(s) = \frac{1}{\sigma^2 s^2 - (3\sigma + \sigma^2)s + 1} \tag{11.29}$$

$$U^1(s) = \frac{-s\sigma + (\sigma + 1)}{\sigma^2 s^2 - (3\sigma + \sigma^2)s + 1} \tag{11.30}$$

We then find the roots of the denominator as $\delta_1 = \frac{(x+y)}{2}$ and $\delta_2 = \frac{(x-y)}{2}$, where $x = \sigma(3 + \sigma)$ and $y = \sigma\sqrt{(\sigma + 5)(\sigma + 1)}$. For $U^0(s) = P^0(s)/Q^0(s)$, using the rational expansion theorem stated in Chapter 10 (Theorem 10.1), we obtain

$$a_1 = -\frac{\delta_1}{\left\{(2\sigma^2/\delta_1) - (3\sigma + \sigma^2)\right\}}$$

$$a_2 = -\frac{\delta_2}{\left\{(2\sigma^2/\delta_2) - (3\sigma + \sigma^2)\right\}}$$

Thus, we have $U_0^0 = Y_0 = 1$, $U_1^0 = Y_2 = (3+\sigma)\sigma$, $U_2^0 = Y_4 = (6+4\sigma+4\sigma^2+\sigma^3)\sigma$. Similarly, for $U^1(s) = P^1(s)/Q^1(s)$, we obtain

$$a_1 = \frac{\sigma - (\sigma+1)\delta_1}{(2\sigma^2/\delta_1) - (3\sigma + \sigma^2)}$$

$$a_2 = \frac{\sigma - (\sigma+1)\delta_2}{(2\sigma^2/\delta_2) - (3\sigma + \sigma^2)}$$

Similarly, we have $U_0^1 = Y_1 = (1+\sigma)$, $U_1^1 = Y_3 = (2+4\sigma+\sigma^2)\sigma$, $U_2^1 = Y_5 = (3+9\sigma+8\sigma^2+5\sigma^3+\sigma^4)\sigma$. Substituting these values of Y_i ($i = 0, \ldots, 5$) in Equation (11.17) we obtain the processing time. These expressions can be readily verified from Equations (11.18) and (11.19). Note that in order to obtain the Y_i's for higher values of m, one has to obtain the roots of a higher degree polynomial. But once the roots are obtained, computing Y_i is easy.

11.2.4 Asymptotic Analysis

In this section we explore the ultimate performance limits of this load distribution strategy by increasing the number of installments n or increasing the number of processors m. In other words, we want to obtain the following expressions:

$$T(m, \infty) = \lim_{n \to \infty} T(m, n) \tag{11.31}$$

$$T(\infty, n) = \lim_{m \to \infty} T(m, n) \tag{11.32}$$

A. Performance for $m = 1$, $n \to \infty$.   Since $m = 1$, only Equation (11.31) needs to be evaluated. For this, consider the processing time given by Equation (11.10). We have the following two cases:

Case i. $\sigma < 1$
When $\sigma < 1$, Equation (11.10) can be modified as

$$T(1, n) = \left(\frac{1 - \sigma^{n+1}}{2 - \sigma^n - \sigma^{n+1}}\right) wT_{cp} \tag{11.33}$$

Now, taking limits as $n \to \infty$ in Equation (11.33) we have

$$T(1, \infty) = \left(\frac{1}{2}\right) wT_{cp} \tag{11.34}$$

Case ii. $\sigma \geq 1$
Now, the processing time given by Equation (11.10) can be modified as

$$T(1, n) = \left(\frac{\sigma^{n+1} - 1}{\sigma^{n+1} + \sigma^n - 2}\right) wT_{cp} \tag{11.35}$$

Taking limits as $n \to \infty$ in Equation (11.35), we have

$$T(1, \infty) = \left(\frac{\sigma}{\sigma + 1}\right) wT_{cp} \tag{11.36}$$

It may be recalled that the expressions given by Equations (11.34) and (11.36) are the same as those given in Chapter 10 for $m = 1$. In fact, a comparison of the timing diagrams reveals the fact that the strategy is indeed the same for both networks.

B. Performance for $m \geq 2$ as $n \to \infty$.   Consider Equations (11.18) and (11.19). Each of the Y_i $(i = 0, \ldots, mn - 1)$ can be rewritten in terms of σ alone. Further, let us denote the coefficient of σ^j in Y_i $(i = 0, 1, \ldots, mn - 1)$ as $C(i, j)$. Hence, we obtain the following expressions:

$$C(i, 0) = 1, \quad i = 0, \ldots, m - 1 \tag{11.37}$$

$$C(i, 0) = 0, \quad i = m, \ldots, mn - 1 \tag{11.38}$$

$$C(0, j) = 0, \quad j = 1, \ldots, mn - 1 \tag{11.39}$$

$$C(i, j) = \sum_{p=0}^{i-1} (i - p)C(p, j - 1), \tag{11.40}$$

$$\text{for } i = 1, \ldots, m - 1 \text{ and } j = 1, \ldots, mn - 1$$

$$C(km + i, j) = \sum_{p=0}^{i} (m - i)C((k - 1)m + p, j - 1)$$

$$+ \sum_{p=i+1}^{m-1} (m - p)C((k - 1)m + p, j - 1) \tag{11.41}$$

$$+ \sum_{p=m}^{m+i-1} (m + i - p)C((k - 1)m + p, j - 1)$$

$$\text{for } i = 0, \ldots, m - 1, \quad k = 1, \ldots, n - 1,$$

$$\text{and } \quad j = 1, \ldots, mn - 1$$

Let

$$Y = \sum_{i=0}^{mn-1} Y_i \tag{11.42}$$

Define the quantity $P(j)$ as

$$P(j) = \sum_{k=0}^{n-1} \sum_{i=0}^{m-1} C(km + i, j) \tag{11.43}$$

where $P(j)$ is the coefficient of σ^j in Y. Then, Equation (11.42) can be rewritten as

$$Y = \sum_{j=0}^{mn-1} P(j)\sigma^j \tag{11.44}$$

Then, using Equations (11.37) through (11.41), Equation (11.43) can be written as

$$P(j) = m \sum_{k=0}^{n-1} \{mC(km, j-1) + (m-1)C(km+1, j-1) + \cdots$$

$$+ C(km+m-1, j-1)\}, \quad \text{for } j = 1, \ldots, mn-1 \tag{11.45}$$

Now, taking the limit as $n \to \infty$ in Equation (11.44). We obtain

$$\lim_{n \to \infty} Y = \sum_{j=0}^{\infty} P(j)\sigma^j \tag{11.46}$$

To evaluate this, consider $P(j)$ as given by Equation (11.43). That is,

$$\lim_{n \to \infty} P(j) = \sum_{k=0}^{\infty} \sum_{p=0}^{m-1} C(km+p, j) \tag{11.47}$$

It can easily be shown that as $n \to \infty$,

$$\sum_{k=0}^{\infty} C(km+p, j) = \sum_{k=0}^{\infty} C(km+p+1, j),$$

$$\text{for } p = 0, \cdots, m-2 \tag{11.48}$$

Hence, using Equation (11.48) in Equation (11.47) we obtain

$$\lim_{n \to \infty} P(j) = \left\{ \frac{m(m+1)}{2} \right\} \lim_{n \to \infty} P(j-1) \tag{11.49}$$

From Equation (11.37) we know that

$$P(0) = m \tag{11.50}$$

Hence, as $n \to \infty$, from Equation (11.44) we obtain

$$\lim_{n \to \infty} Y = m\Omega(K\sigma) \tag{11.51}$$

where

$$K = \frac{m(m+1)}{2} \tag{11.52}$$

and $\Omega(K\sigma) = \{1 + K\sigma + (K\sigma)^2 + \cdots\}$. Equation (11.51) can be further simplified by imposing conditions on the factor $K\sigma$. Before doing so, we will derive some useful expressions as $n \to \infty$. The value of α_m as given by Equation (11.14) can be written as

$$T(m, n) = \left(\frac{N}{N+Y} \right) wT_{cp} \tag{11.53}$$

where

$$N = Y_0 + \sigma \left\{ \sum_{i=0}^{m-1} \sum_{k=0}^{n-1} (m-i)Y_{km+i} \right\} \tag{11.54}$$

and Y is given by Equation (11.42). Now, we will evaluate Equation (11.53) as two cases based on the range of values that the factor $K\sigma$ can take.

Case i. $K\sigma < 1$.

Let us rewrite Equation (11.54) as

$$N = Y_0 + \left\{ m \sum_{k=0}^{n-1} Y_{km} + (m-1) \sum_{k=0}^{n-1} Y_{km+1} \right.$$
$$\left. + \cdots + \sum_{k=0}^{n-1} Y_{km+m-1} \right\} \sigma \qquad (11.55)$$

Further, writing each of the above Y_{km+i}, $(i = 0, 1, \ldots, m-1)$ in terms of $C(i, j)$ and taking $n \to \infty$ we obtain

$$\lim_{n\to\infty} N = Y_0 + \lim_{n\to\infty} \left[\left(\frac{K\sigma}{m} \right) \left\{ \sum_{j=0}^{mn-1} P(j)\sigma^j \right\} \right] \qquad (11.56)$$

which can be rewritten using Equation (11.49) as

$$\lim_{n\to\infty} N = 1 + K\sigma\Omega(K\sigma) \qquad (11.57)$$

Using Equations (11.51) and (11.57) in Equation (11.53) we obtain Equation (11.31) as

$$T(m, \infty) = \left(\frac{1 + K\sigma\Omega(K\sigma)}{1 + (m + K\sigma)\Omega(K\sigma)} \right) wT_{cp} \qquad (11.58)$$

Hence, when $K\sigma < 1$, $\Omega(K\sigma) = 1/(1 - K\sigma)$. Substituting this in $T(m, \infty)$ as given by Equation (11.58), we get

$$T(m, \infty) = \left(\frac{1}{m+1} \right) wT_{cp} \qquad (11.59)$$

Case ii. $K\sigma \geq 1$.

Consider the processing time given by Equation (11.53), together with Equations (11.44) and (11.54). With some algebraic manipulations we rewrite Equations (11.54) and (11.44) as

$$N = 1 + K\sigma R_1(\sigma) \qquad (11.60)$$

$$Y = mR_2(\sigma) \qquad (11.61)$$

where $R_1(\sigma)$ and $R_2(\sigma)$ are polynomials in σ, and are given by

$$R_1(\sigma) = \frac{1}{K} \left[\sum_{i=0}^{m-1} \sum_{k=0}^{n-1} (m-i) \left\{ \sum_{j=0}^{mn-1} C(km+i, j)\sigma^j \right\} \right] \qquad (11.62)$$

$$R_2(\sigma) = \frac{1}{m} \left\{ \sum_{j=0}^{mn-1} P(j)\sigma^j \right\} \qquad (11.63)$$

Further, it can be seen that the coefficient of σ^j in $R_2(\sigma)$ is greater than or equal to the coefficient of σ^j in $R_1(\sigma)$ for all j. Using Equations (11.60) and (11.61),

Equation (11.53) can be rewritten as

$$T(m, n) = \left\{ \cfrac{1}{1 + \cfrac{m R_2(\sigma)}{1 + K\sigma R_1(\sigma)}} \right\} w T_{cp} \tag{11.64}$$

Since $R_1(\sigma) \le R_2(\sigma)$, from Equation (11.64) we obtain

$$T(m, n) \le \left\{ \cfrac{1}{1 + \cfrac{m R_1(\sigma)}{1 + K\sigma R_1(\sigma)}} \right\} w T_{cp} \tag{11.65}$$

Now, as $n \to \infty$, we obtain

$$T(m, \infty) \le \left(\frac{K\sigma}{K\sigma + m} \right) w T_{cp} \tag{11.66}$$

This serves as an upper bound on the processing time $T(m, \infty)$. Because of the difficulty in obtaining a specific relation between $R_1(\sigma)$ and $R_2(\sigma)$, we give a loose lower bound for $T(m, \infty)$ as follows. It can be verified that $R_2(\sigma) < (m+1)R_1(\sigma)/2$. Then, from Equation (11.64), we obtain

$$T(m, n) > \left\{ \cfrac{1}{1 + \cfrac{m}{\left(\frac{1}{R_2(\sigma)} + \frac{K\sigma}{(m+1)/2} \right)}} \right\} w T_{cp} \tag{11.67}$$

Now, as $n \to \infty$, we obtain

$$T(m, \infty) > \left(\frac{\sigma}{\sigma + 1} \right) w T_{cp} \tag{11.68}$$

which serves as a very loose lower bound on $T(m, \infty)$.

Figure 11.5a–d shows the behavior of the processing time $T(m, n)$ against n. It can be seen from these graphs that, for a given σ, when $K\sigma < 1$ the processing time converges to a value given by Equation (11.59); and whenever $K\sigma > 1$, the processing time, as $n \to \infty$, is bounded below by the value given by the RHS of Equation (11.66). However, when $K\sigma = 1$, the RHS of Equation (11.66) becomes equal to the LHS. This phenomenon can be observed very clearly in Figure 11.5b for $m = 4.0$ and $\sigma = 0.1$. The value of this bound as given by Equation (11.66) is 0.2 and as n increases, $T(4, n)$ always lies above this value. Further, a close observation of these graphs reveals the fact that, for any given value of σ, there exists an optimal number of processors for which the processing time is minimum beyond a certain value of n. This can be observed clearly when $\sigma = 0.1$. The system with five processors ($m = 4$) gives better time performance than any other m for $n > 4$. The same behavior can be observed for all values of σ. In fact, this result will become apparent when we study the behavior of $T(m, n)$ against m. However, an important point to be noted at this juncture is that the optimal number of processors depends on both σ and n. In practice, σ is a network parameter and cannot be varied without disturbing the network. However, the parameter n can be software-tuned, and hence performance enhancement of a system can be obtained by a judicious choice of this parameter. As an example, consider Figure 11.5(c) where $\sigma = 0.5$. When $n \ge 2$, the three processor system ($m = 2$) gives better time performance.

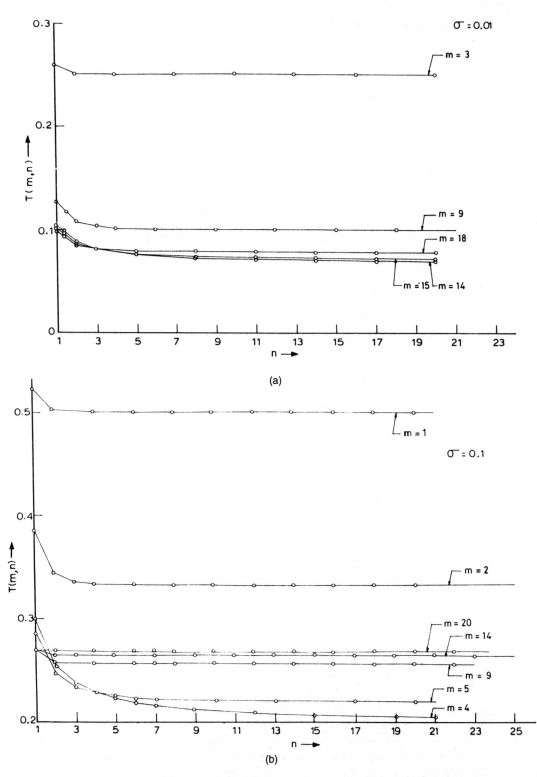

FIGURE 11.5   (a) $T(m, n)$ and n for $\sigma = 0.01$ (with Front End): (b) $T(m, n)$ and n for $\sigma = 0.1$ (with Front End)

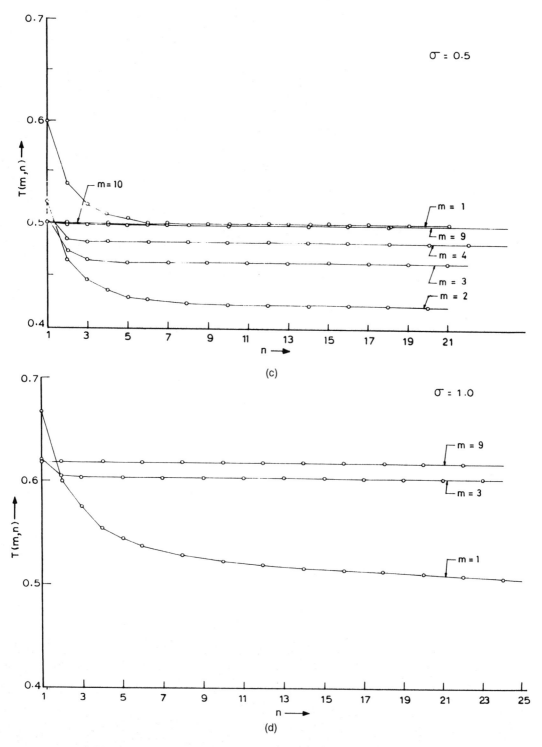

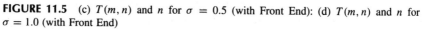

FIGURE 11.5 (c) $T(m, n)$ and n for $\sigma = 0.5$ (with Front End): (d) $T(m, n)$ and n for $\sigma = 1.0$ (with Front End)

But for $n = 1$, a higher number of processors $(m > 2)$ performs better. Although the foregoing discussion highlights some important features of the behavior of processing time with respect to the number of installments, a better insight into the system's performance is gained by observing its behavior with respect to the number of processors. We do this in the following section.

C. Performance as $m \to \infty$. Unlike the analysis carried out for an infinite number of installments, the analytical evaluation of Equation (11.32) is difficult. Hence, we obtain these limiting values computationally.

Figure 11.6a–d shows the behavior of processing time with respect to m. From these figures, it may be observed that for a given value of σ, and when $n \geq 2$, the processing time decreases to a minimum value for a finite m and then increases again. This value of m for which the processing time is a minimum is shown as m^* in these figures. It may be recalled at this juncture that the existence of this m^* was also observed while analyzing the behavior of processing time with respect to n. Further, from Figures 11.6a–d, it may be noted that, after $m = m^*$, the processing time increases and finally saturates to $T(\infty, 1)$, given by

$$T(\infty, n) = T(\infty, 1) = \left(\frac{2}{1 + \sqrt{1 + \frac{4}{\sigma}}} \right) w T_{cp} \qquad (11.69)$$

This expression appears in the single-installment case discussed in Chapter 8. Toward the end of this discussion, we provide a proof of this saturation phenomenon. For the sake of comparison, we have shown the performance bounds shown in Equations (11.59), (11.66), (11.68), and (11.69) as A, B, C, and D, respectively, in Figure 11.6a–d. As claimed, C serves as a very loose lower bound. It may also be observed from the graphs that B serves as an upper bound for all m satisfying the condition $K\sigma \geq 1$. However, it is interesting to note that for all $m \geq \left\lceil \sqrt{1 + \frac{4}{\sigma}} \right\rceil$, D serves as a tighter upper bound than B. The above condition can be derived from Equations (11.66) and (11.69). In Figures 11.6a–d, we have also shown the $T(m, \infty)$ curve (denoted as $n = \infty$). An overview of Figure 11.6 reveals that for lower values of σ, the performance of the system shows greater sensitivity to the parameter n. In fact, this can also be observed from Figure 11.5a–d. This observation is relevant from a practical perspective since it is always desirable to keep the value of σ as low as possible.

Now we shall prove a result on the saturation limit of the processing time $T(m, n)$ with respect to m.

Theorem 11.1. For all $n \geq 2$, as the number of processors in the system tends to infinity, the processing time $T(m, n)$ approaches $T(\infty, 1)$, that is, $T(\infty, n) = T(\infty, 1)$.

Proof. According to the notation followed earlier $Y_{(n-1)m}$ is the load assigned to p_0 in the first installment when there are $(m+1)$ processors in the network. We will first show that $Y_{(n-1)m} \to 0$ as $m \to \infty$. We will prove this by contradiction. Suppose $Y_{(n-1)m} \to \alpha > 0$ as $m \to \infty$. We know that each $Y_{(n-1)m+i} > \alpha$ (when $Y_{(n-1)m+i}$ is the first installment to p_i, $i > 0$). This means that $\sum_{i=0}^{m} Y_{(n-1)m+i} > (m+1)\alpha$.

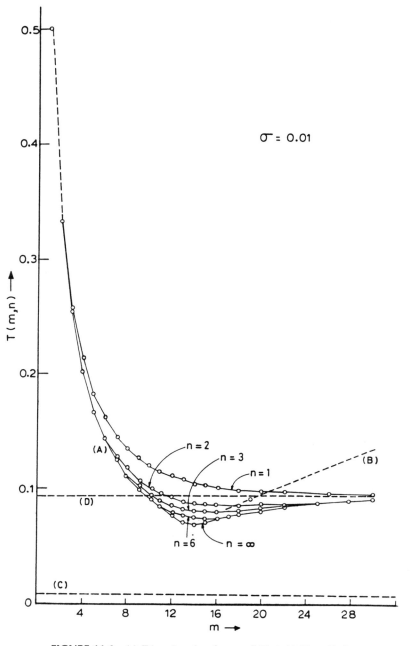

FIGURE 11.6   (a) $T(m, n)$ and m for $\sigma = 0.01$ (with Front End)

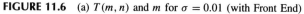

Thus, as $m \to \infty$, $\lim_{m \to \infty} \sum_{i=0}^{m} Y_{(n-1)m+i} \to \infty$, contradicting the fact that $\sum_{i=0}^{m} Y_{(n-1)m+i} \le 1$. Hence, $Y_{(n-1)m} \to 0$ as $m \to \infty$. Thus, the time taken by p_0 to compute $Y_{(n-1)m}$ also tends to zero as $m \to \infty$. From Figure 11.4, note that the communication delay of the total load in the second installment is less than the time taken by p_0 to compute $Y_{(n-1)m}$. Hence, the total load in the second installment also

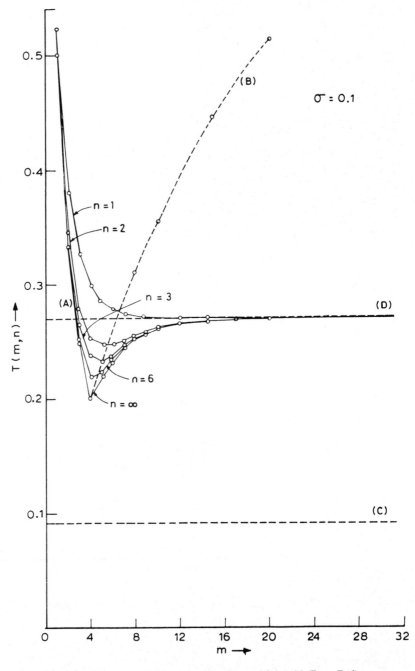

FIGURE 11.6   (b) $T(m, n)$ and m for $\sigma = 0.1$ (with Front End)

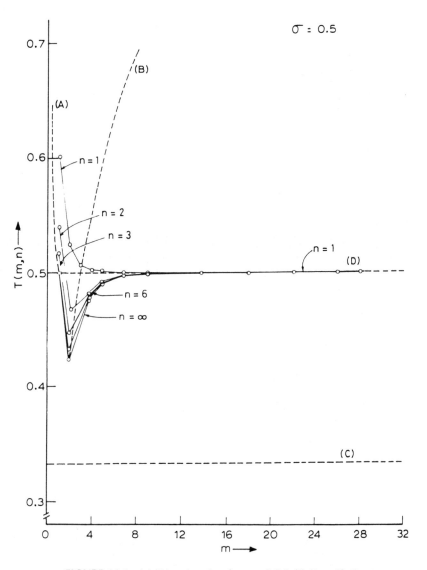

FIGURE 11.6   (c) $T(m, n)$ and m for $\sigma = 0.5$ (with Front End)

tends to zero as m tends to infinity. Similarly, all the subsequent installments will have zero loads. Hence the theorem follows.   □

However, it may be noted that this value of $T(\infty, n)$ for a given σ is nonoptimal (except when $n = 1$) since we can obtain a better time performance by keeping the number of processors as m^*, which is evident from Figures 11.6a–d. For a given n and a particular value of m there exists a range of σ for which this m is optimal. This is shown in Figure 11.7. Note that when $n = 1$ (that is, single installment) the result in Chapter 8 holds and $m \to \infty$ gives the minimum processing time for all σ. Further, from Figure 11.7, when $\sigma = 0.91$ and when $n = 3$, both $m = 1$ and $m = 2$ give the same time performance as $T(1, 3) = T(2, 3) = 0.56043$. From a practical

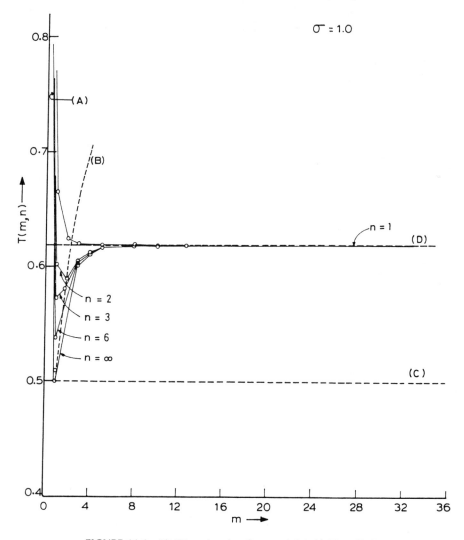

FIGURE 11.6   (d) $T(m, n)$ and m for $\sigma = 1.0$ (with Front End)

point of view, the value of σ is expected to be small. In this case, Figure 11.7 shows that the optimal number of processors is more when σ is low, for a given number of installments. This can also be observed from Figure 11.6. For example, for $n = 6$, when $\sigma = 0.01$, $m^* = 14$ and when $\sigma = 0.1$, $m^* = 4$. Thus, Figures 11.5, 11.6, and 11.7 highlight the trade-off relationships between the number of processors and the number of installments to be used in a given system.

11.3 ANALYSIS FOR WITHOUT-FRONT-END PROCESSORS

In this section, following the rules stated in Section 11.1, we study the performance of the multi-installment strategy for the without-front-end case. Here, we assume that

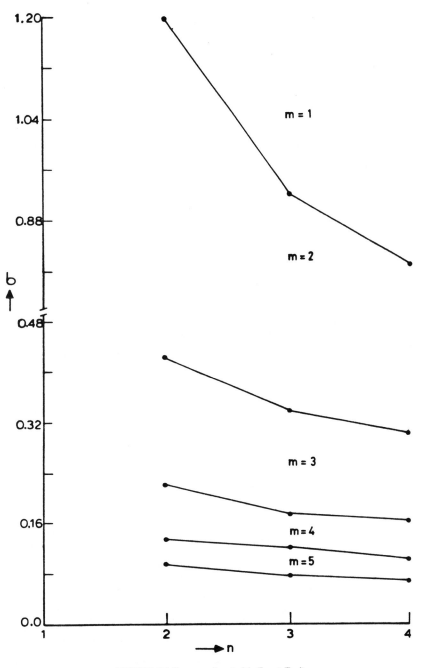

FIGURE 11.7 σ and n (with Front End)

the condition stated in Equation (5.131) is satisfied by all the links in the network, and all the processors take part in the computation process.

11.3.1 Closed-Form Expressions for $m = 1$ and 2

Case i. $m = 1$

The timing diagram for this case is as shown in Figure 11.8a. Let the load fractions in the kth installment for p_1 and p_0 be $\alpha_{k,1}$ and $\alpha_{k,0}$. Then, from the timing diagram we write the following recursive equations:

$$\alpha_{1,k} = \alpha_{0,k} \left(\frac{w_0}{w_1} \right), \quad k = 0, \ldots, n - 1 \tag{11.70}$$

The normalizing equation is given by

$$\sum_{k=0}^{n-1} (\alpha_{1,k} + \alpha_{0,k}) = 1 \tag{11.71}$$

Using Equation (11.70) in Equation (11.71) we obtain the total load computed by processor p_0 as

$$\sum_{k=0}^{n-1} \alpha_{0,k} = \frac{1}{1 + \frac{w_0}{w_1}} \tag{11.72}$$

From the timing diagram, the processing time is given by

$$T(1, n) = \left(\sum_{k=0}^{n-1} \alpha_{1,k} \right) w_1 T_{cp} + \left(\sum_{k=0}^{n-1} \alpha_{0,k} \right) z_0 T_{cm} \tag{11.73}$$

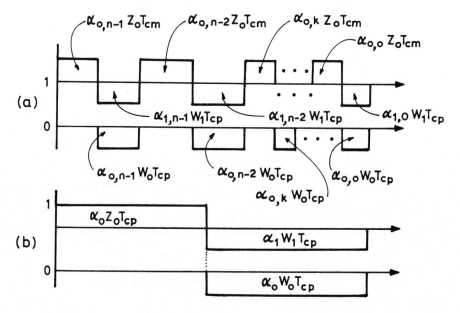

FIGURE 11.8   (a) Timing Diagram: Without Front End ($m = 1$, $n > 1$) (b) Timing Diagram: Without Front End ($m = 1$, $n = 1$)

Now, using Equation (11.72) in Equation (11.73) we obtain

$$T(1, n) = \frac{w_0 T_{cp} + z_0 T_{cm}}{1 + \frac{w_0}{w_1}} \tag{11.74}$$

It is easily verified that the processing time is the same as in the single-installment strategy, the timing diagram for which is shown in Figure 11.8b for comparison.

Case ii. $m = 2$

The timing diagram for this case is shown in Figure 11.9. It can be seen that the processor p_1 does not begin computing until all the n installments have been communicated to p_0. On the other hand, the root processor p_2 performs computation during the time interval in which p_1 communicates the load to p_0, and continues to do so until p_1 is free to receive the next installment. The following are the recursive equations for this case:

$$Y_0 w_0 T_{cp} = Y_1 w_1 T_{cp} \tag{11.75}$$

$$Y_2 w_0 T_{cp} = (Y_0 + Y_1) \, z_1 T_{cm} \tag{11.76}$$

$$Y_k w_0 T_{cp} = Y_{k-1} z_1 T_{cm}, \qquad k = 3, \ldots, n-1 \tag{11.77}$$

The load α_2 on p_2 is given by

$$\alpha_2 w_2 T_{cp} = Y_0 \left(w_0 T_{cp} + z_0 T_{cm} \right) + \sum_{i=2}^{n-1} Y_i z_0 T_{cm} \tag{11.78}$$

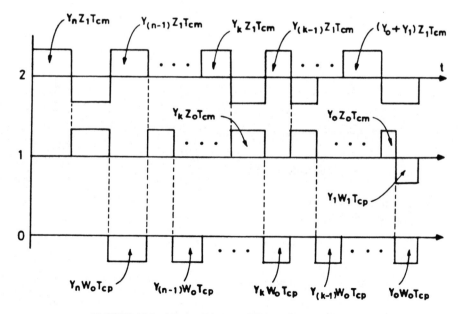

FIGURE 11.9   Timing Diagram: Without Front End ($m = 2$)

The normalizing equation is given by

$$\alpha_2 + \sum_{i=0}^{n-1} Y_i = 1 \tag{11.79}$$

Now, we will solve these equations and obtain the closed-form expression for the processing time. From Equations (11.75) through (11.79), we have $(n+2)$ equations with $(n+2)$ unknowns. This set of equations can be recursively solved by expressing each of the Y_i $(i = 3, \ldots, n-1)$ given by Equation (11.77) in terms of Y_0 as

$$Y_k = Y_0 \left(1 + \frac{w_0}{w_1}\right)\left(\frac{z_1\delta}{w_0}\right)^{k-1}, \quad k = 3, \ldots, n-1 \tag{11.80}$$

Similarly, the load on p_2 can be found using Equations (11.78) and (11.80) as

$$\alpha_2 = Y_0 \left\{ \left(\frac{w_0 + z_0\delta}{w_2}\right) + \left(1 + \frac{w_0}{w_1}\right)\left(\frac{z_0\delta}{w_2}\right)\sum_{k=2}^{n-1}\left(\frac{z_1\delta}{w_0}\right)^{k-1} \right\} \tag{11.81}$$

Now, using Equation (11.79), we obtain Y_0 as

$$Y_0 = \frac{1}{1 + \frac{w_0}{w_1} + (1 + \frac{w_0}{w_1})(1 + \frac{z_0\delta}{w_2})\sum_{k=2}^{n-1}\left(\frac{z_1\delta}{w_0}\right)^{k-1} + \left(\frac{w_0+z_0\delta}{w_2}\right)} \tag{11.82}$$

Now, the processing time can be computed from Figure 11.9 as

$$T(2,n) = \alpha_2 w_2 T_{cp} + \sum_{i=0}^{n-1} Y_i z_1 T_{cm} \tag{11.83}$$

Using Equation (11.82) in Equations (11.80) and (11.81) and then substituting in Equation (11.83) we obtain $T(2, n)$ as

$$T(2,n) =$$

$$Y_0 \left[\alpha_2 w_2 T_{cp} + \left\{1 + \frac{w_0}{w_1} + \left(1 + \frac{w_0}{w_1}\right)\sum_{k=2}^{n-1}\left(\frac{z_1\delta}{w_0}\right)^{k-1}\right\} z_1 T_{cm} \right] \tag{11.84}$$

where Y_0 and α_2 are given by Equations (11.82) and (11.81).

11.3.2 Load Distribution Equations for $m \geq 3$

The timing diagram for this case is as shown in Figure 11.10. The following are the recursive equations:

$$Y_1 w_1 T_{cp} = Y_0 w_0 T_{cp} \tag{11.85}$$

$$Y_i w_i T_{cp} = Y_{i-1} w_{i-1} T_{cp} + \sum_{j=0}^{i-2} Y_j z_{i-2} T_{cm} \tag{11.86}$$

$$i = 2, \ldots, m-1$$

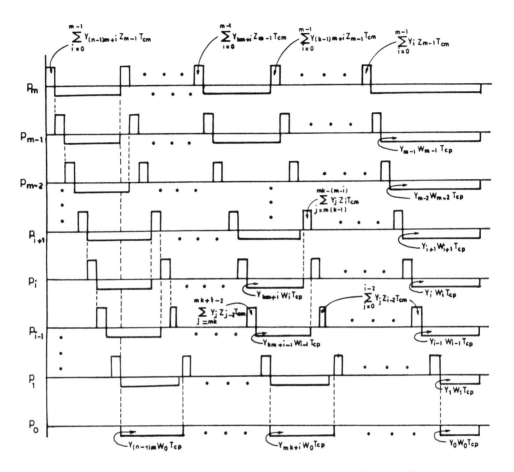

FIGURE 11.10   Timing Diagram: Without Front End ($m \geq 3$)

$$Y_{km} w_0 T_{cp} = \sum_{p=1}^{m-1} \sum_{j=m(k-1)}^{km-p} Y_j z_{m-p} T_{cm}$$

$$k = 1, \ldots, n-1$$

(11.87)

$$Y_{km+i} w_i T_{cp} = Y_{km+i-1} w_{i-1} T_{cp}$$

$$- \sum_{j=m(k-1)}^{km-(m-i)} Y_j z_i T_{cm} + \sum_{j=km}^{mk+i-2} Y_j z_{i-2} T_{cm}$$

(11.88)

$$i = 1, \ldots, m-1 \text{ and } k = 1, \ldots, n-1$$

The load fraction on p_m is given by

$$\alpha_m = \frac{Y_0 w_0 T_{cp} + \sum_{k=0}^{n-1} \sum_{p=0}^{m-2} \sum_{i=0}^{p} Y_{mk+i} \, z_p T_{cm}}{w_m T_{cp}}$$

(11.89)

11.3.3 Closed-Form Expression for $m \geq 3$

In this section, following the procedure explained for the with-front-end case, the mn recursive equations (11.85) through (11.89), together with the normalizing equation (11.15), are solved for $(mn+1)$ unknowns. The processing time $T(m, n)$ can be obtained from the timing diagram (Figure 11.10) as

$$T(m, n) = \frac{\alpha_m w_m T_{cp} + \sum\limits_{i=0}^{mn-1} Y_i z_{m-1} T_{cm}}{\alpha_m + \sum\limits_{i=0}^{mn-1} Y_i} \tag{11.90}$$

For the special case of homogeneous networks with $w_i = w$ and $z_i = z$ for all i, we can derive a closed-form expression for the processing time. To do so, we follow the same procedure as adopted for the with-front-end case. We obtain equations analogous to Equations (11.18) and (11.19) as

$$Y_i = Y_{i-1} + \left(\sum_{j=0}^{i-2} Y_j \right) \sigma \tag{11.91}$$

$$\text{for } i = 1, 2, \ldots, m - 1$$

$$Y_{km+i} = \left\{ \sum_{p=0}^{i} (m - 1 - i) \, Y_{m(k-1)+p} \right.$$

$$\left. + \sum_{p=i+1}^{m-1} (m - p) \, Y_{m(k-1)+p} + \sum_{p=m}^{m+i-2} (m + i - p - 1) \, Y_{m(k-1)+p} \right\} \sigma,$$

$$\text{for } i = 0, \ldots, m - 1, \text{ and } k = 1, 2, \ldots, n - 1 \tag{11.92}$$

Denoting the recurrence relation for each i in Equation (11.91) and (11.92) as U_k^i $(i = 0, \ldots, m - 1)$, using the relation $U_k^i = Y_{km+i}$, we have

$$U_0^i = Y_i, \qquad i = 0, \ldots, m - 1 \tag{11.93}$$

$$U_k^i = \left\{ \sum_{q=0}^{i} (m - 1 - i) \, U_{p-1}^q \right.$$

$$+ \sum_{q=i+1}^{m-1} (m - q) \, U_{p-1}^q$$

$$\left. + \sum_{q=m}^{m+i-2} (m + i - q - 1) \, U_p^{q-m} \right\} \sigma + 1, \tag{11.94}$$

$$\text{for } i = 0, \ldots, m - 1$$

Following the procedure given for the with-front-end case, we obtain the generating function $U^i(s)$ from Equations (11.93) and (11.94) as

$$U^i(s) = \left\{ \sum_{q=0}^{i} (m - 1 - i)g \cdot U^q(s) \right.$$

$$+ \sum_{q=i+1}^{m-1} (m - q)s \cdot U^q(s)$$

$$\left. + \sum_{q=m}^{m+i-2} (m + i - q - 1) \, U^{q-m}(s) \right\} \sigma + 1,$$

(11.95)

$$\text{for } i = 0, \ldots, m - 1.$$

Thus we have m equations with m unknowns $U^i(s)$ ($i = 0, 1, \ldots, m - 1$). To each of these equations, we can apply the rational expansion theorem and suitably choose the required coefficients following the steps shown in Example 11.2.

11.3.4 Asymptotic Analysis

In this section we explore the ultimate performance limits of this load distribution strategy with respect to the number of installments n and the number of processors m in a homogeneous network. In other words, we want to evaluate the expressions shown in Equations (11.31) and (11.32). However, since we have three separate cases for the without-front-end case, we deal with each of these cases independently.

A. Performance as $n \to \infty$ and $m = 1$.   As it has been pointed out in Case (i) in Section 11.3.1, when $m = 1$ (two processor network) this load distribution strategy is the same as the single-installment strategy and hence

$$T(1, \infty) = \lim_{n \to \infty} T(1, n) = T(1, 1) = \left(\frac{zT_{cm} + wT_{cp}}{2} \right)$$

(11.96)

B. Performance as $n \to \infty$ and $m = 2$.   The closed-form expression given by Equation (11.84) for a homogeneous network can be rewritten as

$$T(2, n) = \frac{(1 + \sigma + 2\sigma^2 + 2\sum_{k=3}^{n-1} \sigma^k)wT_{cp} + (2 + 2\sigma + 2\sum_{k=3}^{n-1} \sigma^{k-1})zT_{cm}}{3 + 3\sigma + 2\sigma^2 + 2(1 + \sigma)\sum_{k=3}^{n-1} \sigma^{k-1}}$$

(11.97)

Now we evaluate Equation (11.31) using the fact that $\sigma < 1$. Thus, Equation (11.97) reduces to

$$T(2, \infty) = \lim_{n \to \infty} T(2, n) = \left(\frac{(1 + \sigma)^2}{3 + \sigma^2} \right) wT_{cp}$$

(11.98)

In the with-front-end case, in order to evaluate Equations (11.31) and (11.32), we derived some intermediate conditions shown in Equations (11.48) and (11.49). However, in the without-front-end case, derivation of such conditions is difficult. This is because of the difficulty in obtaining an exact closed-form solution for $T(m, n)$.

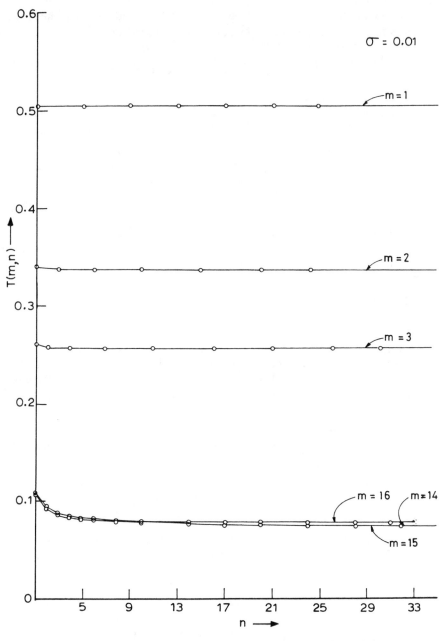

FIGURE 11.11   (a) $T(m, n)$ and n for $\sigma = 0.01$ (without Front End)

Hence, we present numerical results in order to study the behavior of the processing time.

Figures 11.11a–c show the behavior of $T(m, n)$ and n for different values of σ. For comparison purposes we have shown the plots for the same values of σ as in the with-front-end case. Here, too, the behavior is similar to that of the with-front-end

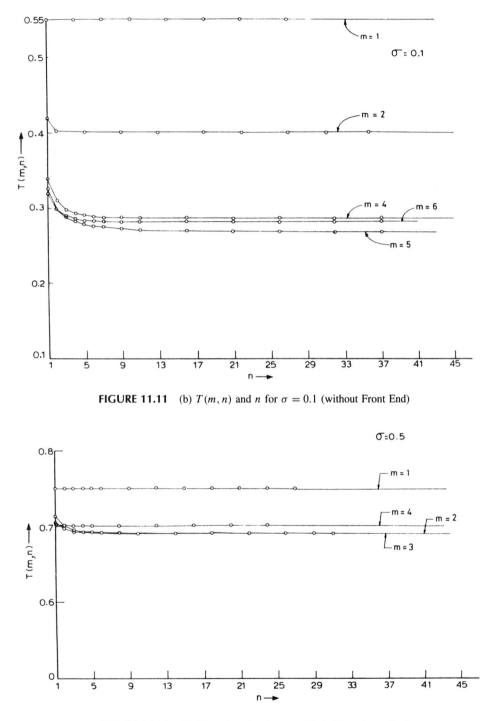

FIGURE 11.11   (b) $T(m, n)$ and n for $\sigma = 0.1$ (without Front End)

FIGURE 11.11   (c) $T(m, n)$ and n for $\sigma = 0.5$ (without Front End)

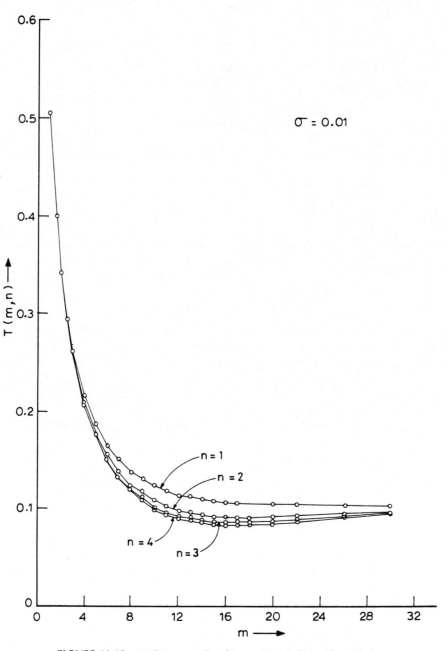

FIGURE 11.12 (a) $T(m, n)$ and m for $\sigma = 0.01$ (without Front End)

case. However, as one expects, the number of processors that gives the best time performance $(m = m^*)$ differs. The variation of $T(m, n)$ against m is shown in Figure 11.12a–c. Here, too, the behavior of the processing time with respect to m is qualitatively similar to that of the with-front-end case.

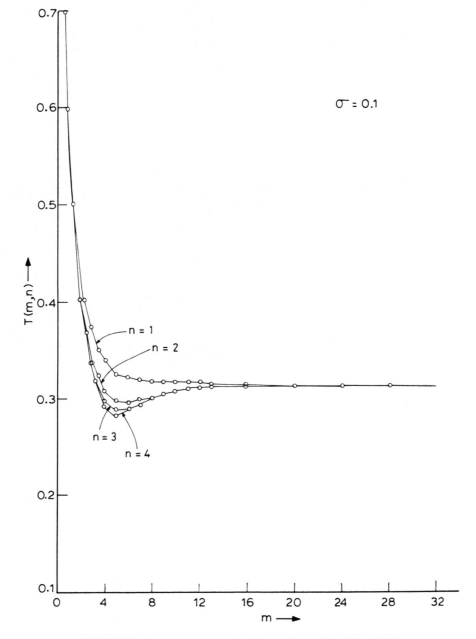

FIGURE 11.12   (b) $T(m, n)$ and m for $\sigma = 0.1$ (without Front End)

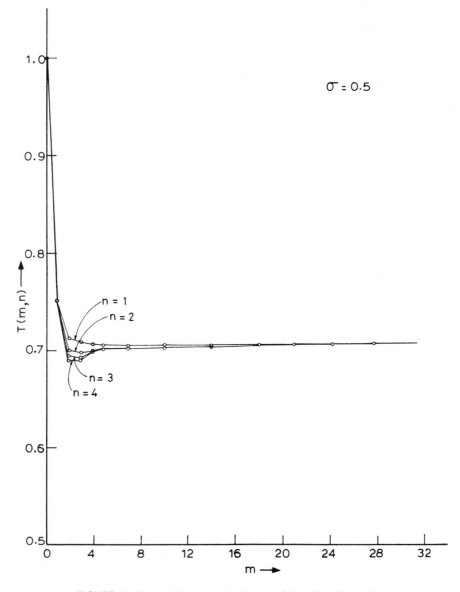

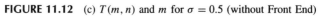

FIGURE 11.12   (c) $T(m, n)$ and m for $\sigma = 0.5$ (without Front End)

11.4 CONCLUDING REMARKS

Following are the highlights of this chapter:

- The performance of the multi-installment strategy of load distribution for linear networks was studied.
- Recursive equations for a heterogeneous network were developed and partial closed-form expressions for the processing times were derived for a homogeneous network.
- To study the ultimate performance limits of the network, an asymptotic analysis was carried out with respect to the number of installments and the number of processors. Some bounds on the processing time were obtained in the with-front-end case. Since an exact closed-form expression could not be derived for the without-front-end case, only a computational study was carried out.

BIBLIOGRAPHIC NOTES

Most of the material presented in this chapter is taken from Bharadwaj (1994). As in Chapter 10, the generating functions approach has been adopted from Graham *et al.* (1989).

CHAPTER 12

Multi-Job Load Distribution in Bus Networks

In previous chapters, we investigated efficient ways of distributing a single divisible load to minimize the processing time under the premise that this divisible load constitutes a single job. However, most practical distributed computing systems operate in an environment where multiple jobs (each constituting a single divisible load) may be submitted. In this chapter we propose an efficient procedure to handle such multiple jobs in a distributed computing network, using some of the results obtained in earlier chapters. A straightforward application of the single-job scheme in this situation is to take up each job sequentially only after the processing of the previous job is complete. In this chapter, we propose a more sophisticated multi-job scheme. This scheme exploits the special structure of a divisible load to yield a better time performance than that obtained by a straightforward application of the single-job scheme.

In this chapter, we will consider the following two architectures: (i) bus network with a control processor, and (ii) bus network without a control processor.

12.1 BUS NETWORK WITH A CONTROL PROCESSOR

Consider first the case where the network model consists of a buffer for incoming jobs, a control processor for distributing the processing load, and m processors attached to a bus (Figure 12.1). The jobs, on arrival, wait in the buffer for service. The buffer is assumed to be sufficiently large so that no jobs are turned away or lost. It is also assumed that the service discipline is *first-in first-out* (FIFO). Under the supervision of the control processor, the first of the jobs waiting in the buffer can

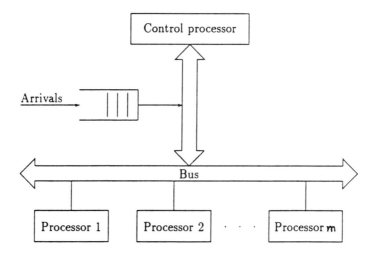

FIGURE 12.1   Bus Network with Load Origination at a Control Processor

be delivered to the network for processing. The control processor partitions and distributes the processing load among the m processors connected through a bus type communication medium. All the processors are equipped with front ends and each processor may have a different computing speed.

As before, we denote the bus communication speed parameter as z and the processor speed parameters as w_i ($i = 1, \ldots, m$). In addition to these, the following notations will be used throughout this chapter:

$\hat{\alpha}_i^q$: The fraction of the entire processing load of the qth job that is assigned to the ith processor in the *single-job scheme*.

α_i^q: The fraction of the entire processing load of the qth job that is assigned to the ith processor in the *multi-job scheme*.

T_f^q: The finish time of the entire processing load of the qth job.

T_{cm}^q: The time that it takes to communicate the entire load of the qth job over the channel when $z = 1$.

T_{cp}^q: The time that it takes for each processor to compute the entire load of the qth job when $w_i = 1$.

The timing diagrams for the bus network with load origination at a control processor in the single-job scheme and the multi-job scheme are depicted in Figures 12.2 and 12.3, respectively. It is assumed that at the initial time ($t = 0$), the buffer already contains more than one job, and all the processors are idle. The control processor begins distributing the first available job to the processors in the network. The load distribution for the single-job scheme is shown in Figure 12.2 with the condition for each job that all the processors stop computing at the same instant in time. Load distribution of the second job is started only after completing the processing of the first job. Therefore, starting with the second job, each processor has considerable idle time between consecutive jobs.

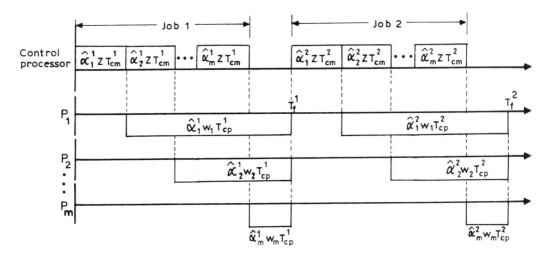

FIGURE 12.2   Timing Diagram: Single-Job Scheme (Load Origination at a Control Processor)

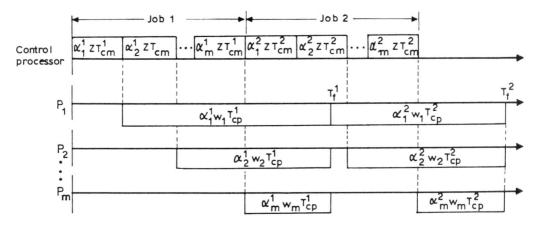

FIGURE 12.3   Timing Diagram: Multi-Job Scheme (Load Origination at a Control Processor)

The proposed multi-job scheme, on the other hand, is based on the idea that one would like to reduce the idle time between two consecutive jobs. Therefore, in this scheme, the control processor need not wait until the finish time of the previous job and can start distributing the next job immediately after it finishes distributing the previous job. In this process, those processors that have finished receiving their processing load prior to the completion of the previous job's computation (T_f^1) can start their computation immediately after T_f^1. Clearly, one can significantly reduce the overall processing time in this multi-job scheme. We will comment on the optimality of the multi-job scheme later.

In Chapter 4, we obtained closed-form solutions to find $\hat{\alpha}_i^q$ for the optimal load allocation for each processor in the single-job scheme. Here, we will briefly review these solutions for completeness and notational consistency. Following this, we will examine the recursive algorithm to find α_i^q for $q \geq 2$ for the optimal load allocation in the multi-job scheme.

12.1.1 Closed-Form Solution for the Single-Job Scheme

Since distribution of the processing load is done in the same fashion for every job in the single-job scheme and for the first job in the multi-job scheme, the closed-form solutions to find $\hat{\alpha}_i^q$ and α_i^1 are the same. Thus, we will only review the case of finding $\hat{\alpha}_i^q$ for the qth job in the single-job scheme.

Based on the fact that the minimum processing time occurs when all processors finish their computation at the same time instant, the following set of equations can be obtained from Figure 12.2. Although Figure 12.2 shows the timing diagram for the first job and the second job only, it is easy to see that it can be used to obtain the closed-form solution to find the optimum fraction $\hat{\alpha}_i^q$ for the general qth job also.

$$\hat{\alpha}_i^q w_i T_{cp}^q = \hat{\alpha}_{i+1}^q z T_{cm}^q + \hat{\alpha}_{i+1}^q w_{i+1} T_{cp}^q \qquad i = 1, 2, \ldots, m-1 \tag{12.1}$$

This equation can be solved as

$$\hat{\alpha}_{i+1}^q = \left\{ \frac{w_i T_{cp}^q}{z T_{cm}^q + w_{i+1} T_{cp}^q} \right\} \hat{\alpha}_i^q = k_i \hat{\alpha}_i^q$$

$$= k_i k_{i-1} \cdots k_1 \hat{\alpha}_1^q, \qquad i = 1, 2, \ldots, m-1 \tag{12.2}$$

where

$$k_i = \frac{\hat{\alpha}_{i+1}^q}{\hat{\alpha}_i^q} = \frac{w_i T_{cp}^q}{z T_{cm}^q + w_{i+1} T_{cp}^q} \qquad i = 1, 2, \ldots, m-1 \tag{12.3}$$

Here, k_i can be directly found from the system parameters (w_i, z) and the size of the qth job (T_{cm}^q, T_{cp}^q). Since the fractions of the total processing load should sum to one, $\hat{\alpha}_1^q$ can be obtained from the normalization equation as:

$$\sum_{i=1}^{m} \hat{\alpha}_i^q = \left\{ 1 + \sum_{i=1}^{m-1} \left(\prod_{j=1}^{i} k_j \right) \right\} \hat{\alpha}_1^q = 1 \tag{12.4}$$

Once $\hat{\alpha}_1^q$ is found, one can calculate the rest of the load fractions $(\hat{\alpha}_2^q, \hat{\alpha}_3^q, \ldots, \hat{\alpha}_m^q)$ by using Equation (12.3). Note that the single-job scheme is optimal if only a single job is to be processed. When multiple jobs are involved it is not optimal, as the following sections will demonstrate.

12.1.2 Algorithm for the Multi-Job Scheme

Case i.   When $T_f^{q-1} \geq z T_{cm}^{q-1} + z T_{cm}^q$, for $q \geq 2$

Here we will consider the case in which the distribution of the qth job is started immediately after the control processor finishes communicating the $(q-1)$th job and is finished before the completion of the $(q-1)$th job's computation (T_f^{q-1}). This is shown in Figure 12.4. In this case, the algorithm to find α_i^q is very simple. Note that Figure 12.4 shows the timing diagram for only the first two jobs, and the communication time for each fraction of load is abbreviated to only its corresponding

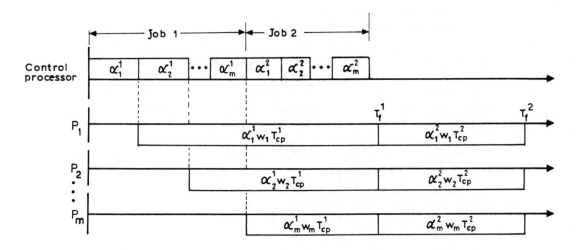

FIGURE 12.4 Timing Diagram: Multi-Job Scheme with $T_f^1 \geq zT_{cm}^1 + zT_{cm}^2$ (Load Origination at a Control Processor)

fraction (for example, $\alpha_1^1 zT_{cm}^1$ written as α_1^1). For our purposes one may think of the first job as the $(q-1)$th job and the second job as the qth job.

Each processor can simultaneously start its computation of the qth job immediately after T_f^{q-1} and finish its computation at the same time for an optimal solution. Therefore, the processing time in each processor is the same. Thus,

$$\alpha_1^q w_1 T_{cp}^q = \alpha_2^q w_2 T_{cp}^q = \alpha_3^q w_3 T_{cp}^q = \cdots = \alpha_m^q w_m T_{cp}^q \qquad (12.5)$$

From these equations we can write

$$\alpha_i^q = \left(\frac{w_1}{w_i}\right)\alpha_1^q, \qquad i = 1, 2, \ldots, m \qquad (12.6)$$

Using the normalization equation, we have

$$\sum_{i=1}^{m} \alpha_i^q = \sum_{i=1}^{m} \left(\frac{w_1}{w_i}\right)\alpha_1^q = 1 \qquad (12.7)$$

from which we obtain

$$\alpha_1^q = \left(\sum_{i=1}^{m} \frac{w_1}{w_i}\right)^{-1} \qquad (12.8)$$

$$\alpha_i^q = \left(\frac{w_1}{w_i}\right)\alpha_1^q, \qquad i = 1, 2, \ldots, m \qquad (12.9)$$

Note that since there is no wasted time between the consecutive jobs in every processor, the total required processing time for the qth job ($T_f^q - T_f^{q-1}$) is minimized.

Case ii. When $T_f^{q-1} < zT_{cm}^{q-1} + zT_{cm}^q$, for $q \geq 2$

Here we will consider the case when T_f^{q-1} occurs during the communication process of the qth job. That is, some of the processors that have received their processing load before T_f^{q-1} can start their computation immediately after T_f^{q-1} while others, which have not received their processing load yet, have to wait for some time for their processing load to be delivered. This is shown in Figure 12.5. Again one can think of the first job as the $(q-1)$th job and the second job as the qth job. The processing time of the $(q-1)$th job's processing load (T_f^{q-1}) occurs during the communication of the nth fraction of the qth job's load. Let Γ_i denote the time interval between T_f^{q-1} and the time that the ith processor receives its processing load corresponding to the qth job. Thus, processors p_1 to p_{n-1} can begin their computation immediately after T_f^{q-1} while $p_n, p_{n+1}, \ldots, p_m$ have to wait $\Gamma_n, \Gamma_{n+1}, \ldots, \Gamma_m$ periods of time, respectively, to receive their processing load and then begin their computation at times $(T_f^{q-1} + \Gamma_n), (T_f^{q-1} + \Gamma_{n+1}), \ldots, (T_f^{q-1} + \Gamma_m)$, respectively.

Now, we will present an algorithm to find the α_i^q that minimizes the total solution time. The processing time of p_1 to p_{n-1} is the same since they start and finish their computation simultaneously. Thus,

$$\alpha_1^q w_1 T_{cp}^q = \alpha_2^q w_2 T_{cp}^q = \cdots = \alpha_{n-1}^q w_{n-1} T_{cp}^q \qquad (12.10)$$

Therefore,

$$\alpha_i^q = \left(\frac{w_1}{w_i}\right)\alpha_1^q, \qquad i = 1, 2, \ldots, n-1 \qquad (12.11)$$

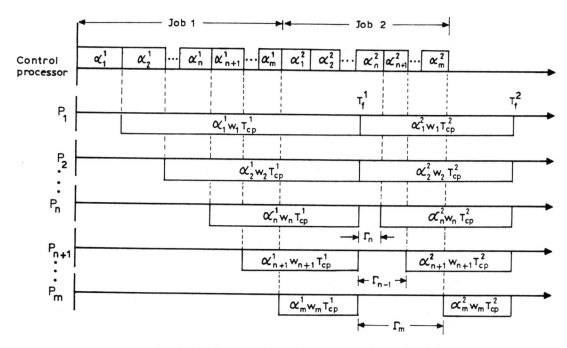

FIGURE 12.5 Timing Diagram: Multi-Job Scheme with $T_f^1 < zT_{cm}^1 + zT_{cm}^2$ (Load Origination at a Control Processor)

The next step is to find an expression for Γ_i, which is the time interval between T_f^{q-1} and the time instant at which the ith processor receives its processing load.

$$\Gamma_i = (\alpha_1^q + \alpha_2^q + \cdots + \alpha_i^q) z T_{cm}^q - \alpha_m^{q-1} w_m T_{cp}^{q-1}, \quad i = n, n+1, \ldots, m \quad (12.12)$$

The processing time of the ith processor is therefore

$$
\begin{aligned}
\alpha_i^q w_i T_{cp}^q &= \alpha_1^q w_1 T_{cp}^q - \Gamma_i \\
&= \alpha_1^q w_1 T_{cp}^q - \left(\sum_{k=1}^{i} \alpha_k^q \right) z T_{cm}^q + \alpha_m^{q-1} w_m T_{cp}^{q-1}, \quad i = n, n+1, \ldots, m
\end{aligned}
$$
$$(12.13)$$

Now consider the time taken by the nth processor to compute its processing load, that is, the processing time when $i = n$.

$$\alpha_n^q w_n T_{cp}^q = \alpha_1^q w_1 T_{cp}^q - (\alpha_1^q + \alpha_2^q + \cdots + \alpha_{n-1}^q + \alpha_n^q) z T_{cm}^q + \alpha_m^{q-1} w_m T_{cp}^{q-1}$$

Here α_n^q can be expressed as a function of α_1^q since $\alpha_2^q, \alpha_3^q, \ldots, \alpha_{n-1}^q$ have been expressed as functions of α_1^q previously.

$$
\begin{aligned}
\alpha_n^q &= \left\{ \frac{w_1 T_{cp}^q - \left(\sum_{i=1}^{n-1} \frac{w_1}{w_i} \right) z T_{cm}^q}{z T_{cm}^q + w_n T_{cp}^q} \right\} \alpha_1^q + \frac{\alpha_m^{q-1} w_m T_{cp}^{q-1}}{z T_{cm}^q + w_n T_{cp}^q} \\
&= u_n^q \alpha_1^q + v_n^q
\end{aligned}
$$
$$(12.14)$$

Here u_n^q and v_n^q are constants that are functions of the system parameters (z, w_i), the computation size of the $(q-1)$th job (T_{cp}^{q-1}), the size of the qth job (T_{cp}^q, T_{cm}^q), and (α_m^{q-1}). Here, α_m^{q-1} is assumed to be a known value because it is computed when the $(q-1)$th job is distributed. Thus,

$$u_n^q = \frac{w_1 T_{cp}^q - \left(\sum_{i=1}^{n-1} \frac{w_1}{w_i} \right) z T_{cm}^q}{z T_{cm}^q + w_n T_{cp}^q} \quad (12.15)$$

$$v_n^q = \frac{\alpha_m^{q-1} w_m T_{cp}^{q-1}}{z T_{cm}^q + w_n T_{cp}^q} \quad (12.16)$$

Let us consider the case for the next processor, that is, when $i = n + 1$.

$$
\begin{aligned}
\alpha_{n+1}^q w_{n+1} T_{cp}^q &= \alpha_1^q w_1 T_{cp}^q - \Gamma_{n+1} \\
&= \alpha_1^q w_1 T_{cp}^q - (\alpha_1^q + \alpha_2^q + \cdots + \alpha_{n-1}^q + \alpha_n^q + \alpha_{n+1}^q) z T_{cm}^q \\
&\quad + \alpha_m^{q-1} w_m T_{cp}^{q-1}
\end{aligned}
$$

Again α_{n+1}^q can be expressed as a function of α_1^q as

$$\alpha_{n+1}^q = \left\{ \frac{w_1 T_{cp}^q - \left(\sum_{i=1}^{n-1} \frac{w_1}{w_i} + u_n^q\right) z T_{cm}^q}{z T_{cm}^q + w_{n+1} T_{cp}^q} \right\} \alpha_1^q + \frac{\alpha_m^{q-1} w_m T_{cp}^{q-1} - v_n^q z T_{cm}^q}{z T_{cm}^q + w_{n+1} T_{cp}^q}$$

$$= u_{n+1}^q \alpha_1^q + v_{n+1}^q$$

where u_{n+1}^q and v_{n+1}^q are also constants since u_n^q and v_n^q have been found previously.

One can see that this procedure can be continued up to the case where $i = m$. Then, every fraction that the processor should calculate to achieve the minimum solution time is found as a function of α_1^q. Once all α_i^q have been found, α_1^q can be calculated from the normalization equation,

$$1 = \sum_{i=1}^{n-1} \alpha_i^q + \sum_{i=n}^{m} \alpha_i^q$$

$$= \left(\sum_{i=1}^{n-1} \frac{w_1}{w_i}\right) \alpha_1^q + \sum_{i=n}^{m} (u_i^q \alpha_1^q + v_i^q) \tag{12.17}$$

$$= \left(\sum_{i=1}^{n-1} \frac{w_1}{w_i} + \sum_{i=n}^{m} u_i^q\right) \alpha_1^q + \sum_{i=n}^{m} v_i^q$$

As a summary of this section, let us rephrase the algorithm to find α_i^q in the case $T_f^{q-1} < z T_{cm}^{q-1} + z T_{cm}^q$, for $q \geq 2$.

$$u_i^q = \frac{w_1 T_{cp}^q - \left(\sum_{k=1}^{n-1} \frac{w_1}{w_k} + \sum_{k=n}^{i-1} u_k^q\right) z T_{cm}^q}{z T_{cm}^q + w_i T_{cp}^q}, \tag{12.18}$$

$$i = n, n+1, \ldots, m$$

$$v_i^q = \frac{\alpha_m^{q-1} w_m T_{cp}^{q-1} - \left(\sum_{k=n}^{i-1} v_k^q\right) z T_{cm}^q}{z T_{cm}^q + w_i T_{cp}^q}, \quad i = n, n+1, \ldots, m \tag{12.19}$$

$$\alpha_1^q = \frac{1 - \sum_{i=n}^{m} v_i^q}{\sum_{i=1}^{n-1} \frac{w_1}{w_i} + \sum_{i=n}^{m} u_i^q} \tag{12.20}$$

$$\alpha_i^q = \begin{cases} \left(\dfrac{w_1}{w_i}\right) \alpha_1^q & i = 1, 2, \ldots, n-1 \\ u_i^q \alpha_1^q + v_i^q & i = n, n+1, \ldots, m \end{cases} \tag{12.21}$$

where it is assumed that $\sum_{i=n}^{n-1} u_i^q = 0$ and $\sum_{i=n}^{n-1} v_i^q = 0$.

Though the above algorithm is straightforward, it should be noted that we must know the value of the index n (that is, in which fraction of the $(q + 1)$th job is T_f^{q-1} located) in order to implement the algorithm. Actually, it may seem impossible to determine the location of T_f^{q-1} because, to do this, all values of α_i^q should be calculated first, which in turn requires the location of T_f^{q-1}.

But this dilemma can be resolved using the following recursive algorithm: First, identify the location of T_f^{q-1} by using the values of $\hat{\alpha}_i^q$ calculated in the single-job scheme. Since only the values of the system parameters and the size of the qth job are required to calculate $\hat{\alpha}_i^q$, one can easily compute $\hat{\alpha}_i^q$ by the closed-form solution described in the previous section. Next, the location of T_f^{q-1} can be obtained by using these values of $\hat{\alpha}_i^q$. Once the location of T_f^{q-1} is known, a fresh set of *tentative* α_i^q can be computed by the algorithm described in the previous section.

In the next step, one investigates the location of T_f^{q-1} as shown in Figure 12.6. If the location of T_f^{q-1} is changed from $\hat{\alpha}_n^q$ to α_{n+1}^q or even to $\alpha_{n+2}^q, \alpha_{n+3}^q, \ldots$, then one simply increases the value of n to the corresponding new value, $n + 1, n + 2, \ldots$ and so on, and calculates the values of α_i^q again. The process is repeated until the location of T_f^{q-1} is not changed when comparing the location of T_f^{q-1} with the previous values of α_i^q and with the new values of α_i^q at the time of each iteration. Note that when it is said that the position or location of T_f^{q-1} is changed it means that the fraction in which T_f^{q-1} is located is changed. The value of T_f^{q-1} itself is not changed since it depends only on the previous job's load.

Let us consider an example. Suppose that there is a bus network with five processors. For the second job, first calculate $\hat{\alpha}_i^2$ by the closed-form solution with the single-job scheme $(\hat{\alpha}_1^2, \hat{\alpha}_2^2, \ldots, \hat{\alpha}_5^2)$. If T_f^1 occurs during the communication of the second fraction $(\hat{\alpha}_2^2)$, set $n = 2$ and calculate the new values of α_i^2 by the algorithm of the multi-job scheme $(\alpha_1^2, \alpha_2^2, \ldots, \alpha_5^2)$. Now if T_f^1 occurs during the communication of the fourth fraction (α_4^2) when reidentifying the location, reset $n = 4$ and recalculate α_i^2. If the location of T_f^1 still occurs during the communication of α_4^2 after recalculation and reidentification, then stop. In practice, however, it is rarely the case that the location of T_f^1 is changed after the second iteration.

Note that the value of n never decreases in each iteration. It always increases. This is because the earlier parts of the fractions (e.g., α_1^2, α_2^2) become smaller and the latter parts of the fractions (e.g., $\alpha_{m-1}^2, \alpha_m^2$) become larger with each iteration.

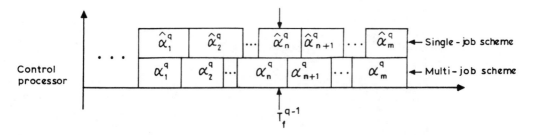

FIGURE 12.6 Communication Timing Diagram: Single-Job Scheme and Multi-Job Scheme (Load Origination at a Control Processor)

12.1.3 Is This Multi-Job Scheme Optimal?

For a single job, the load distribution strategy is optimal if the finish time of each processor is the same. But what about the multi-job scheme? Is this optimality condition still valid in the multi-job scheme? It turns out that for a given load distribution sequence and network configuration, the multi-job scheme is indeed optimal. This will be shown through the following argument.

For each individual job in the multi-job scheme, the minimum finish time occurs when all the processors finish computing at the same time instant; otherwise, one can improve the finish time by transferring the load from busy processors to idle ones. The question is: Will this still hold when one considers the performance criterion to be the overall processing time of all jobs? For instance, if there are ten jobs in the system, is this multi-job scheme also optimal in terms of the tenth job's processing time? To answer this question in the negative, one might come up with a strategy to close the gaps Γ_n to Γ_m and achieve a time performance that is less than the multi-job scheme. However, there will be serious disadvantages in closing these gaps and the result will actually be worse for the following three reasons. First, the processing time will be higher for the first job and possibly for some of the next jobs. This is because, except for the last job, the other jobs will not have the property that each of their load fractions complete processing at the same instant in time. The second problem is that the distribution of a given job will depend not only on its own size but also on the size of the other jobs. Since this is a purely deterministic system it is not possible to determine the size of a future job which may not even exist. Finally one cannot actually close the gaps if the computational load of the $(q-1)$th job is small (that is, T_{cp}^{q-1} is small) and the communication load of the qth job is relatively large (that is, T_{cm}^q is large). Therefore, the proposed multi-job scheme is an optimal load distribution strategy.

Another point to note here is that in the single job scheme, described in previous chapters, it was assumed that all the processors are free right from the time when the job is taken up for processing. This assumption was also true in the straightforward application of the single-job scheme given in this chapter (Section 12.1.1). In contrast, in the multi-job scheme proposed here, a processor might be busy processing the previous job while its predecessor is processing the next job. Thus, in the multi-job scheme the above assumption is relaxed. In fact, this is the reason for its optimal performance.

12.2 BUS NETWORK WITHOUT A CONTROL PROCESSOR

The bus network to be examined here does not have a control processor. The jobs are assumed to arrive directly at a buffer that routes them to one of the processors connected to the bus (Figure 12.7). Without loss of generality, we will assume this processor to be p_1. Processor p_1 distributes the processing load of the received job among the other processors. Each processor is equipped with a front end for communication offloading. As before, it is assumed here that each processor may have a different computing speed. Note that this model is similar to a single-level tree network with equal communication link speeds.

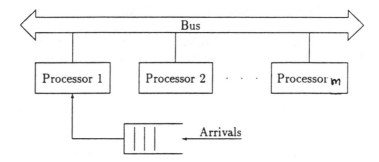

FIGURE 12.7   Bus Network with Load Origination at a Computing Processor.

As one might guess, the solution procedure to find the best fractions for optimal load distribution is very similar to the case of a network with load origination at a control processor. In particular, the closed-form solutions to find $\hat{\alpha}_i^q$ (single-job scheme) and α_i^1 are exactly the same and need not be repeated here. On the other hand, the algorithm to find α_i^q for $q \geq 2$ here is similar, but not identical, to that for a network with load origination at a control processor. The difference is that the originating processor (p_1) in this case does not need to communicate its own fraction (α_1^q) of the load. The following will describe the procedure to find α_i^q.

Case i.   When $T_f^{q-1} \geq (1 - \alpha_1^{q-1})z T_{cm}^{q-1} + (1 - \alpha_1^q)z T_{cm}^q$

This case is shown in Figure 12.8. The resulting equations are similar to Equations (12.8) and (12.9). However, there is a slight difference. In the case where the load is distributed by a control processor, the total amount of the communication

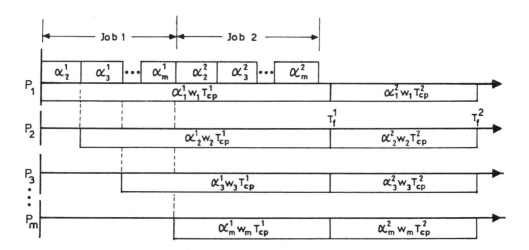

FIGURE 12.8   Timing Diagram: Multi-Job Scheme with $T_f^1 \geq (1 - \alpha_1^1)z T_{cm}^1 + (1 - \alpha_1^2)z T_{cm}^2$
(Load Origination at a Computing Processor)

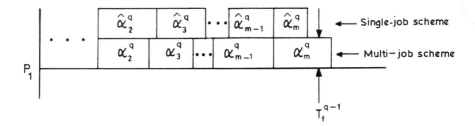

FIGURE 12.9 Communication Timing Diagram: Single-Job Scheme and Multi-Job Scheme (Load Origination at a Computing Processor)

time for one job is independent of how the control processor assigns the fractions (α_i^q) or where T_f^{q-1} is located. That is, the total amount of the communication time for the qth job was a fixed value (zT_{cm}^q). But in the case where the load is distributed by a computing processor, it is not. Since the total amount of the communication time in this case is $(\alpha_2^q + \alpha_3^q + \cdots + \alpha_m^q)zT_{cm}^q = (1 - \alpha_1^q)zT_{cm}^q$, there is a strong dependence on the value of α_1^q. In other words, the smaller the value of α_1^q, the larger the total communication time, and vice versa. Therefore, it is possible for the following case to exist. When first determining the location of T_f^{q-1} in the algorithm given in Section 12.1.2, using the values of the load allocation fractions in the single-job scheme $(\hat{\alpha}_2^q, \hat{\alpha}_3^q, \ldots, \hat{\alpha}_m^q)$, T_f^{q-1} is located after p_1 finishes communicating the qth job. So one might calculate the new values of the fractions (α_i^q) simply by using Equations (12.8) and (12.9). But when identifying the location of T_f^{q-1} again after calculation, it is possible that the new location of T_f^{q-1} is placed before the end of the communication, as in Figure 12.9. This is because, as mentioned before, the earlier fractions become smaller and the later fractions become larger in the multi-job scheme when compared to the single-job scheme. If this happens, then $T_f^{q-1} < (1 - \alpha_1^{q-1})zT_{cm}^{q-1} + (1 - \alpha_1^q)zT_{cm}^q$.

Another thing that must be pointed out here is that, as one can see in Figure 12.9, it takes less time to communicate the qth job in the single-job scheme than in the multi-job scheme because the total communication time in the latter case is longer than in the former case. However, the total processing time $(T_f^q - T_f^{q-1})$ to compute the qth job's processing load in the single-job scheme takes longer than that in the multi-job scheme. This is so because if the load allocation fractions calculated in the single-job scheme are used in the multi-job scheme, then, for jobs after the first one, each processor does not finish its computation at the same instant in time. This increases the processing time. The reason lies in the fact that the single job load fractions are based on the assumption that there is some waiting time.

Case ii.   When $T_f^{q-1} < (1 - \alpha_1^{q-1})zT_{cm}^{q-1} + (1 - \alpha_1^q)zT_{cm}^q$

Again, the resulting equations are very similar to those in the earlier section (see Equations (12.19) to (12.21). The only difference is that the summation term in the numerator of u_i^q is $\sum_{k=2}^{n-1} \left(\frac{w_1}{w_k}\right)$ in the case where the network is equipped with a control processor, while in this case, the summation term in the numerator of u_i^q is $\sum_{k=1}^{n-1} \left(\frac{w_1}{w_k}\right)$. Note that while processing a single job we are using a single installment strategy.

12.3 PERFORMANCE EVALUATION

Based on the previous results, some performance evaluation results were computed for various cases: the single-job scheme and the multi-job scheme for the network with load origination at a control processor; and the network with load origination at a computing processor. In each graph, the overall finish time (total solution finish time) is plotted against the number of jobs.

The simulation is done for the case in which the total number of jobs is ten. There are five processors in the network, and it is assumed that the values of the channel speed, the computing speed of each processor, and communication load for every job are equal to unity (that is, $z = 1$, $w_i = 1$, $T_{cm}^i = 1$, for all i).

In Figure 12.10, the overall processing time is plotted against the number of jobs when the computational load of every job is 6 ($T_{cp}^q = 6$ for all q), which is a medium load. Since the computational load for every job is the same, the total processing time is linear in the single-job scheme. Clearly, the multi-job scheme is superior to the single-job scheme in terms of the overall processing time.

Figures 12.11 and 12.12 plot the processing time when the computational load of the first half of the jobs is 10 ($T_{cp}^q = 10$, for $q = 1, 2, \ldots, 5$, that is, a heavy

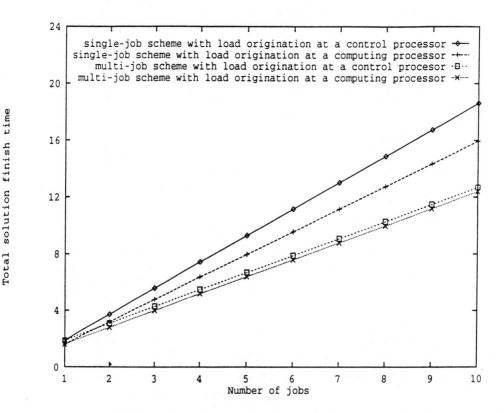

FIGURE 12.10   Overall Processing Time When $T_{cp}^q = 6$ for All q.

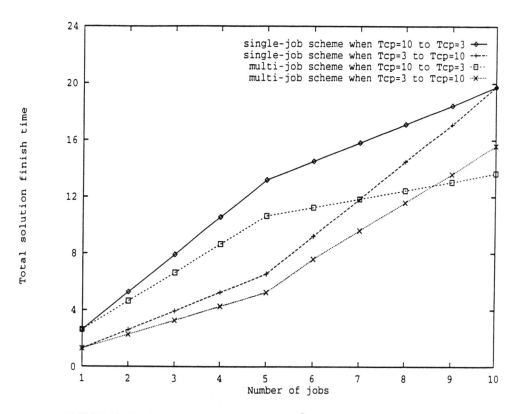

FIGURE 12.11 Overall Processing Time When $T_{cp}^q = 10$ for $q = 1, \ldots, 5$ and $T_{cp}^q = 3$ for $q = 6, \ldots, 10$ and Vice Versa (Load Origination at a Control Processor)

computational load) and that of the second half of the jobs is 3 ($T_{cp}^q = 3$, for $q = 6, 7, \ldots, 10$, that is, a light computational load). Naturally, the total processing time of the last job in the single-job scheme is the same regardless of the order in which the computational load is assigned, although there is some difference in the processing times of the jobs in the middle of the sequence of jobs. However, for the multi-job scheme, assigning the job with the heavy computational load first, and the one with the light computational load last, causes a reduction of the overall processing time. This is because processing the heavy computational load first results in a timing diagram like Figure 12.4 rather than like Figure 12.5. If there are several heavy jobs ahead of the light jobs, the load distribution will be done much ahead of the time of its computation and this means that there is no wasted time, thus reducing the waiting time between consecutive jobs. Therefore, if it is possible to assign the order of service at one's convenience—if, that is, the service discipline is not restricted to FIFO—assigning heavy computational load first can reduce the overall processing time.

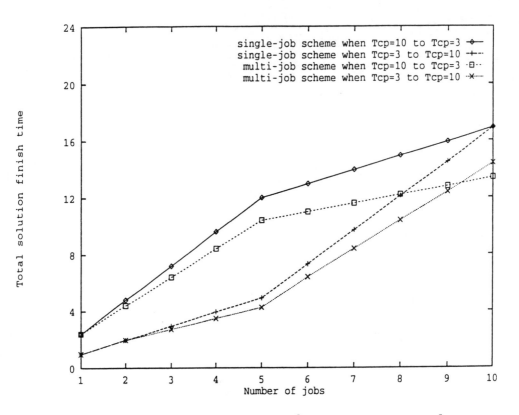

FIGURE 12.12   Overall Processing Time When $T_{cp}^q = 10$ for $q = 1, \ldots, 5$ and $T_{cp}^q = 3$ for $q = 6, \ldots, 10$ and Vice Versa (Load Origination at a Computing Processor).

12.4 CONCLUDING REMARKS

The following are the highlights of this chapter:

- A computational algorithm to determine optimal load distribution in a bus-oriented network, processing several arbitrarily divisible loads, was presented.
- It was found that the algorithm converges very quickly to the optimal value.

BIBLIOGRAPHIC NOTES

Most of the material presented in this chapter is taken from Sohn and Robertazzi (1993a).

CHAPTER **13**

Future Research Directions

Research in the area of *scheduling arbitrarily divisible loads* is of very recent origin and was stimulated by the requirements of processing large volumes of data in a parallel and distributed computing environment. This research also has potential applications in operations research, in problems involving transportation, facility location, and, in general, resource allocation.

The main thrust of research in this area has concentrated on determining the fraction of the total processing load that should be allocated to each processor so that a given load can be processed in minimum time, subject to communication delays associated with load transfers. This book collates, and provides a unified treatment of many of the results obtained earlier in the literature, with emphasis on design and analysis of load distribution strategies. However, research in this area is by no means complete. The analytical tractability of the methodology described in this book naturally suggests many directions for further research. We will briefly discuss some of those research directions here.

In the case of the single-installment strategy (for single-level tree and linear networks) optimality conditions for achieving minimum processing time were proved in this book (Chapter 5). In Chapters 10 and 11, it was assumed that these optimality conditions also hold for the multi-installment strategy, although a formal proof for this assertion was not provided. Though this assumption appears to be intuitively valid, it would be of interest to obtain a rigorous proof. Similarly, these optimality conditions may be extended to multi-level tree networks and to other load distribution strategies (for example, the one given in Chapter 9). In fact, for a multi-level tree, the conditions that identify redundant processor-link pairs have to be generalized. This would be an interesting and useful research problem.

Another potential topic of research would be to prove the optimal sequence and optimal arrangement results (as in the case of the single-installment strategy given in Chapter 7) for the multi-installment strategy for single-level tree networks. This is likely to pose considerable difficulties as the general set of recursive equations is not straightforward to solve. However, it appears intuitively that the results on optimal sequencing and arrangement (as in the case of single-installment strategy) may still continue to hold. A formal proof for this assertion for multi-installment strategy could lead to a more general result.

In the case of heterogeneous linear networks, a closed form for processing time is not available in the literature so far. This is most probably due to the complicated combinatorial terms that appear in the expressions for individual load fractions while solving the recursive equations. However, it will be useful to obtain a closed-form solution for a heterogeneous linear network. Once this closed-form solution is obtained, optimal sequencing of load distribution and optimal arrangement of processors and links can also be attempted.

In the case of linear networks, the front ends were not fully utilized in the multi-installment strategy presented in this book. It would be interesting to explore the possibility of improving the time performance further by a better utilization of front ends as was done for the single installment strategy described in Chapter 9.

The system model adopted in this book is approximate. From the example shown in Chapter 5, we can see that the results are not too different from the exact model so far as the optimality conditions and the processing time are concerned. However, if we incorporate the communication latency, the asymptotic behavior of time performance will change in a significant way. For example, the processing time with respect to the number of processors, and number of installments, will first decrease to a minimum and then increase as the cumulative time delay due to communication latency becomes prominent, thus specifying a maximum number of processors that should be used to achieve the minimum processing time. It is worth exploring such behavior of processing time by directly including communication latency in the model. In a recent paper, this has been studied in some detail for linear, bus, star, tree, ring, and hypercube networks (for this and all other references in this discussion, see the Bibliographic Notes at the end of this chapter). Similarly, one might also incorporate into the model the fact that, in practice, the divisibility property of any load is governed by a divisibility factor (defined in Chapter 2) and, further, load fractions have to be sent in packets of fixed length. This practical scenario can give rise to additional optimality considerations that need study.

The multi-job scheme (Chapter 12) is of practical importance and a useful future research direction can consider a similar problem in the context of general tree and linear networks. A related problem of interest is one in which each processor need not be available right from the beginning of the computational process, but may have a release time (the earliest time at which the processor will be able to take up the processing of its own load fraction) associated with it. A recent study in this area considers a heterogeneous distributed computing system in which arbitrarily divisible processing loads originate at every node. Depending on the volume of the load at each node, heavily loaded nodes send a part of their loads to lightly loaded nodes through a packet broadcast network, which is subject to communication delays. These delays depend on the bandwidth allocated for each load transfer. The objective is to minimize the processing time by dynamically allocating optimal communication bandwidths for load transfer by each heavily loaded processor. The load transfer problem is specified in terms of time-varying load transfer rates that are expressed as piecewise constant functions of time. However, the research addressing the problem of multiple load origination points in a network is not complete. This is an important topic for future research.

Though this book considers only two types of networks, namely, single-level tree/star and linear networks, it appears possible to extend these results to other network architectures such as ring, hypercube, mesh, multi-level tree, and so on. Recently, scheduling of divisible loads has been studied for homogeneous hypercube and mesh networks. In these studies the broadcast type of communication model (or a multi-port regimen, as opposed to the single-port regimen used in this book) is adopted. Communication delay is expressed as a linear function of the size of the load fraction and the number of layers that need to be traversed to communicate this load fraction to a given node. A processor equivalence concept is used to replace all the processors in a layer by a single equivalent processor, thus converting the network into a linear one. An asymptotic analysis is carried out to study the behavior of standard performance measures such as speedup and utilization against the number of layers. However, in these studies only a homogeneous network is considered and there is considerable scope to obtain practically useful results by extending the model to general heterogeneous networks.

Other recent studies utilizing the paradigm of scheduling divisible loads consider the design and analysis of algorithms for scheduling a collection of both divisible and indivisible jobs to loosely coupled multiprocessor systems. However, in such studies, the effect of communication delay is not explicitly accounted for. On the other hand, there has been some effort to take into account interprocessor communication delays that occur during the actual execution of the job, and also the effect of failure of one or several processors and the subsequent redistribution of unprocessed loads to achieve optimality.

Although the models for processors and communication links adopted in this book are assumed to be deterministic, in reality they are not so. There have been attempts to extend some of the load distribution strategies presented in this book to systems that are subject to time-varying processor and channel speeds, modeled as stochastic quantities. This variation in speed is attributed to unknown background jobs, executed and communicated by various nodes, that limit the available capacity of the processors and channels.

This book presents important theoretical developments in the area of scheduling divisible loads and does not cover the issues related to implementation of these strategies on real parallel or distributed computing systems. However, the issues related to the implementation of these strategies are important not only from the applications viewpoint but also from the viewpoint of realistic performance evaluation. These implementation issues are a separate subject of study in themselves in the context of arbitrarily divisible loads just as they are in conventional load balancing and scheduling problems. These issues are not covered in this book and form an important direction for future research.

While the above discussion focuses on several useful research directions that are possible, or have seen recent developments, the following discussion will explore a few potential application areas that might use the concepts presented in this book either in its present form or with suitable modifications. These applications are somewhat different from the ones we have already mentioned.

First we will discuss the applicability of these concepts to multiprogramming environments. There has been extensive and continuing work on multiprogramming and multiprocessor scheduling, task allocation, and load balancing. One approach to the problem could be that when a processor has a processing load to distribute, it can request from each of the other processors the amount of processing effort that they are willing to *donate*. The ideas presented here can then be used to determine the allocations of load by transforming the donated effort to a parameter representing the *speed* of each processor for the given job. This is a nontrivial problem, as donating effort to a new process effectively reduces the amount of processor capacity available for already resident processes. There are several questions to be addressed here regarding the determination of donated effort, the process mix, and the scheduling policy (round robin, leveled queues, and so on) of each processor. Even for a simple load sharing algorithm there are certain basic questions for which answers are not currently available. For instance, assuming that each processor has a large memory, one could save time by transporting data to processors well in advance of actual computation. But the true benefit from this strategy would depend on how accurately one could predict the future load situation at each processor. Alternatively, it might be better to hold off data transfer until it is clearly known which processors have excess capacity.

Another aspect of the problem involves process termination. When a process terminates on a processor, the computational effort that was being used for that process is now available. The question then becomes whether this extra capability should be used for other processes still running on the processor or whether it should be allocated to other processes, imported from an external source or newly initiated. Note that importing a process fragment from another processor imposes a communication delay that must be taken into account.

Imposing real-time constraints adds another level of difficulty. In general, though obtaining schedules for multiprocessors with real-time constraints is intractable, heuristic algorithms often perform well. The basic problem is that an optimal schedule may involve temporary idling of some resources so that they are available for processes with time constraints. However, most scheduling algorithms developed for uniprocessor systems tend to do just the opposite, that is, they keep resources continuously busy. The effect of introducing divisible processes to such systems remains an open question.

A final complication results from the queueing of processes. Queueing will result whenever a scheduling algorithm does not allow every submitted process to be instantly taken up for processing. Such a scheduling algorithm, to maintain the performance of processes that are already being executed, will not allow the immediate execution, on arrival, of some incoming processes that may degrade the overall multiprocessor performance. There are a number of intriguing questions to be addressed here. One involves the best queueing discipline to use in a mixed environment of divisible and indivisible processes. The fact that some processes are divisible opens up new possibilities in comparison to traditional indivisible scheduling policies. Another question involves flow control—that is, which process should receive immediate attention and which should be delayed to maintain system performance.

This question will probably have different answers depending on the context, that is, whether some processes need to be executed in real time, or which among the divisible or indivisible processes get priority. A last question involves the best place to perform queueing—that is, should the data for the processes be queued at the point of origination (at a processor) until capacity becomes available, or should it be distributed as soon as possible?

The ideas behind scheduling of divisible loads can also be used to formulate and solve certain practical problems that are somewhat similar to the classical transportation and facility location problems. For example, consider the following problem: There is a location where certain raw materials are available (for example, a mine or a sea port). These have to be transported to various locations (production centers) to be processed into a finished marketable product. The number of transport vehicles available at the starting point are limited. Hence, if we choose one of the production centers to be the first to receive its share of the raw material, then the others have to wait until this delivery has been made. This is equivalent to the communication delay considered in this book. For obvious reasons we would like to see that the raw material is processed in the shortest possible time, which would mean that all the production centers must finish processing at the same time. One can immediately observe the analogy with a single-level tree network processing an arbitrarily divisible load. Yet this problem has a number of subtle differences with the single-level tree model. For example, the model of the communication delay needs modification since it may have to absorb the transportation cost, too. The possibility of some of the trucks delivering goods to one production center while the others deliver to another requires a different variation. A multi-port communication regimen (as opposed to the single-port regimen we have been using) in a distributed computing system is equivalent to this model. Further, suppose there is only a single transport vehicle and it delivers goods to various production centers in a fixed sequence. This can be likened to the linear network model. Other possibilities also exist.

The inverse problem to this can be as follows. Suppose a finite number of possible locations for production centers (with some prespecified maximum feasible capacities, which in turn may depend on environmental considerations or state laws) are available. Then one can think of choosing a subset of them that will process the load in minimum time under the above conditions. As a case in point, a location with a very high capacity plant may be less preferable to several locations with small capacities if the former is far away compared to the latter group of locations.

To conclude, in this book a number of new load distribution strategies for arbitrarily divisible loads are presented and analyzed. However, from the applications viewpoint, divisible load theory is still at an incipient stage. The model adopted in this book seems to be a good starting point in understanding the physics of the load distribution process in a distributed computing system. In a practical scenario, the processing loads may neither be arbitrarily divisible, nor strictly indivisible. In contrast to the results in the area of scheduling indivisible jobs, which depend mostly on heuristic algorithms, the approach given here offers many analytical results. Hence, we feel that this approach can serve as a basis for understanding complex scheduling problems.

BIBLIOGRAPHIC NOTES

A recent work that includes the communication latency in the delay model is by Blazewicz and Drozdowski (1994). In this study the communication latency is referred to as communication startup cost.

Redistribution of divisible loads that originate at more than one processor in a DCS is addressed in Haddad (1994).

The problem of scheduling divisible loads in hypercube and mesh architectures is studied in Blazewicz and Drozdowski (1995) and Blazewicz and Drozdowski (1996), respectively.

The problem of scheduling a mix of both divisible and indivisible jobs is addressed by Bataineh and Al-Asir (1994), while considerations of interprocessor communication time and failure models are the subject matters in Bataineh and Al-Ibrahim (1994).

Sohn and Robertazzi (1995a, b) study the effect of time-varying processor and channel speeds and provide a stochastic analysis of the optimal load distribution strategy. They also present extensive numerical computations to support their results.

A starting point for tackling the implementation issues could be based on techniques and architectural details presented in Thomson-Leighton (1992), Quinn (1987), Hwang and Briggs (1989), Sloman and Kramer (1987), DeCegama (1989), Siegel (1990), and Coulouris and Dollimore (1988).

The application of the concepts presented in this book to variants of the classical transportation and facility location problems has some similarities with the solution concepts in resource allocation problems studied in the literature; for instance, see Ibaraki and Katoh (1988), where a general formulation of this problem with several applications and methods of solution are discussed.

Bibliography

Anger, F.D., Hwang, J.J., and Chow, Y.C., "Scheduling with Sufficient Loosely Coupled Processors," *J. of Parallel and Distributed Computing,* Vol. 9, No. 1, 1990, pp. 87–92.

Atallah, M.J. et al., "Models and Algorithms for Coscheduling Compute-Intensive Tasks on a Network of Workstations," *J. of Parallel and Distributed Computing,* Vol. 16, No. 4, 1992, pp. 319–327.

Bataineh, S. and Al-Alsir, B., "An Efficient Scheduling Algorithm for Divisible and Indivisible Tasks in Loosely Coupled Multiprocessor Systems," *Software Engineering J.,* Vol. 9, 1994, pp. 13–18.

Bataineh, S. and Al-Ibrahim, M., "Effect of Fault-Tolerance and Communication Delay on Response Time in a Multiprocessor System with a Bus Topology," *Computer Comm.* Vol. 17, 1994, pp. 843–851.

Bataineh, S., Hsiung, T., and Robertazzi, T.G., "Closed Form Solutions for Bus and Tree Networks of Processors Load Sharing a Divisible Job," *IEEE Trans. Computers,* Vol. 43, No. 10, 1994, pp. 1184–1196.

Bataineh, S. and Robertazzi, T.G., "Bus Oriented Load Sharing for a Network of Sensor Driven Processors," *IEEE Trans. Systems, Man, and Cybernetics,* Vol. 21, No. 5, 1991, pp. 1202–1205.

Bataineh, S. and Robertazzi, T.G., "Ultimate Performance Limits for Networks of Load Sharing Processors," *Proc. Conf. Information Sciences and Systems,* Princeton Univ., Princeton, N.J., 1992, pp. 794–799.

Bertsekas, D.P. and Tsitsiklis, J.N., *Parallel and Distributed Computation: Numerical Methods,* Prentice-Hall, Englewood Cliffs, N.J., 1989.

Bharadwaj, V., "Distributed Computation with Communication Delays: Design and Analysis of Load Distribution Strategies," PhD diss., Indian Institute of Science, Bangalore, India, 1994.

Bharadwaj, V., Ghose, D., and Mani, V., "Design and Analysis of Load Distribution Strategies for Infinitely Divisible Loads in Distributed Computing Networks with Communication Delays," Technical Report 422/GC/01-92, Department of Aerospace Engineering, Indian Institute of Science, Bangalore, Oct. 1992a.

Bharadwaj, V., Ghose, D., and Mani, V., "A Study of Optimality Conditions for Load Distribution in Tree Networks with Communication Delays," Technical Report 423/GI/02-92, Department of Aerospace Engineering, Indian Institute of Science, Bangalore, Dec. 1992b.

Bharadwaj, V., Ghose, D., and Mani, V., "Optimal Sequencing and Arrangement in Distributed Single-Level Networks with Communication Delays," *IEEE Trans. Parallel and Distributed Systems,* Vol. 5, No. 9, 1994a, pp. 968–976.

Bharadwaj, V., Ghose, D., and Mani, V., "Multi-installment Load Distribution Strategy for Linear Networks with Communication Delays," *First International Workshop on Parallel Processing,* Dec. 26–29, Bangalore, India, 1994b.

Bharadwaj, V., Ghose, D., and Mani, V., "An Efficient Load Distribution Strategy for a Distributed Linear Network of Processors with Communication Delays," *Computers and Mathematics with Applications,* Vol. 29, No. 9, 1995a, pp. 95–112.

Bharadwaj, V., Ghose, D., and Mani, V., "Multi-Installment Load Distribution in Tree Networks with Delays," *IEEE Trans. Aerospace and Electronic Systems,* Vol. 31, No. 2, 1995b, pp. 555–567.

Bhatt, S.N. et al. "Scattering and Gathering Messages in Networks of Processors," *IEEE Trans. on Computers,* Vol. 42, No. 8, 1993, pp. 938–949.

Binder, J.D., "Massively Parallel Supercomputers: Has Their Time Come?" *Aerospace America,* Vol. 32, No. 5, 1994, pp. 16–18.

Blazewicz, J. and Drozdowski, M., "Distributed Processing of Divisible Jobs with Communication Startup Costs," Research Report RA-94/006, Institute of Computing Science, Poznan University of Technology, Poznan, Poland, Dec. 1994.

Blazewicz, J. and Drozdowski, M., "Scheduling Divisible Jobs on Hypercubes," *Parallel Computing,* Vol. 21, No. 12, 1995, pp. 1945–1956.

Blazewicz, J. and Drozdowski, M., "The Performance Limits of a Two-Dimensional Network of Load Sharing Processors," *Foundations of Computing and Decision Sciences,* Vol. 21, No. 1, 1996, pp. 3–15.

Bokhari, S.H., *Assignment Problems in Parallel and Distributed Computing,* Kluwer, Boston, Mass., 1987.

Carlson, B.D., Evans, E.D., and Wilson, S.L., "Search Radar Detection and Track with Hough Transform. Part I: System Concept. Part II: Detection Statistics. Part III: Detection Performance with Binary Integration," *IEEE Trans. Aerospace and Electronic Systems,* Vol. 30, No. 1, 1994, pp. 102–108; 109–115; 116–125.

Casavant, T.L. and Kuhl, J.G., "A Taxonomy of Scheduling in General-Purpose Distributed Computing Systems," *IEEE Trans. Software Eng.,* Vol. 14, No. 1, 1988, pp. 141–154.

Cheng, Y.C. and Robertazzi, T.G., "Distributed Computation with Communication Delays," *IEEE Trans. Aerospace and Electronic Systems,* Vol. 24, No. 6, 1988, pp. 700–712.

Cheng, Y.C. and Robertazzi, T.G., "Distributed Computation for a Tree Network with Communication Delays," *IEEE Trans. Aerospace and Electronic Systems,* Vol. 26, No. 3, 1990, pp. 511–516.

Choudhary, A.N. and Ponnusamy, R., "Implementation and Evaluation of Hough Transform Algorithms on a Shared-Memory Multiprocessor," *J. of Parallel and Distributed Computing,* Vol. 12, No. 2, 1991, pp. 178–188.

Coffman, E.G., Jr., ed., *Computer and Job-Shop Scheduling Theory,* John Wiley, New York, 1976.

Coffman, E.G., Jr., Garey, M.R., and Johnson, D.S., "An Application of Bin-packing to Multiprocessor Scheduling," *SIAM J. on Computing,* Vol. 7, No. 1, 1978, pp. 1–17.

Coulouris, G.F., and Dollimore, J., *Distributed Systems: Concepts and Design,* Addison-Wesley, Workingham, England, 1988.

DeCegama, A.L., *Parallel Processing Architectures and VLSI Hardware,* Prentice-Hall, Englewood Cliffs, N.J., 1989.

Fernandez-Baca, D., "Allocating Modules to Processors in a Distributed System," *IEEE Trans. Software Eng.,* Vol. 15, No. 11, 1989, pp. 1427–1436.

Gerogiannis, D. and Orphanoudakis, S.C., "Load Balancing Requirements in Parallel Implementations of Image Feature Extraction Tasks," *IEEE Trans. Parallel and Distributed Systems,* Vol. 4, No. 9, 1993, pp. 994–1013.

Ghose, D. and Mani, V., "Distributed Computation with Communication Delays: Asymptotic Performance Analysis," *J. of Parallel and Distributed Computing,* Vol. 23, No. 3, 1994, pp. 293–305.

Graham, R.L., Knuth, D.E., and Patashnik, O., *Concrete Mathematics,* Addison-Wesley, Reading, Mass., 1989.

Haddad, E., "Communication Protocol for Optimal Redistribution of Divisible Load in Distributed Real-Time Systems," *Proc. ISMM Int'l. Conf. Intelligent Information Management Systems,* 1994, pp. 39–42.

Hwang, K. and Briggs, F.A., *Computer Architecture and Parallel Processing,* McGraw-Hill, New York, 1989.

Ibaraki, T. and Katoh, N., *Resource Allocation Problems: Algorithmic Approaches*, MIT Press, Cambridge, Mass., 1988.

Kim, H.J. et al., "Optimal Configuration of Host-Satellite System for Load Distribution," Preprint, 1993.

Kim, H.J., Jee, G.I., and Lee, J.G., "Optimal Load Distribution for Tree Network Processors," *IEEE Trans. Aerospace and Electronic Systems,* Vol. 32, No. 2, 1996, pp. 607–612.

Kim, S.D., Nichols, M.A., and Siegel, H.J., "Modelling Overlapped Operation between the Control Unit and Processing Elements in an SIMD Machine," *J. of Parallel and Distributed Computing,* Vol. 12, No. 4, 1991, pp. 329–342.

Krishnamurti, R. and Ma, E., "An Approximation Algorithm for Scheduling Tasks on Varying Partition Sizes in Partitionable Multiprocessor Systems," *IEEE Trans. Computers,* Vol. 41, No. 12, 1992, pp. 1572–1579.

Lee, C.-H., Lee, D., and Kim, M., "Optimal Task Assignment in Linear Array Networks," *IEEE Trans. Computers,* Vol. 41, No. 7, 1992, pp. 877–880.

Leighton, F. T., *Introduction to Parallel Algorithms and Architectures: Arrays, Trees, Hypercubes,* Morgan Kaufmann, San Mateo, Calif., 1992.

Lewis, T.G., El-Rewini, H., and Kim, I.K., *Introduction to Parallel Computing,* Prentice-Hall, Englewood Cliffs, N.J., 1992.

Mani, V. and Ghose, D., "Distributed Computation in Linear Networks: Closed-Form Solutions," *IEEE Trans. Aerospace and Electronic Systems,* Vol. 30, No. 2, 1994, pp. 471–483.

Murthy, C.S.R. and Selvakumar, S., "Scheduling Parallel Programs for Execution on Multiprocessors," *Proc. CSA Silver Jubilee Workshop on Computing and Intelligent Systems,* Bangalore, India, 1993, pp. 91–115.

Nation, W.G., Maciejewski, A.A., and Siegel, H.J., "A Methodology for Exploiting Concurrency Among Independent Tasks in Partitionable Parallel Processing Systems," *J. of Parallel and Distributed Computing,* Vol. 19, No. 3, 1993, pp. 271–278.

Norman, M.G. and Thanisch, P., "Models of Machines and Computation for Mapping in Multicomputers," *ACM Computing Surveys,* Vol. 25, No. 3, 1993, pp. 263–302.

Peng, D.-T. and Shin, K.G., "Optimal Scheduling of Cooperative Tasks in a Distributed System Using an Enumerative Method," *IEEE Trans. Software Eng.,* Vol. 19, No. 3, 1993, pp. 253–267.

Price, C.C. and Salama, M.A., "Scheduling of Precedence-Constrained Tasks on Multiprocessors," *The Computer Journal,* Vol. 33, No. 3, 1990, pp. 219–229.

Quinn, M.J., *Designing Efficient Algorithms for Parallel Computers,* McGraw-Hill, New York, 1987.

Reed, D.A. and Grunwald, D.C., "The Performance of Multicomputer Interconnection Networks," *Computer,* Vol. 20, No. 1, 1987, pp. 63–73.

Robertazzi, T.G., "Processor Equivalence for a Linear Daisy Chain of Load Sharing Processors," *IEEE Trans. Aerospace and Electronic Systems,* Vol. 29, No. 4, 1993, pp. 1216–1221.

Royden, H.L., *Real Analysis,* 3rd ed., Macmillan, New York, 1988.

Saad, Y. and Schultz, M.H., "Data Communication in Parallel Architectures," *Parallel Computing,* Vol. 11, No. 2, 1989, pp. 131–150.

Shin, K.G. and Chen, M.S., "On the Number of Acceptable Task Assignments in Distributed Computing Systems," *IEEE Trans. Computers,* Vol. 39, No. 1, 1990, pp. 99–110.

Shirazi, B.A. and Hurson, A.R., eds., Special Issue on Scheduling and Load Balancing, *J. of Parallel and Distributed Computing,* Vol. 16, No. 4, 1992, pp. 271–394.

Shirazi, B.A., Hurson, A.R., and Kavi, K.M., eds., *Scheduling and Load Balancing in Parallel and Distributed Systems,* IEEE Computer Society Press, Los Alamitos, Calif., 1995.

Shivaratri, N., Krueger, P., and Singhal, M., "Load Sharing Policies in Locally Distributed Systems," *Computer,* Vol. 25, No. 12, 1992, pp. 33–44.

Siegel, H.J., *Interconnection Networks for Large-Scale Parallel Processing: Theory and Case Studies,* 2nd ed., McGraw-Hill, New York, 1990.

Sloman, M. and Kramer, J., *Distributed Systems and Computer Networks,* Prentice-Hall, Englewood Cliffs, N.J., 1987.

Sohn, J. and Robertazzi, T.G., "A Multi-Job Load Sharing Strategy for Divisible Jobs on Bus Networks," CEAS Technical Report 665, State Univ. New York at Stony Brook, Apr. 1993a.

Sohn, J. and Robertazzi, T.G., "Optimal Load Sharing for a Divisible Job on a Bus Network," *Proc. Conf. Information Sciences and Systems,* Johns Hopkins Univ., Baltimore, Md., 1993b, pp. 835–840.

Sohn, J. and Robertazzi, T.G., "An Optimum Load Sharing Strategy for Divisible Jobs with Time-Varying Processor Speed and Channel Speed," CEAS Technical Report 706, State Univ. N.Y. at Stony Brook, Jan. 1995a.

Sohn, J. and Robertazzi, T.G., "An Optimum Load Sharing Strategy for Divisible Jobs with Time-Varying Processor Speed," *Proc. Eighth Int'l. Conf. Parallel and Distributed Computer Systems*, Orlando, Fla., 1995b, pp. 27–32.

Sohn, J. and Robertazzi, T.G., "Optimal Divisible Job Load Sharing for Bus Networks," *IEEE Trans. Aerospace and Electronic Systems,* Vol. 32, No. 1, 1996, pp. 34–40.

Stankovic, J.A., "An Application of Bayesian Decision Theory to Decentralized Control of Job Scheduling," *IEEE Trans. Computers,* Vol. 34, No. 1, 1985, pp. 117–130.

Stankovic, J.A. et al., "Implications of Classical Scheduling Results for Real-Time Systems," *Computer*, Vol. 28, No. 6, 1995, pp. 16–25.

Stone, H.S., "Multiprocessor Scheduling with the Aid of Network Flow Algorithms," *IEEE Trans. Software Engineering,* Vol. 3, No. 1, 1977, pp. 85–93.

Swami, A., Young, H.C., and Gupta, A., "Algorithms for Handling Skew in Parallel Task Scheduling," *J. of Parallel and Distributed Computing,* Vol. 16, No. 4, 1992, pp. 363–377.

Tantawi, A.N. and Towsley, D., "Optimal Static Load Balancing in Distributed Computer Systems," *J. of ACM,* Vol. 32, No. 2, 1985, pp. 445–455.

Tenney, R.R. and Sandell, N.R., Jr., "Detection with Distributed Sensors," *IEEE Trans. Aerospace and Electronic Systems,* Vol. 17, No. 4, 1981, pp. 501–510.

Tzafestas, S. and Triantafyllakis, A., "Deterministic Scheduling in Computing and Manufacturing Systems: A Survey of Models and Algorithms," *Math. and Computers in Simulation,* Vol. 35, No. 5, 1993, pp. 397–434.

Veltman, B., Lageweg, B.J., and Lenstra, J.K., "Multiprocessor Scheduling with Communication Delays," *Parallel Computing,* Vol. 16, No. 2–3, 1990, pp. 173–182.

Weber, R., "On a Conjecture About Assigning Jobs to Processes of Different Speeds," *IEEE Trans. Automatic Control,* Vol. 38, No. 1, 1993, pp. 166–170.

Xu, J., "Multiprocessor Scheduling of Processors with Release Times, Deadlines, Precedence, and Exclusion Relations," *IEEE Trans. Software Engineering,* Vol. 19, No. 1, 1993, pp. 139–154.

Index

Additional Advances Board Titles

Scheduling and Load Balancing in Parallel and Distributed Systems
Behrooz A. Shirazi, Ali R. Hurson, and Krishna M. Kavi

Parallel Computers
Theory and Practice
Thomas L. Casavant, Pavel Tvrdík, and František Plášil

Emerging Trends in Database and Knowledge Base Machines
Mahdi Abdelguerfi and Simon Lavington

Instruction-Level Parallel Processors
H.C. Torng and Stamatis Vassiliadis

IEEE Computer Society Press Publications

The world-renowned Computer Society Press publishes, promotes, and distributes a wide variety of authoritative computer science and engineering texts. These books are available in two formats: 100 percent original material by authors preeminent in their field who focus on relevant topics and cutting-edge research, and reprint collections consisting of carefully selected groups of previously published papers with accompanying original introductory and explanatory text.

Submission of proposals: For guidelines and information on CS Press books, send e-mail to cs.books@computer.org or write to the Acquisitions Editor, IEEE Computer Society Press, P.O. Box 3014, 10662 Los Vaqueros Circle, Los Alamitos, CA 90720-1314. Telephone +1 714-821-8380. FAX +1 714-761-1784.

IEEE Computer Society Press Proceedings

The Computer Society Press also produces and actively promotes the proceedings of more than 130 acclaimed international conferences each year in multimedia formats that include hard and softcover books, CD-ROMs, videos, and on-line publications.

For information on CS Press proceedings, send e-mail to cs.books@computer.org or write to Proceedings, IEEE Computer Society Press, P.O. Box 3014, 10662 Los Vaqueros Circle, Los Alamitos, CA 90720-1314. Telephone +1 714-821-8380. FAX +1 714-761-1784.

Additional information regarding the Computer Society, conferences and proceedings, CD-ROMs, videos, and books can also be accessed from our web site at www.computer.org.

6/11/96